21ST CENTURY
RESIDENTIAL
LANDSCAPE DESIGN

21ST CENTURY
RESIDENTIAL
LANDSCAPE DESIGN

DEAN HERALD

PHOTOGRAPHY BY DANNY KILDARE

images
Publishing

Published in Australia in 2012 by
The Images Publishing Group Pty Ltd
ABN 89 059 734 431
6 Bastow Place, Mulgrave, Victoria 3170, Australia
Tel: +61 3 9561 5544 Fax: +61 3 9561 4860
books@imagespublishing.com
www.imagespublishing.com

Copyright © The Images Publishing Group Pty Ltd 2012
The Images Publishing Group Reference Number: 978

All rights reserved. Apart from any fair dealing for the purposes of private study, research, criticism or review as permitted under the Copyright Act, no part of this publication may be reproduced, stored in a retrieval system or transmitted in any form by any means, electronic, mechanical, photocopying, recording or otherwise, without the written permission of the publisher.

National Library of Australia Cataloguing-in-Publication entry:

Author:	Herald, Dean.
Title:	21st century residential landscape design / Dean Herald.
ISBN:	9781864704068 (hbk.)
Series:	21st century architecture.
Subjects:	Architecture, Domestic – 21st century.
	Landscape architecture – 21st century.
	Architecture, Modern.

Dewey Number: 728

Edited by Driss Fatih

Designed by The Graphic Image Studio Pty Ltd, Mulgrave, Australia
www.tgis.com.au

Pre-publishing services by United Graphic Pte Ltd, Singapore
Printed by 1010 Printing International Limited in China on 140gsm GoldEast Matt Art

IMAGES has included on its website a page for special notices in relation to this and our other publications. Please visit www.imagespublishing.com.

Contents

6	Introduction
8	Rural Resort
18	Reflections
28	The Pavilion
36	Mirror Image
44	Contemporary Dreams
54	Sydney Living
62	Hidden Valley
72	Sunken Connections
80	Floating Layers
92	The Secret Garden
104	Intimate Hideaway
110	Modern Life
122	Eastern Influence
130	Infinity Blue
140	On Show
148	Resort Style Living
156	Manly Hideaway
164	Set In Stone
172	Urban Movement
180	Chill Out
190	Boardwalk Bathing
194	On The Green
202	Hanging Out
210	On Edge
218	Bushland Oasis
226	Acknowledgements

Introduction

DEAN HERALD

The residential landscape space is unique in so many ways: the land differs from site to site, as do the people who use it. Each client brings individual needs to a project, and these are taken into consideration along with the contours of the land and the architectural influence of the home. Detailed consideration is also given to the functionality of the space and how it will be used, its long-term viability of growth and how all the elements will age.

The fundamentals of the design process, such as drainage and other environmental factors, are always present and must be taken into account for the project to truly be a success. Above all, the residential landscape is unique because it is personal – it provides the opportunity to express individuality right outside our homes and share it with those we care most about.

A residential landscape space comes with few of the rules that are felt in society: it has no dress code and you can choose who enters it. It is a place where memories for both children and adults are formed that will be shared for years to come at family dinners. It's where kids learn to swim, kick a ball, ride a bike, climb a tree and discover the best hiding spot in the world.

Over the last 20 years we have witnessed the residential landscape develop into an accepted extension of the home, which in turn has had a direct influence on modern architecture. The indoor–outdoor connection plays a major role in the placement of rooms in a home and the opening of doorways to connect them. Large doors and windows allow a constant connection with not only external living spaces, but also the smooth tones that planting can bring. The introduction of water, whether in the form of a swimming pool or a pond, builds on this connection with both sight and sound and throughout the design process becomes a strong focal feature. The development of the swimming pool and the opportunities available to influence water in landscapes complete some of the main entertaining features and allow the plant material to play its role.

The ability to entertain is a common desire among clients and this can be expressed in so many different ways. Typically, a love of good food plays a major role and the outdoor cooking experience can be as simple as a barbeque or as complex as a fully equipped outdoor kitchen. The pavilion has also grown in popularity – including all the facilities required to entertain with ease and making it a pleasure to be the host.

21st Century Residential Landscape Design is a collection of 25 projects in which a designed atmosphere has been expressed and developed to the individual needs of my clients. It is a celebration of my firm's philosophy that a perfect relationship can exist between the site, the environment and the architectural style of every home.

Rural Resort

DURAL

I met with the clients for this project on their vacant, 5-acre property to review their desire to build a new home with a strong indoor–outdoor connection. Working together with the house designer, we developed a floor plan providing large glass openings and strong sight lines from a number of locations in the home.

Through a large clear-glass front entry, the position of the pool is immediately apparent with a shallow pond starting against the rear glass and flowing into the pool.

The pool widens – accommodating the spa after a series of floating steppers located at the far end of the pond – as it stretches a further 14.5 metres before reaching the infinity edge, where water overflows to a lower tank. The pool has a firm connection with the entertaining pavilion, which is designed at 45 degrees to the pool to create architectural interest and to allow a better line of sight from the kitchen inside. The pavilion has a large chimney clad in Italian granite. Along with a fireplace and lounge area there is space for a television, which is also visible from within the pool. An electric pizza oven is positioned on the side of the chimney, providing another cooking option. Behind the fireplace is a small bathroom, so there is no need to return to the main house. Alongside the lounge area is an outdoor kitchen fully equipped for entertaining.

All of these items sit on a hardwood timber deck that is suspended over the pool. It also backs onto the tennis court, located behind the pavilion, providing a perfect elevated viewing space. The planting selected to surround the home, pool and pavilion consists of leafless bird of paradise (*Strelitzia reginae* 'Juncea'), Mexican lily (*Beschorneria yuccoides*), century plant (*Agave attenuata*), Japanese sago palm (*Cycas revoluta*), purple fountain grass (*Pennisetum advena* 'Rubrum'), variegated mondo (*Ophiopogon intermedians* 'Stripey White'), blue chalk sticks (*Senecio serpens*) and yellow star jasmine (*Trachelospermum asiaticum*). An advanced Canary Island date palm (*Phoenix canariensis*) was installed next to the pool to provide midday shade and give a horticultural balance to the pavilion structure.

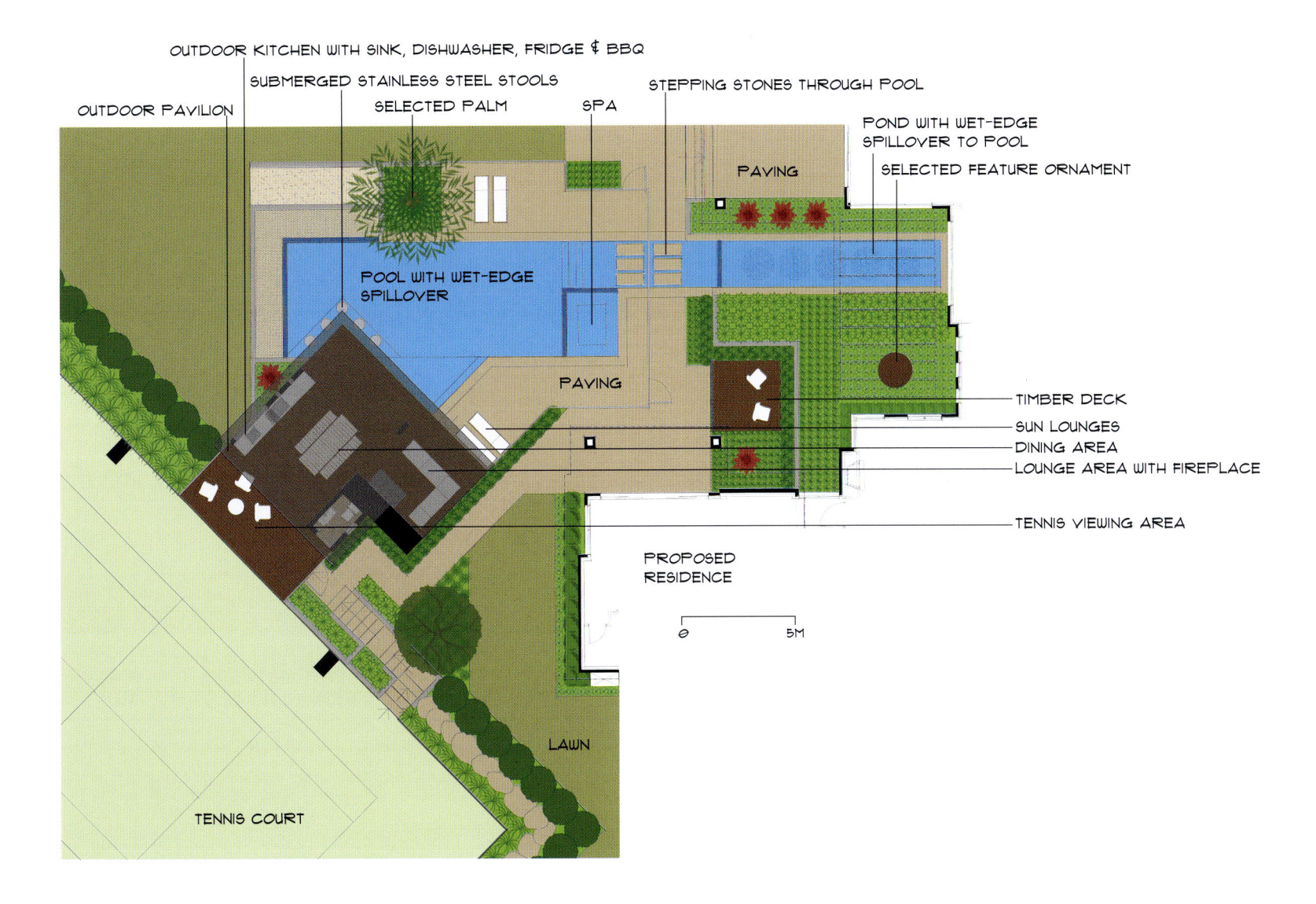

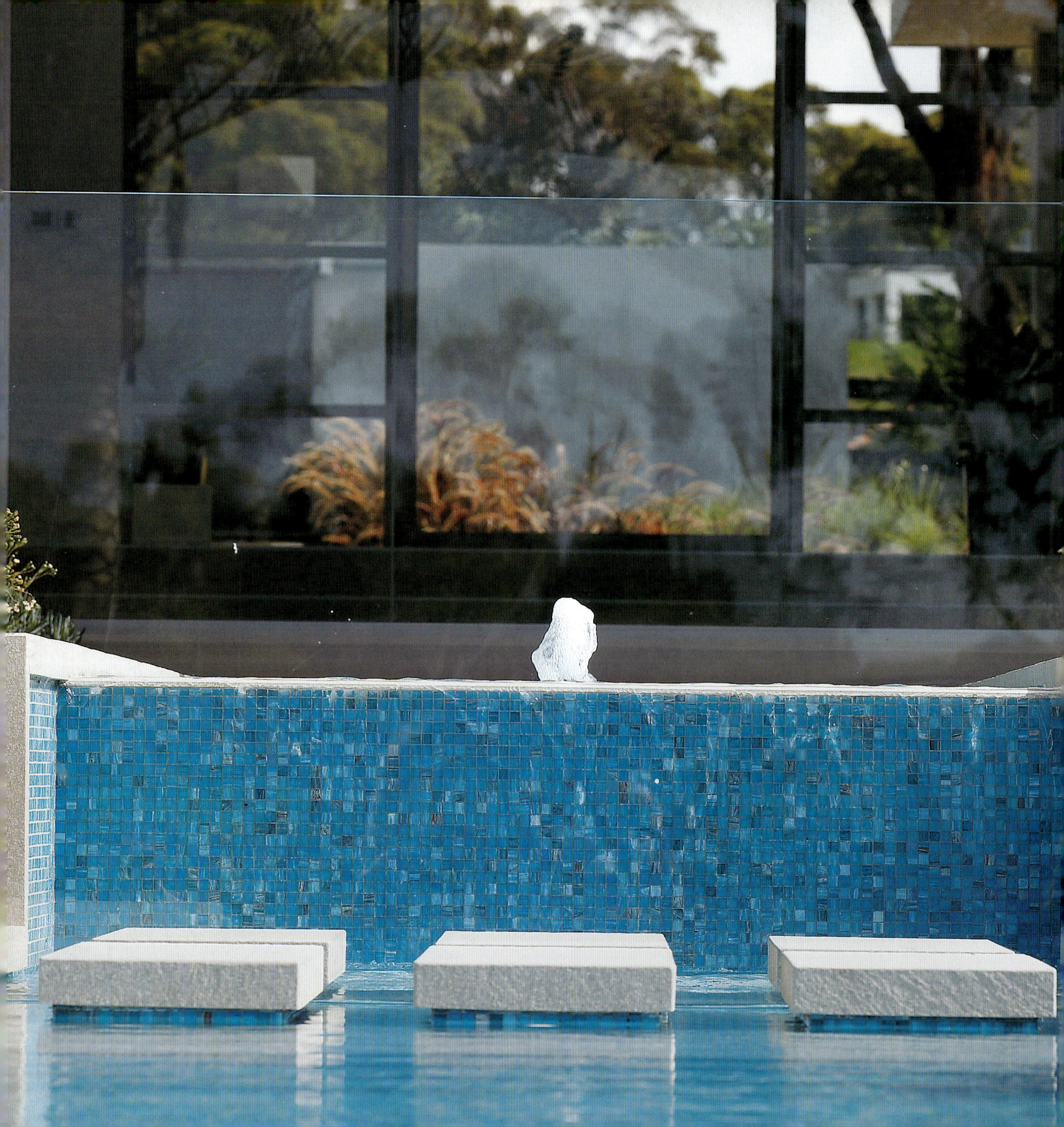

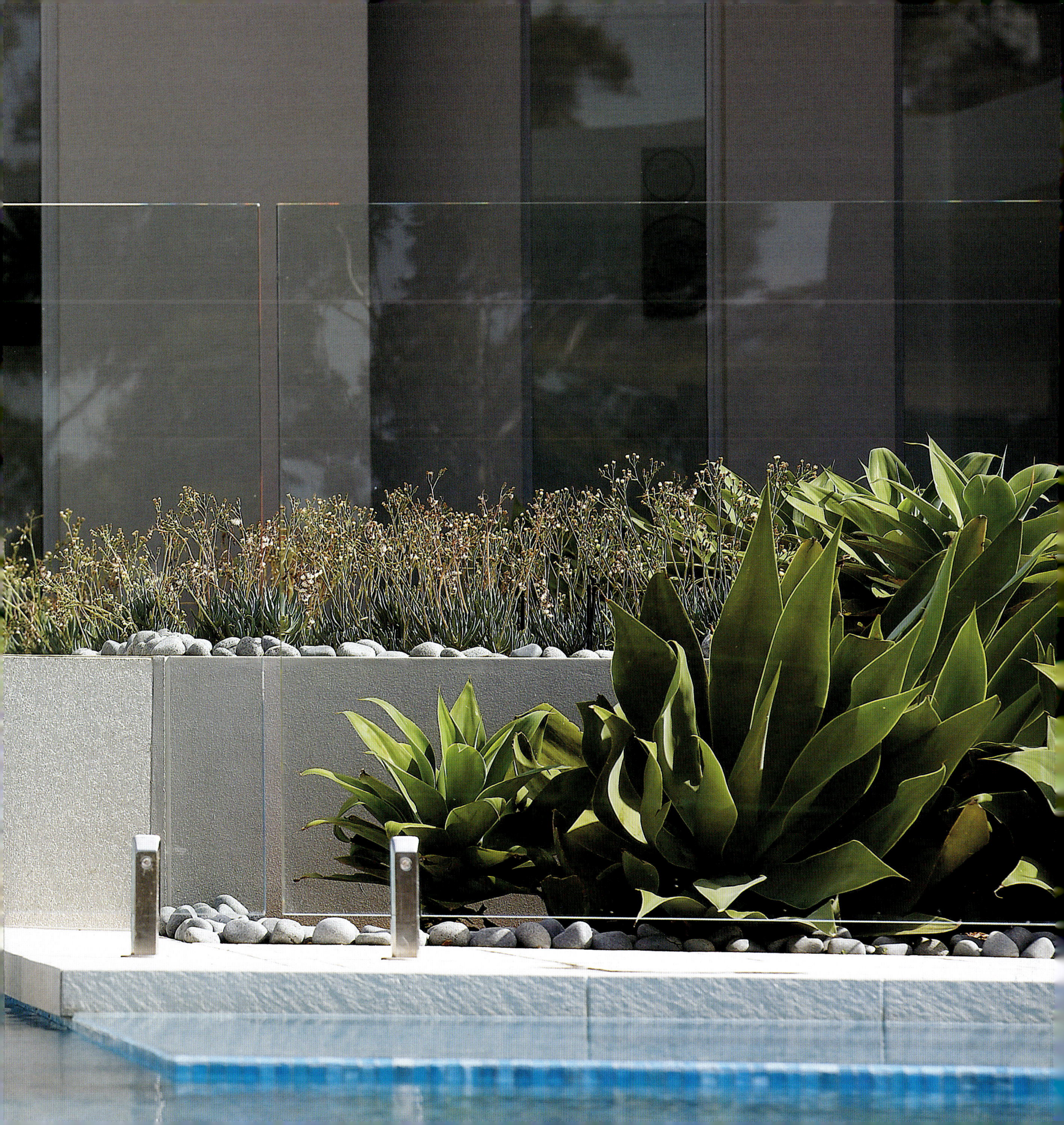

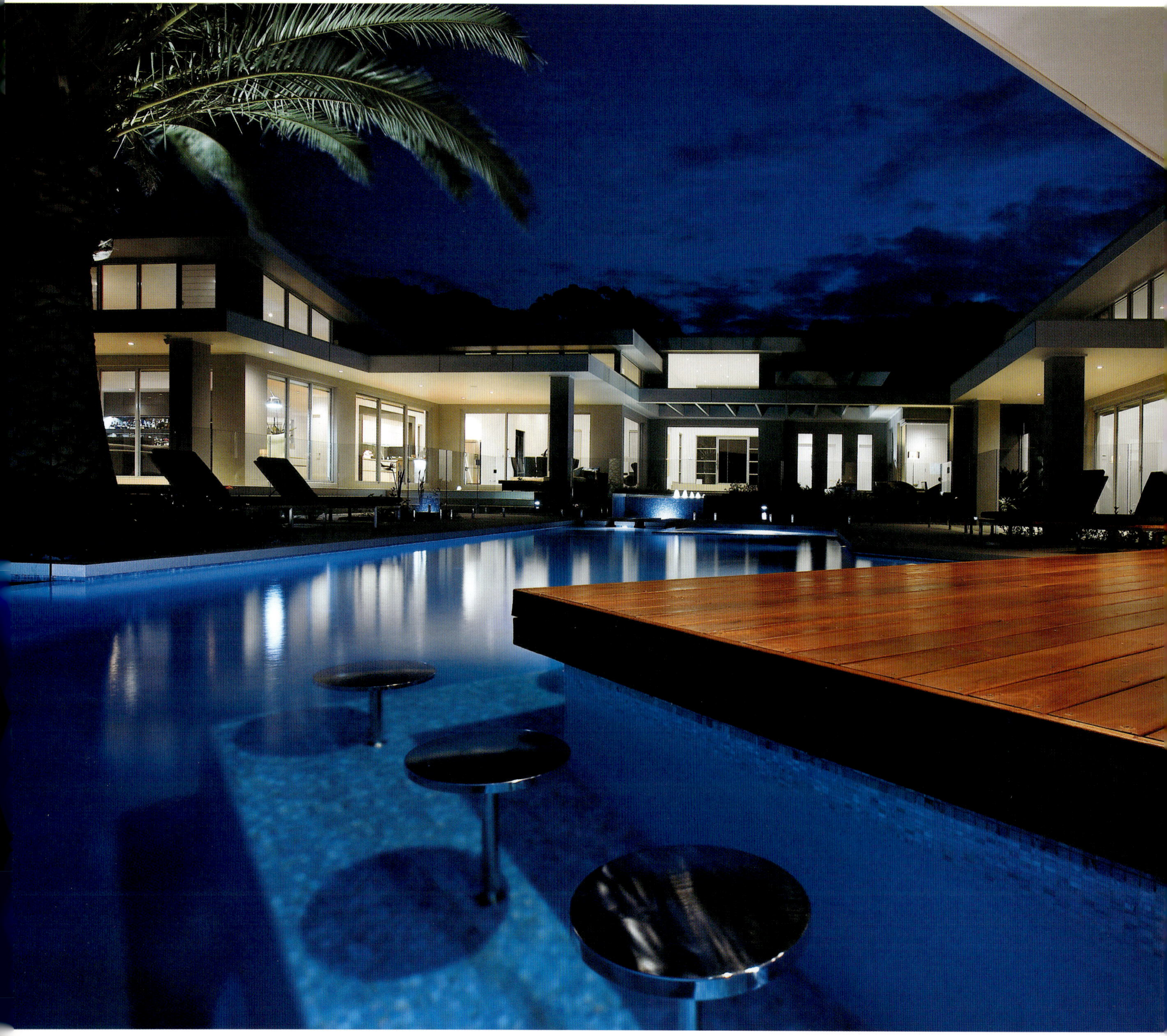

RURAL RESORT 13

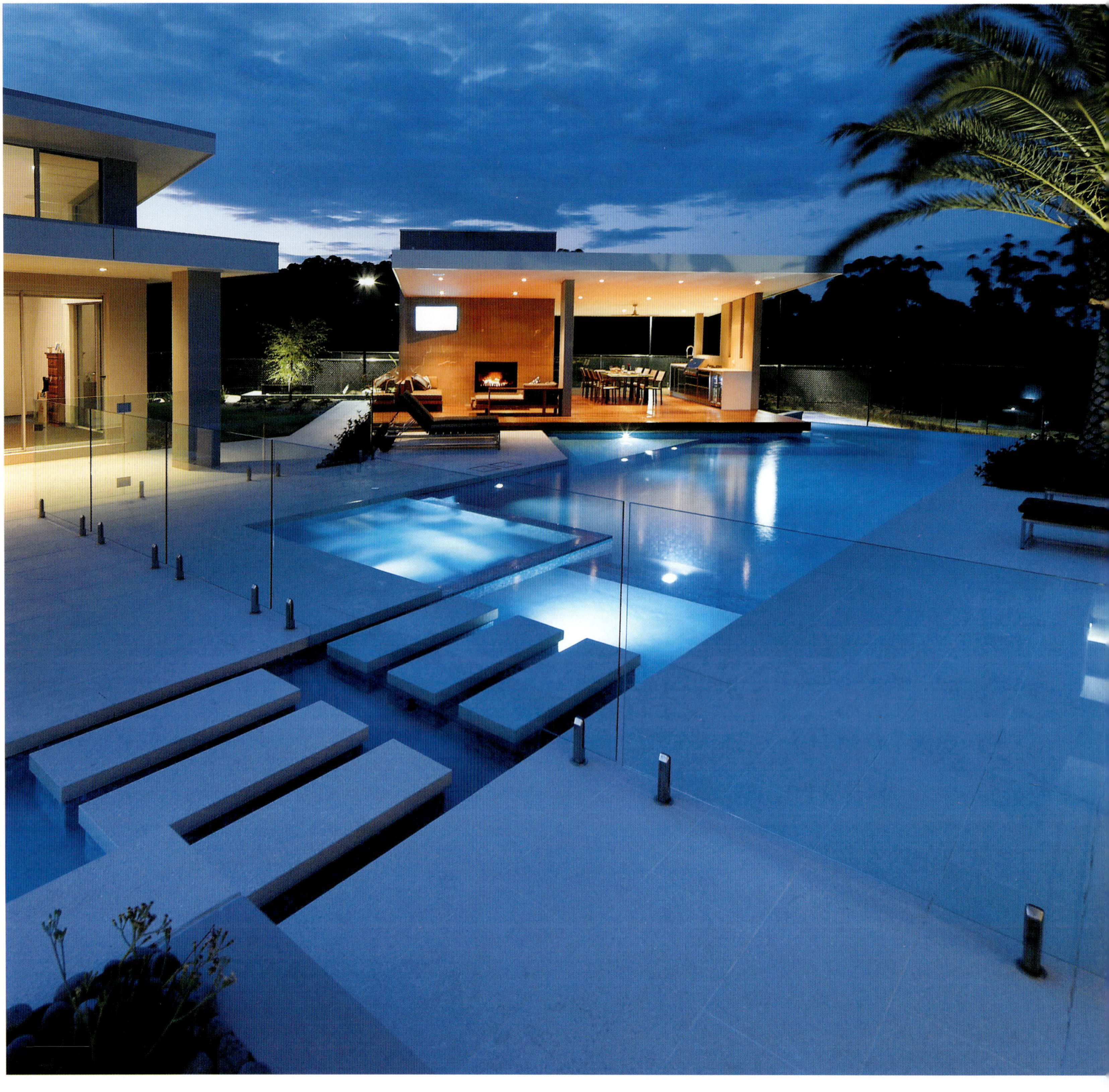

RURAL RESORT 15

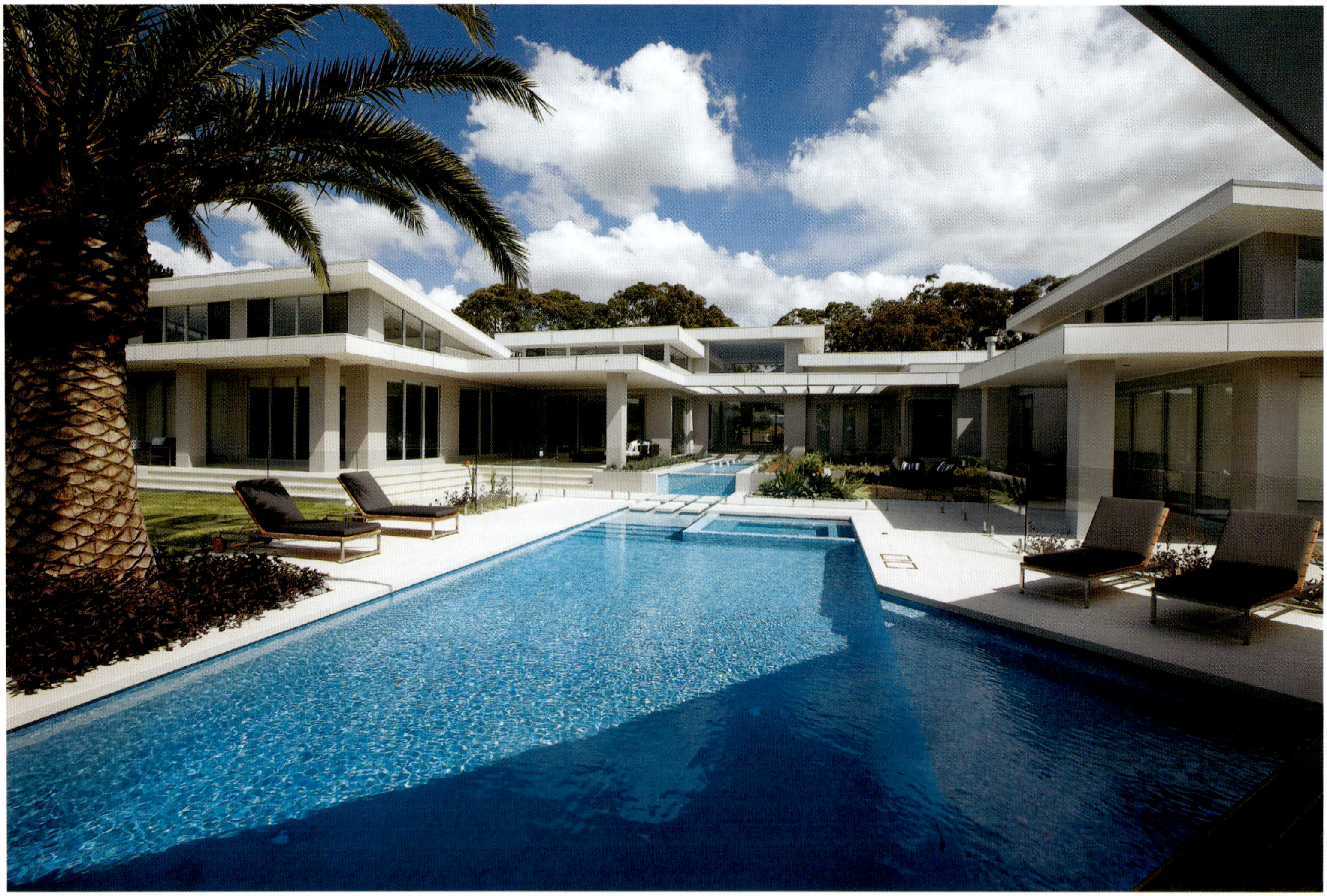

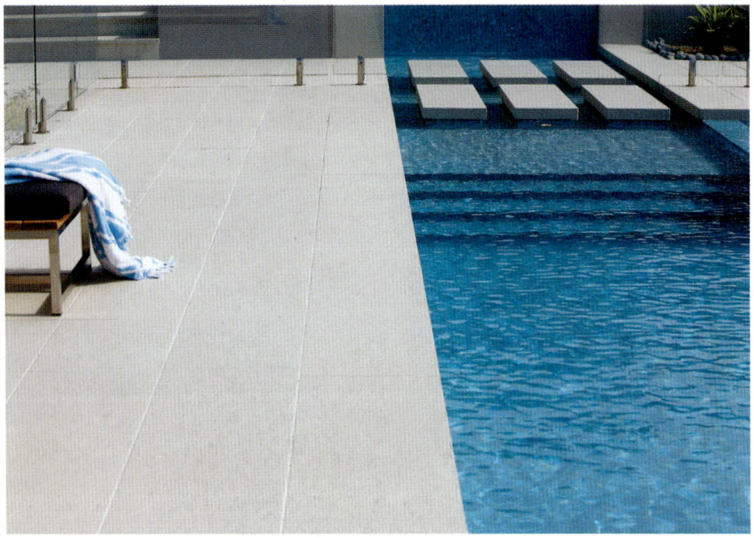

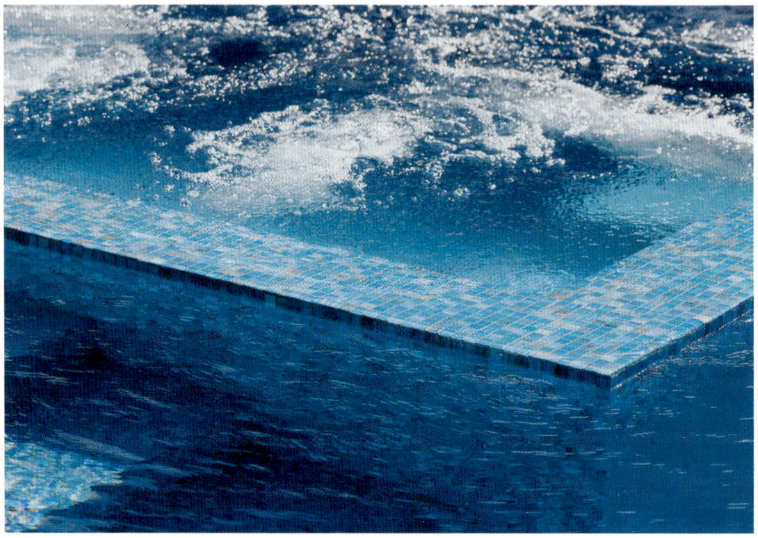

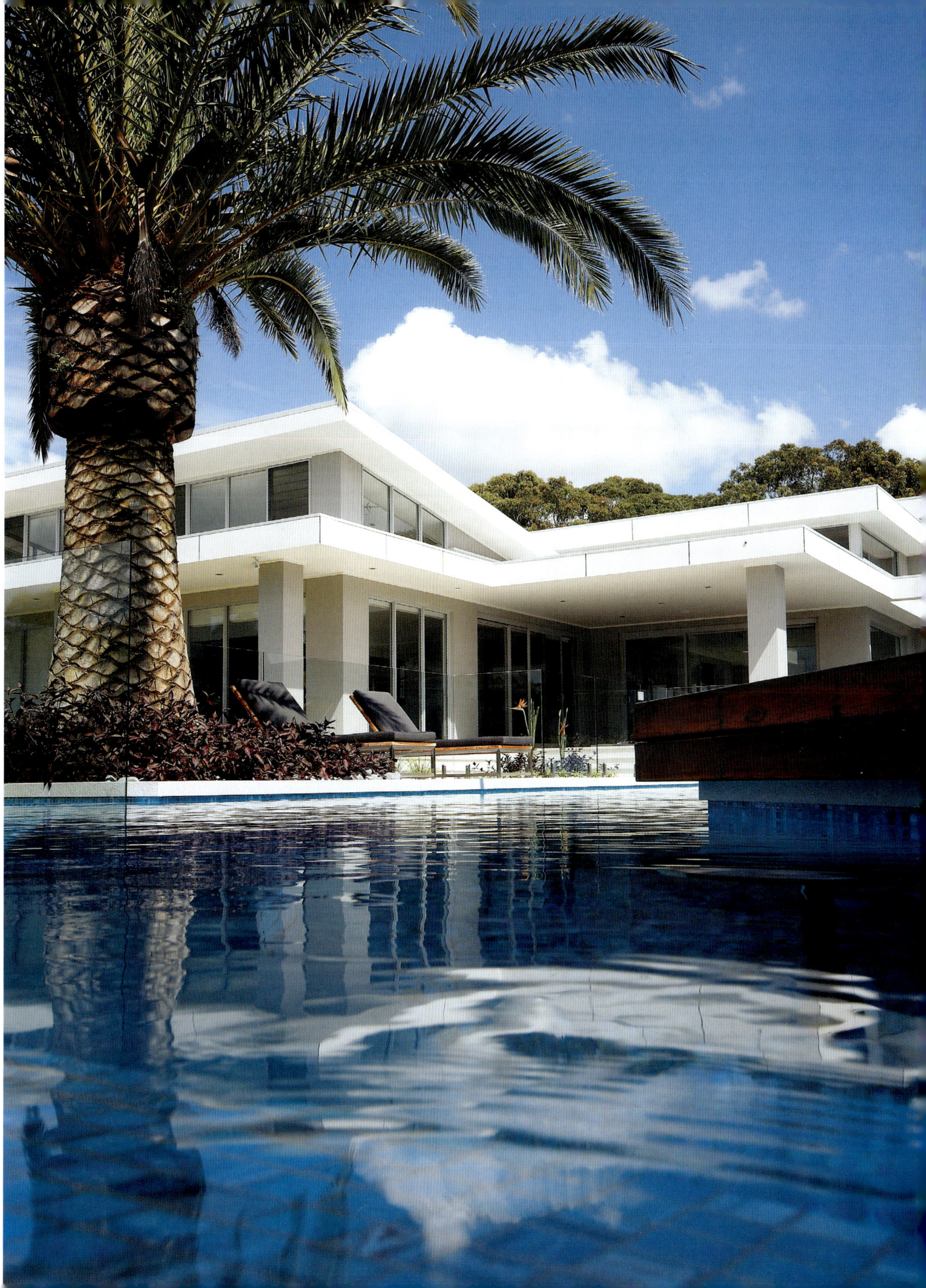

Returning to the Melbourne International Flower and Garden Show for the third time, for what was going to be my seventh show garden in all, I saw it as an important opportunity to not just design and build a garden but to send a message though a designed space that had real meaning and could assist in the greater awareness of a cause. With this in mind I was drawn to the effects that the different forms of mental illness were having on the community and used this as inspiration to form the design.

The look and feel of the garden was designed to offer a relaxing atmosphere while still having a structure of strength as the centrepiece. The colours, textures and plant palette were all selected to play a role, along with the scale of individual items.

Reflections

MELBOURNE

The stepping-stone path that greets visitors at the entry of the garden represents the beginning of the journey. The stepping stones start out large, indicating that the first step to healing is a big one. Each stepper is slightly smaller than the last, representing the positive gains made by continuing along this path. At the end of the path, visitors are faced with a wall that encourages them to turn and take the stairs up to a new space. This represents a poignant moment in the healing process – the 'turning point' for those who suffer – and celebrates the moment they make the decision to take action towards a new direction in their lives.

At the top of the stairs is a space where key elements reside and contribute to the essential message of the garden. Firstly it represents 'life', with the inclusion of fire and water – two essential elements for survival. A roof structure represents the milestone of 'turning your life around'; with its 180-degree curve and large scale it represents how important and what an achievement that milestone is. A timber deck with a simple setting of two chairs is a place of reflection for two people to connect and discuss the private matter of their journey. Surrounding this space is a pond providing the gentle movement of water, which flows over the infinity edge, along with a lush planting palette to soften the structures, as if softening the harshness of the illness or providing a sanctuary from it.

Above this space is the outdoor bathroom, another space of reflection and healing, providing a unique experience in the garden. The ability to bathe outside under the stars is a great experience and is even better if shared with someone you love. A sculptural piece appropriately named *Lovers* was placed within this space to represent what is most important in life.

The plants were selected to enhance the smooth and relaxing tones of the garden. The mass planting of dwarf silver lady tree ferns (*Blechnum gibbum* 'Silver Lady') at the front of the garden provides a clear view of the structure while softening the area. Giant bromeliads (*Alcantarea imperialis* 'Peter Tristram' and *A. imperialis* 'Rubrum'), grey star ctenanthe (*Ctenanthe setosa* 'Grey Star'), rhoeo (*Tradescantia spathacea*) and ti plant (*Cordyline fruticosa* 'Rubra') were added to bring colour among the lush greens. The use of sweeper weeping lilly pilly (*Waterhousia floribunda* 'Sweeper'), slender weavers bamboo (*Bambusa textilis* 'Gracilis') and the Illawarra flame tree (*Brachychiton acerifolius*) continue the theme and also provide dense screening and scale to the roof structure. The relaxing atmosphere of ferns and palms complements the inclusion of bangalow palms (*Archontophoenix cunninghamiana*), bird's nest ferns (*Asplenium nidus*), king ferns (*Todea barbara*) as well as tree ferns (*Cyathea* spp.). Some of these plants make their way to the outdoor bathroom, and the inclusion of bromeliads, with their striking red flowers, adds a little colour and passion to the space.

This garden will mean different things to different people. If we are able to make somebody smile, evoke a thought of compassion, or assist in a personal struggle – then our goal has been achieved.

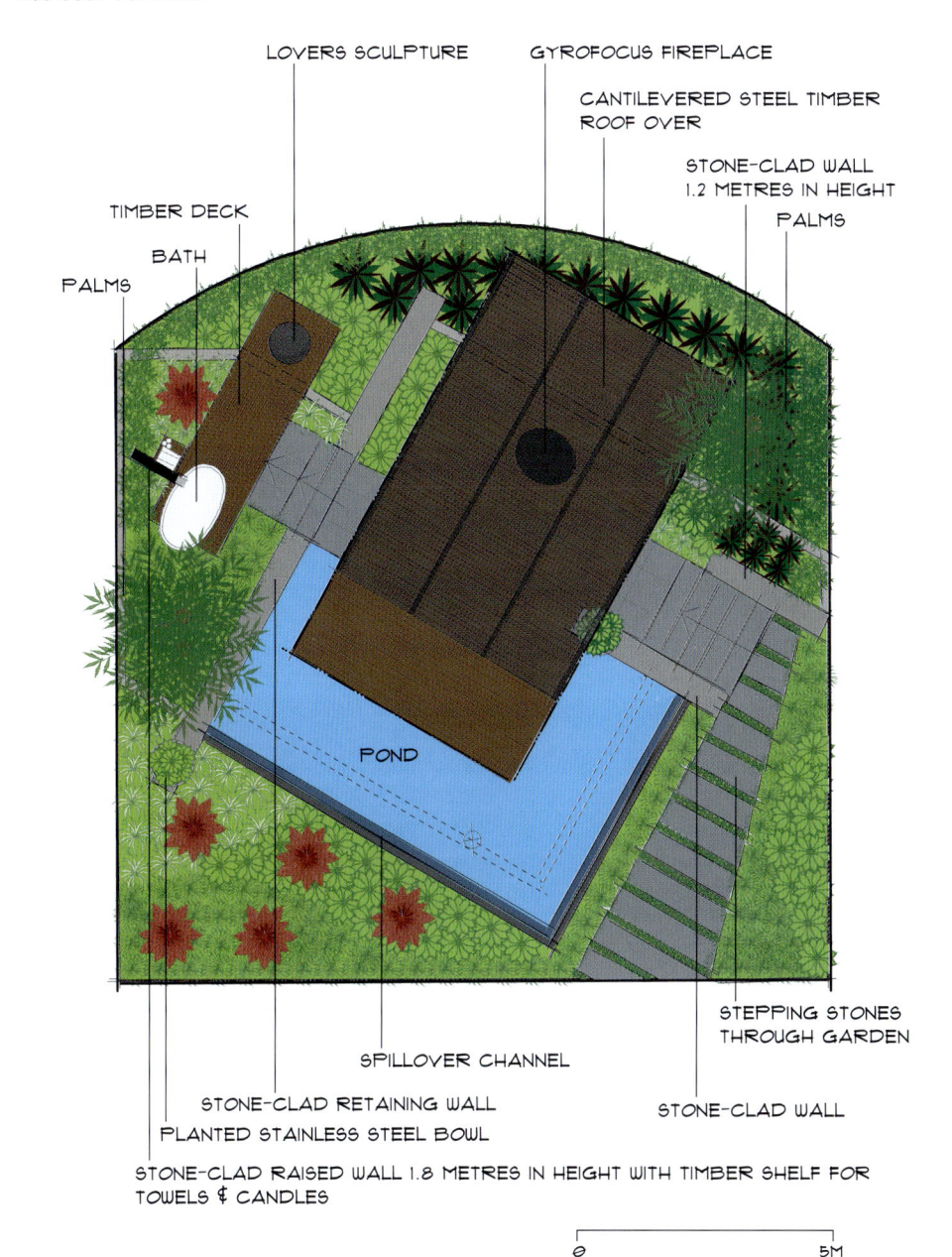

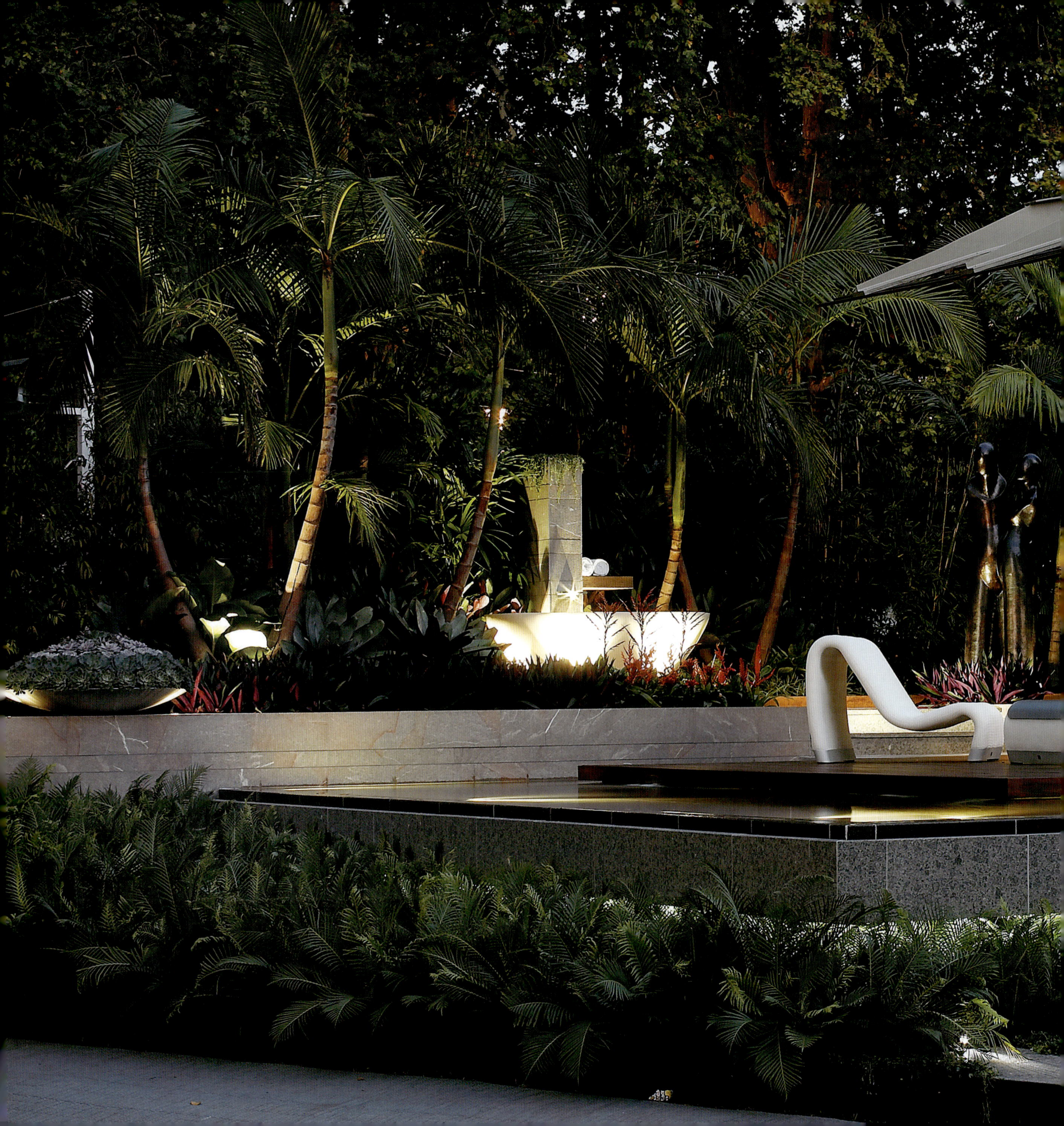

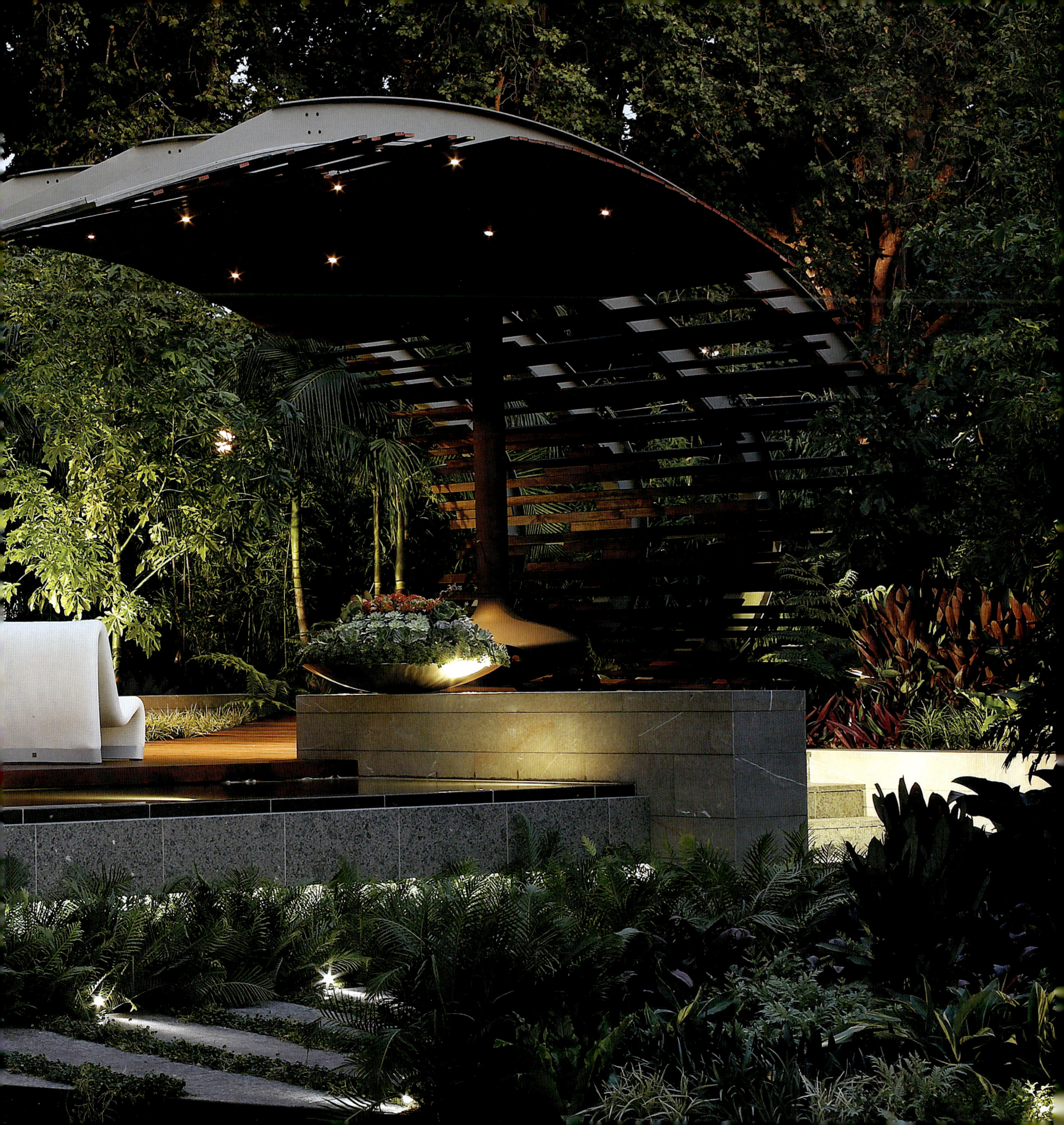

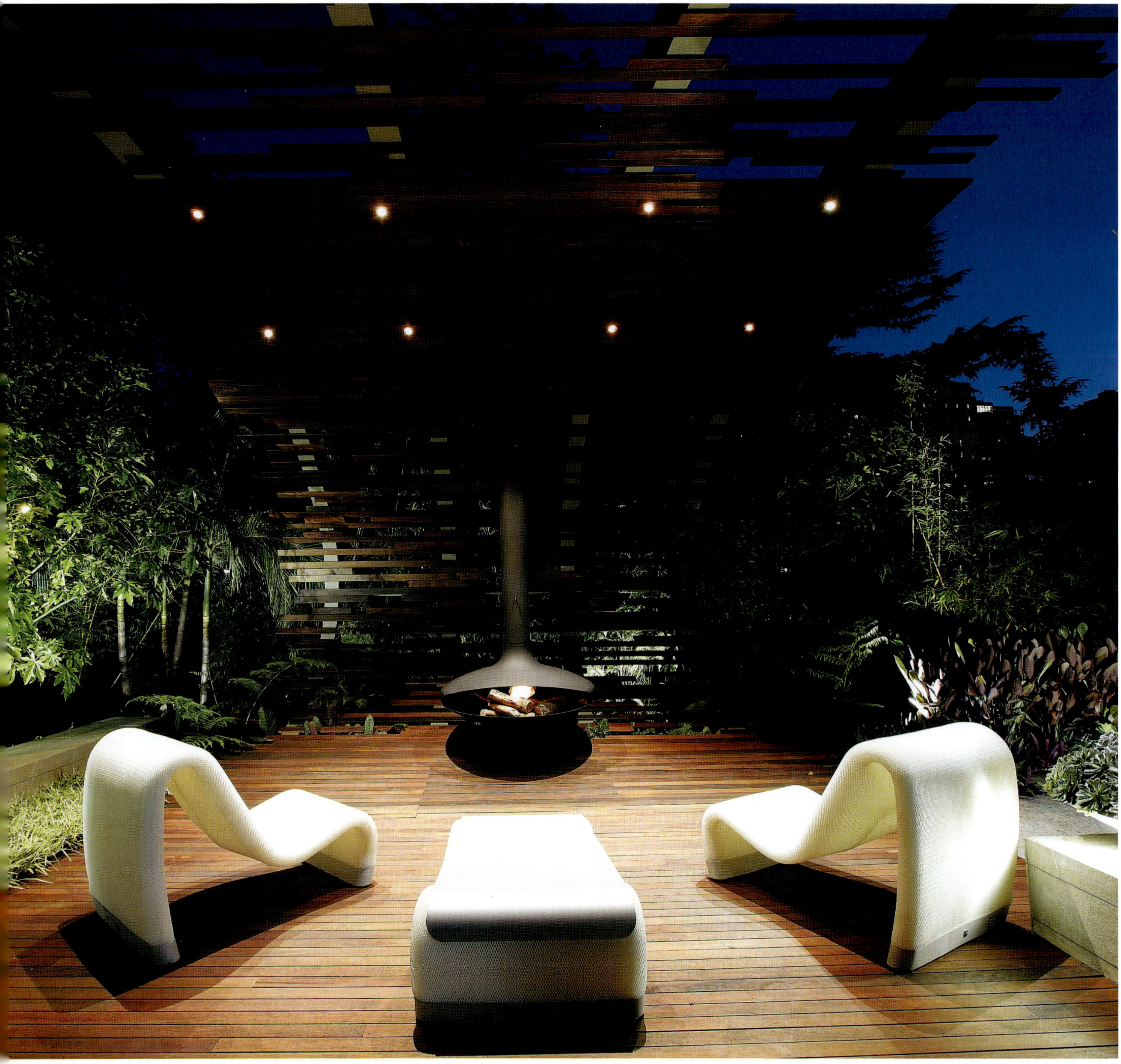

REFLECTIONS 23

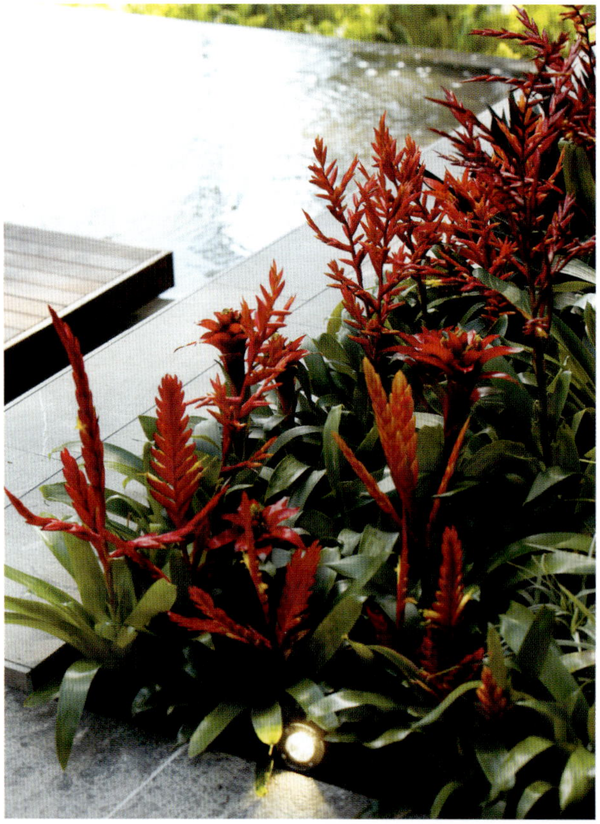

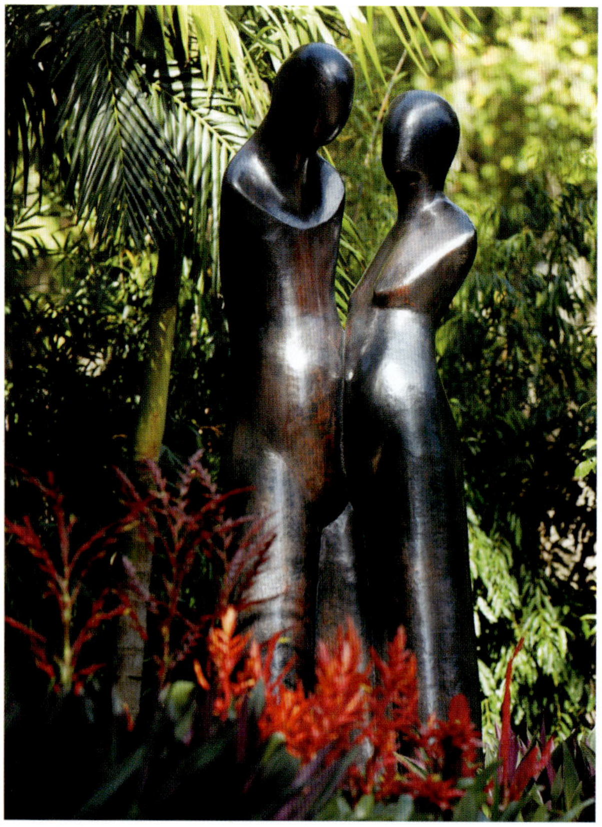

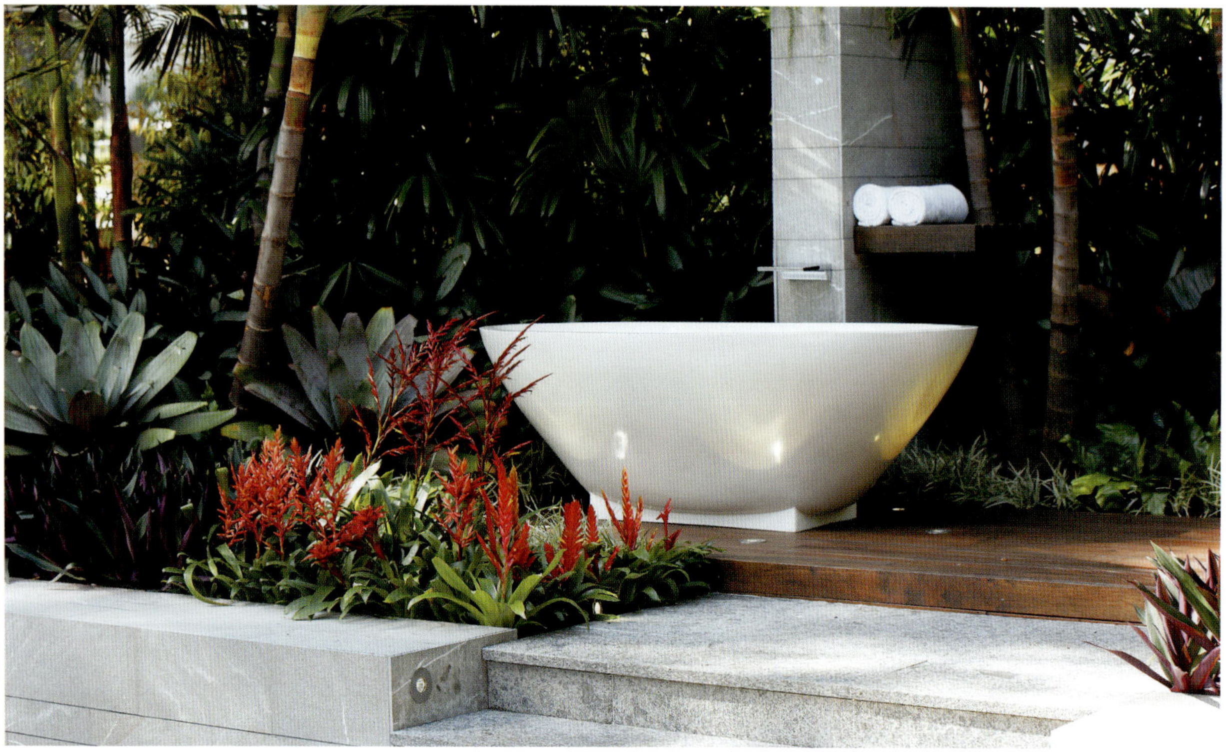

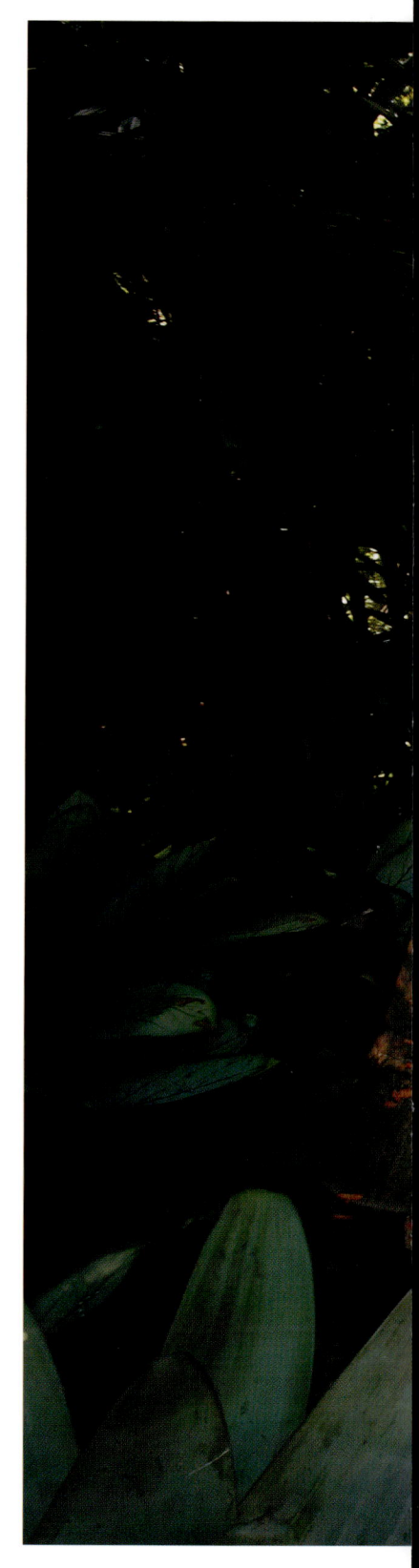

REFLECTIONS 25

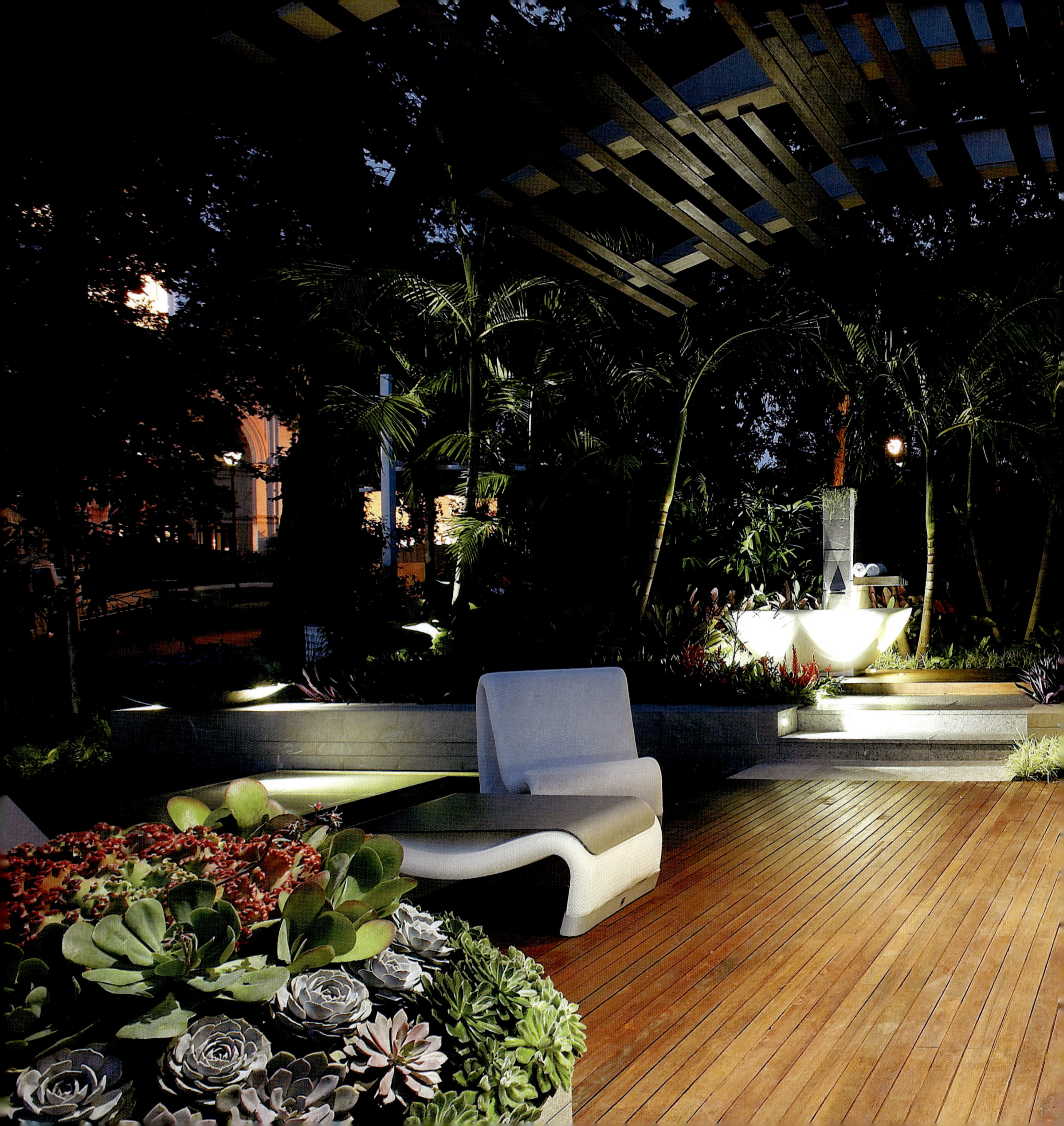

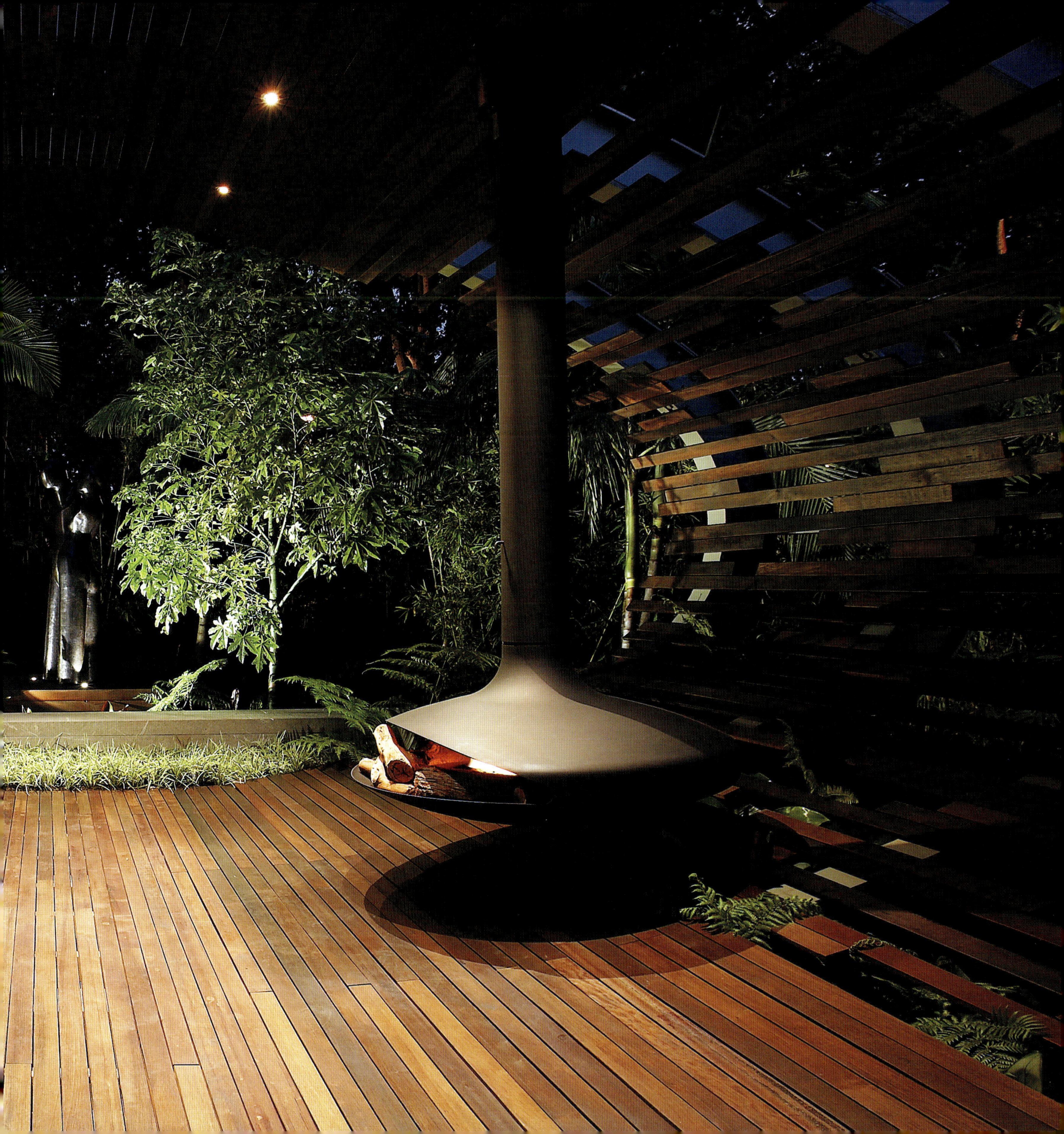

A pavilion can expand the available functional areas within a home, but a well-designed pavilion with full inclusions and a relevant position to other external assets can completely transform how all entertaining is carried out, giving a property an envious reputation.

My brief for this project was to design and build a pavilion that maximises the entertaining opportunities of the property and complements the pool. The scale of the pavilion in relation to the existing house and pool was important in order to display a seamless connection.

Inside, the cooking space consists of an island bench with a commercial-grade teppanyaki hotplate – positioned to overlook the pool so a watchful eye can monitor the children

The Pavilion

DURAL

while they swim. The island bench is also a great way to interact with friends and family while cooking, as people can sit opposite the cook, including them in the conversation.

Set to the wall behind is a 7-metre bench that houses the sink, dishwasher, ice-maker and triple-glazed fridge and ensures that all appliances are on hand when required. The length of bench space is ample for the preparation and serving of food, including pizzas, which can be cooked in the pizza oven installed above in the back wall. The end of the bench provides the perfect location to house wood for the adjoining fireplace. Clad in beige travertine with grey-blue undertones, it acts as a contrasting structural statement at that end of the pavilion. This area is furnished with a lounge and an open fireplace providing a comfortable place to retreat to after the cooking and dining is over, whatever the season.

The pavilion is located right on the edge of the pool, providing an unspoilt relationship between the two. With both structures in a set elevation above natural ground, they take advantage of the natural bushland view and rolling lawn, while maintaining a direct connection with the home.

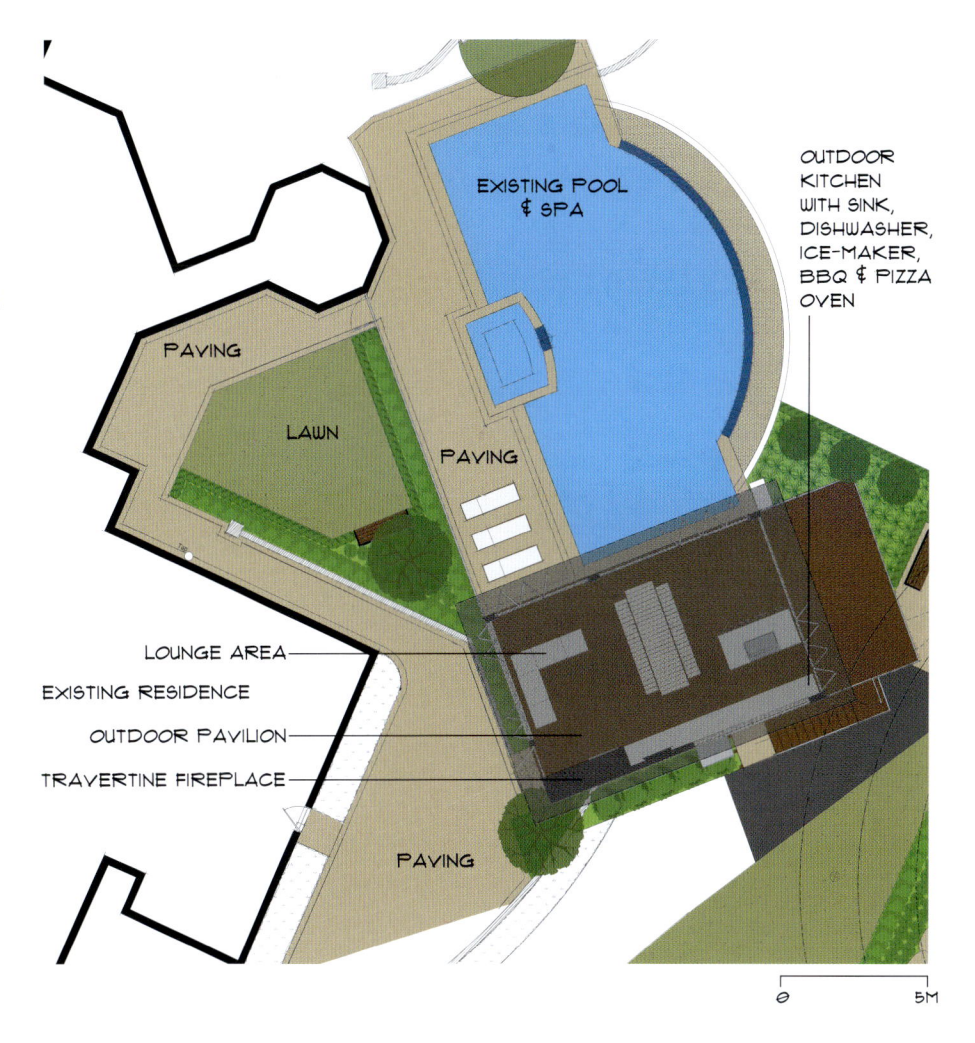

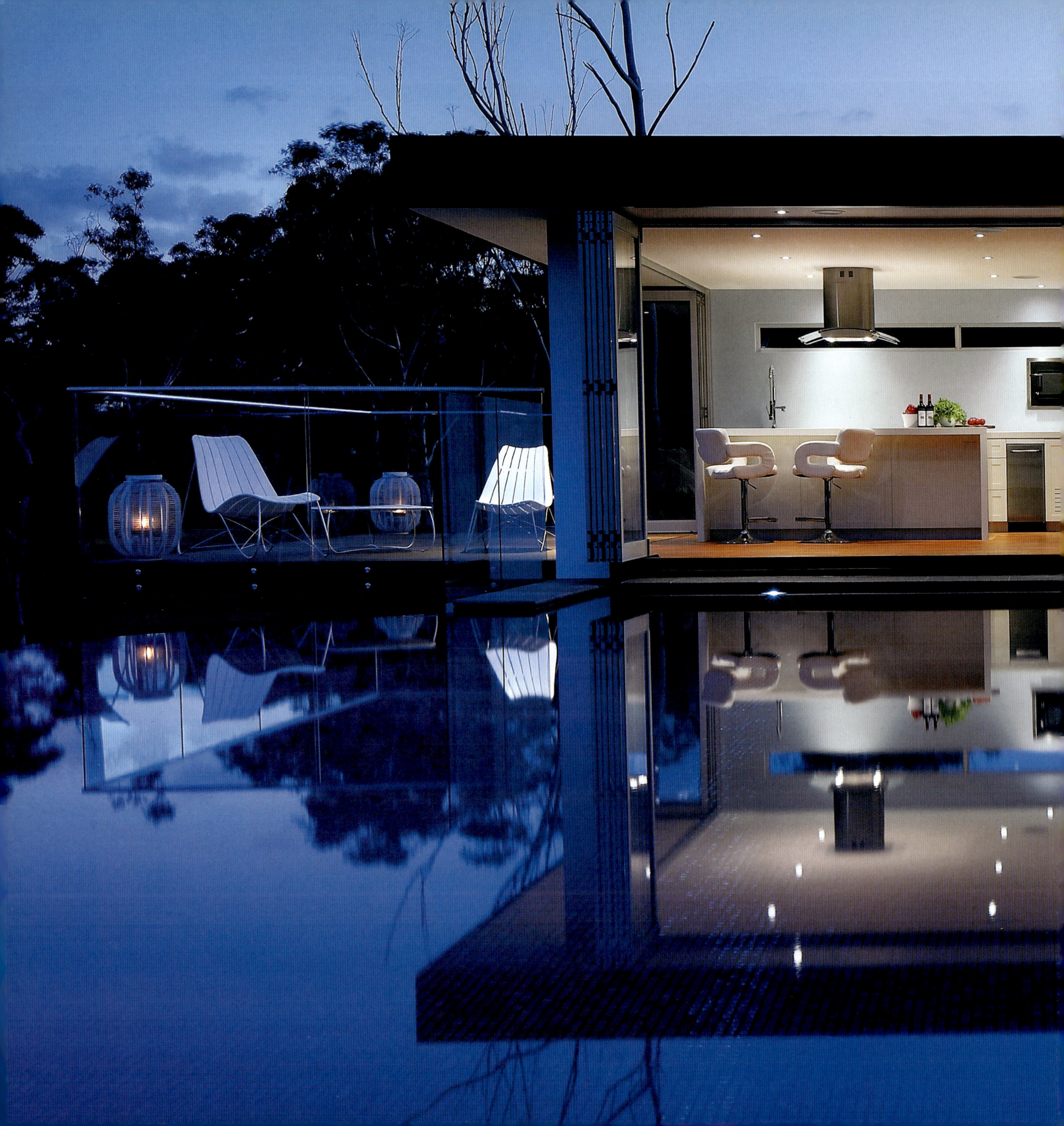

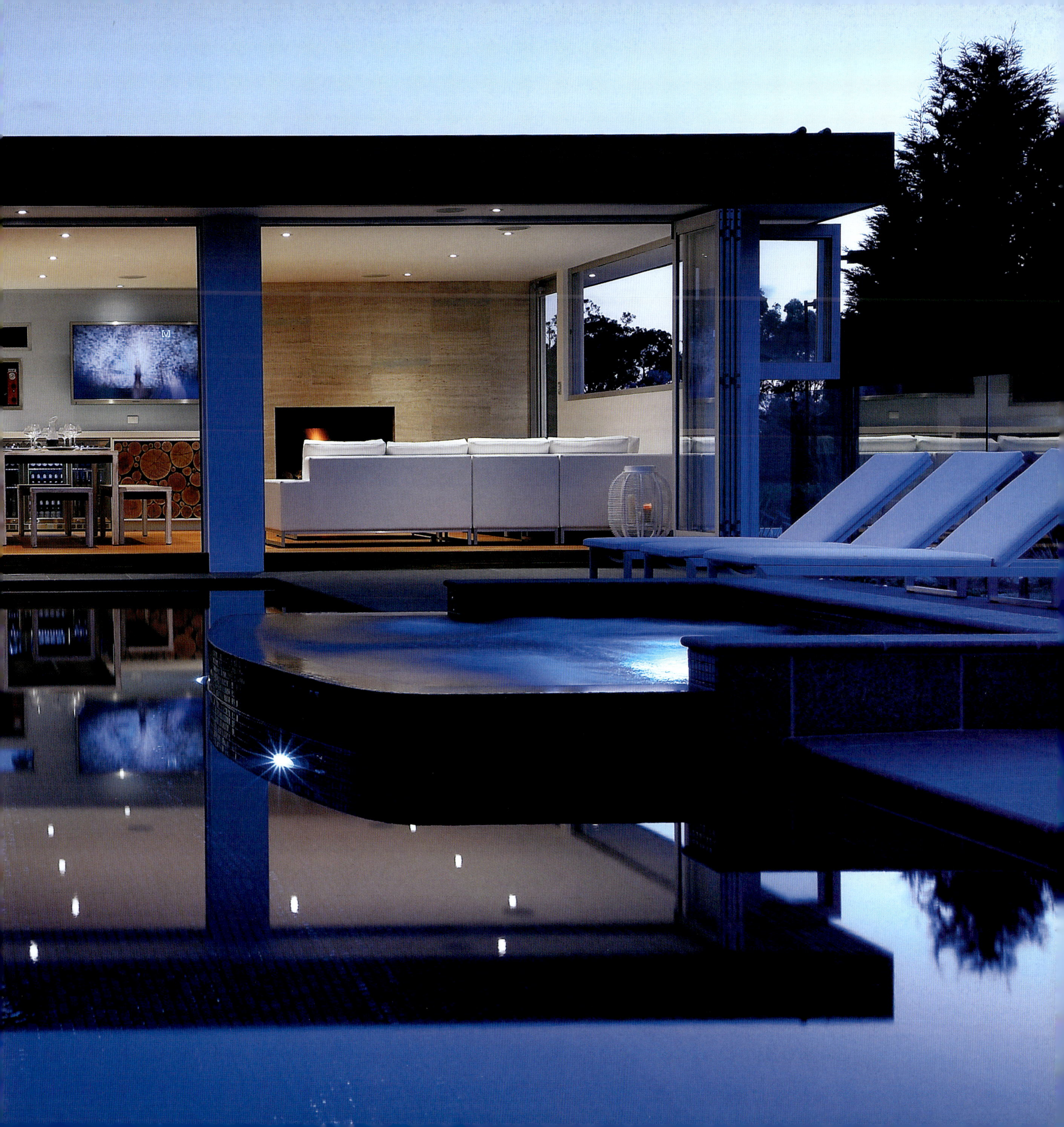

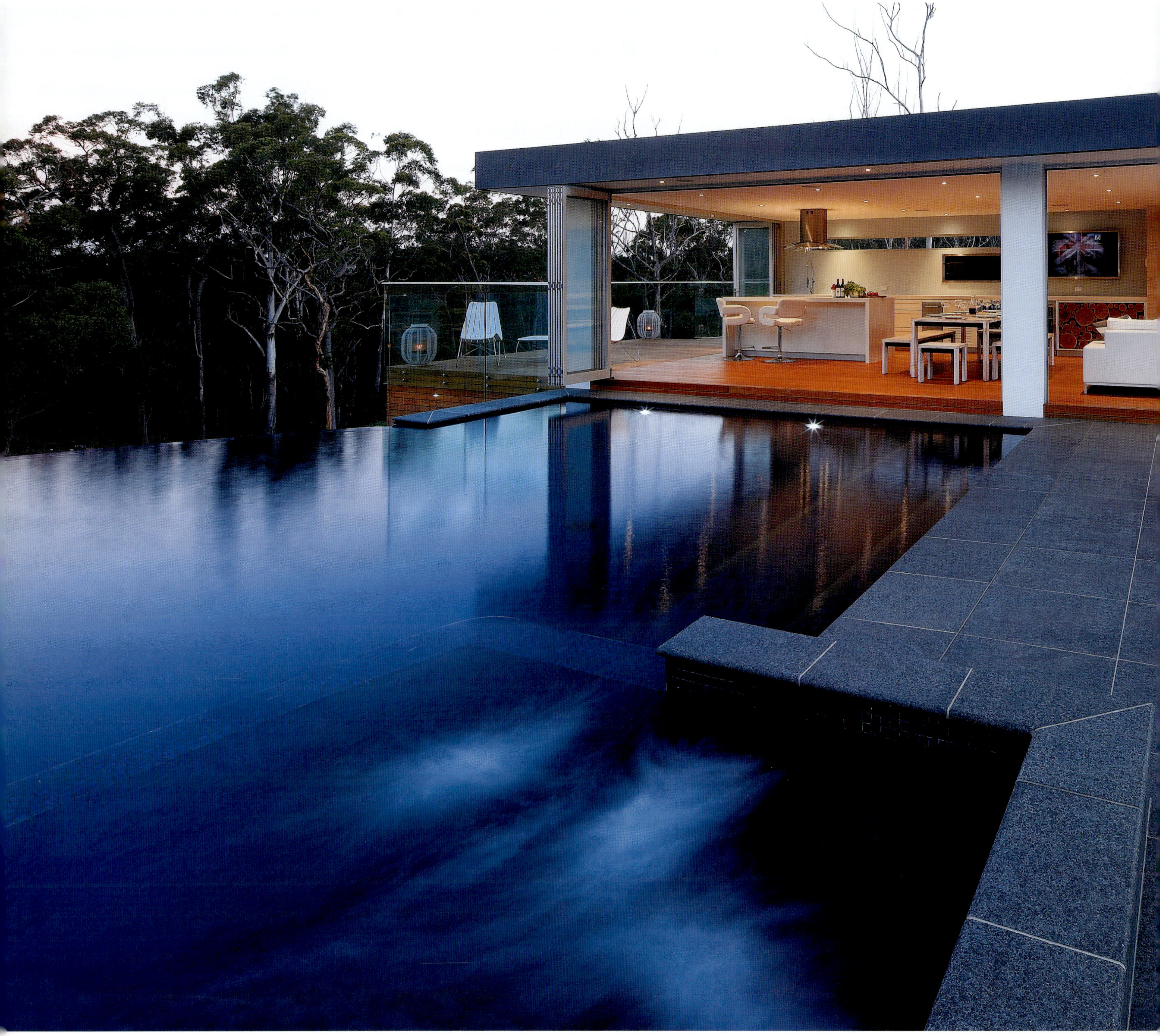

THE PAVILION 33

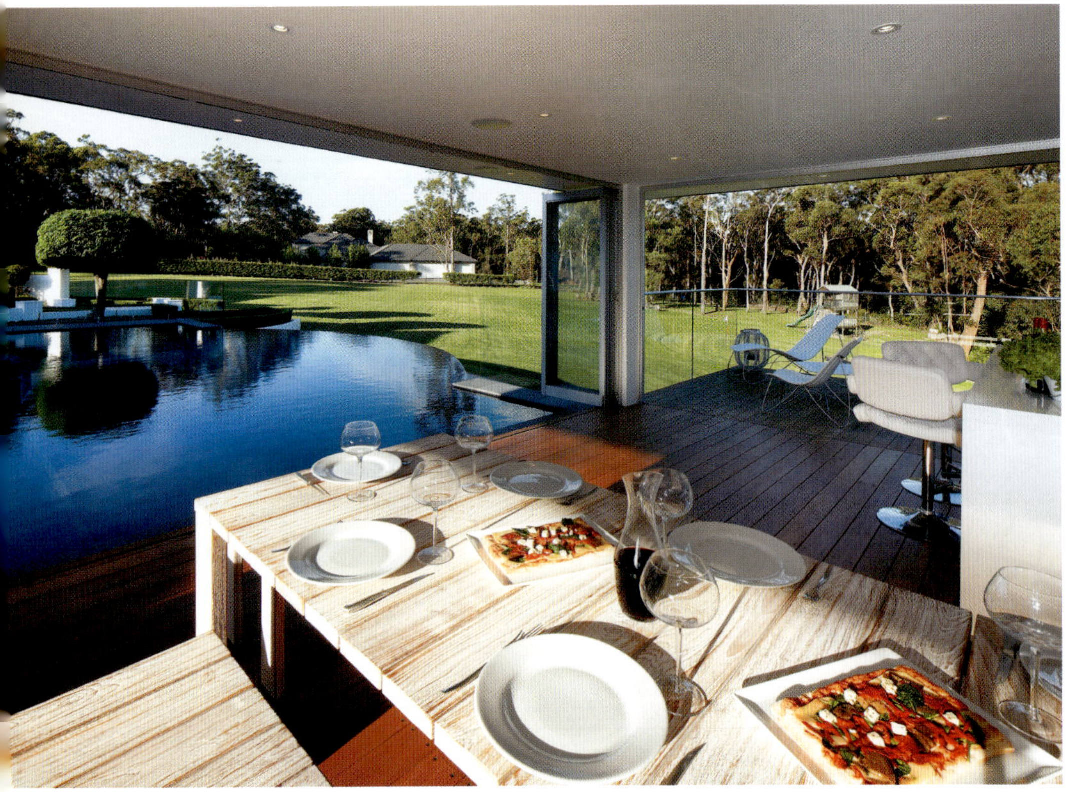

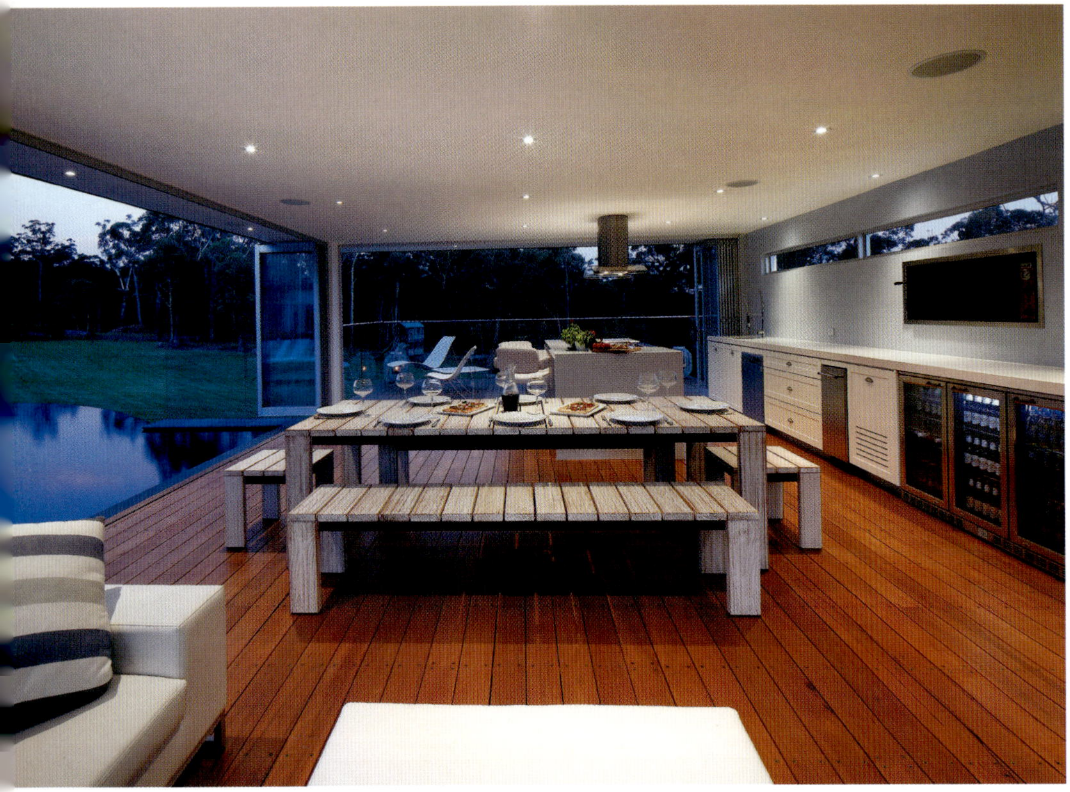

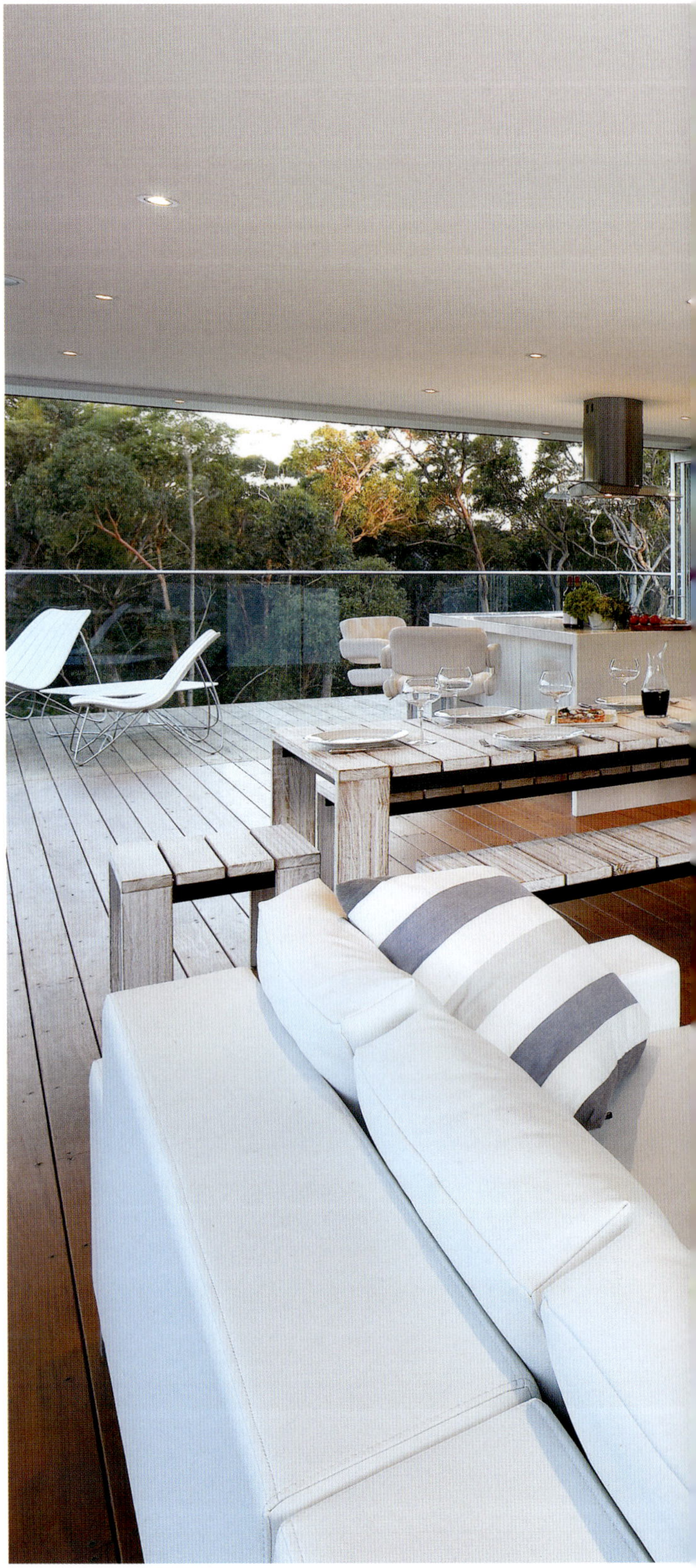

THE PAVILION 35

This project brief, covering an area of 110 square metres, brought many challenges. Throughout the design process, these challenges became opportunities that enabled the clients' wishes to become reality.

The clients were keen to install a swimming pool without losing too much entertaining space from their property and to improve the indoor–outdoor connection. An L-shaped space provided opportunities to achieve the brief in a number of ways. After considering the site and setback requirements, the pool was placed, along with a hot spa, to enable adequate surrounding space for relaxation, along with room for the kids to be kids.

Mirror Image

CLOVELLY

As the pool faces a side street, I thought it was important to enhance the view from the garden and to ensure privacy by providing a raised wall finished with dry-stone cladding. To give the illusion of a larger pool when viewed from the house, a mirror was inserted within this wall. The wall also hides all the pool equipment behind it – a difficult task that is often not given proper consideration in projects covering only a small area. A raised timber deck was installed at the side of the pool to interrupt the rectangular shape and provide a location for the pool chairs and an overhead retractable shade covering.

With the area adjacent to the house less than 3.5 metres wide, mirrors were used to make it appear as large as possible. An etched sculptural design adds an individual feel and point of interest to the functional element of

STONE-CLAD WALL WITH MIRROR AND PLANTING

GATE

SPA

PAVING

SELECTED FEATURE TREES

TIMBER DECK

EXISTING HEDGE

POOL

SUN LOUNGES

SCREEN PLANTING

DECORATIVE MIRROR

OUTDOOR KITCHEN WITH SINK, BBQ & BAR FRIDGE & DISHWASHER

DINING TABLE

LOUNGE AREA

EXISTING RESIDENCE

0   5M

the space. The end result is a generous feel to the dining area, with the outdoor kitchen placed in view of the pool, allowing a strong visual connection while entertaining.

Good screen planting was used throughout the space, including lilly pilly (*Syzygium australe* 'Select Form') at the boundary and ornamental pears (*Pyrus calleryana* 'Chanticleer') as feature trees. Rhoeo (*Tradescantia spathacea*) and century plants (*Agave attenuata*) give a lush feel to the smaller garden beds.

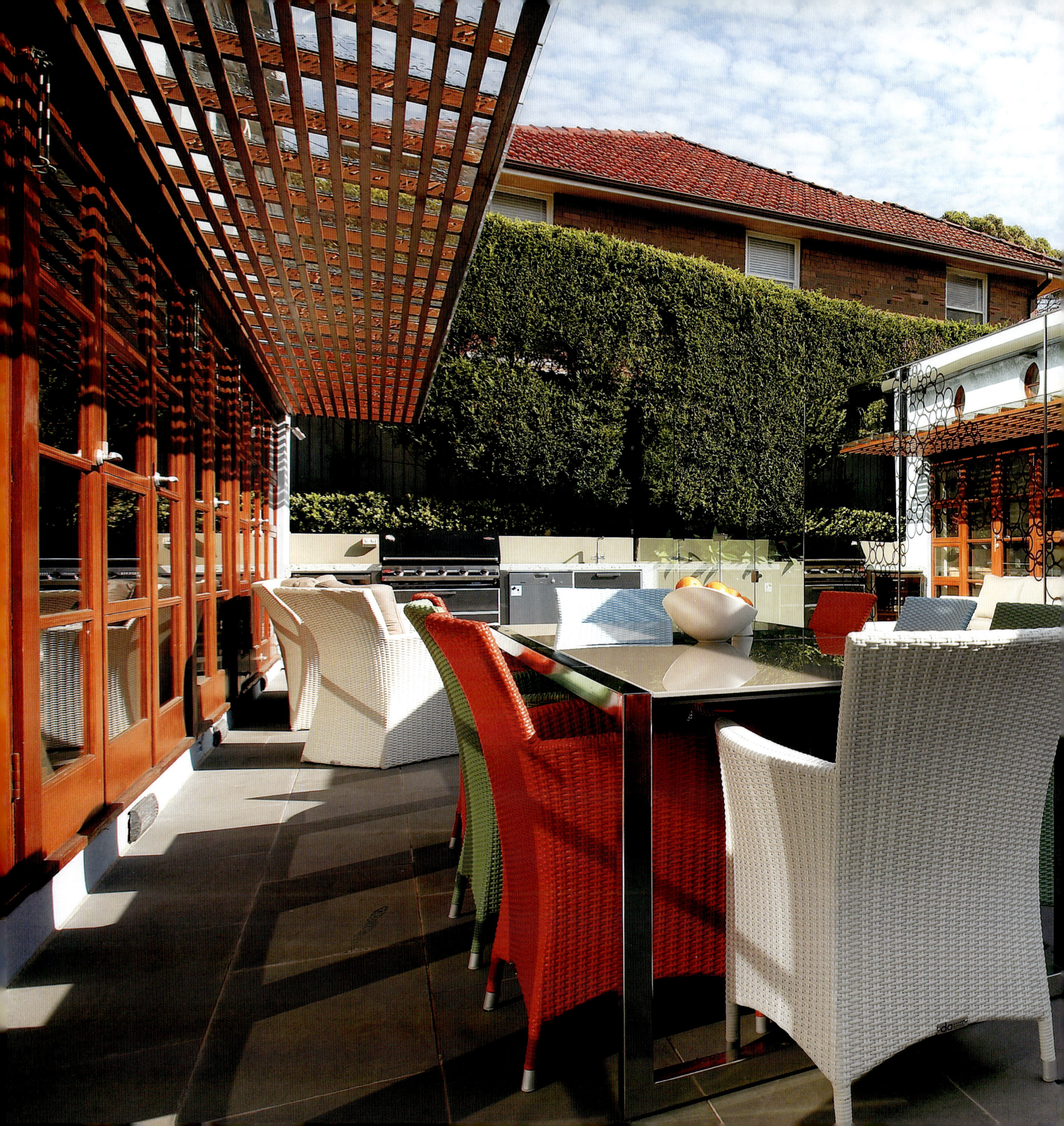

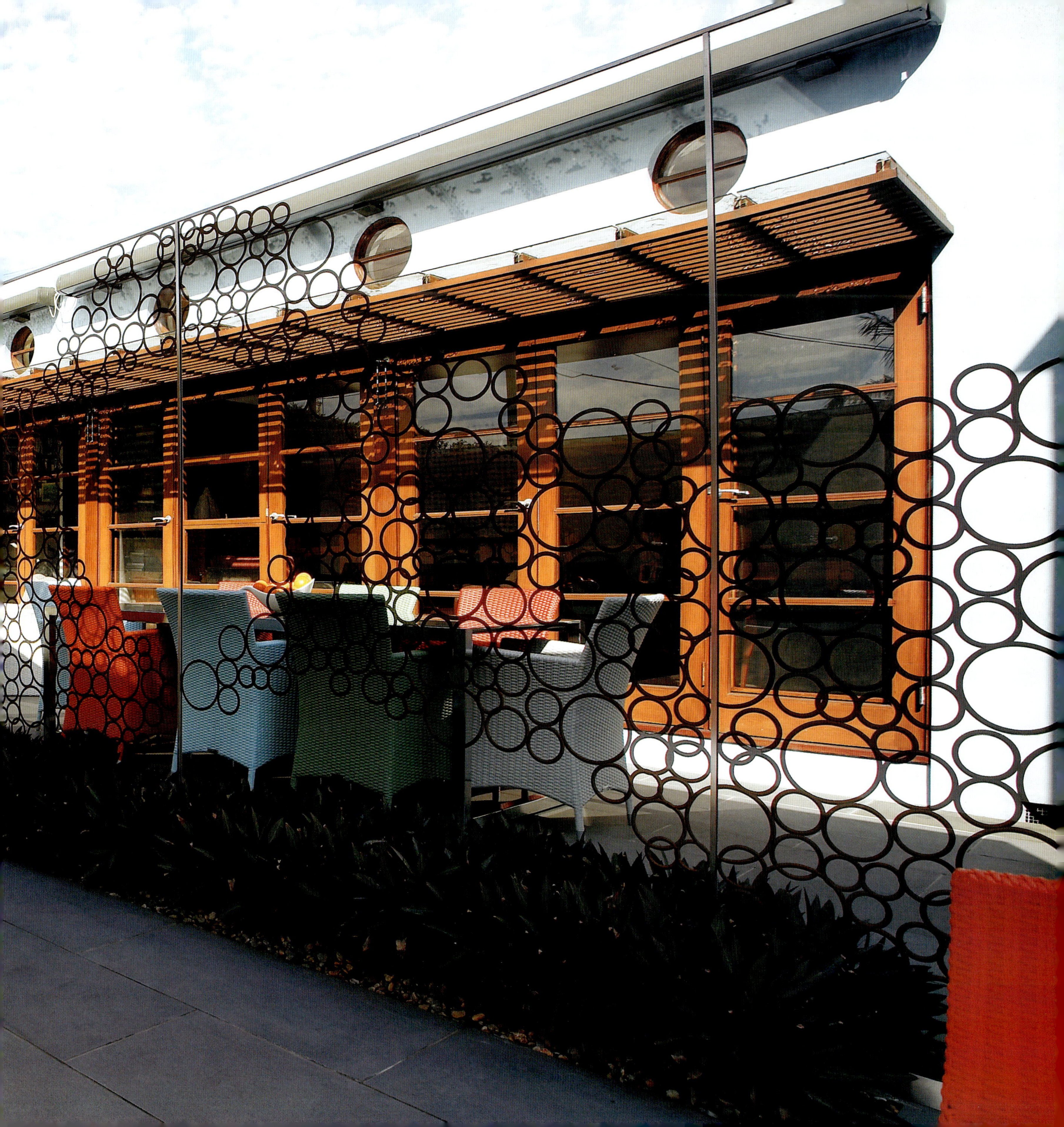

40

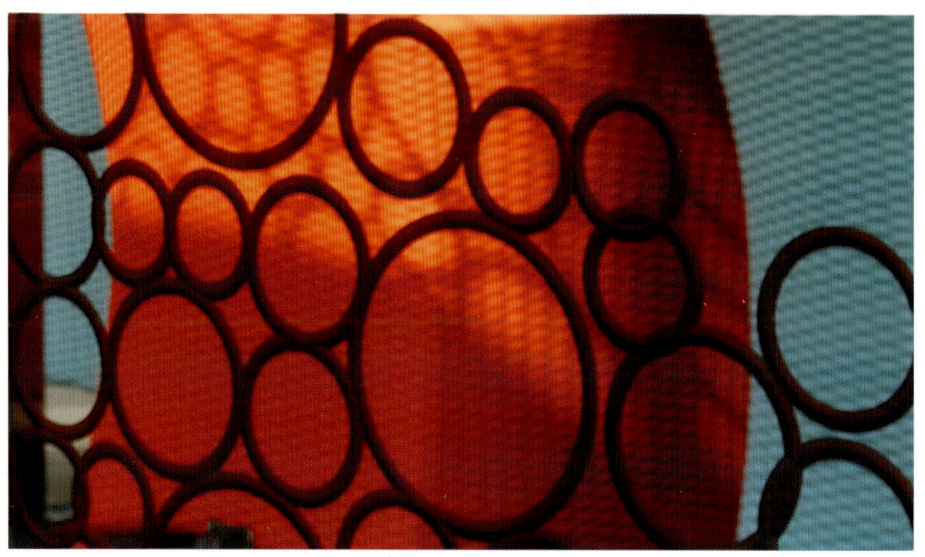

MIRROR IMAGE 41

42

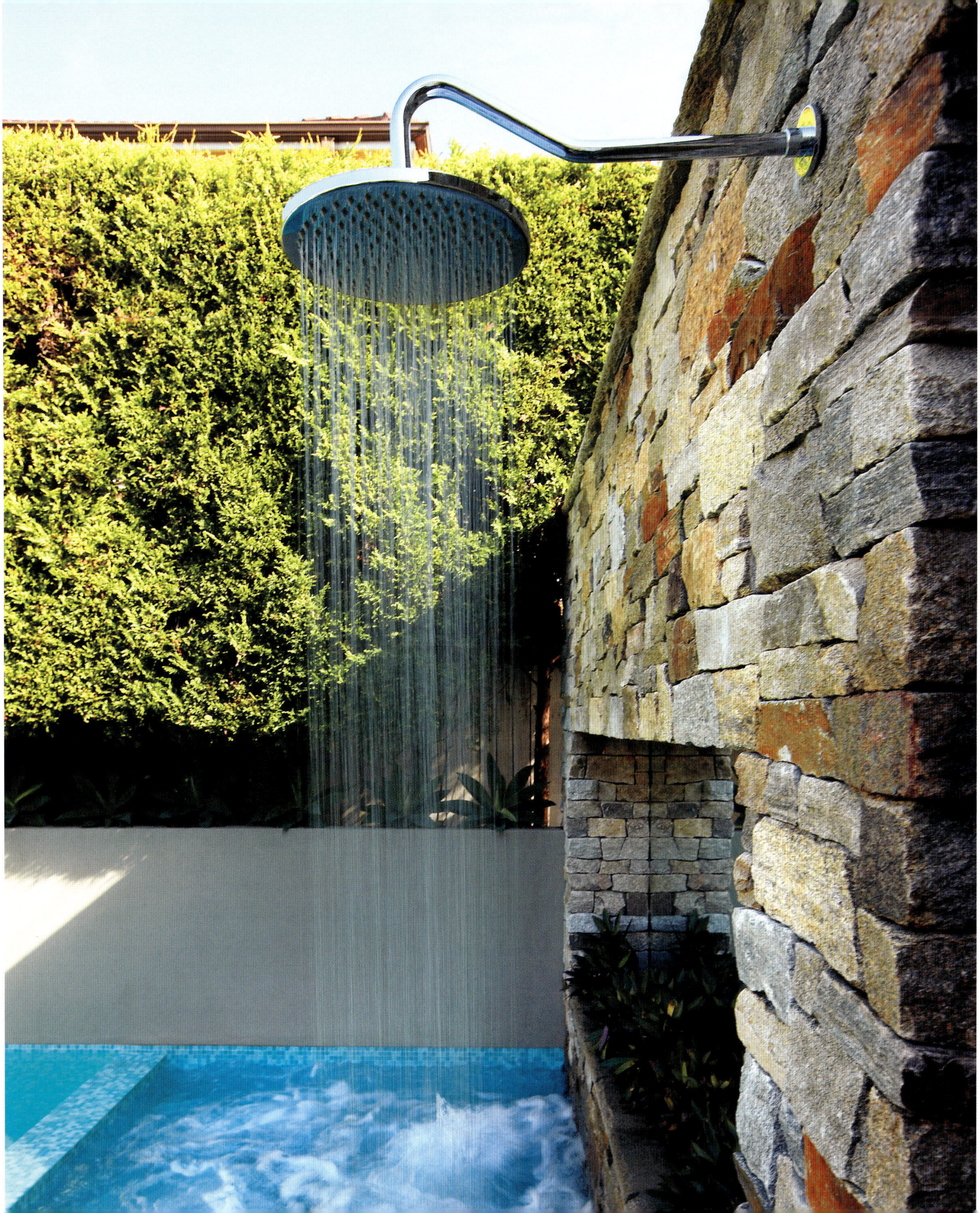

The bold architectural lines of this home presented an exciting opportunity to extend and add to the strong expressions of design through to the exterior spaces. With modern landscape design it is often what you don't design that makes the project a success, giving true meaning to the adage 'less is more'. For this project, restraint was required during the design process to enable the lines of the home to work smoothly with the landscape.

Flowing on from the living areas of the home is the external entertaining area, with the pool set in relation to the lower window vista of the home. The area between is designed in three spaces. First is a cooking area, with a barbecue connected to the dining table for reasons of space and

Contemporary Dreams

LYSTERFIELD

to ensure it didn't dominate the view from the house. The second element is a central concrete platform on which three square concrete plinths have been placed, providing permanent seating to the space at a low elevation. A fire was inserted in the centre plinth, not only adding a central feature but also prolonging the time the space can be used throughout the year. Finally, an outdoor lounge was created in the third area, making a relaxing location in which to retreat. A synthetic, low-maintenance lawn separates these spaces and introduces colour.

Plan labels:
- GABION FEATURE WALL
- CASCADING WATERFALL
- COBBLE INLAY
- WATER TROUGH
- DRIVEWAY
- SELECTED FEATURE BOULDER WITH WATER SPOUTS
- SELECTED FEATURE TREES
- LAWN
- POOL
- CONCRETE
- SELECTED DAYBED
- DECKING
- SPA
- DINING AREA
- FIRE PIT
- OUTDOOR KITCHEN WITH SINK & BBQ
- CONCRETE BENCH
- PROPOSED RESIDENCE
- PAVING
- POND
- WATER TROUGH WITH CASCADING WATER INTO POND
- STEPPING STONES
- SEATING AREA

0   5M

At the other side of the home and partly visible from the main living areas is the study garden. The view through the outer glass walls of the study evokes an impression of being within the garden. The surrounding outer garden walls are clad in travertine stone to define the space and continue the material palette used within the home. For a contemporary view from the study three elements were used: firstly, a simple water feature consisting of a cantilevered concrete plank that transports water to the lower pond; secondly, an organic stepping-stone path with a sitting area to contrast with the controlled lines of the home; and finally, to give a lush green carpet effect to the floor, a single species was used throughout: creeping boobialla (*Myoporum parvifolium*).

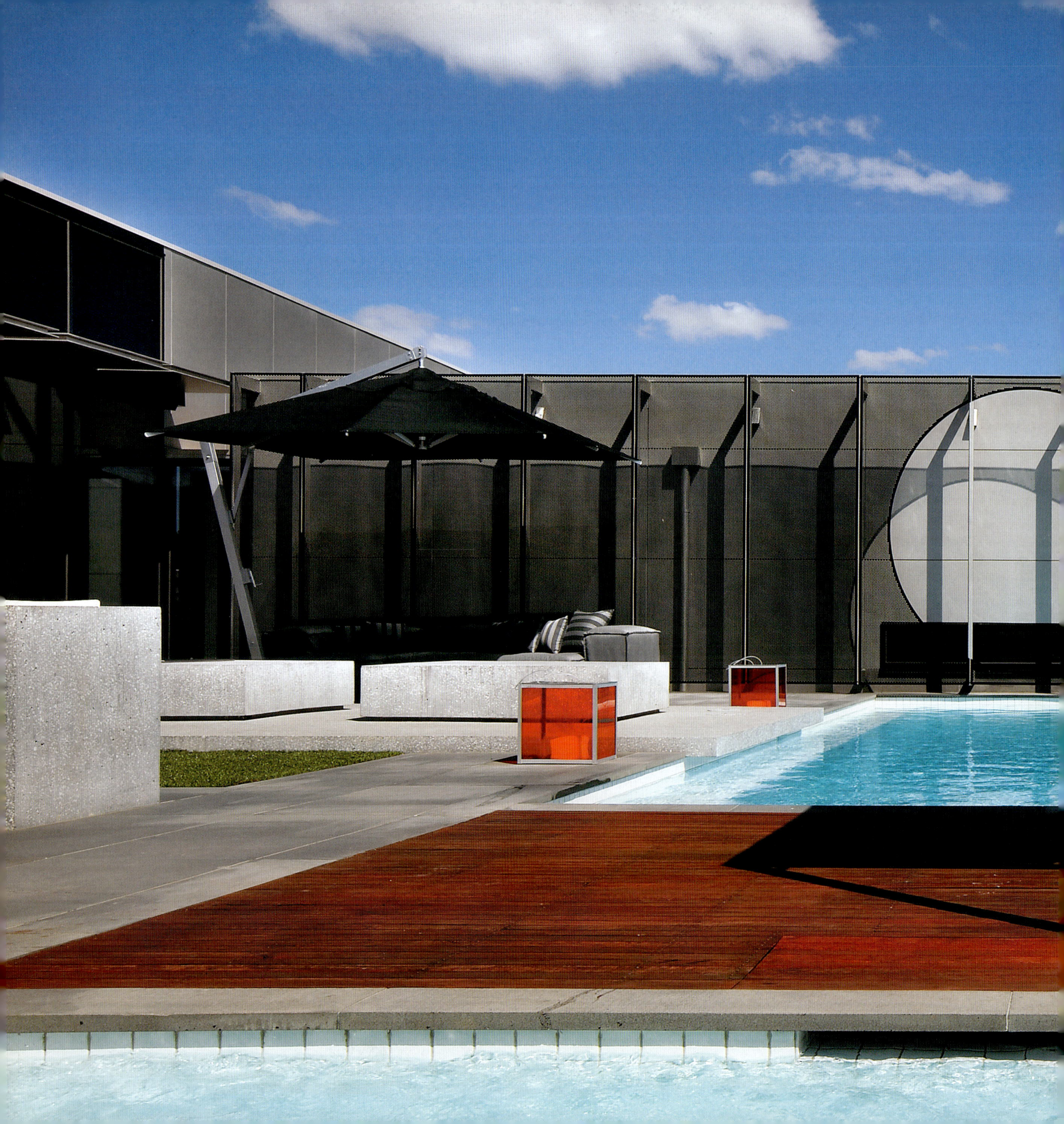

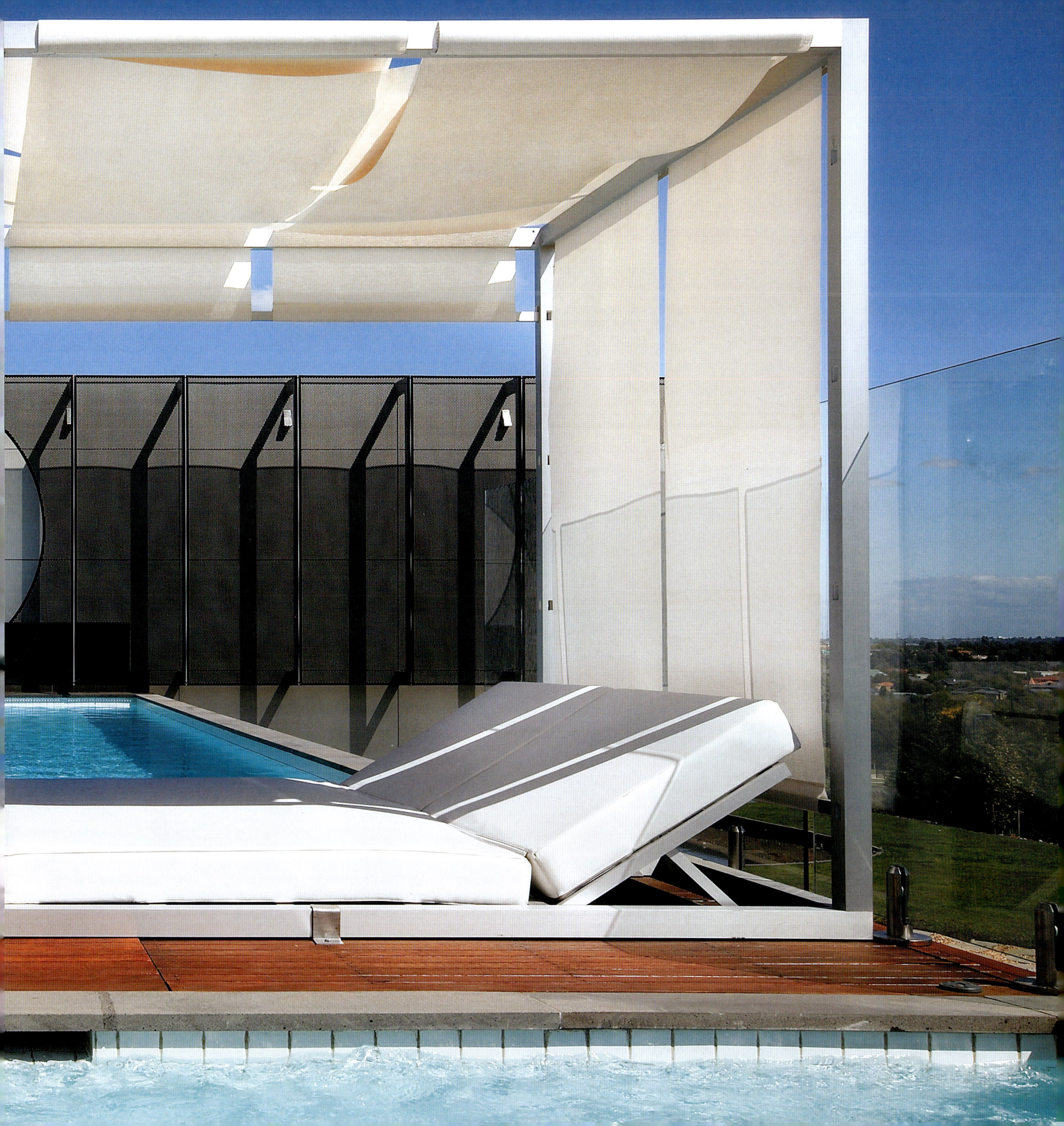

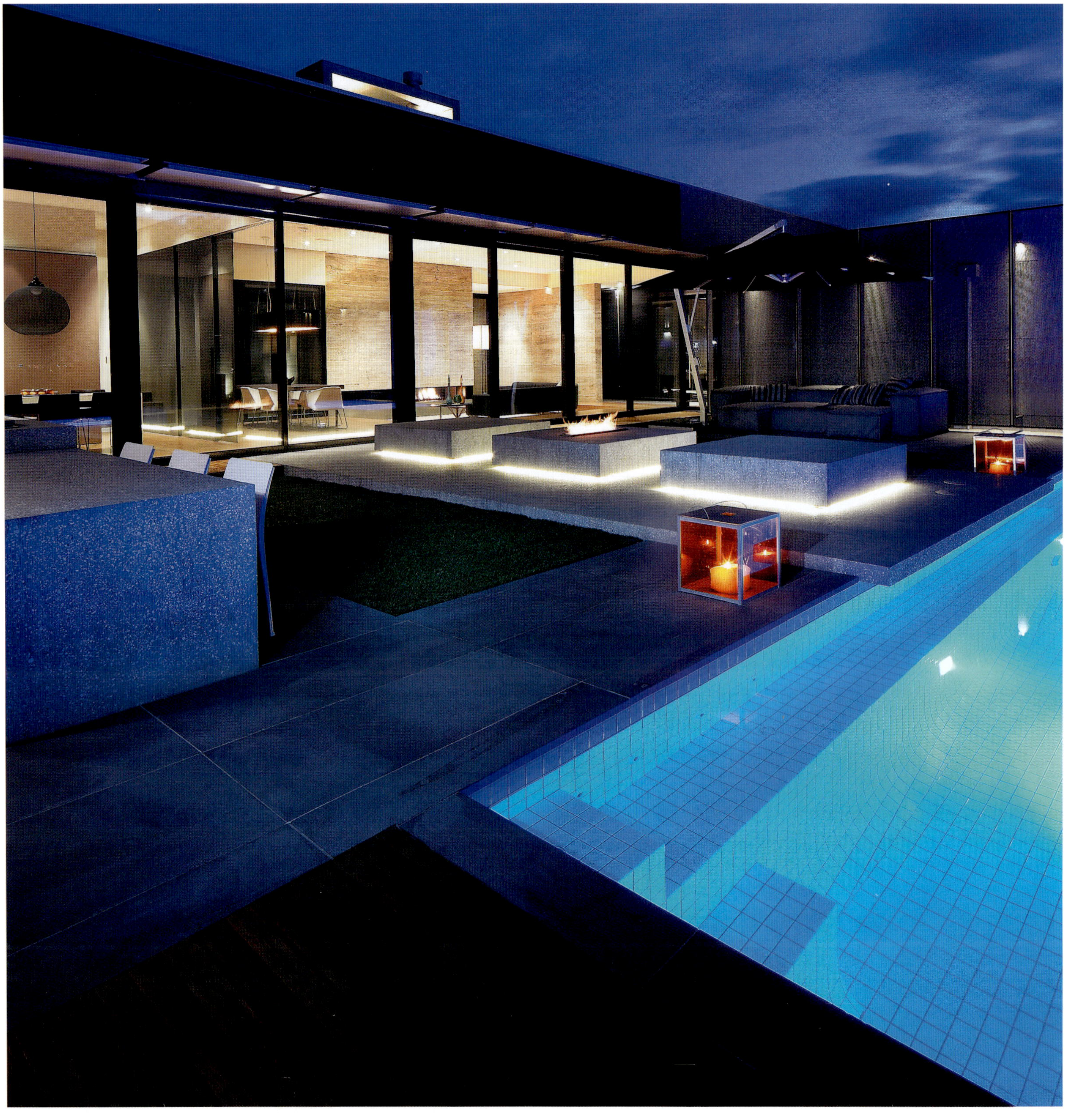

CONTEMPORARY DREAMS 49

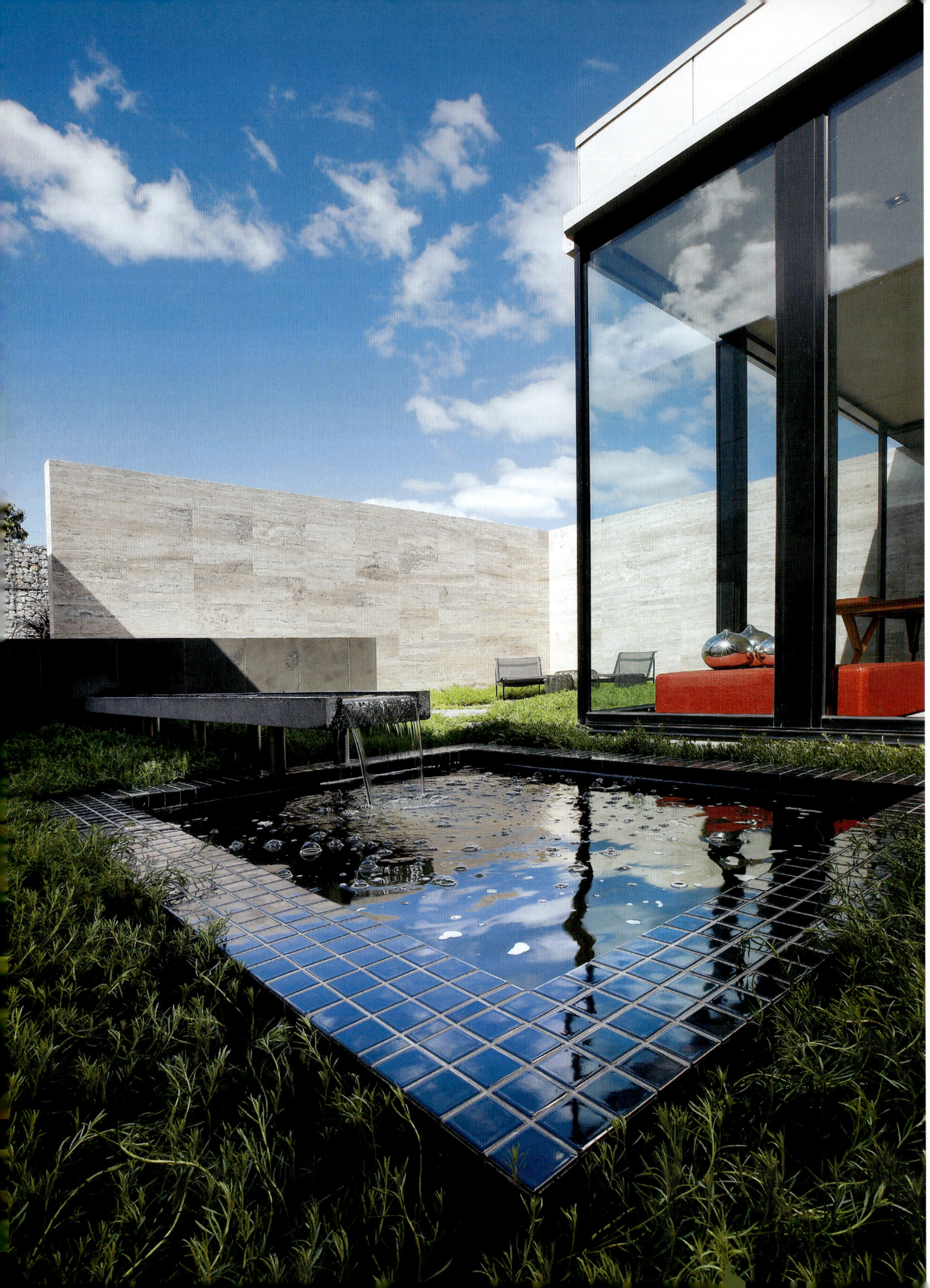
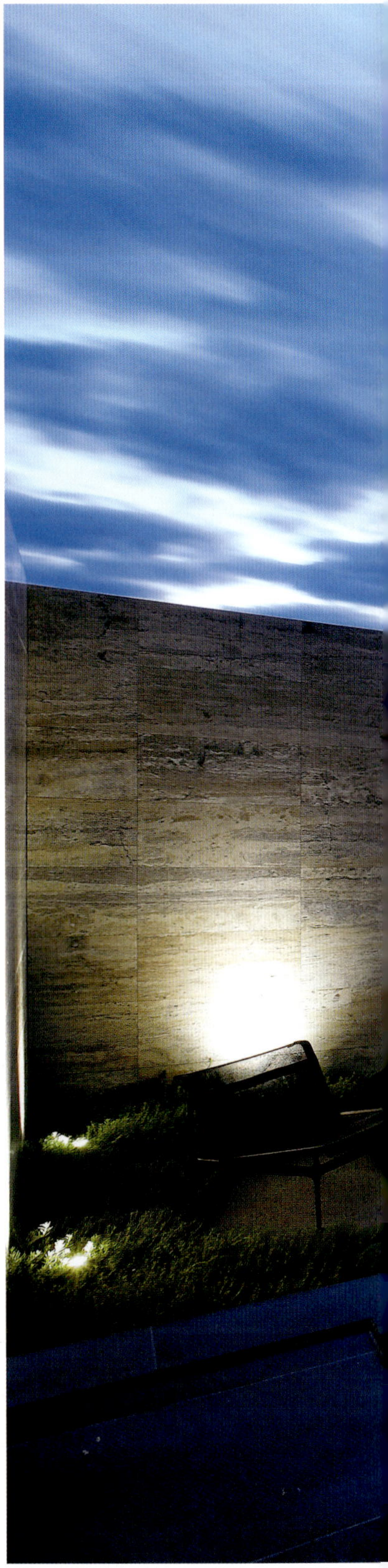

CONTEMPORARY DREAMS 51

52

CONTEMPORARY DREAMS 53

The owners of this property enjoy stunning views of the Sydney Harbour Bridge from the front living areas of their home. They wanted to create a private space to the rear for entertaining family and friends – the indoor/outdoor entertaining area features an open-style pavilion and outdoor kitchen complete with refrigerator, teppanyaki barbecue and pizza oven. With a custom-designed, cantilevered dining table included to make the best use of the available space, the kitchen and hotplate are positioned to enable clear lines of sight to all surrounding areas, including a view up into the home.

To increase the potential for multi-seasonal use, a fireplace was added to the pavilion, enhancing the structure with a strong architectural element. The location of the pavilion ties in well with the swimming pool, with a simple rectangular shape to match the lines of the home and the square dimensions of the rear space. Custom-designed glass separates the spa from the pool, with the placement of the spa enabling a glimpse through to the Harbour Bridge at the front of the property.

The pool's infinity edge maximises its size and provides a stunning feature view from the lower games room of the house. The pool is fully covered with glass mosaic tiles for a continuous look and feel.

The light tone of the travertine floor tiles complements the colour of the swimming pool as well as the lawn and plant selections. The planting theme concentrates on a lush feel

Sydney Living

LONGUEVILLE

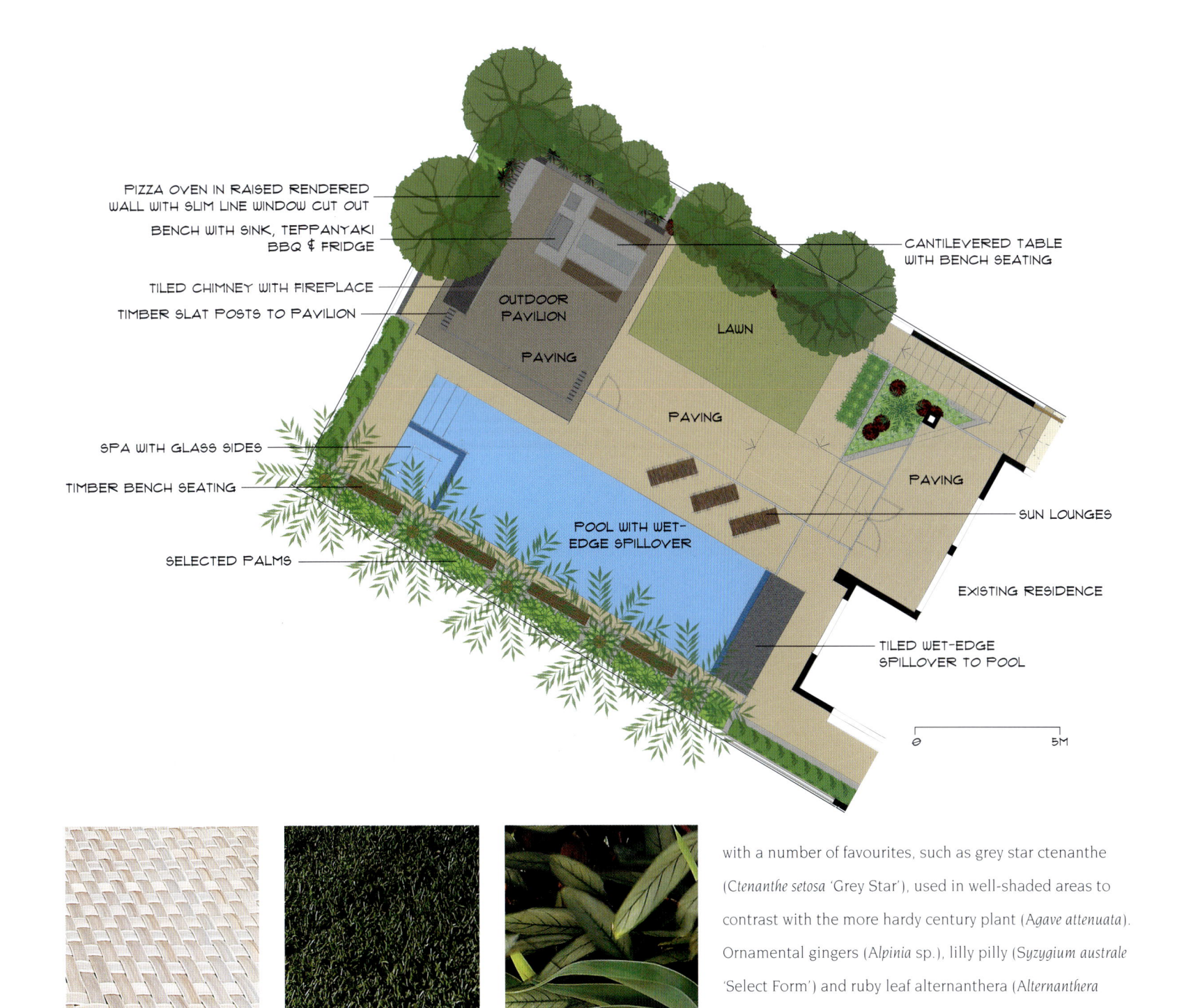

PIZZA OVEN IN RAISED RENDERED
WALL WITH SLIM LINE WINDOW CUT OUT

BENCH WITH SINK, TEPPANYAKI
BBQ & FRIDGE

CANTILEVERED TABLE
WITH BENCH SEATING

TILED CHIMNEY WITH FIREPLACE

TIMBER SLAT POSTS TO PAVILION

OUTDOOR PAVILION

LAWN

PAVING

PAVING

SPA WITH GLASS SIDES

PAVING

TIMBER BENCH SEATING

POOL WITH WET-EDGE SPILLOVER

SUN LOUNGES

SELECTED PALMS

EXISTING RESIDENCE

TILED WET-EDGE SPILLOVER TO POOL

0   5M

with a number of favourites, such as grey star ctenanthe (*Ctenanthe setosa* 'Grey Star'), used in well-shaded areas to contrast with the more hardy century plant (*Agave attenuata*). Ornamental gingers (*Alpinia* sp.), lilly pilly (*Syzygium australe* 'Select Form') and ruby leaf alternanthera (*Alternanthera dentata*) have also been used for colour and form.

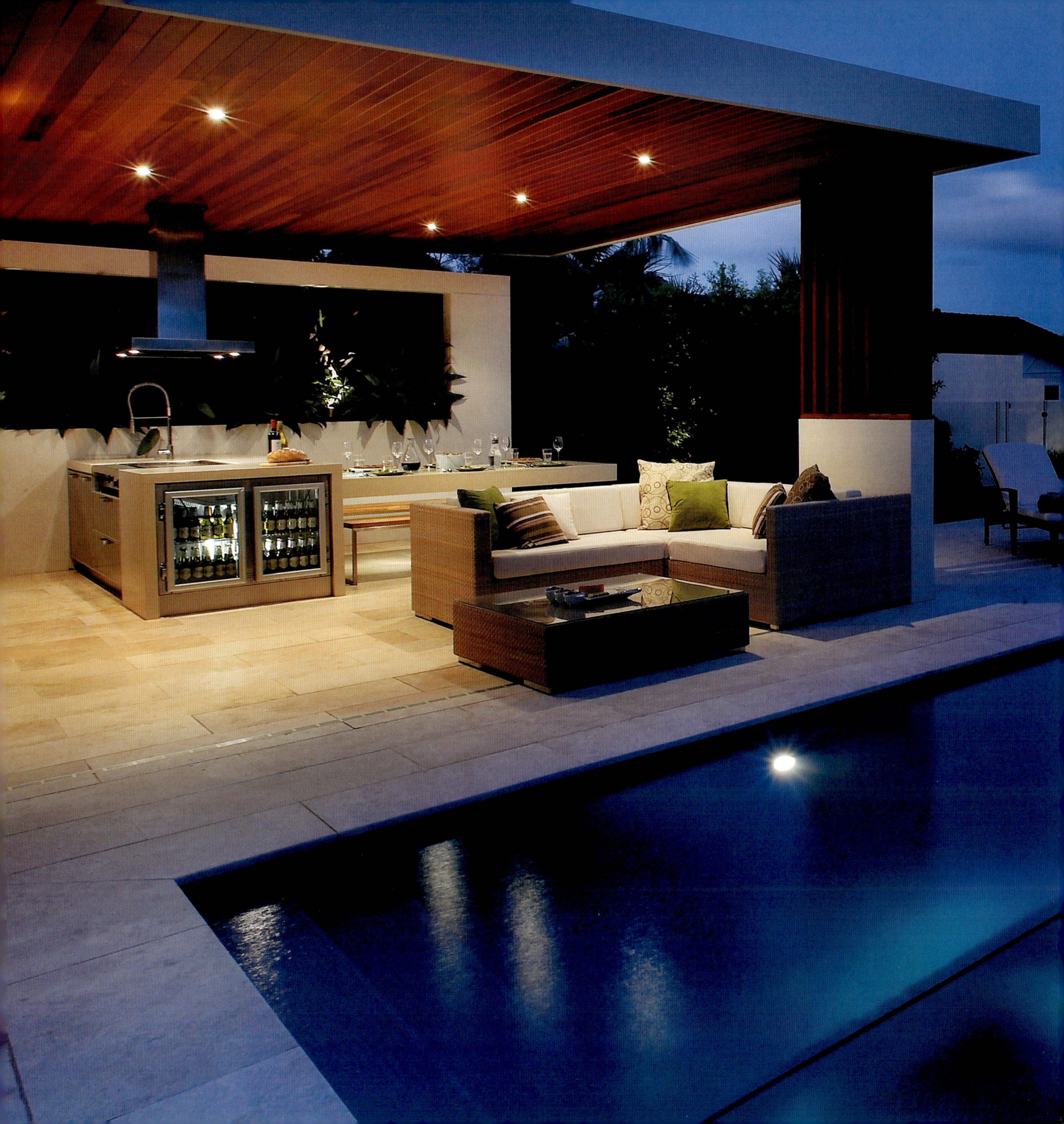

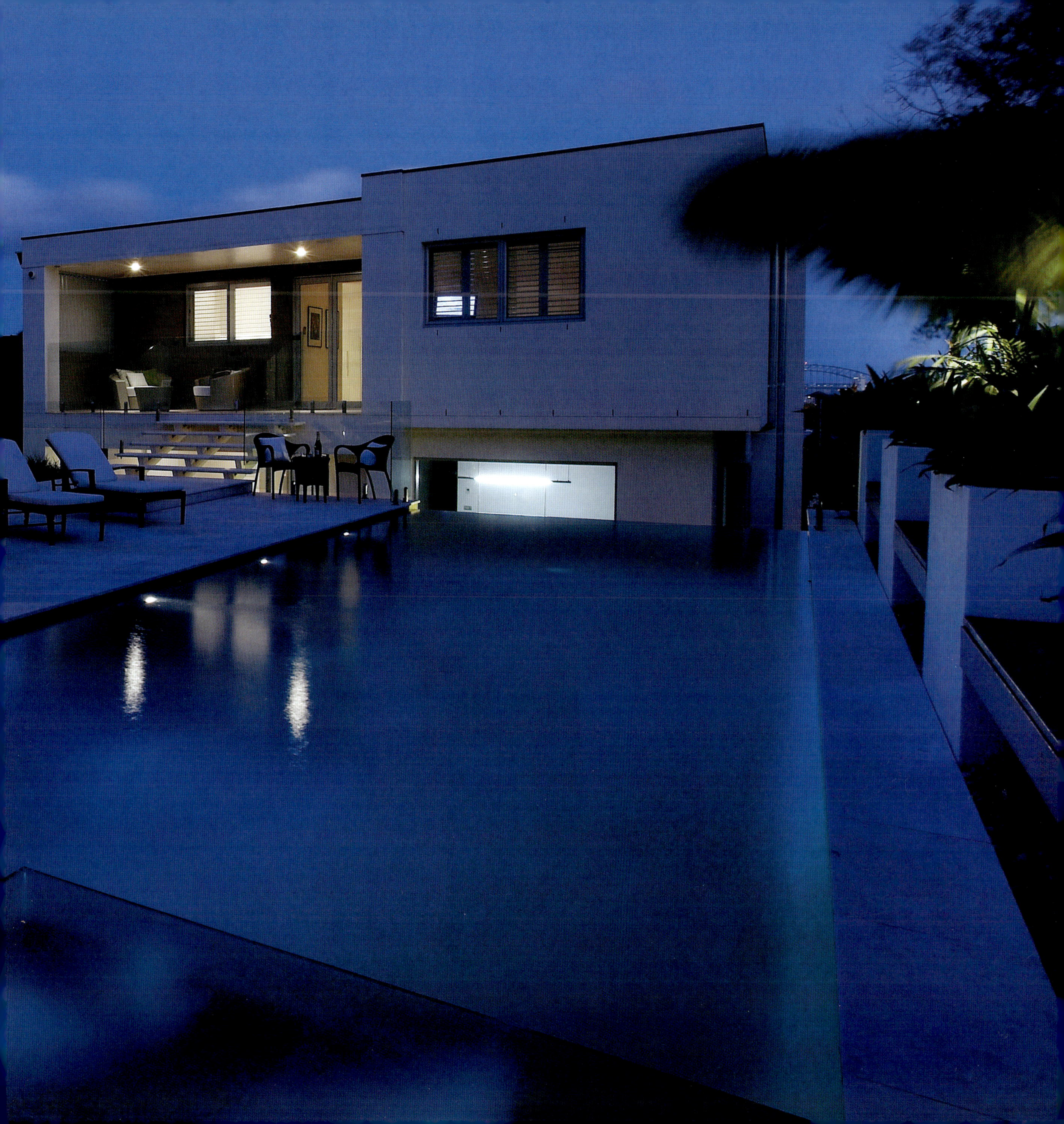

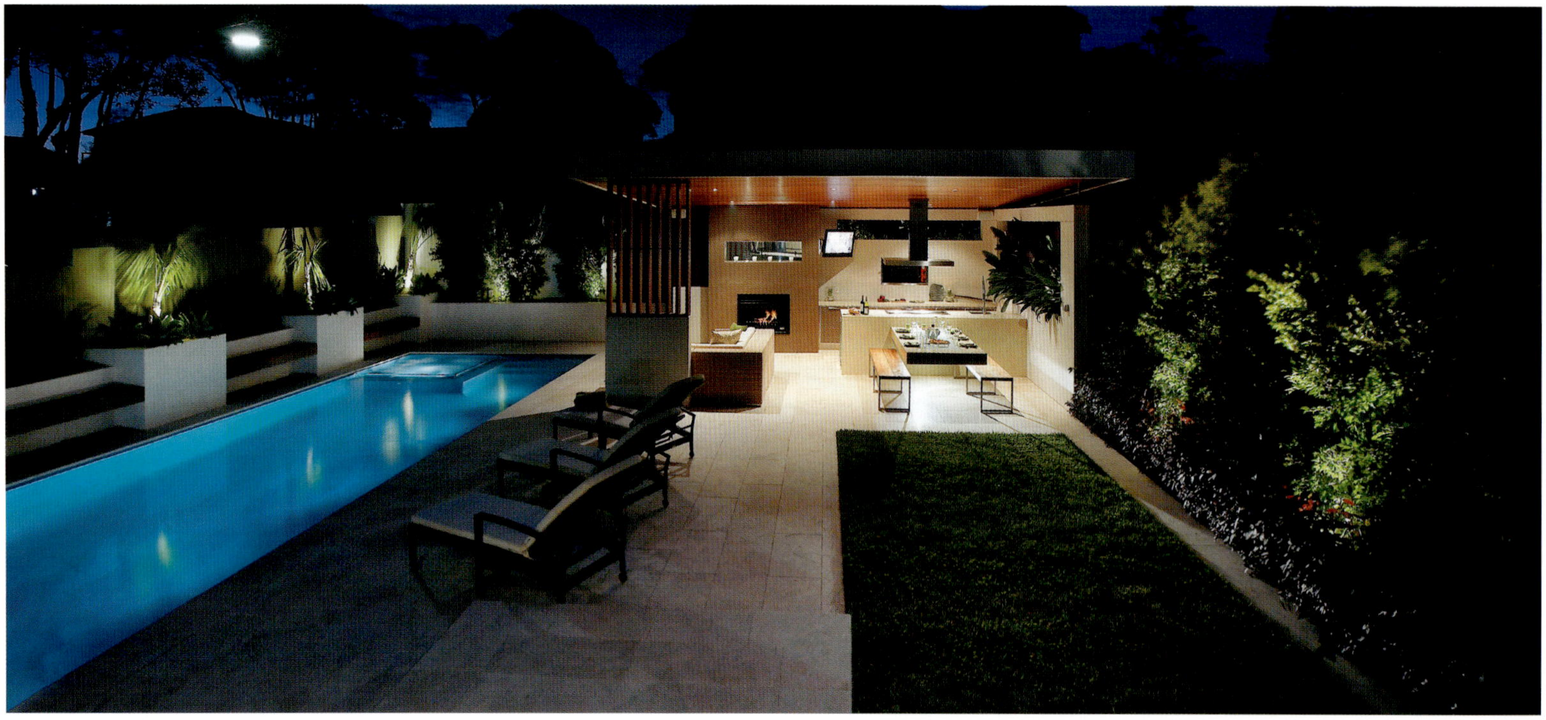

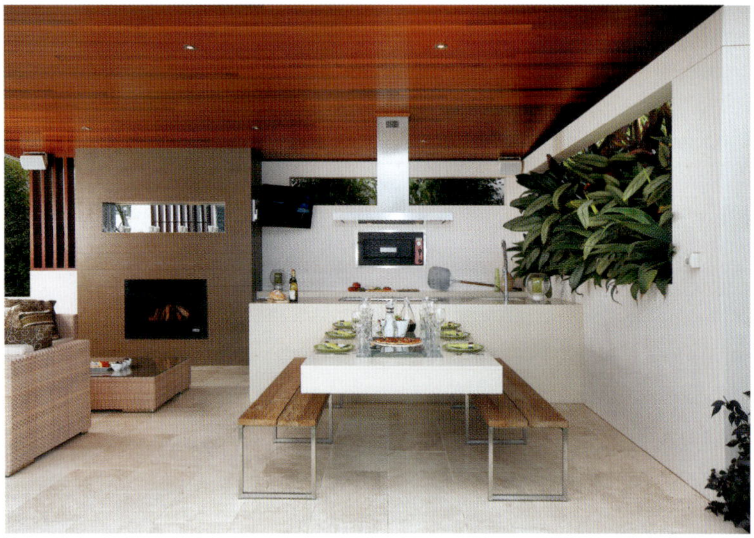

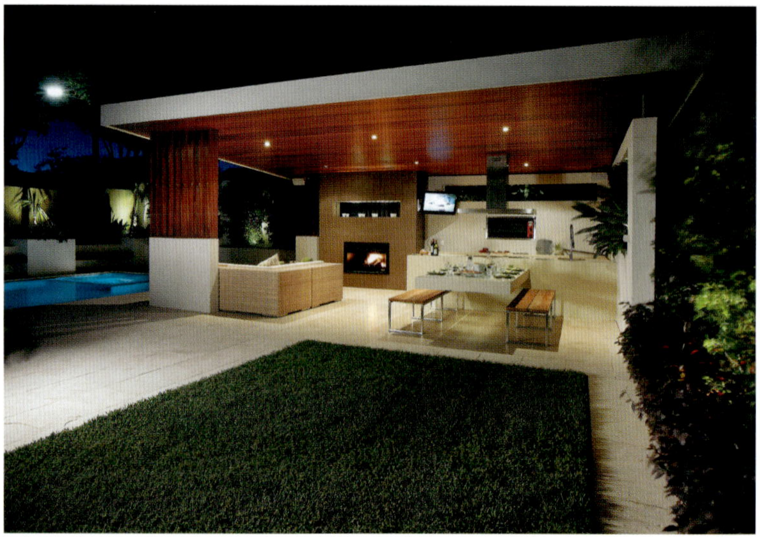

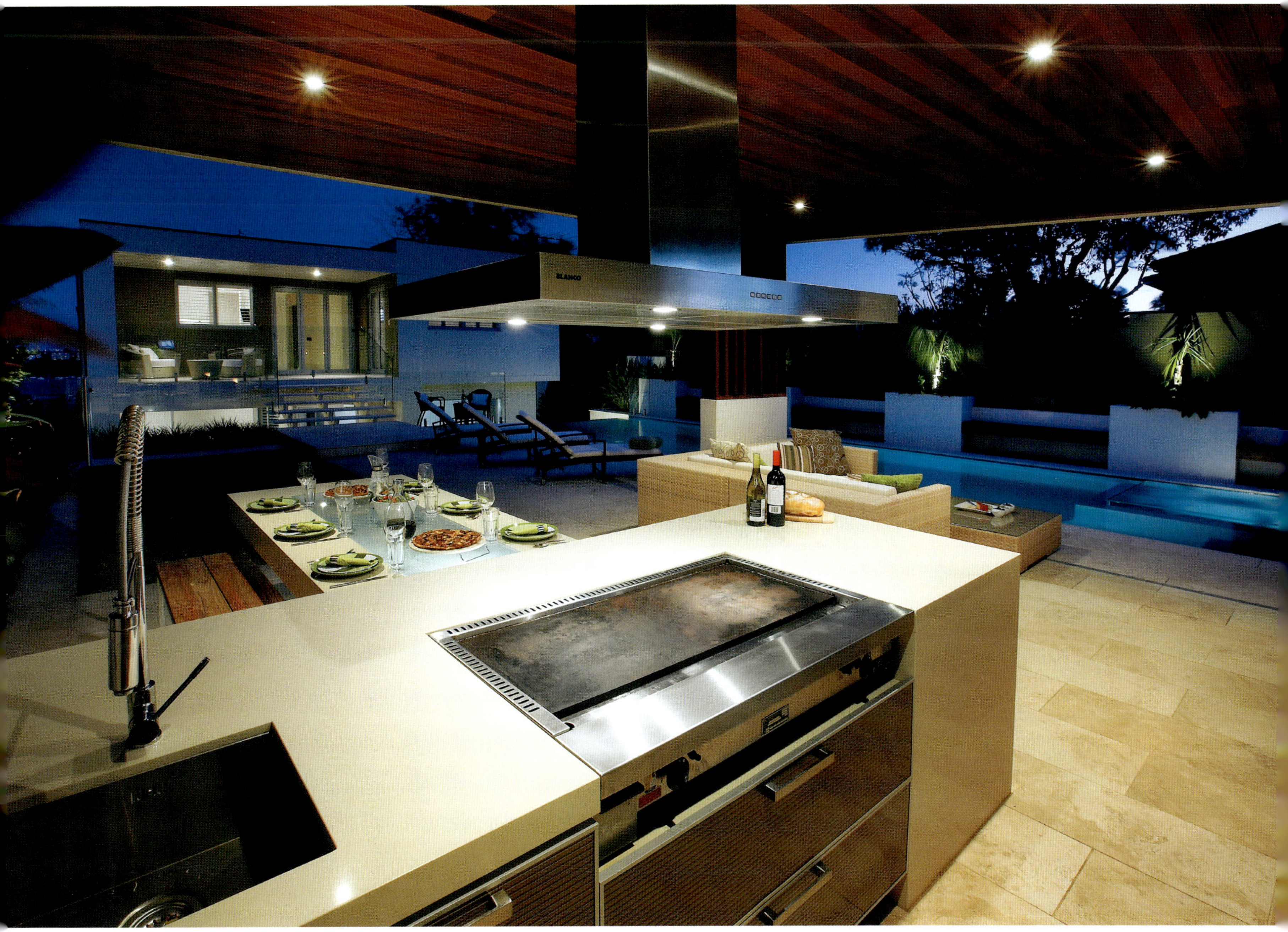

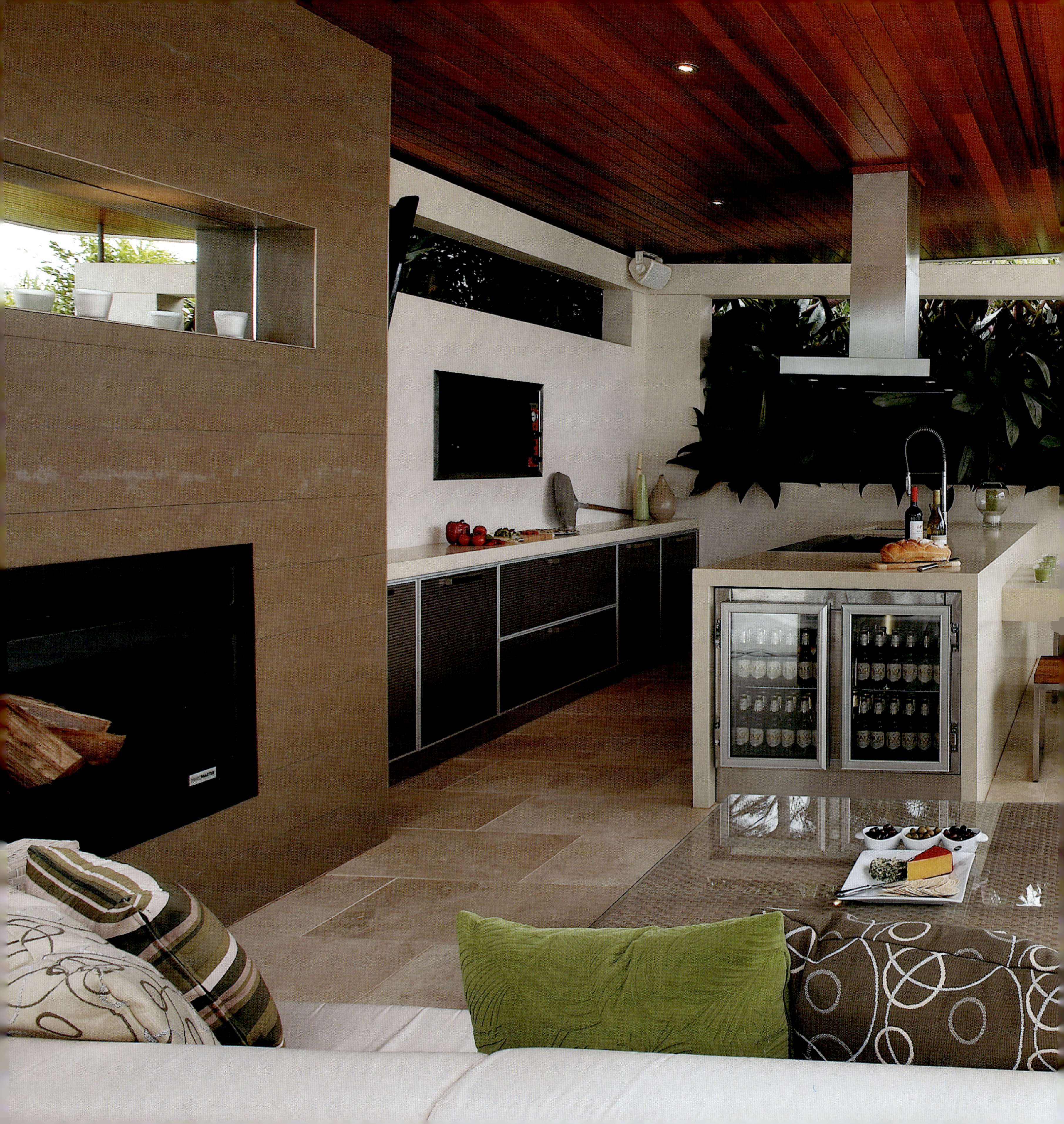

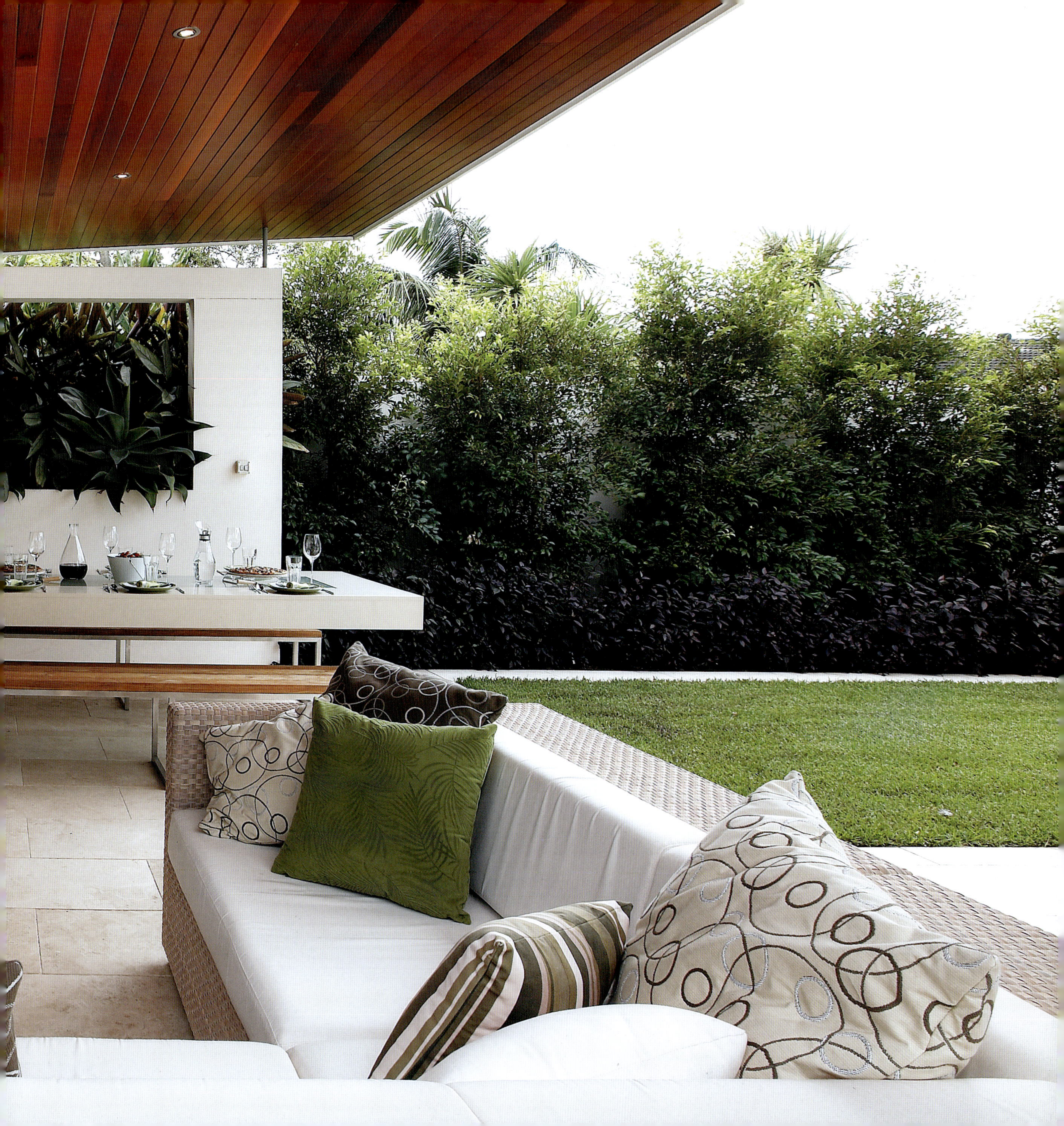

Hidden Valley

DURAL

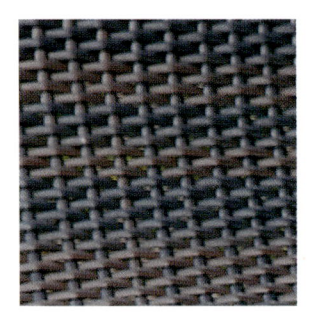

With a large-scale renovation planned for this home, I was approached by the owners to review the best position for their pool and entertaining area. These needed to work with the proposed floor plan and architecture of the house while blending seamlessly with the natural landscape. Set in a valley surrounded by tall eucalyptus trees, the aspect of the land was a critical factor in the entire design process in order to ensure use is maximised during all seasons and to assist with maintenance of the pool and entertaining area.

After considering sight lines from the home, it was clear that the location of the pool would work best at the front of the property. The lie of the land enables an infinity-edge design for the pool structure, which not only adds a visual effect from the house, but also provides a necessary practical element that allows falling leaves to float across the water and fall off the edge into a catchment tank below. Straight lines were used in the pool and spa design – influenced by the architecture of the house – while the outer edge of the pool forms a curve to blend into the natural landscape and take on the form of the existing dam below. A change of level was used to create a defined lower pool area, providing good separation from the higher cooking and dining area outside the sliding doors of the house.

Travertine stone was selected as a suitable flooring material to blend with the colour palette of the home, providing a

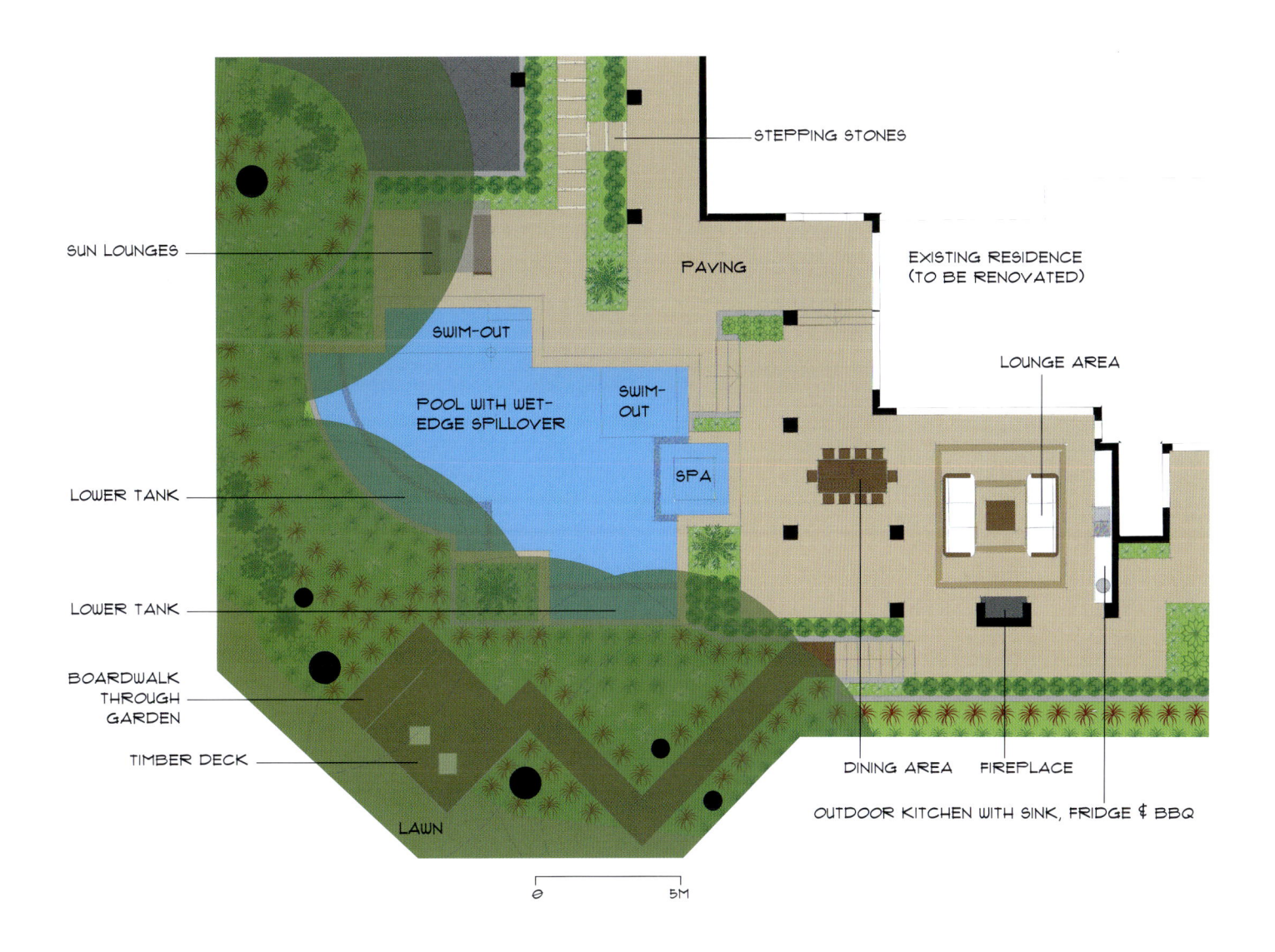

- STEPPING STONES
- PAVING
- EXISTING RESIDENCE (TO BE RENOVATED)
- SUN LOUNGES
- SWIM-OUT
- SWIM-OUT
- LOUNGE AREA
- POOL WITH WET-EDGE SPILLOVER
- LOWER TANK
- SPA
- LOWER TANK
- BOARDWALK THROUGH GARDEN
- TIMBER DECK
- DINING AREA
- FIREPLACE
- LAWN
- OUTDOOR KITCHEN WITH SINK, FRIDGE & BBQ

0 — 5M

mild mottled effect that assists in disguising the leaf stains from the surrounding native trees. Japanese sago palms (*Cycas revoluta*) were planted in selected locations around the pool, providing strong structural features, while variegated mondo (*Ophiopogon intermedians* 'Stripey White') and century plants (*Agave attenuata*) were used to complement the relaxed planting theme.

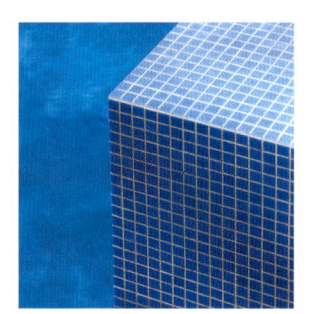

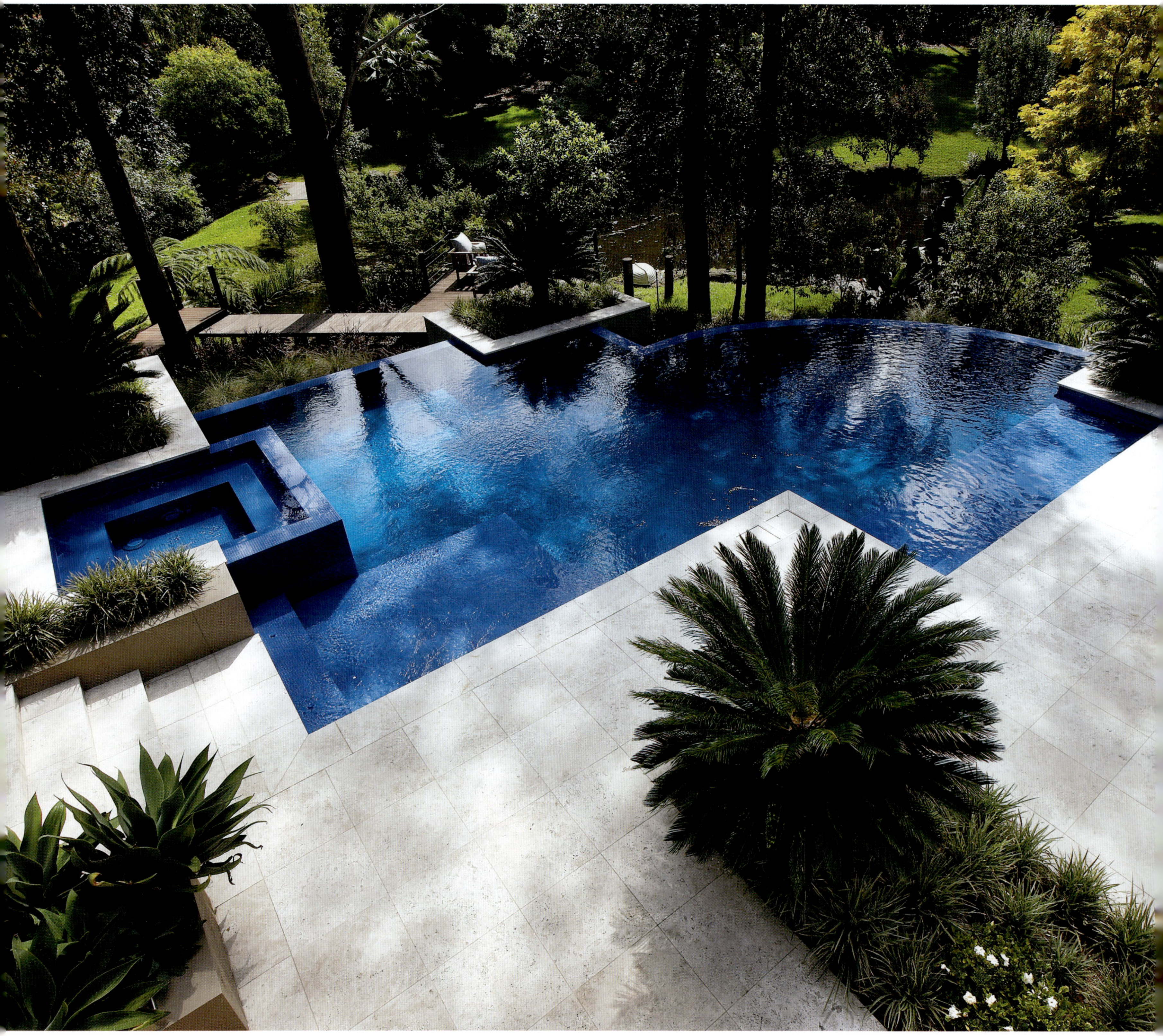

HIDDEN VALLEY 65

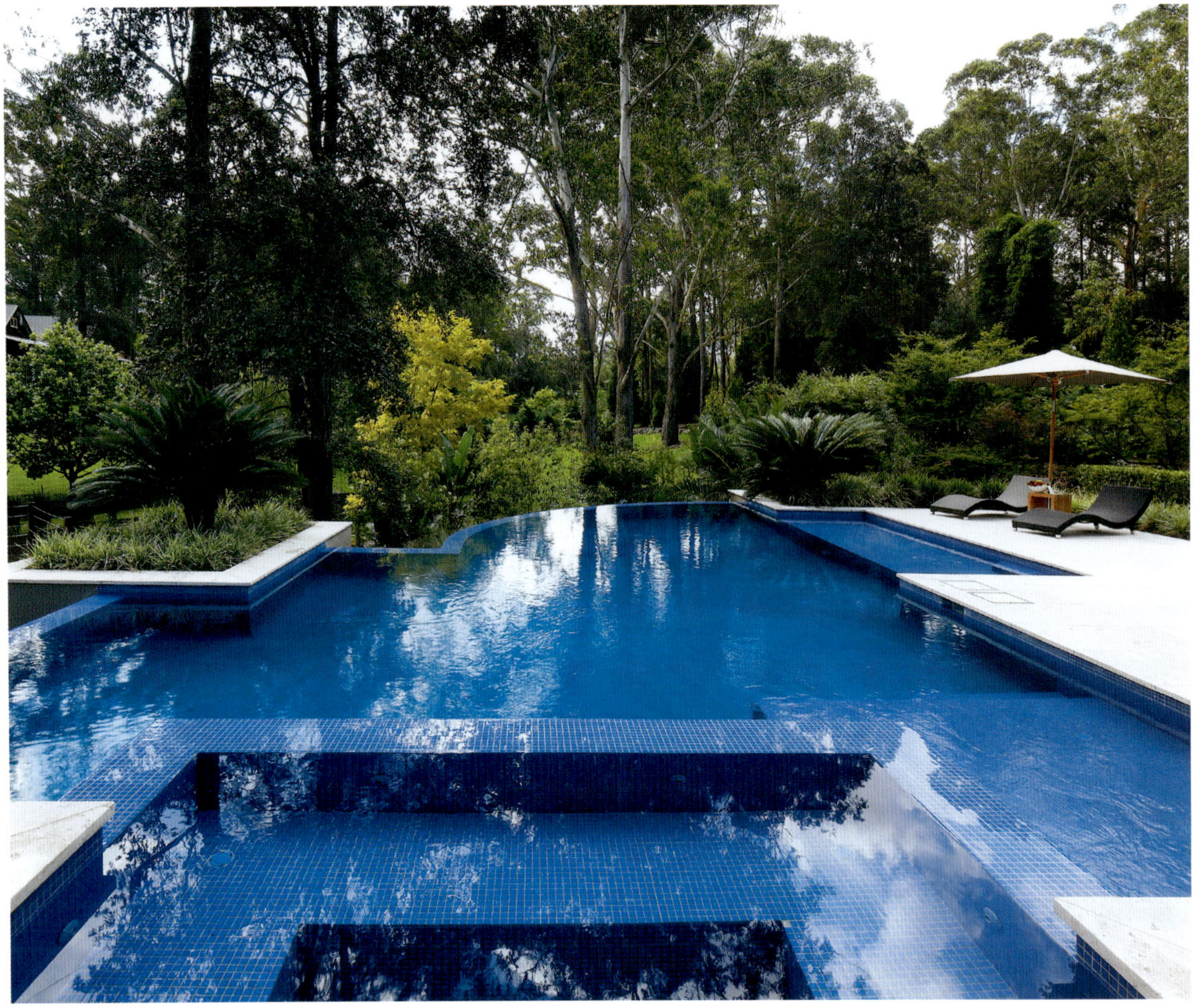

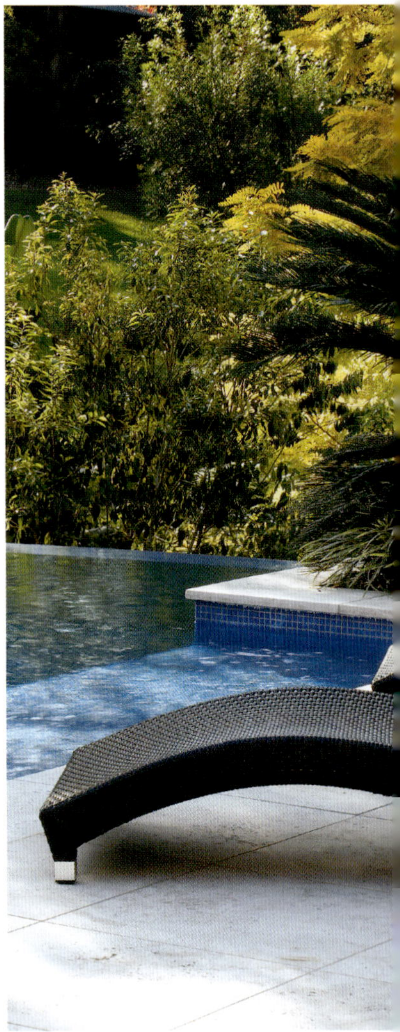

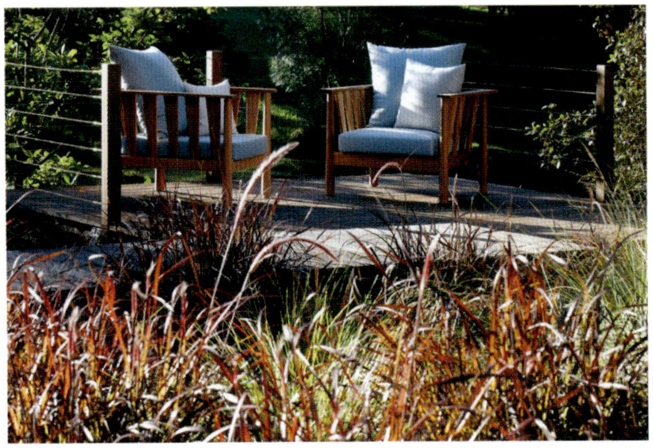

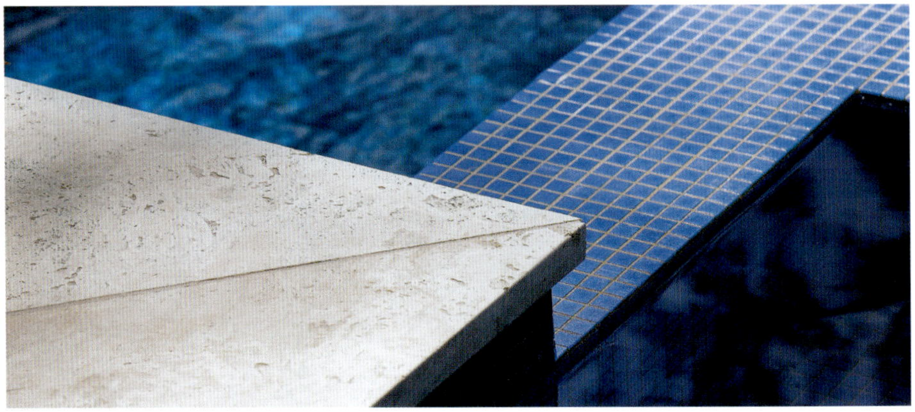

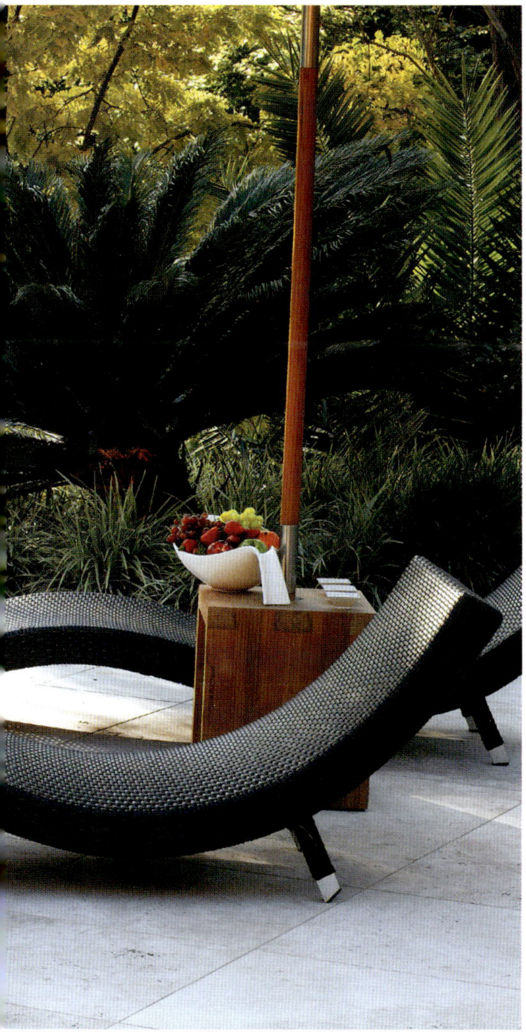

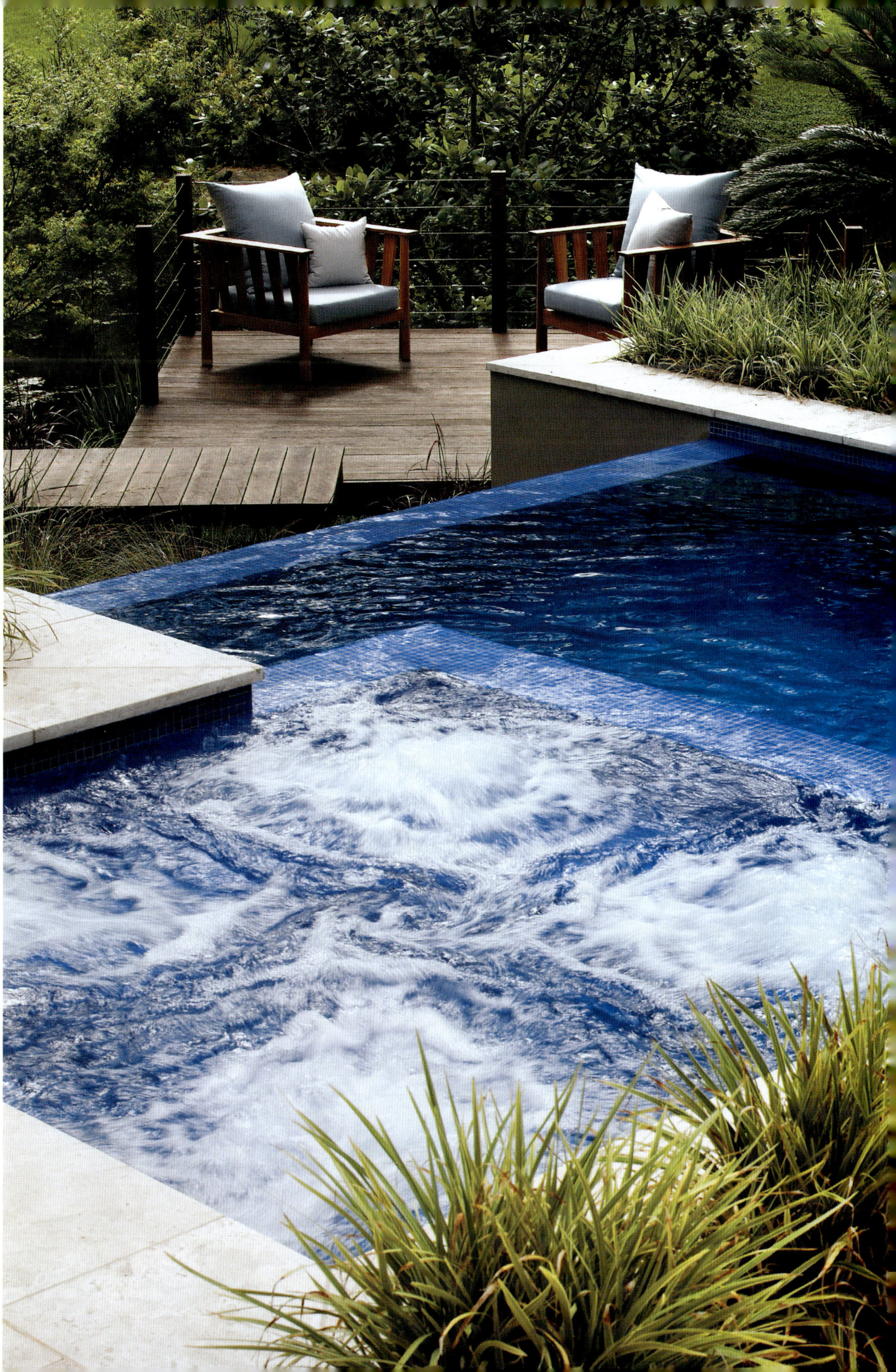

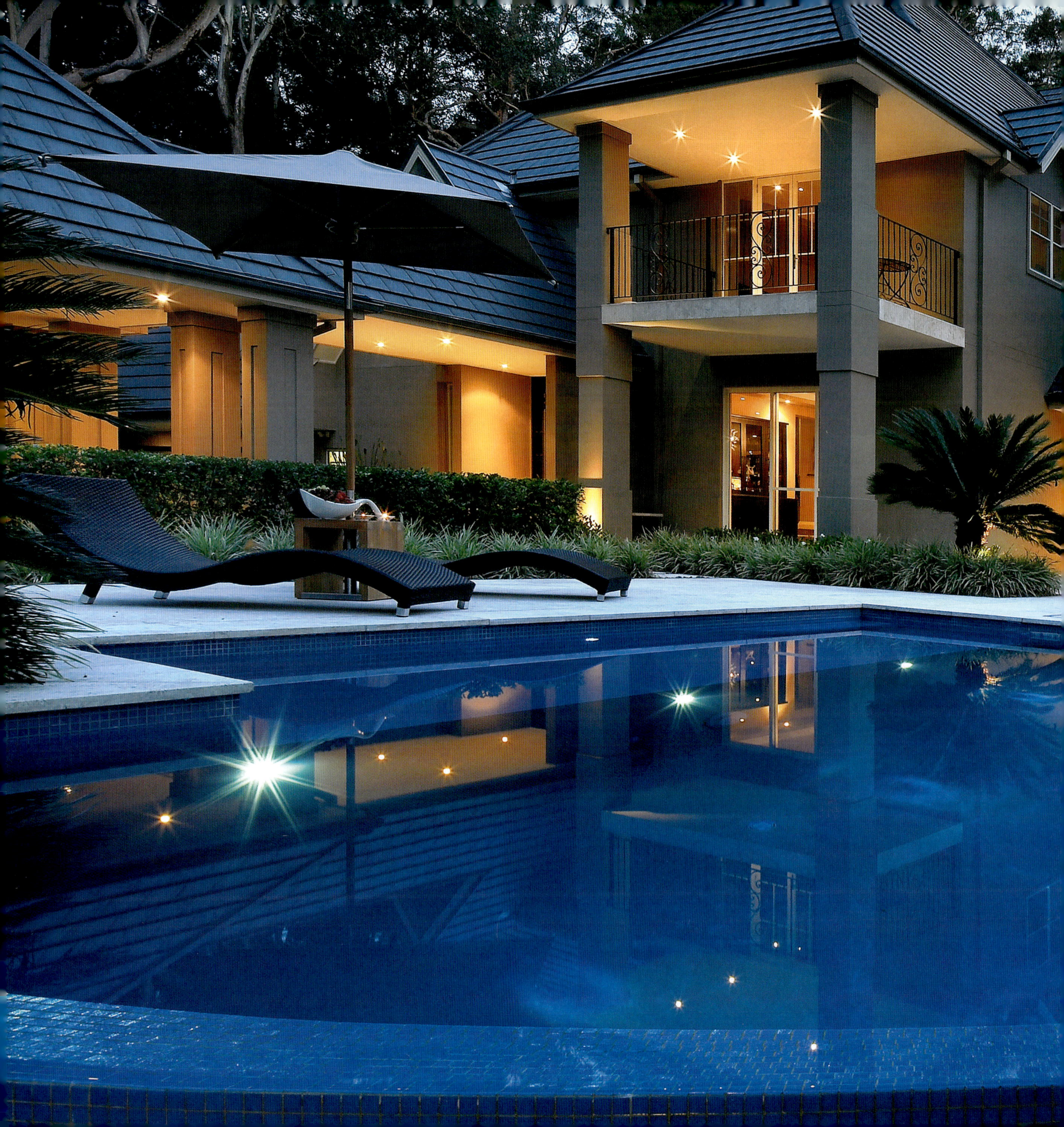

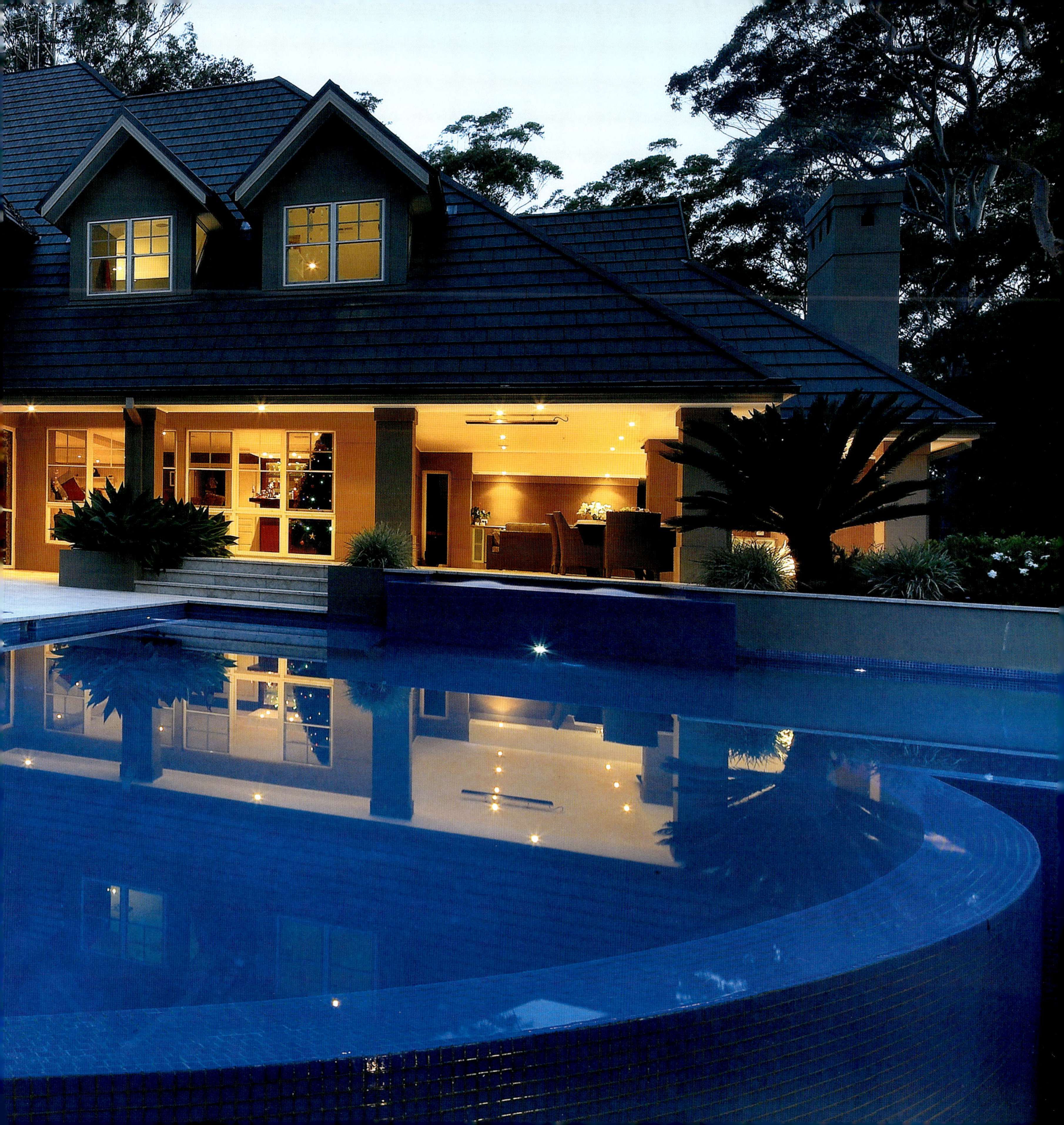

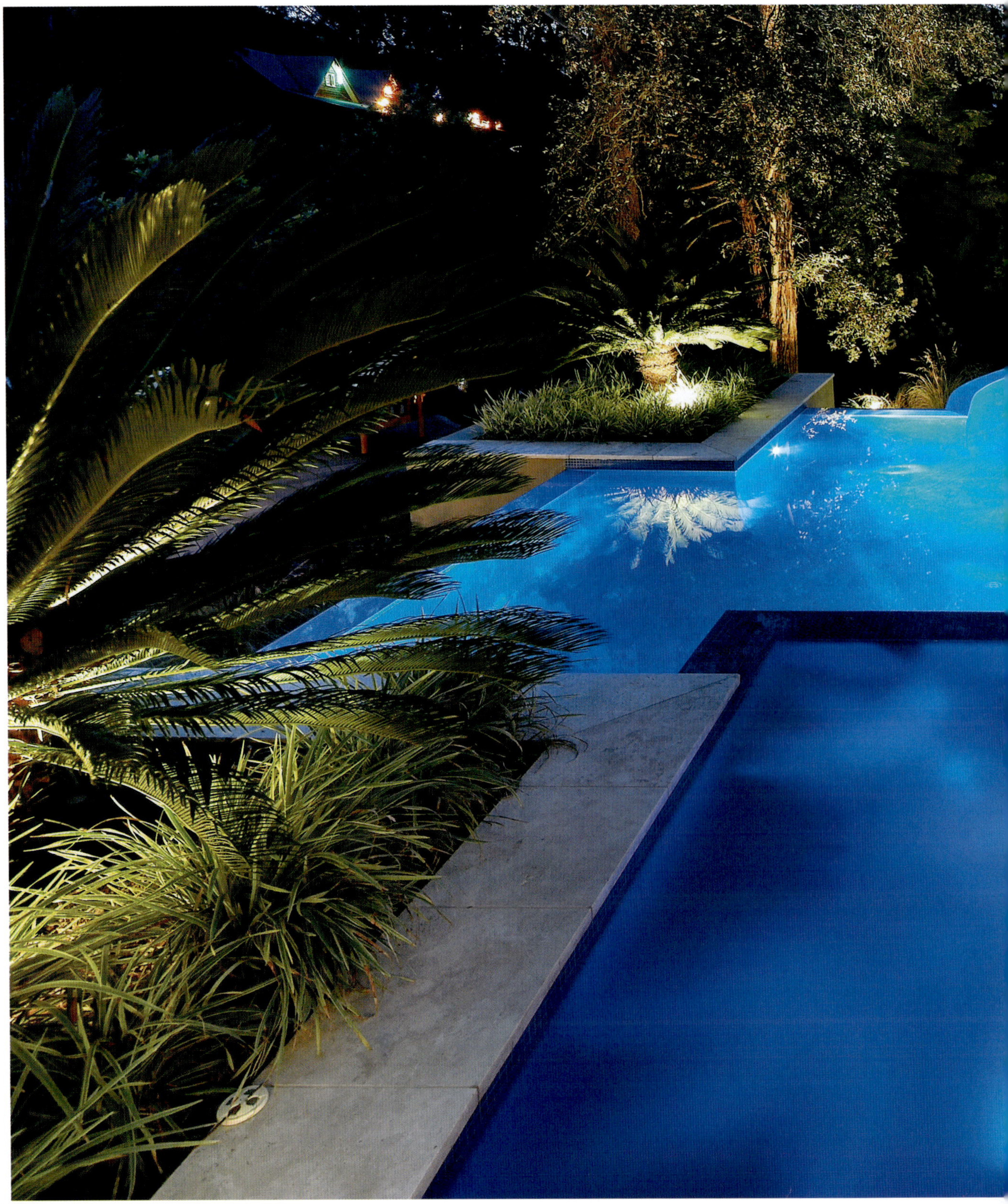

HIDDEN VALLEY 71

For a garden that was showing its age and not relevant to the new owners of this property I was called upon to review how best to update the space to cater for the entertaining they did for their friends and family. The design work was not limited to the external areas but also included the internal space, along with doors and windows.

I began to explore the possibilities of creating dedicated external spaces for each entertainment activity. With the existing pool level set, I saw the opportunity to use a change in levels to help communicate the different areas. With this in mind, a sunken lounge area was created with fixed hardwood bench seating dressed with soft cushions. A Japanese box hedge (Buxus microphylla var. japonica) surrounds

Sunken Connections

GORDON

the seating along with a custom-made stainless steel ice box for convenient storage of drinks. Also within this space is a raised stone wall with a wood fireplace, a timber storage display and a planter box above that softens the structure.

Adjacent to and above this space is a functional outdoor kitchen with all the necessary appliances for entertaining, including a double glass-door refrigerator, a teppanyaki barbecue, a sink and generous bench space for the preparation of meals. This area is covered with a flat roof structure with heaters, making it a usable space during the colder months of the year. The dining area is positioned on a raised deck to give it definition from the large bluestone pavers installed throughout the other areas. I designed and fabricated the table to best suit this location and included an Eco fire in the centre of the area, which creates a great atmosphere in the evening. New retaining walls give shape to the garden and surround the pool while preserving the existing plant assets, such as a rather large mature date palm.

Japanese sago palms (*Cycas revoluta*) were added to the existing plant material, along with little gem magnolias (*Magnolia grandiflora* 'Little Gem'), slender weavers bamboo (*Bambusa textilis* 'Gracilis'), xanadu (*Philodendron* 'Xanadu') variegated mondo (*Ophiopogon intermedians* 'Stripey White') and star jasmine (*Trachelospermum jasminoides*). To maximise views of this new outdoor living space, new frameless glass doors were installed at the rear of the home along with a new kitchen layout and adjoining living and dining area.

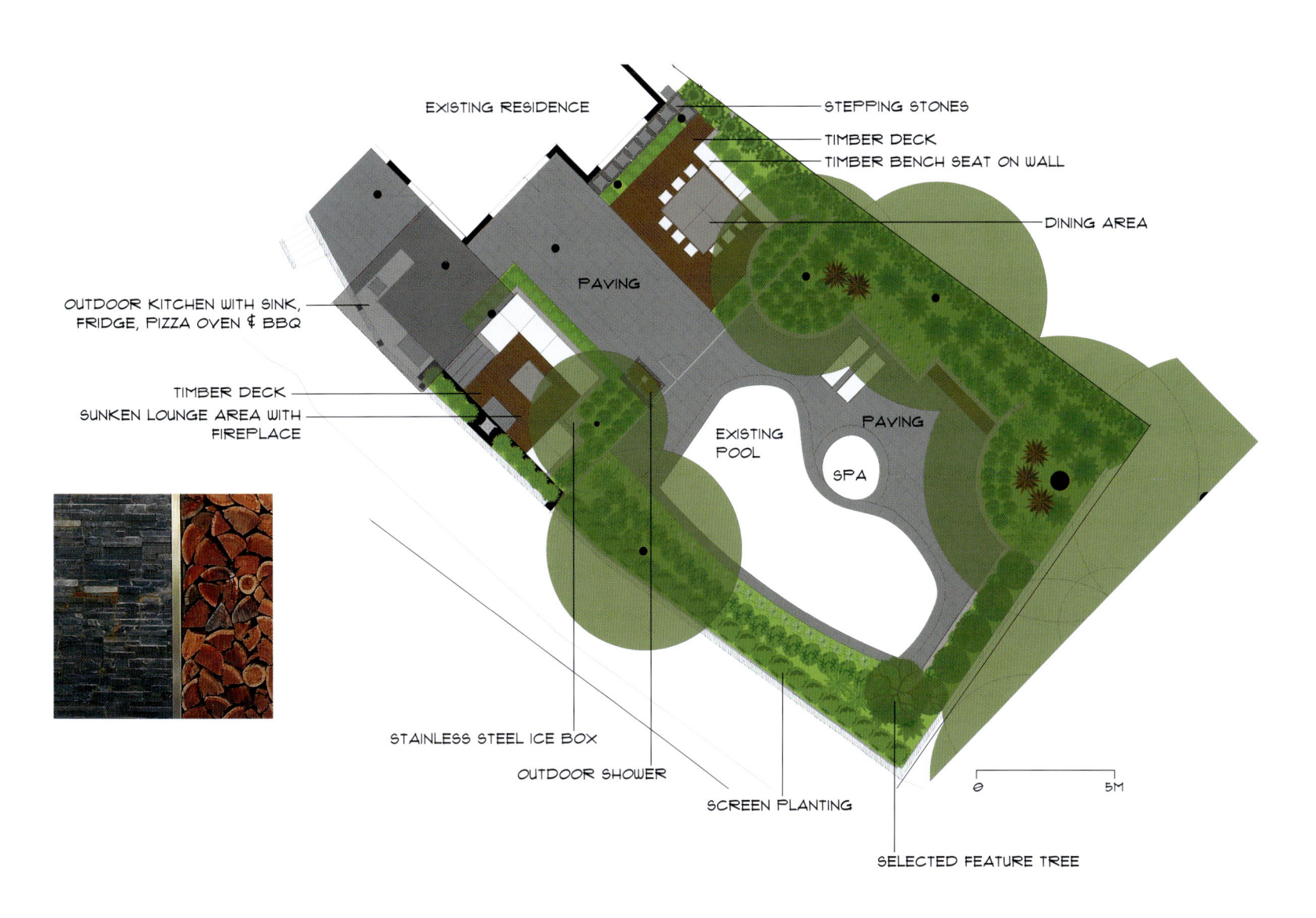

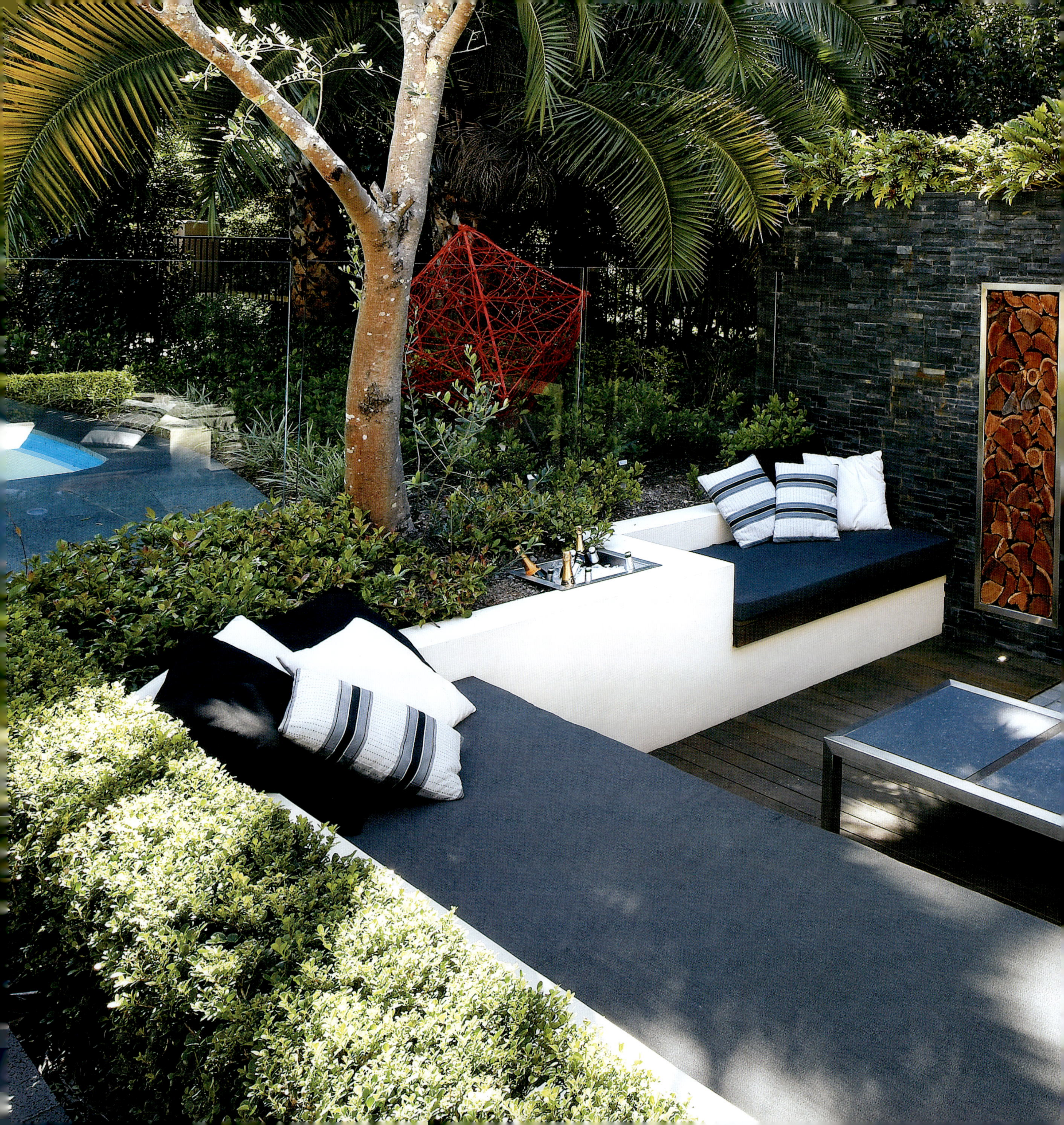

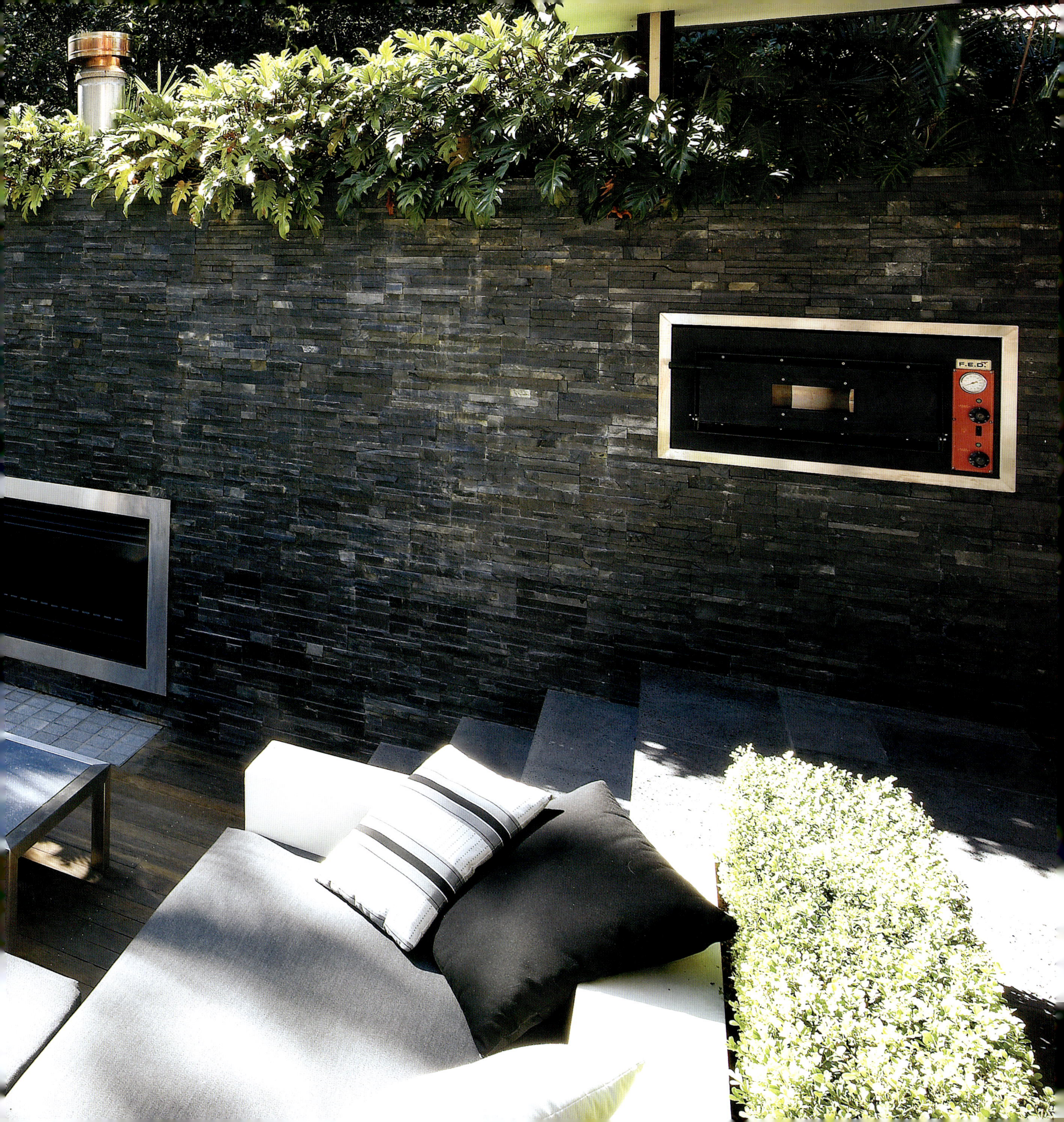
F.E.D.

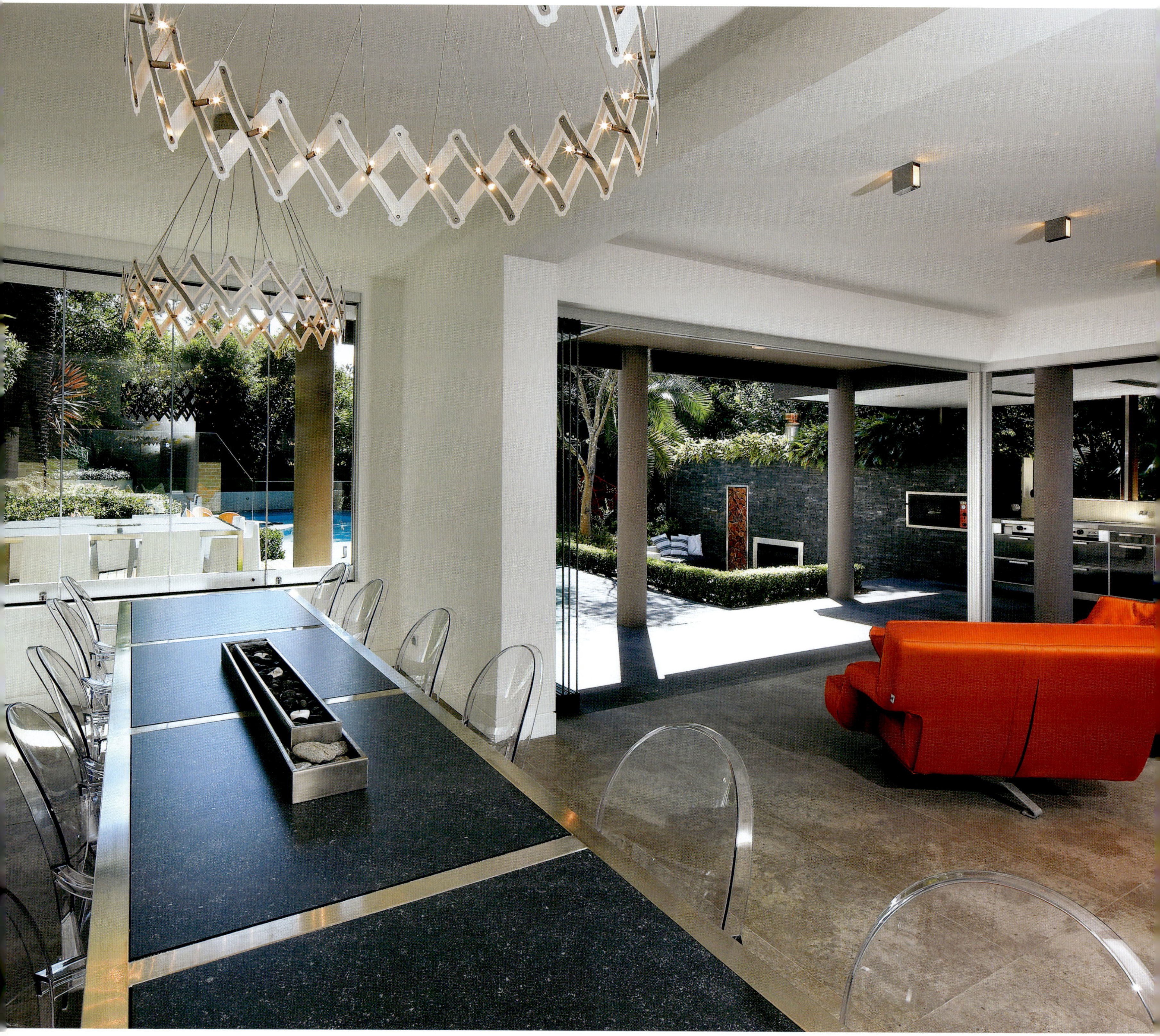

SUNKEN CONNECTIONS 77

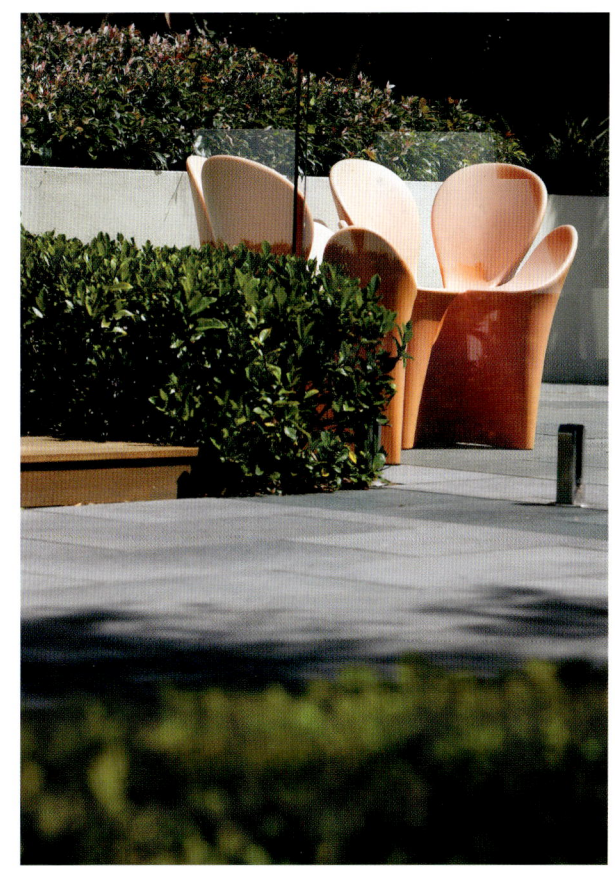

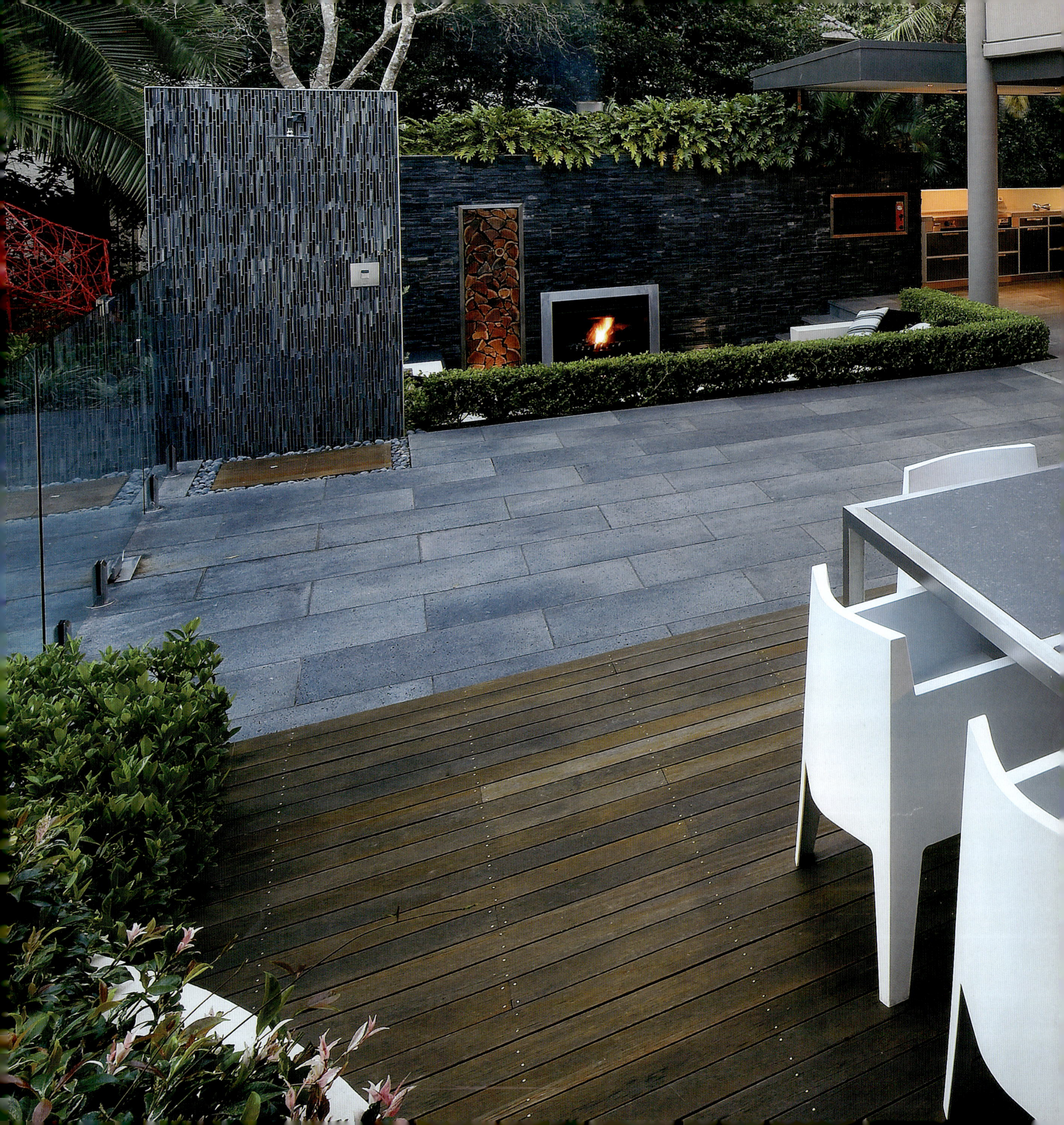

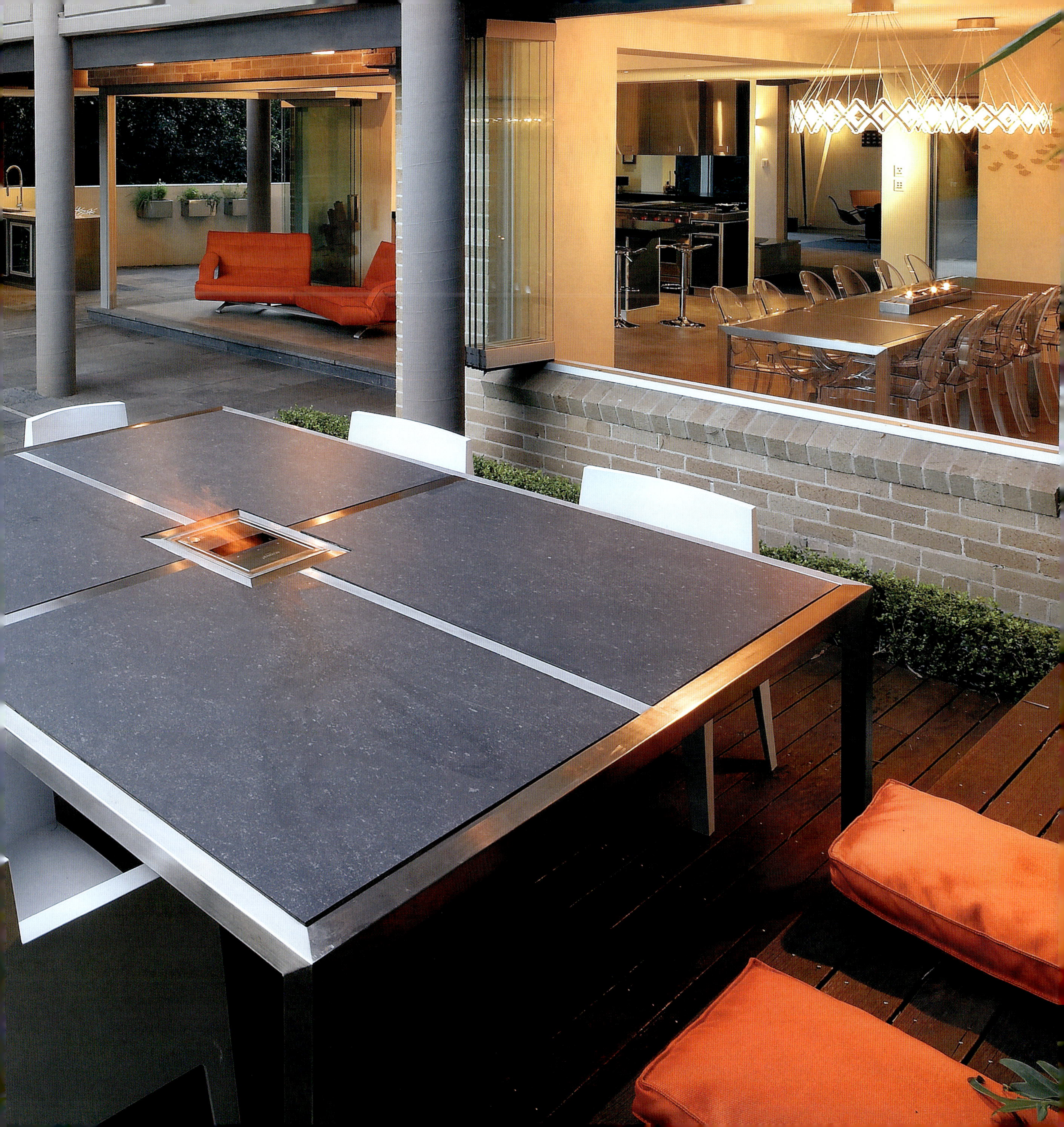

Show gardens are an opportunity for me to be the designer and the client, and to see a result in a short period of time. The Melbourne International Flower and Garden Show is an annual event in which I have participated several times, and I have been fortunate enough to win a gold medal with my team on each occasion.

This design encapsulates the true experience of resort-style living in a residential environment – a design style I have been producing for more than 10 years. The pool plays a central role, around which all elements revolve. Fully tiled in blue glass mosaics, the pool features a vanishing edge, swim-up bar and water feature above, consisting of a stunning stainless steel sphere sculpture.

Floating Layers
MELBOURNE

To one side is a flat-roofed pavilion supported by layered hardwood timber slat posts joining a steel beam above. In this pavilion a hanging kitchen suspended by two steel rods rests against the rear wall, providing a cooking location at one end with the other end for dining. Suspending the bench made the space appear larger by allowing a view through the kitchen area, revealing the sandstone-tiled floor below.

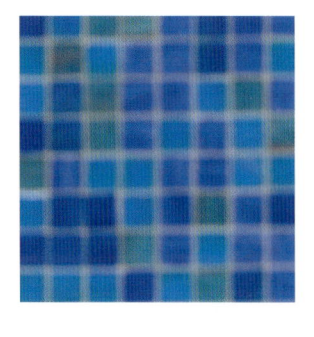

On the other side of the pool is a smaller-scale version of the large pavilion, which houses a swim-up bar with stainless steel stools set within the pool, glass-door refrigerators, storage space and a sink. A custom-made, stainless steel trough was installed in the bench close to the edge of the pool, forming a self-serve bar which can be filled with ice and drinks. A sunken hardwood deck located at the front edge of the pool creates a lounge area offering a line of sight that skims across the water level. At the rear of the

Plan labels:

- STONE-CLAD WALL
- DRAGONS BLOOD FEATURE TREES
- STAINLESS STEEL SCULPTURE
- UPPER POND WITH SPILLOVER
- TIMBER FINS
- SWIM-UP BAR WITH STAINLESS STEEL STOOLS
- SUNKEN BAR WITH SINK & FRIDGE
- CANTILEVERED BENCH WITH BBQ & DINING AREA
- OUTDOOR PAVILION
- OUTDOOR SHOWER
- TIMBER BRIDGE
- SUNKEN LOUNGE AREA
- TIMBER DECK
- POOL WITH SPILLOVER
- PAVING
- TIMBER DECK

0   5M

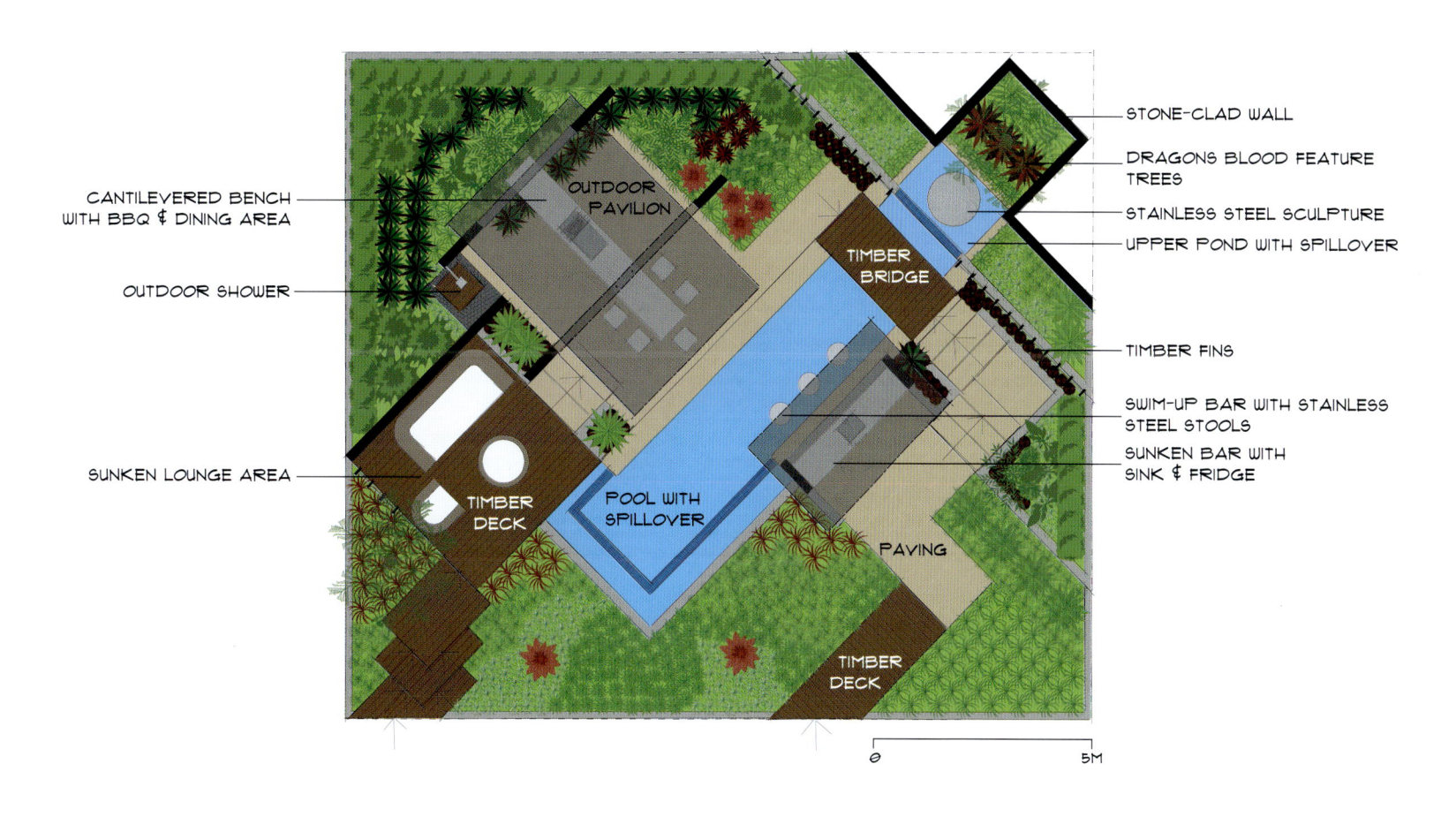

lounge is a stone-clad, dry-stack wall that relates to the wall at the far end of the pool.

Given the large scale of the structures in this project, planting plays a role in reducing the dominance of the built form and in softening hard edges. Dragon's blood trees (*Dracaena draco*) are used as focal points to catch the eye and provide architectural form by way of their material structure. At the lower edge of the pool, mass plantings of purple fountain grass (*Pennisetum advena* 'Rubrum'), turf lily (*Liriope muscari*) and spiny-headed mat rush (*Lomandra longifolia* 'Tanika') were used. Due to the shade cast by the surrounding kitchen pavilion, shade-loving plants, such as grey star ctenanthe (*Ctenanthe setosa* 'Grey Star'), ti plant (*Cordyline fruticosa*) and Japanese sago palm (*Cycas revoluta*), were included in the design.

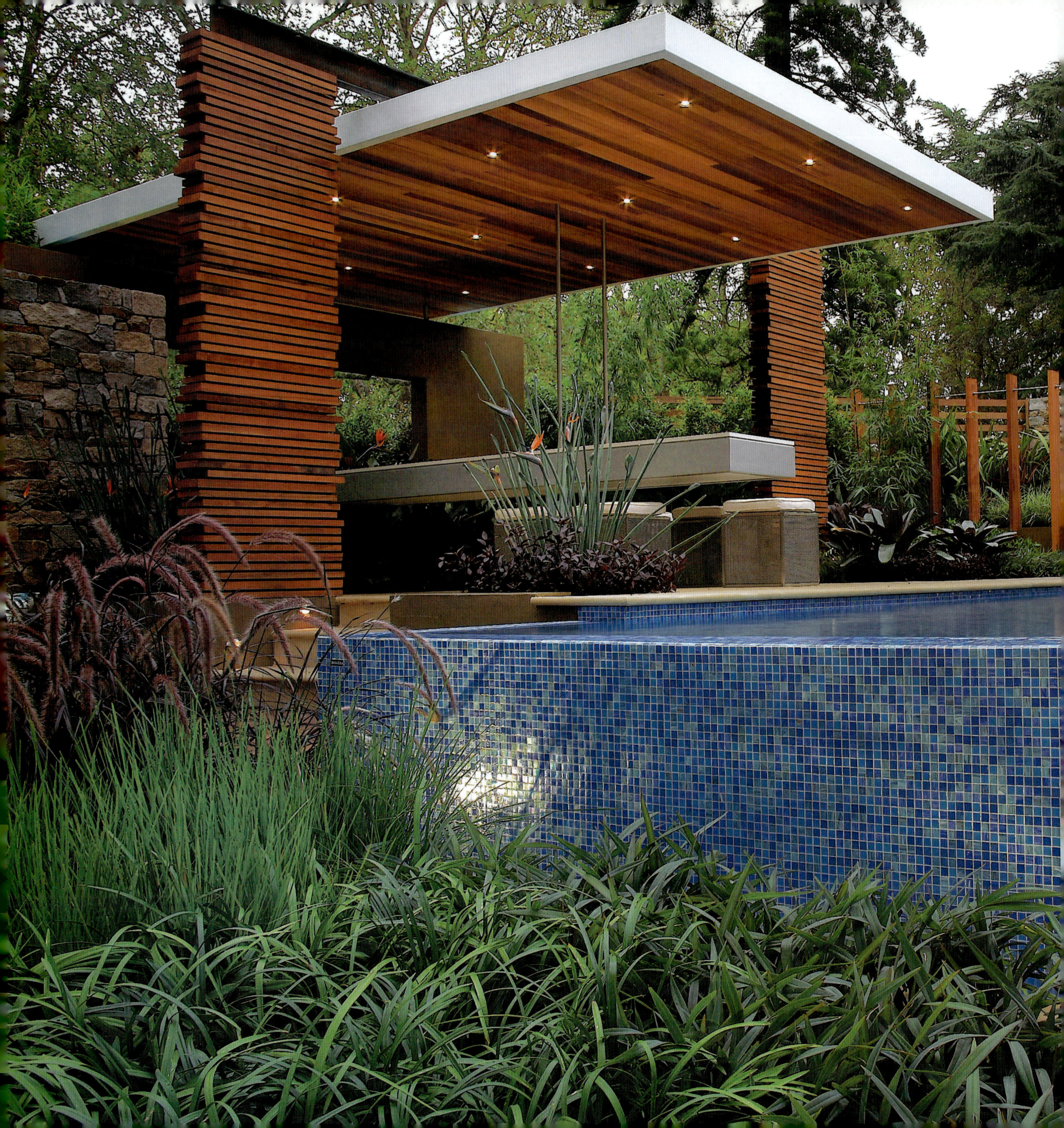

FLOATING LAYERS 83

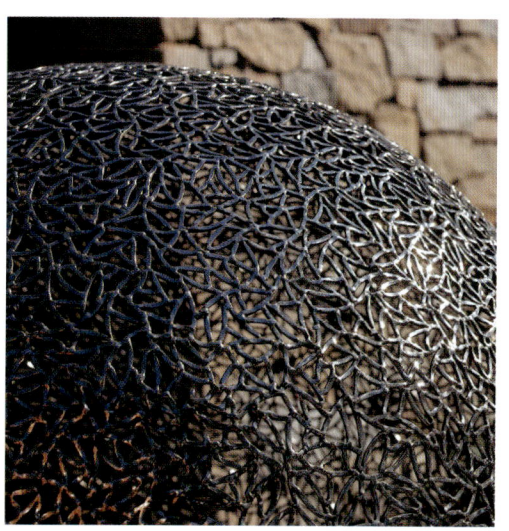

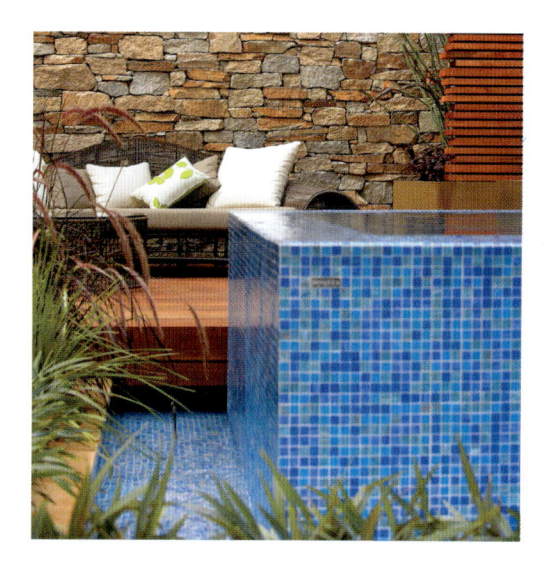

84

FLOATING LAYERS 85

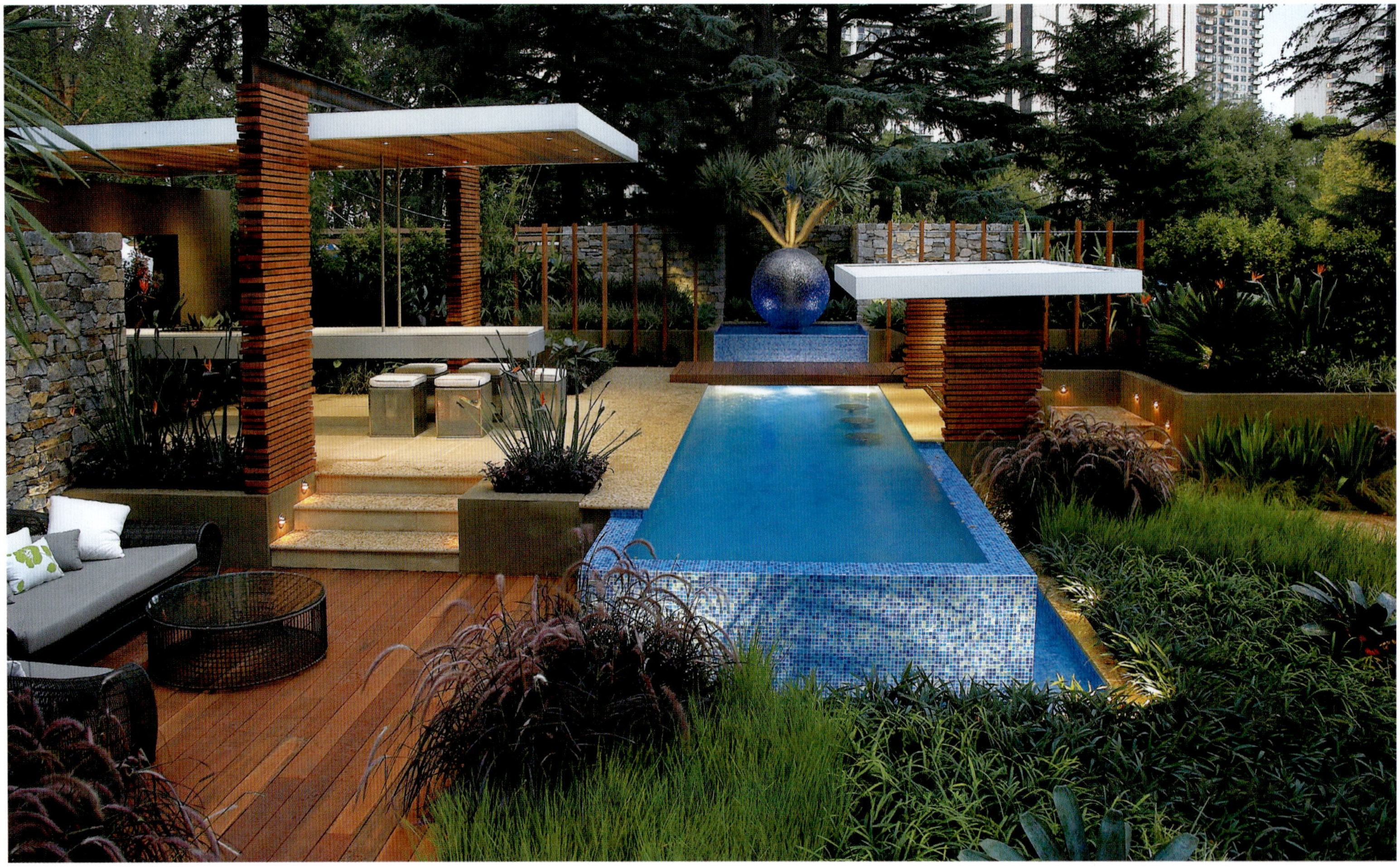

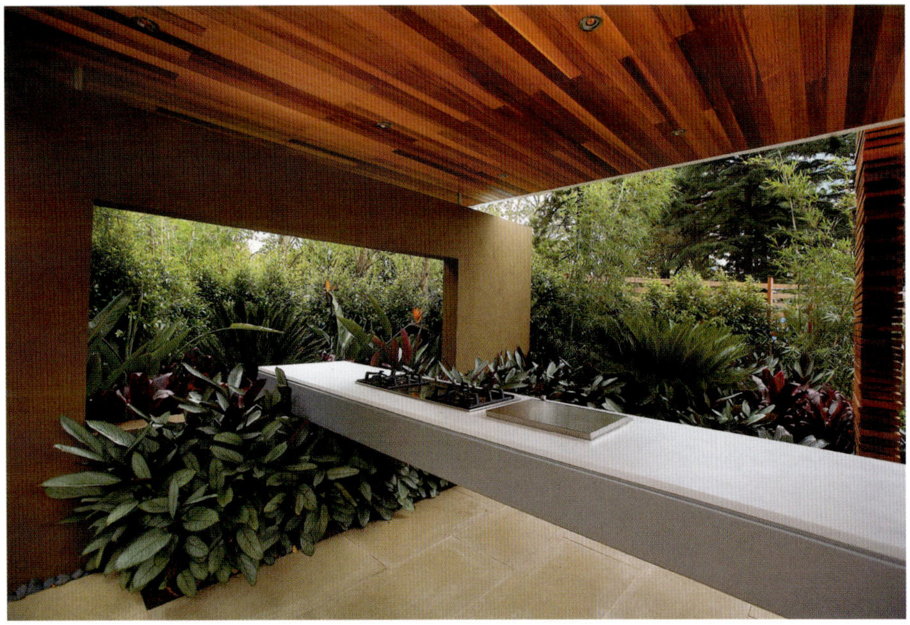

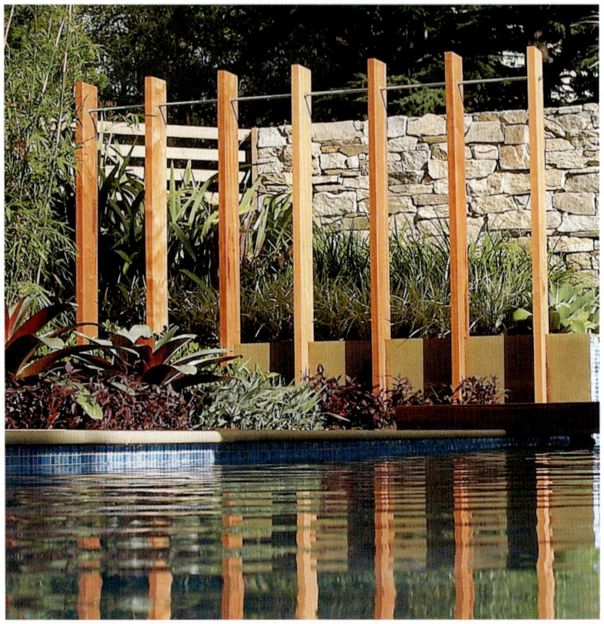

FLOATING LAYERS 87

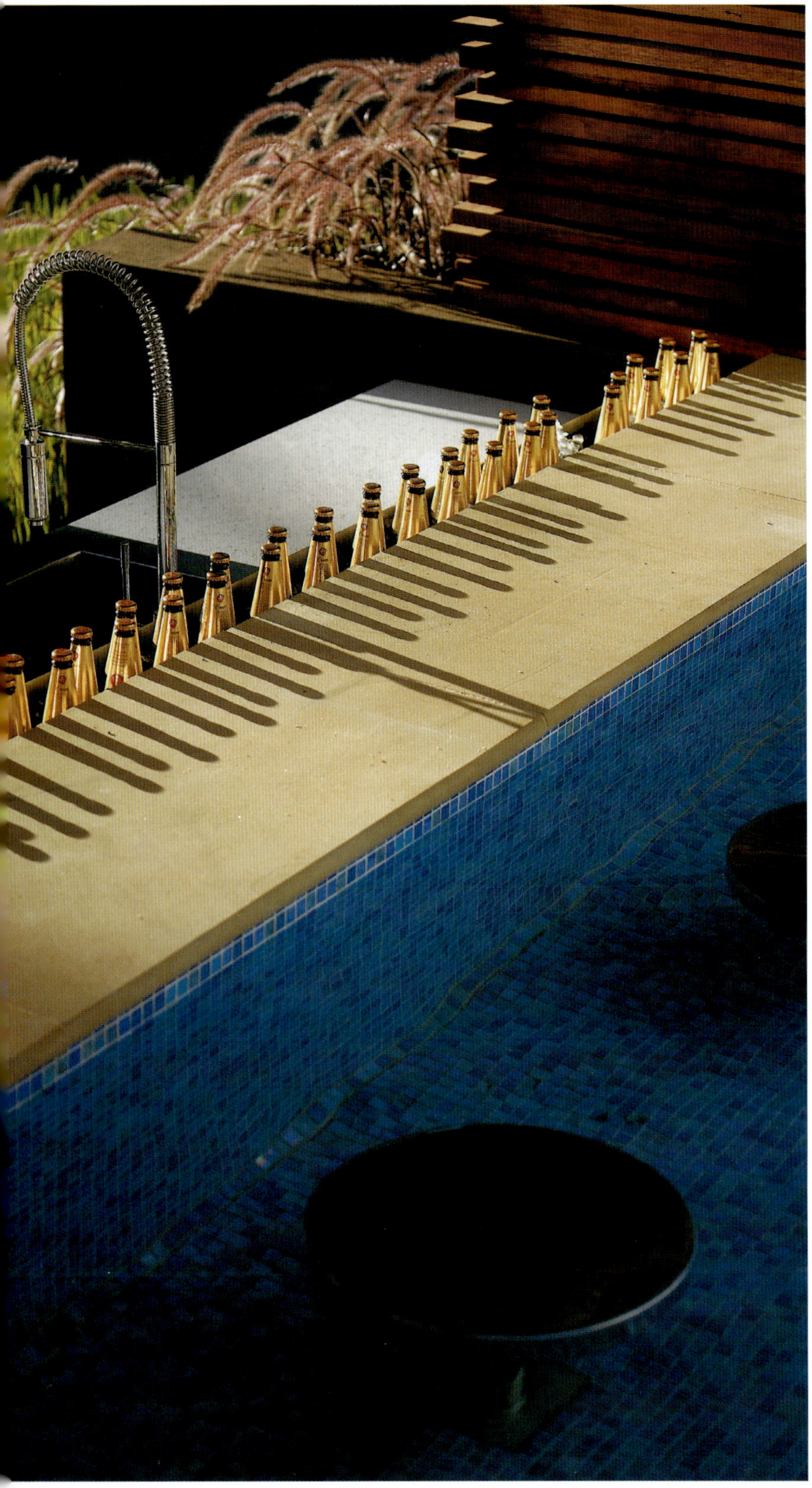

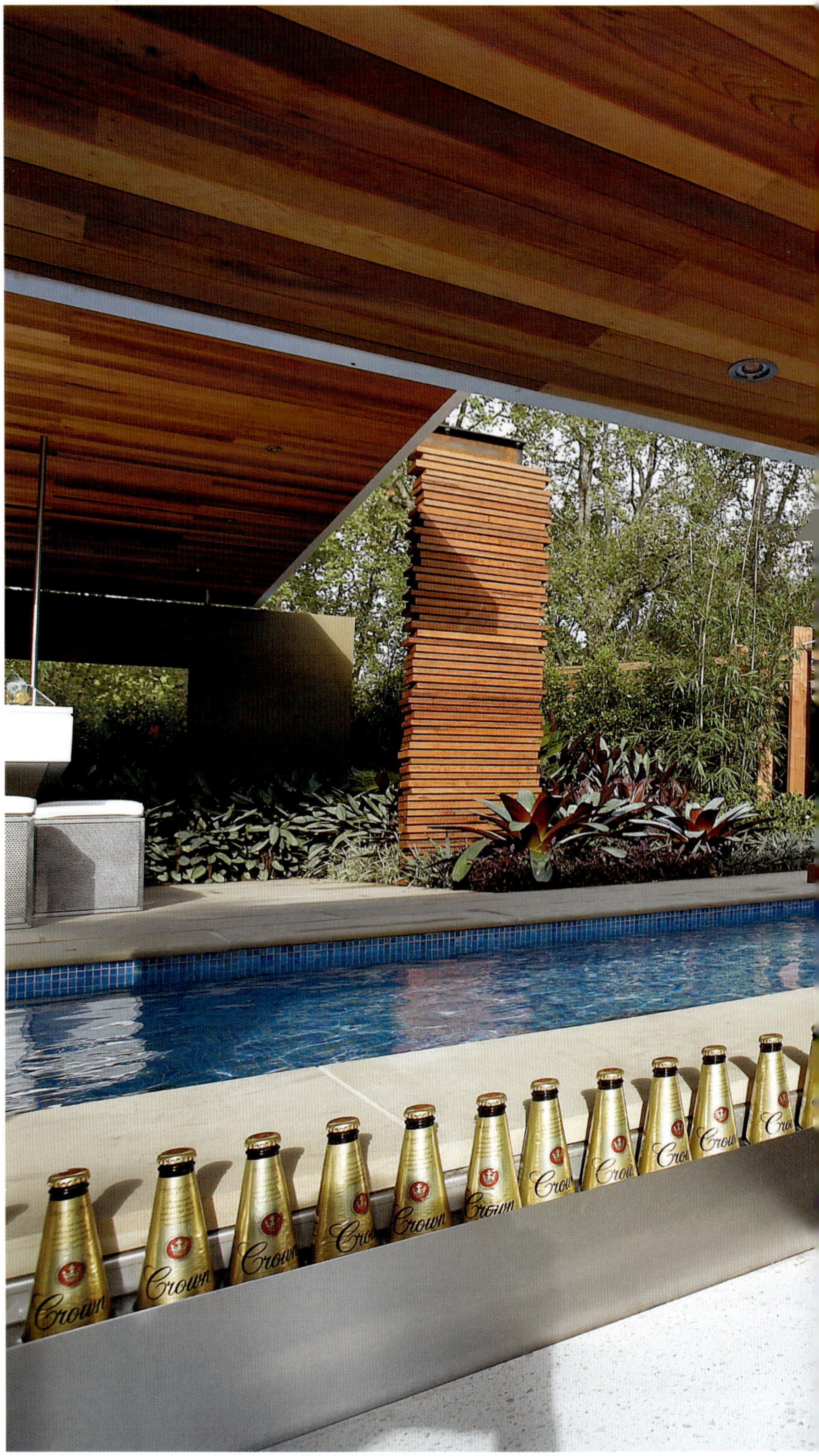
Crown
Crown
Crown
Crown
Crown

FLOATING LAYERS 89

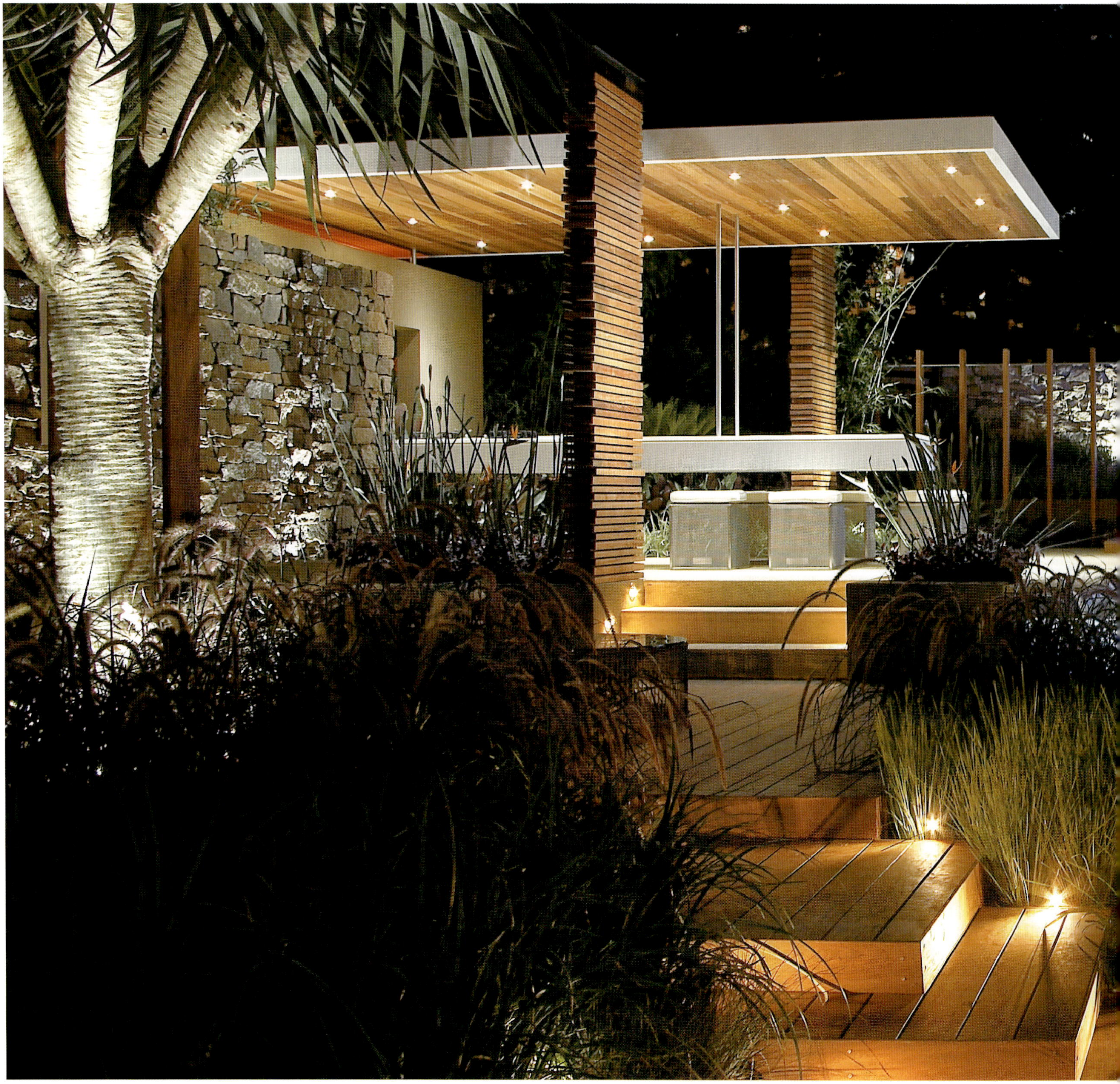

FLOATING LAYERS 91

The Secret Garden

CASTLE HILL

Of all the gardens I have designed and built, this garden is one of the most special to me, due to its significance to my clients. I was asked to design this garden as a memorial after my client lost his son in a tragic accident. Never before had I been given such a meaningful role and responsibility to express a space for such an important reason.

The area of this garden is just over 40 metres by 40 metres and was the horse arena where the children learnt to ride. It sits within a 5-acre property of established formal gardens, which are well maintained with stunning carved sandstone pieces set throughout. Given the setting, I thought a formal tone for the project was most appropriate and the square nature of the arena offered the opportunity to express a strong symmetrical theme.

The centrepiece of the garden is a grand, tiered water feature. A commissioned bronze sculpture of a stallion takes pride of place and provides a strong visual connection to the past. The water feature's central fountain is fitted with 16 bubblers, which provide dramatic movement of the water and begin the flow from the highest point down to the troughs below. These troughs extend to each corner of the garden, dividing the square area into quarters. Three of the troughs end with a large pot, overflowing with water, set within a square pond. At the end of the fourth trough is a Juliet balcony, which is elevated just short of 3 metres above the garden, providing the perfect view.

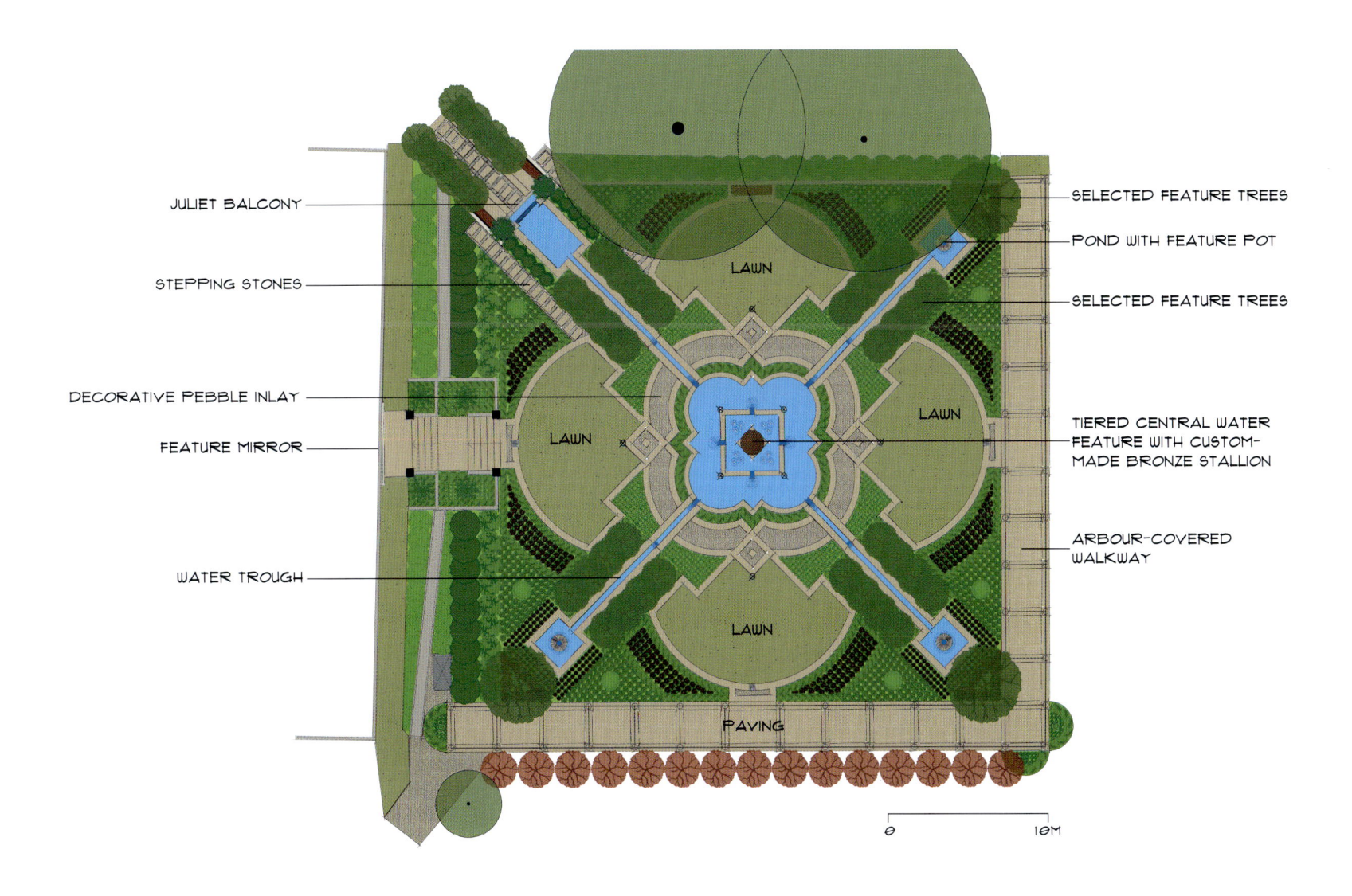

- JULIET BALCONY
- STEPPING STONES
- DECORATIVE PEBBLE INLAY
- FEATURE MIRROR
- WATER TROUGH
- SELECTED FEATURE TREES
- POND WITH FEATURE POT
- SELECTED FEATURE TREES
- TIERED CENTRAL WATER FEATURE WITH CUSTOM-MADE BRONZE STALLION
- ARBOUR-COVERED WALKWAY
- LAWN
- PAVING

0   10M

Positioned on the lower two sides of the garden is a grand colonnade. With a custom-curved, open steel arbour and rustic columns that stretch 70 metres in length, this arbour, with its entwined plantings of ornamental grape (*Vitis vinifera*), embraces the outer edge of the garden while providing two entrance points with a symmetrical view. With the four areas set, the formal planting style was repeated in each quadrant. Avenue-style planting of ornamental pears (*Pyrus calleryana* 'Chanticleer') creates a strong relationship with the four water troughs, while layered plantings of orange jessamine (*Murraya panniculata*) and Japanese box (*Buxus microphylla* 'Japonica') act as fillers beneath.

Combination plantings were used to fill out the larger garden areas encompassing plants such as Chinese fringe flower (*Loropetalum chinense* 'Rubrum'), dwarf Japanese box (*Buxus microphylla* 'Faulkner'), society garlic (*Tulbaghia violacea*), lilly pilly (*Syzygium australe*) and yellow star jasmine (*Trachelospermum asiaticum*). Annuals were used to provide seasonal colour while working with the formal theme.

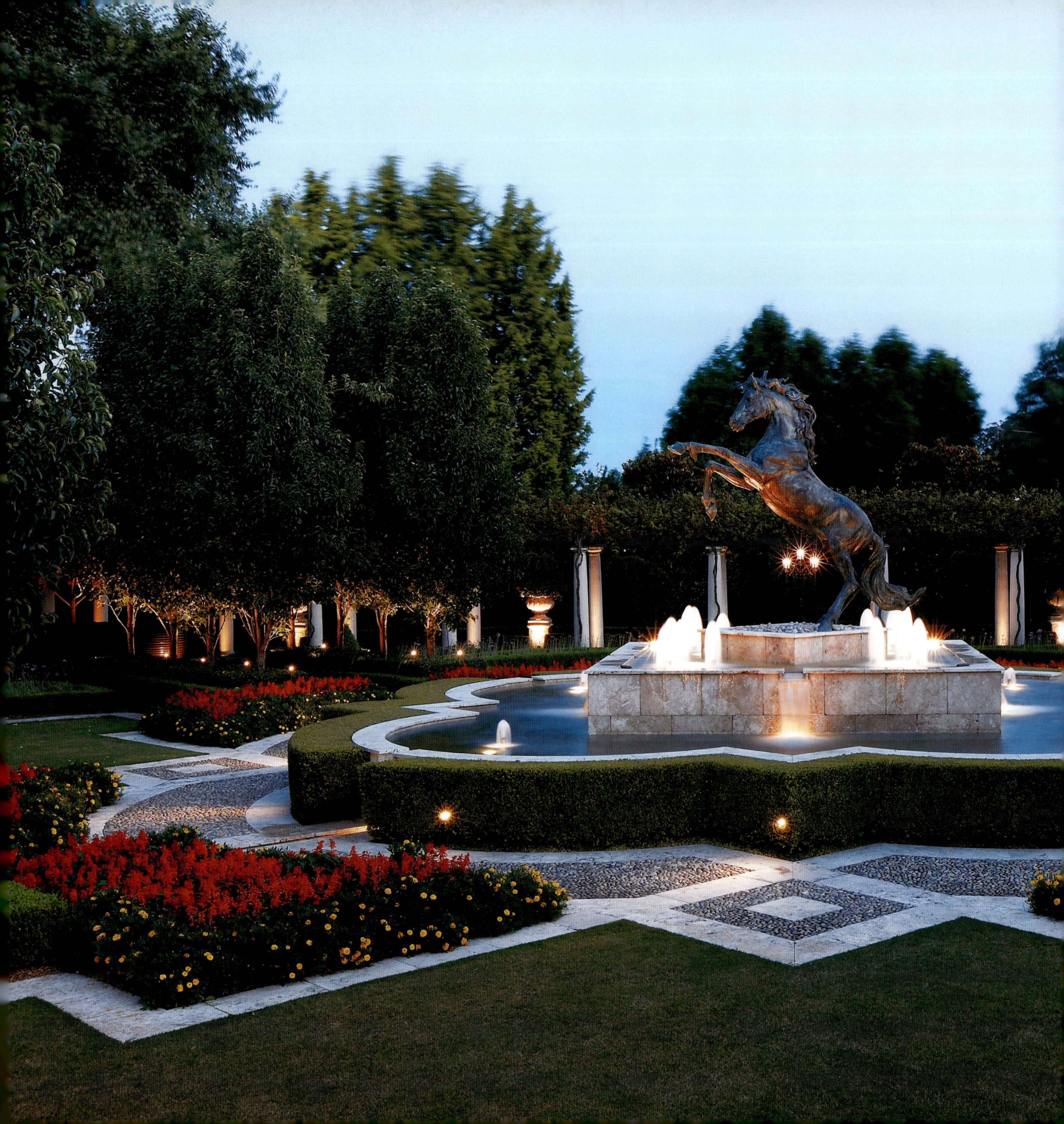

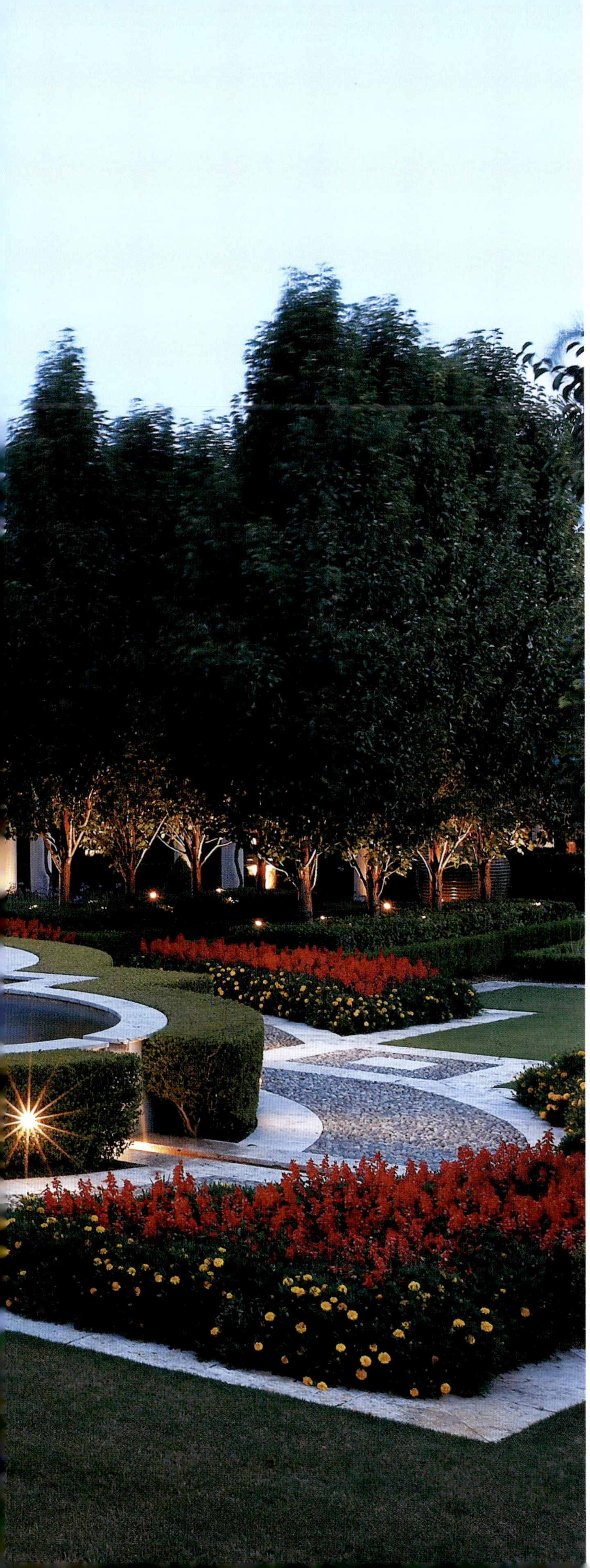
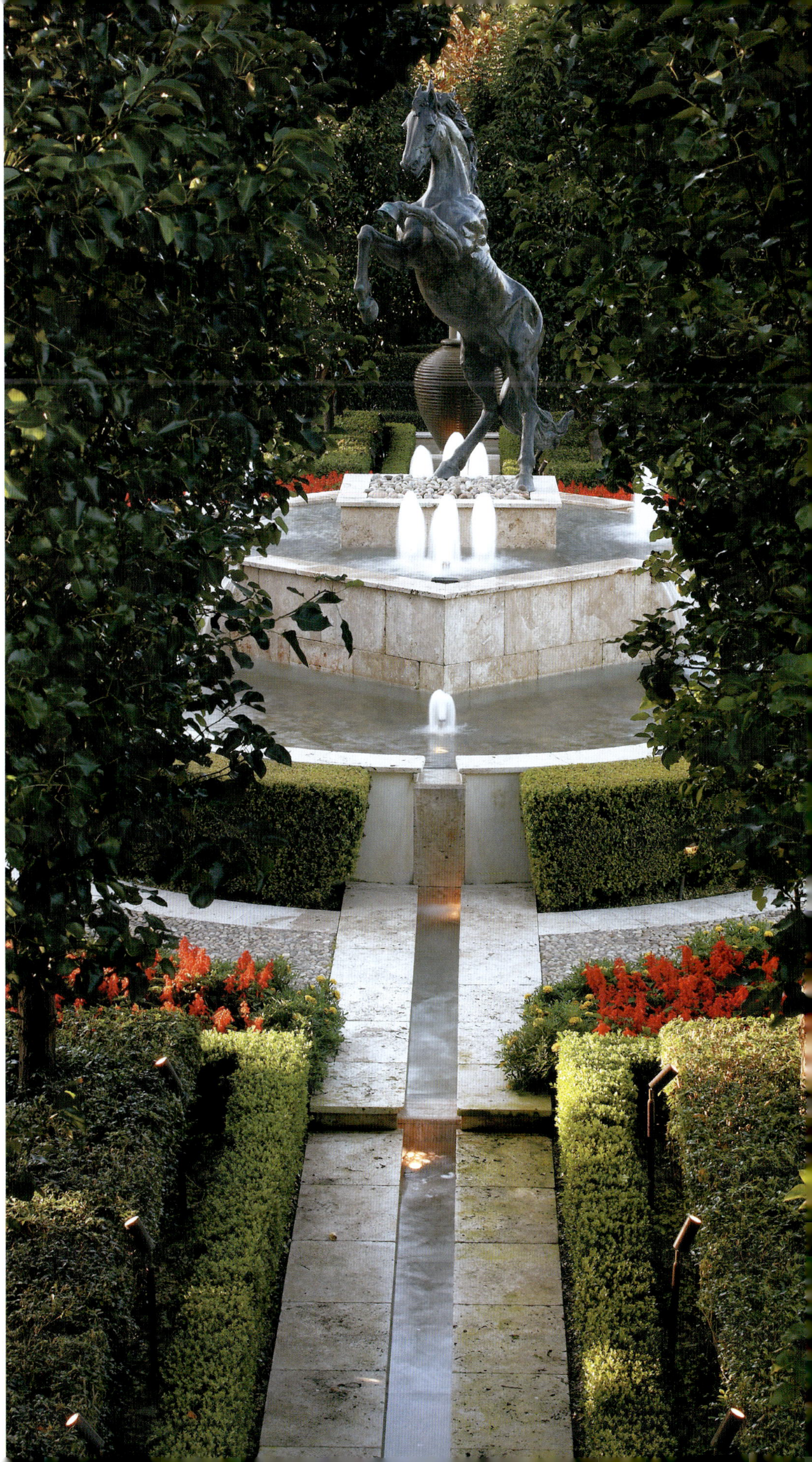

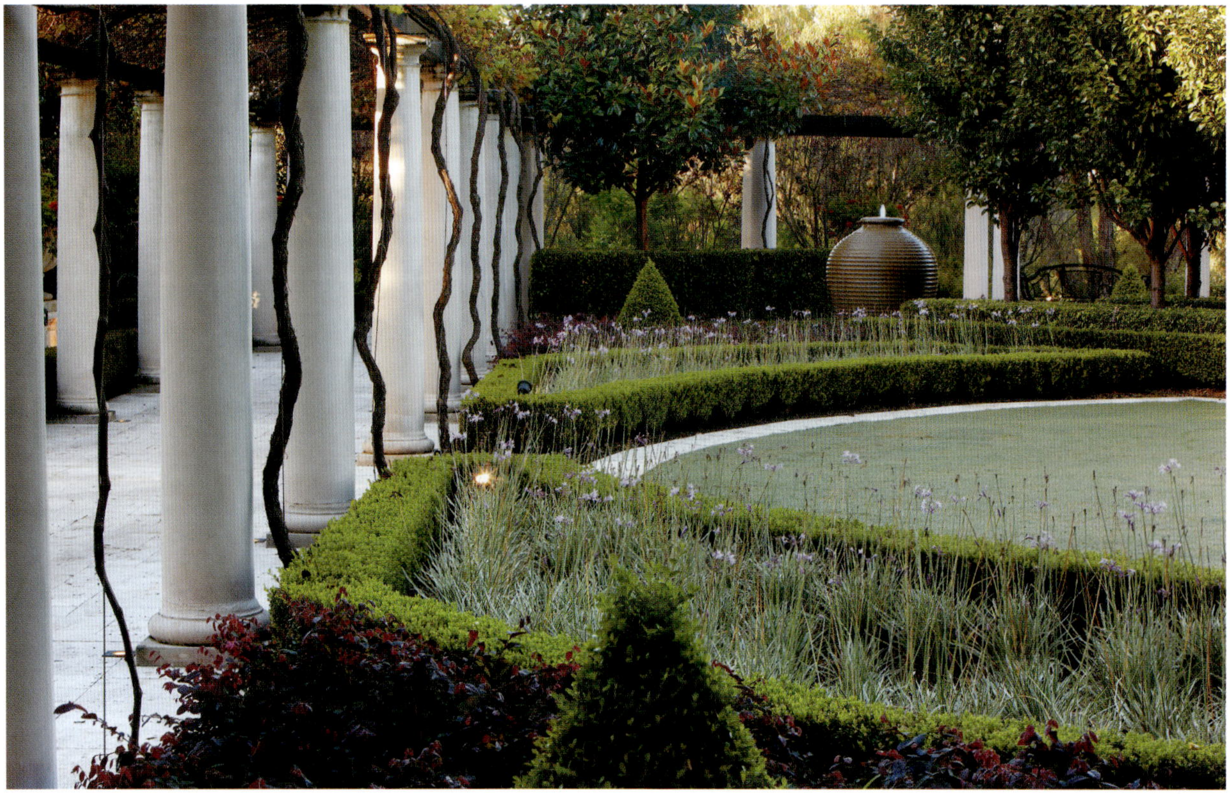

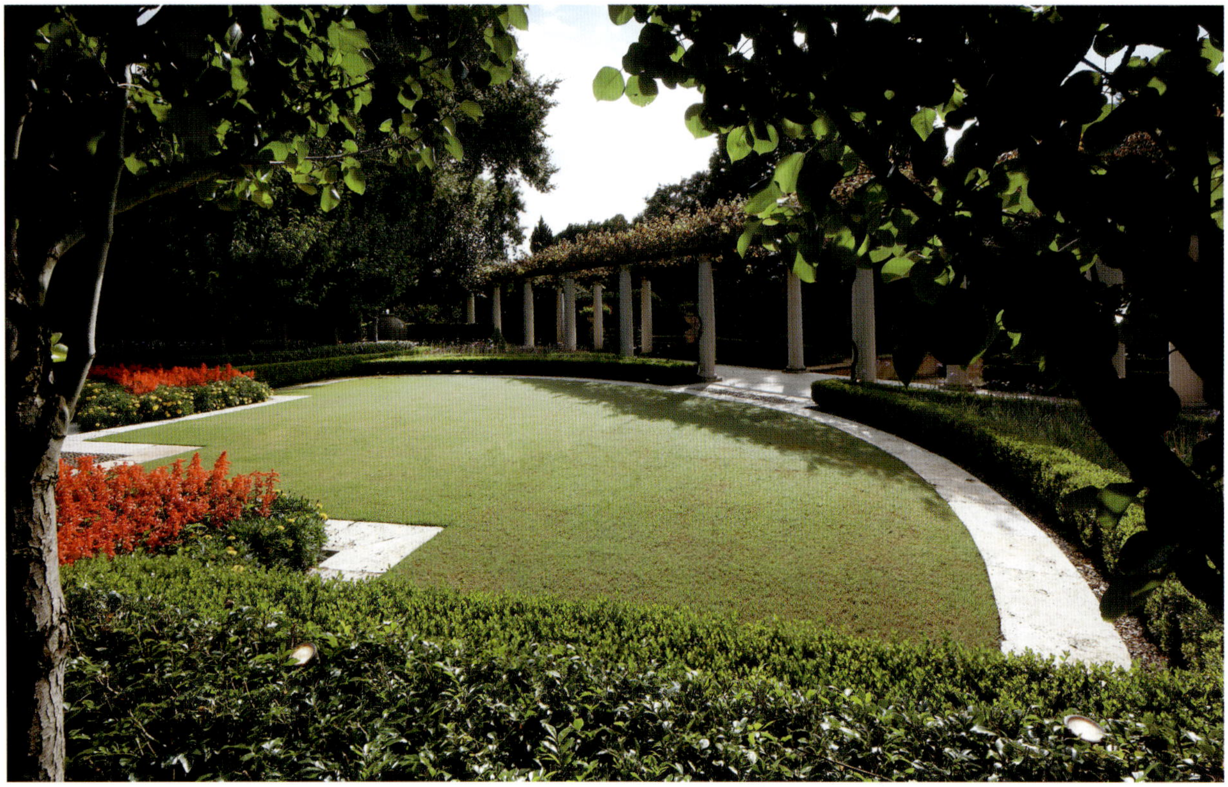

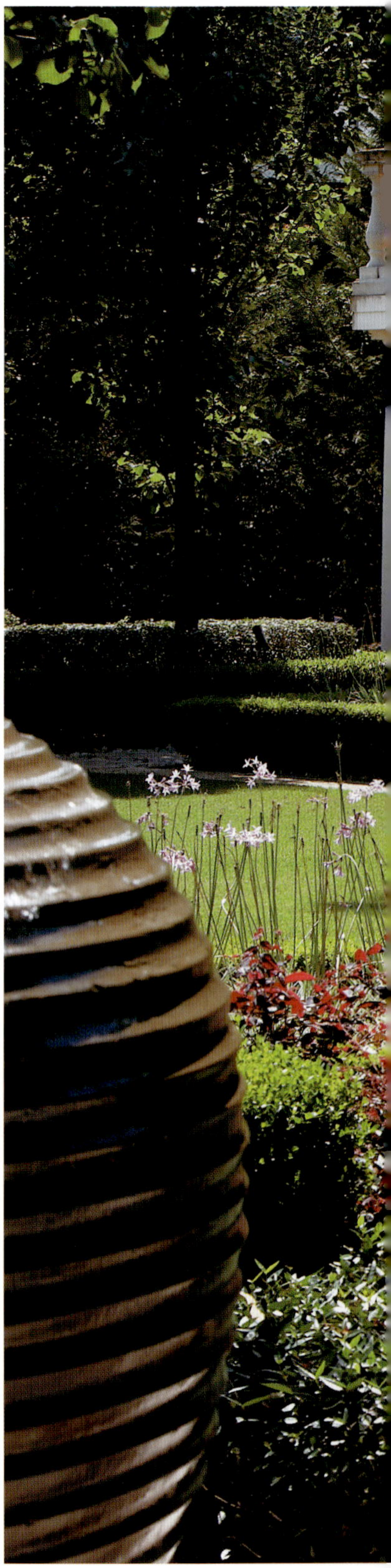

THE SECRET GARDEN 97

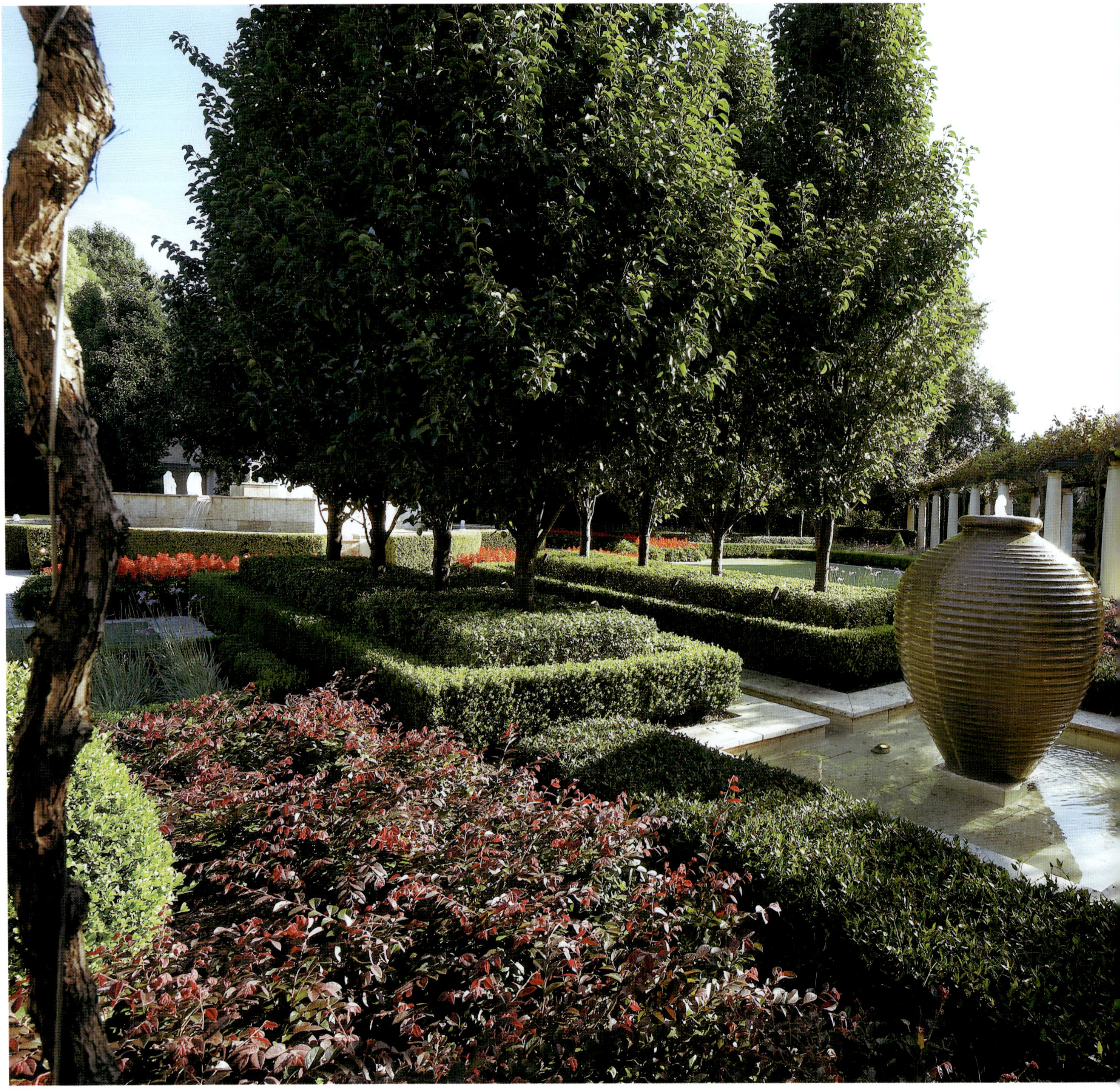

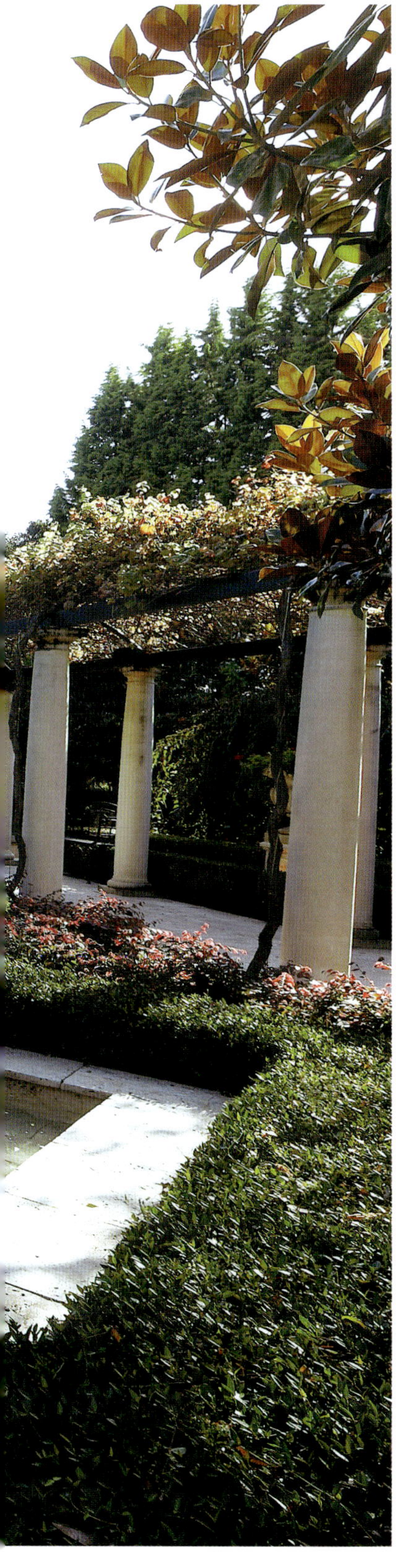
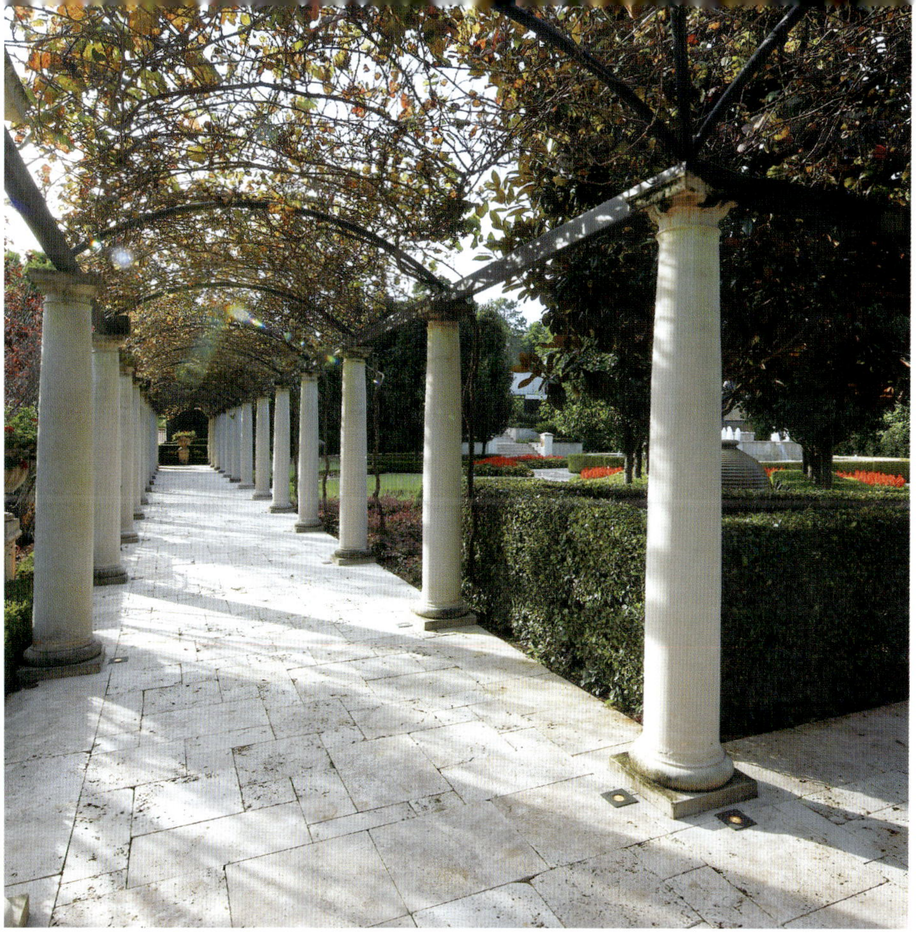
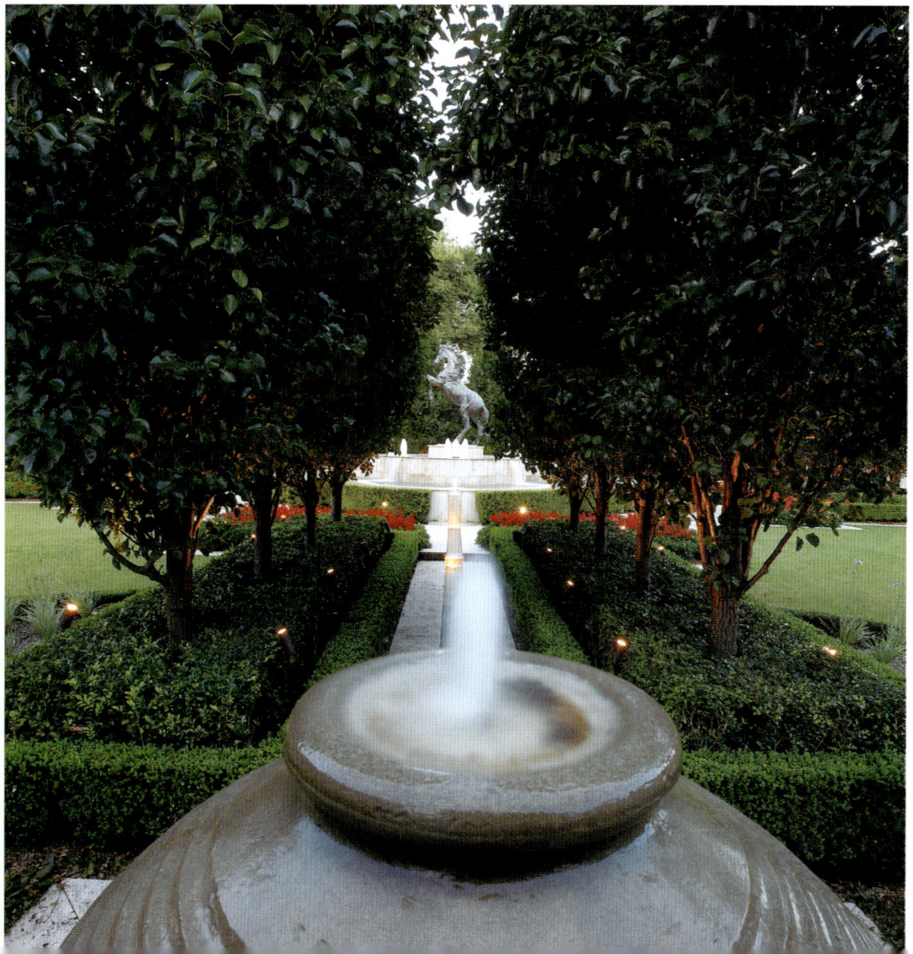

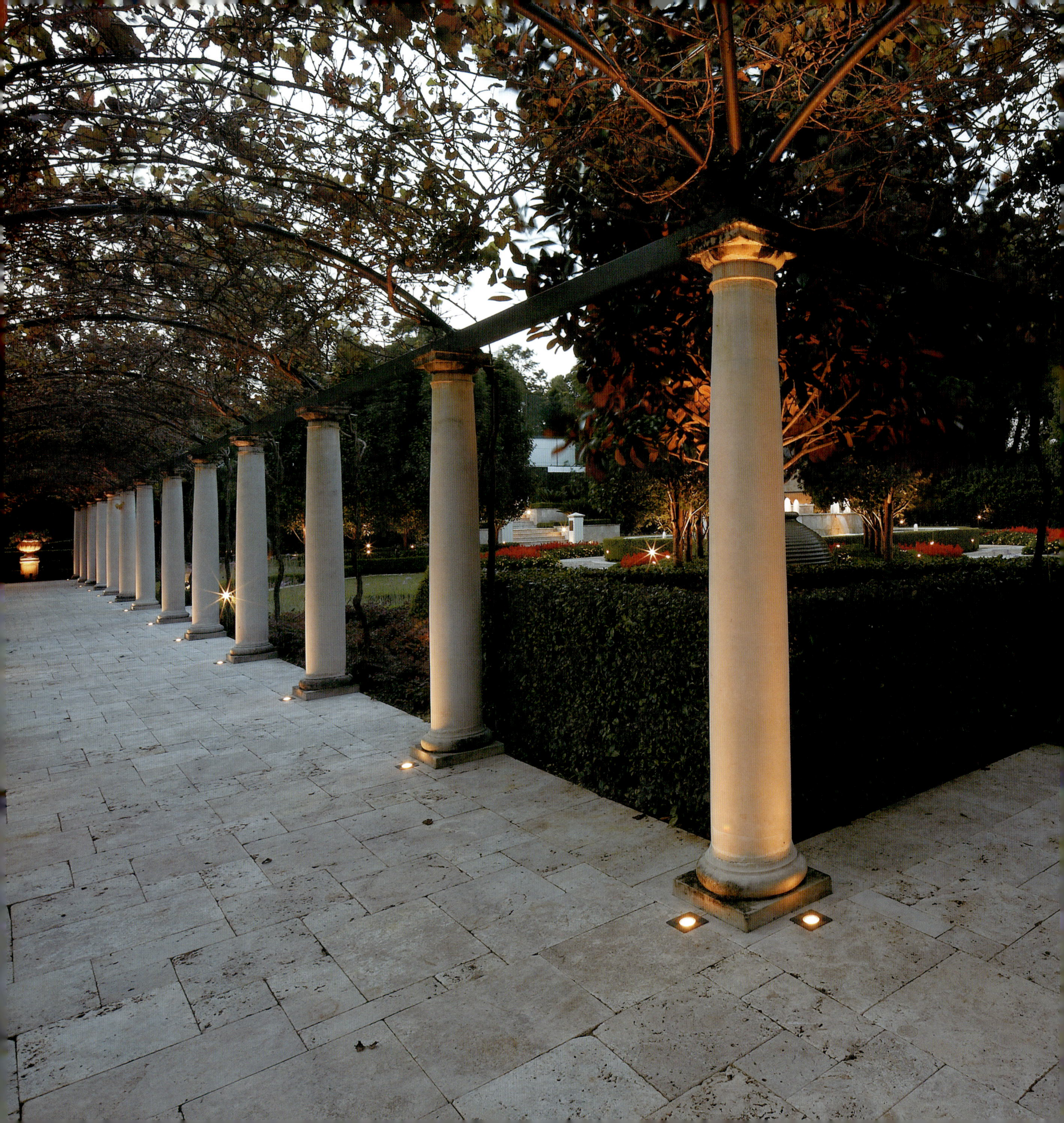

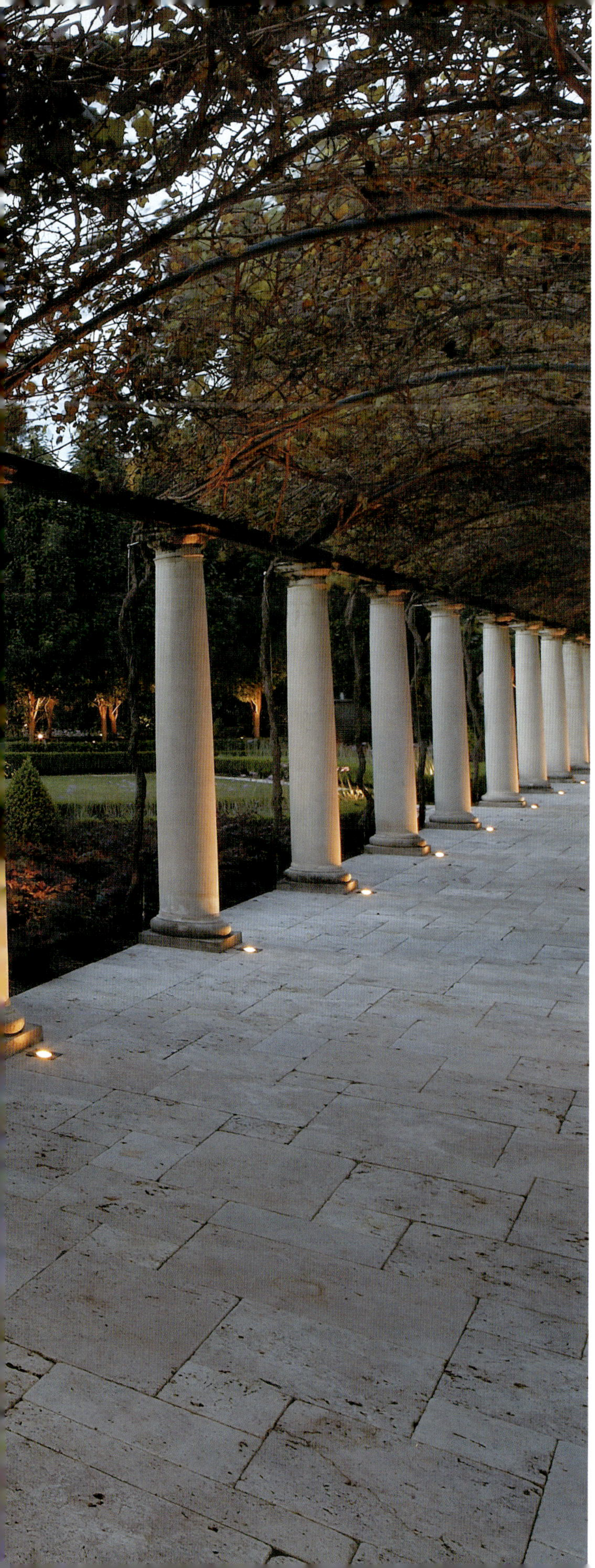

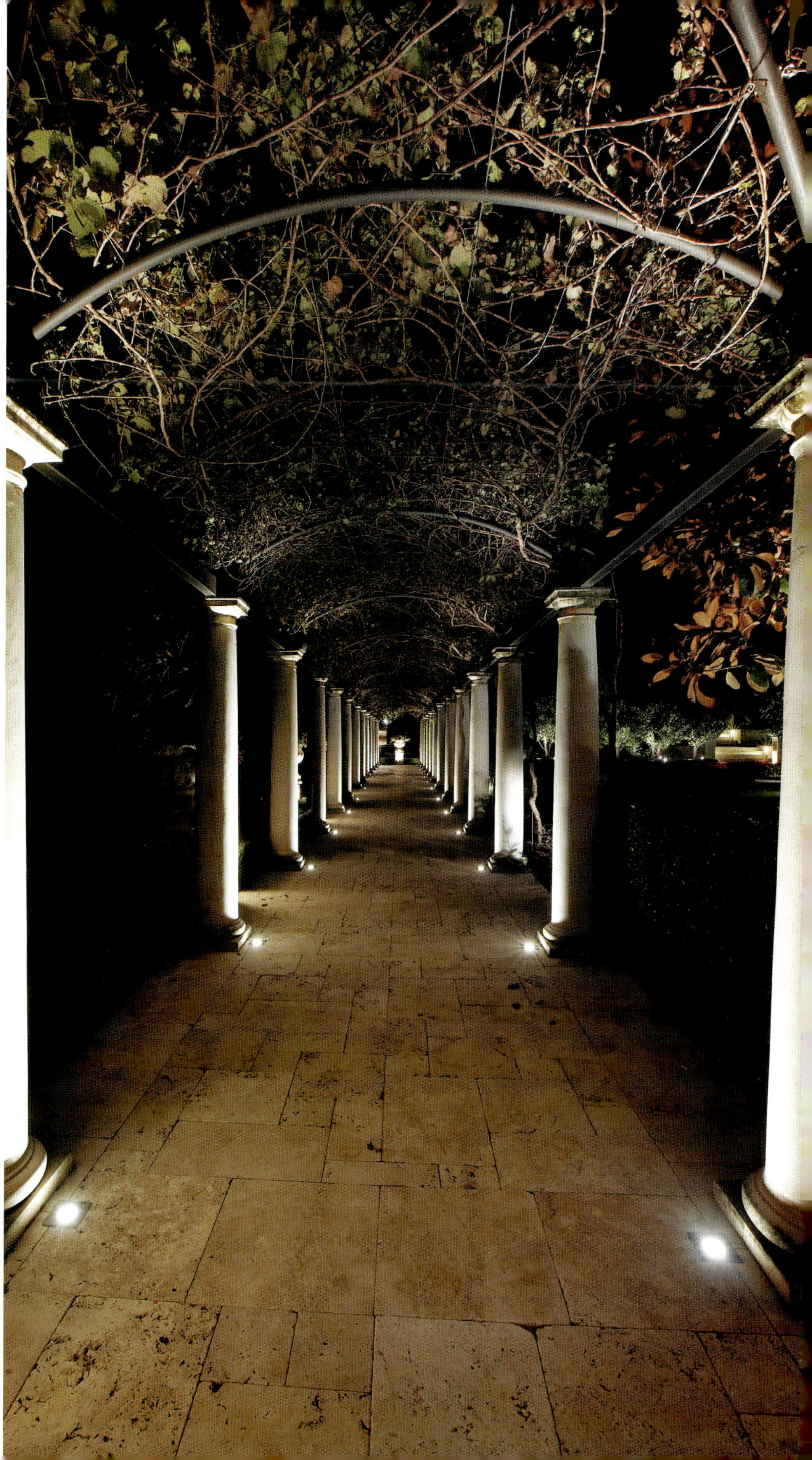

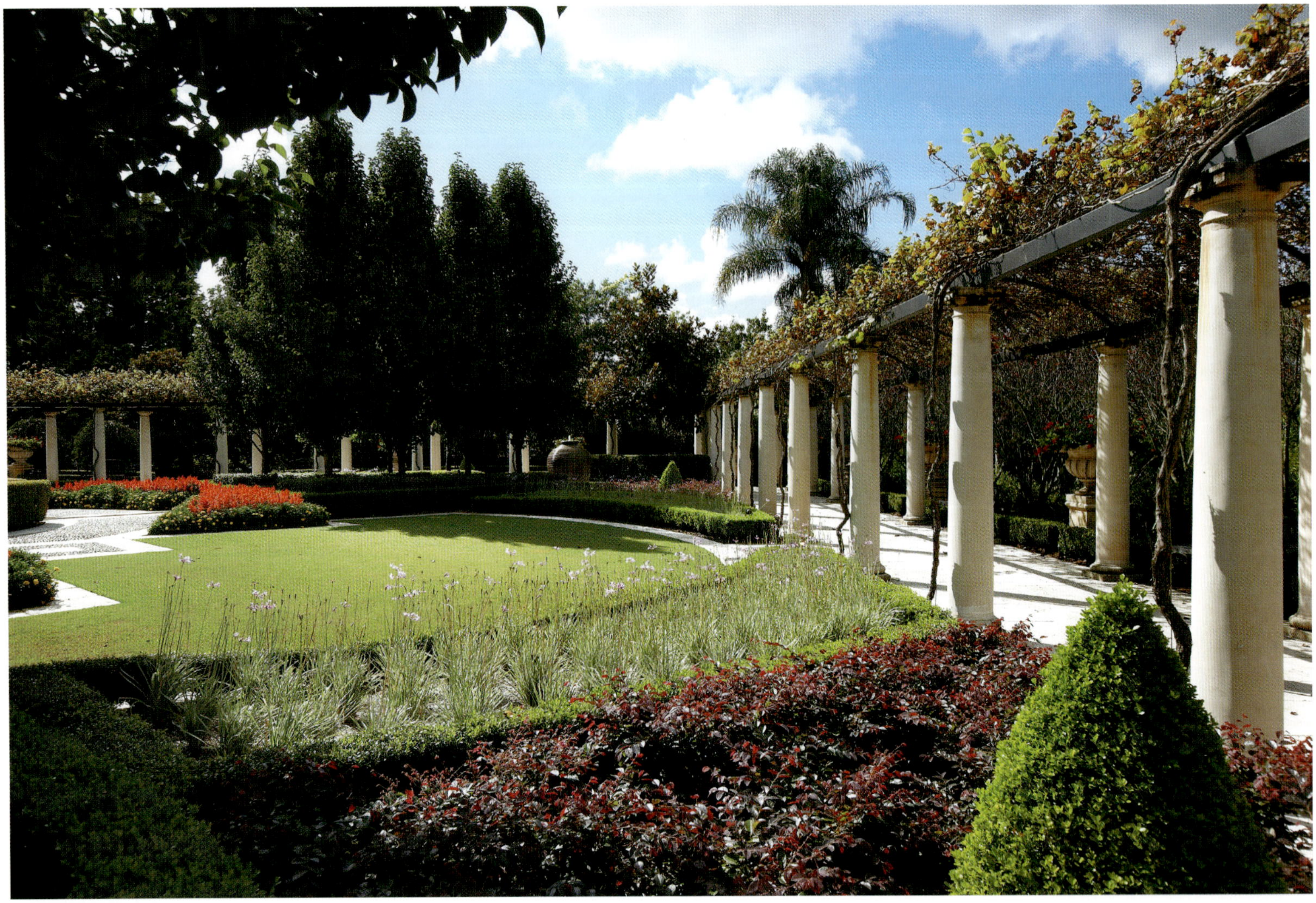

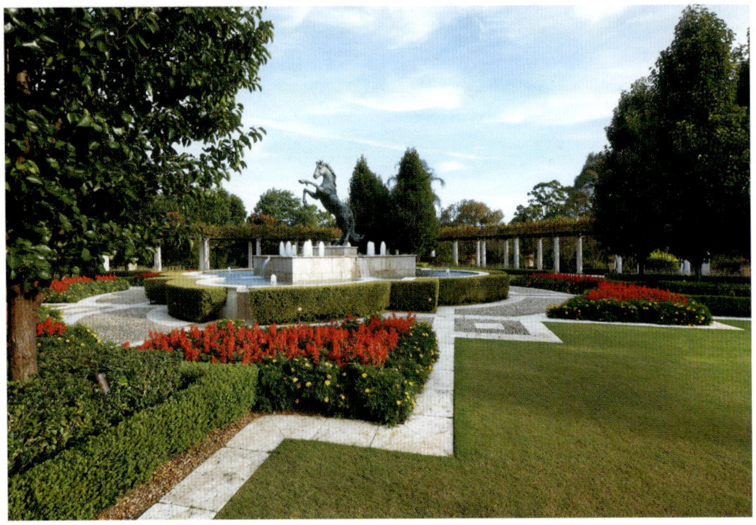

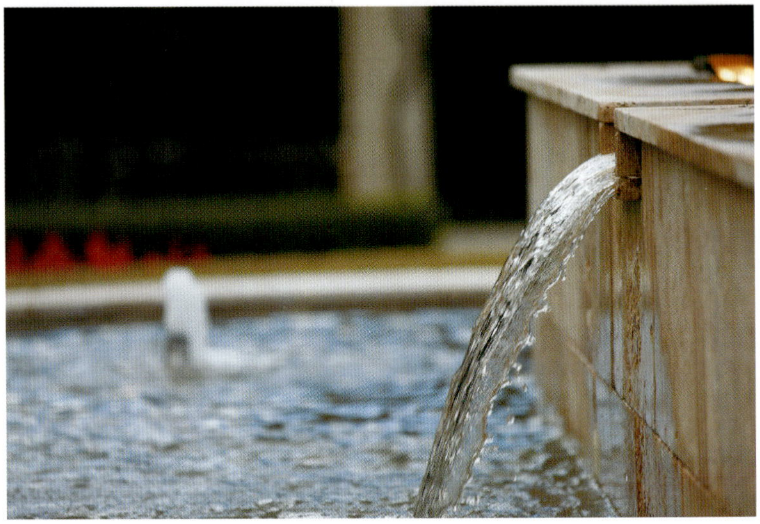

THE SECRET GARDEN 103

The atmosphere of an outdoor bathroom garden differs greatly from other external spaces. It is a place of intimacy and tranquility and offers true seclusion like no other place. This outdoor bathroom was designed off the ensuite of the house, providing not only an extended area of use, but also a permanent view from the room, increasing light and the relationship with the garden. This style of garden requires lush plantings that evoke the feel of a rainforest, which may not suit other areas of the home.

With the ceiling removed and the sky in full view, an outdoor bathroom provides a unique bathing experience – in some ways, it evokes the feeling of a luxurious tropical resort. The privacy of a space like this enables it to be shared

Intimate Hideaway

DURAL

with someone special, pausing time and allowing a true connection. It can be a place of romance – the outdoor bath providing a soothing retreat that is only enhanced with the placement of candles and a bottle of wine.

The outdoor stone bath includes a custom-designed water outlet and is set on a hardwood timber deck. The outlet was mounted on a freestanding tumbled-travertine tiled wall that relates to the internal floor of the ensuite. A long mirror was mounted on the wall to provide a feeling of extra space while reflecting the lush foliage in both corners, as well as serving the practical purpose of a bathroom

STONE-CLAD RAISED PRIVACY WALL WITH MIRROR

OUTDOOR SHOWER

STONE BATH

OPAQUE-GLASS WINDOW

TIMBER DECK

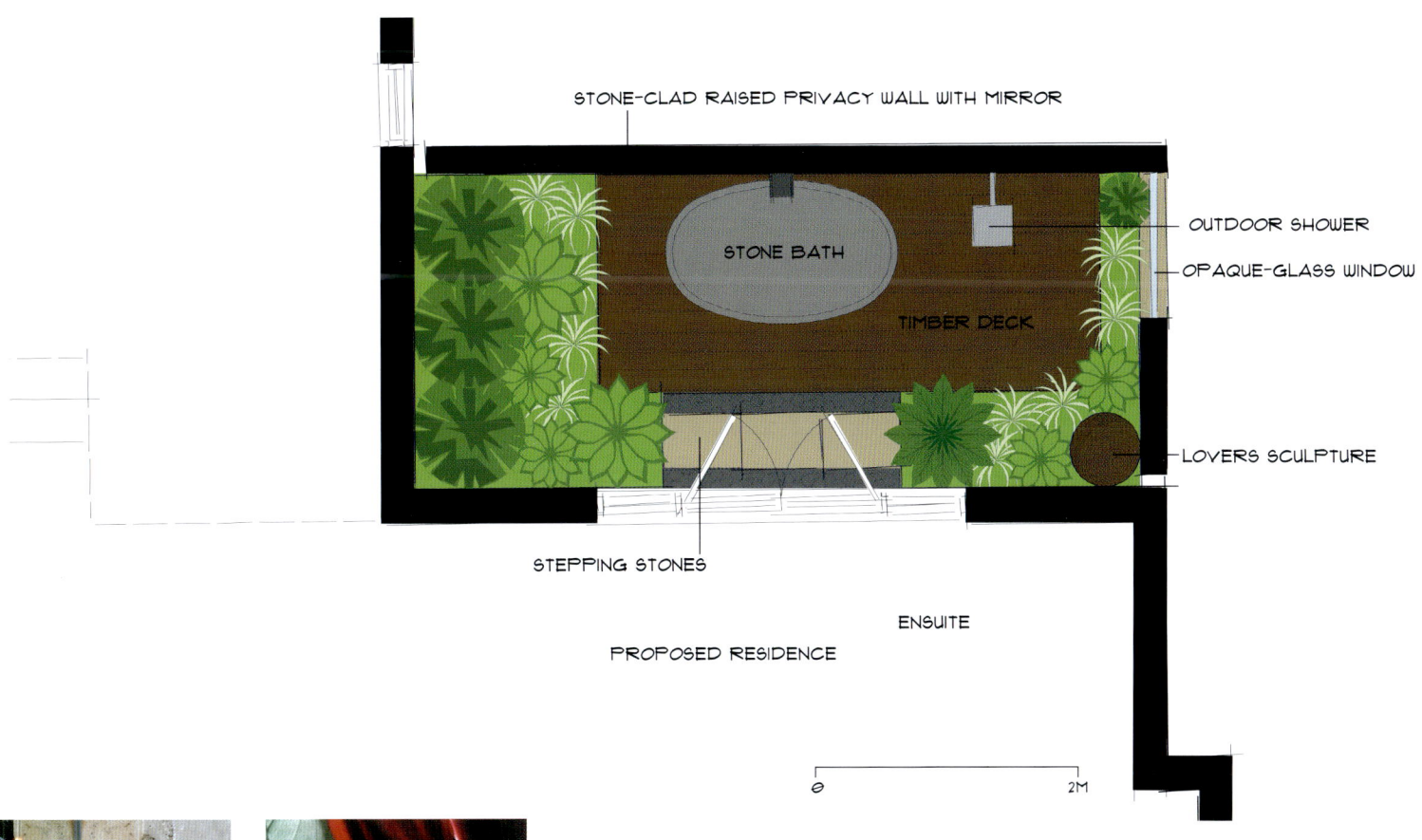

LOVERS SCULPTURE

STEPPING STONES

ENSUITE

PROPOSED RESIDENCE

0   2M

mirror. A shower fitted to the wall in the remaining space of the decking provides a unique showering experience. Among the century plant (A*gave attenuata*) and giant bromeliad (*Alcantarea imperialis* 'Rubrum') sits a bronze sculpture named *Lovers* – a perfect addition to this garden, sitting tastefully and discreetly in the corner.

105

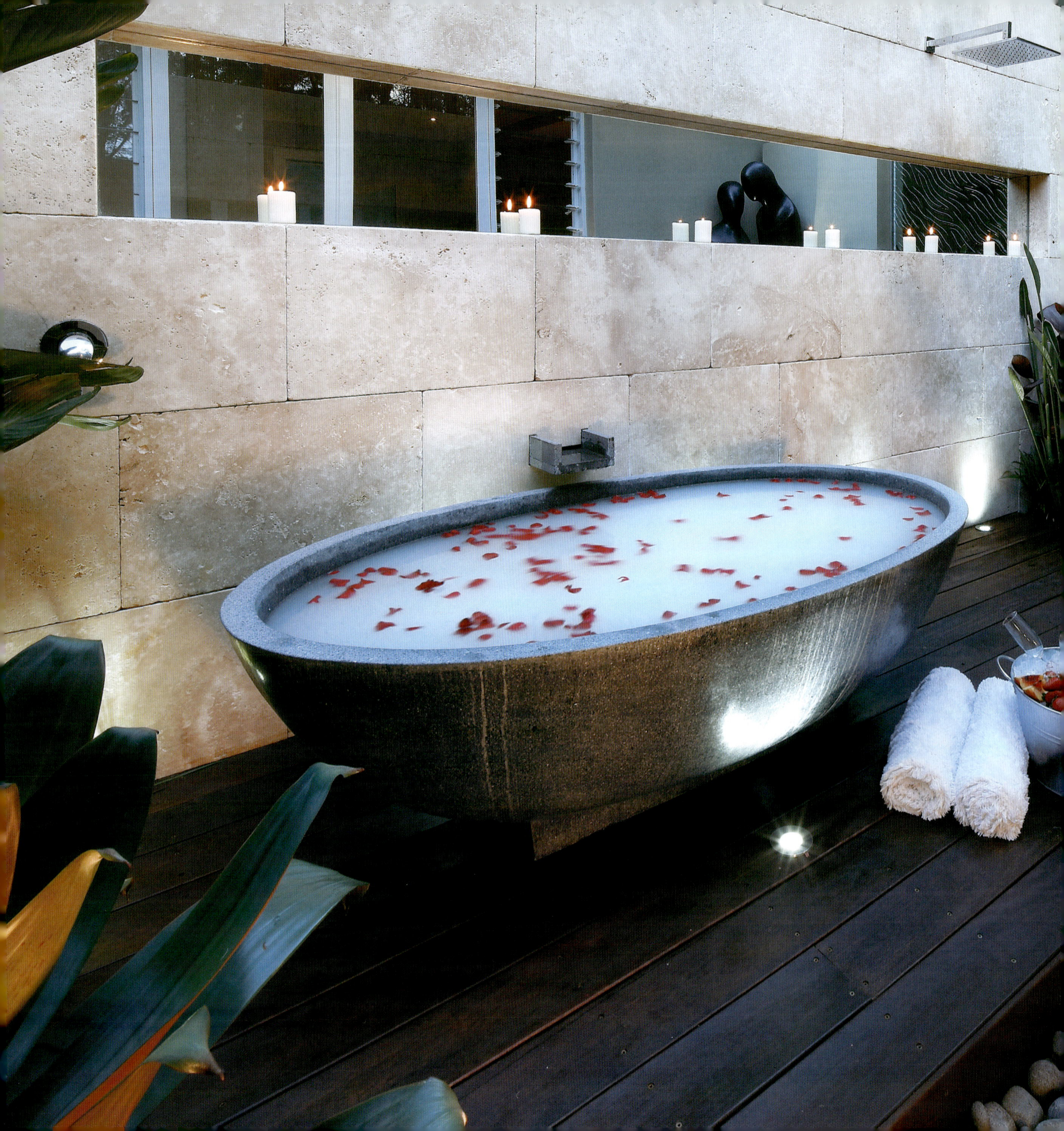

INTIMATE HIDEAWAY 107

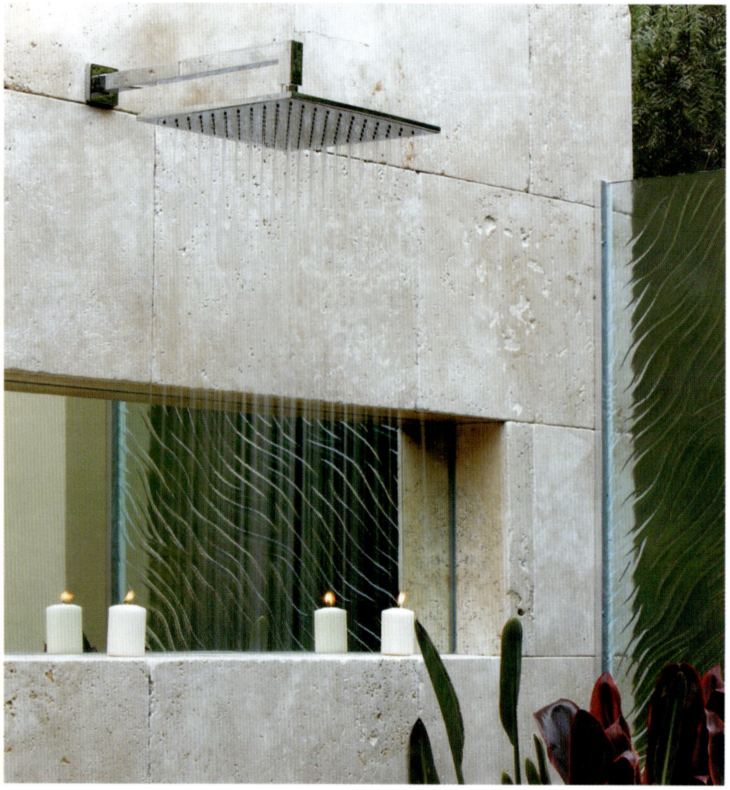

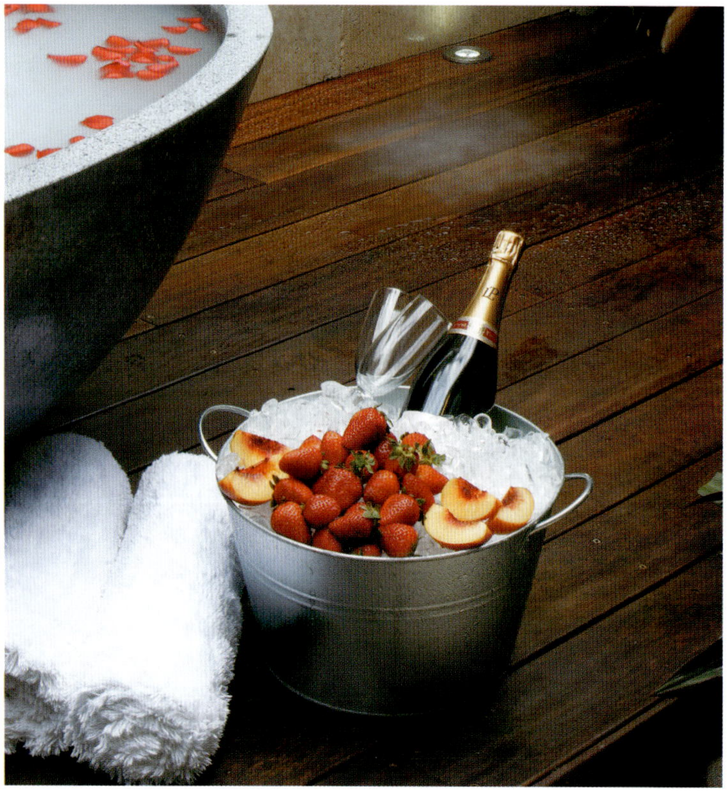

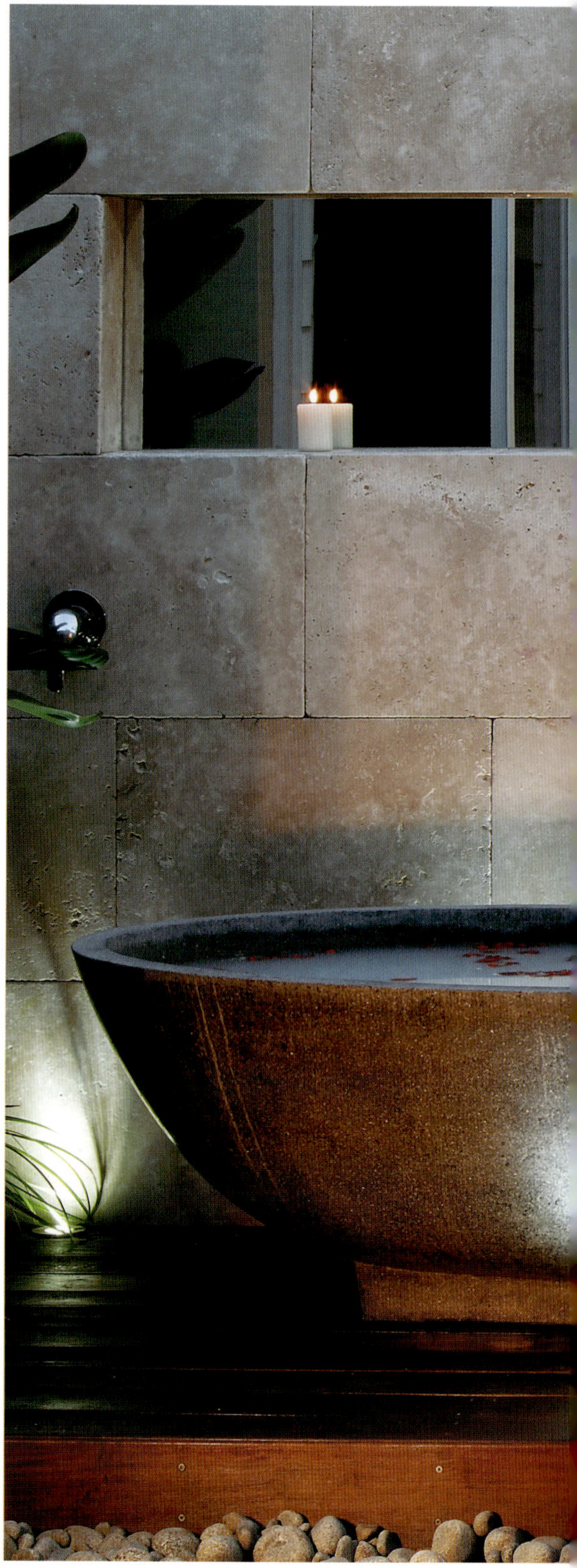

INTIMATE HIDEAWAY 109

I have always been drawn to modern architecture but I am even more so when it is situated on a broad acreage, where there is space for the strong architectural lines of the home to be admired from a distance without interruption from neighbouring properties. It also brings opportunities to reflect the clean and contemporary lines in the landscape, which was part of my clients' brief for this project.

Working closely with the house design team, we were able to ensure that features of the external landscape interact with the architecture of the house. Being involved at such an early stage of the design process allowed me to suggest design ideas connecting the home to the landscape, which

Modern Life

DURAL   is often the fundamental difference between a project that is simply good, and one that is great.

With two-storey glass windows at the rear of the home, I saw the potential to position the pool right against the building, which would provide a constant view from the home while achieving great connection with the outside. Due to the scale of the dwelling, it was important to incorporate a relatively large pool. This was done using clean contemporary lines and incorporating three zones: a large, shallow area; a 15-metre swim lane; and a glass spa, which also acts as a sculpture when not in use.

In the shallow area, three stainless steel bowls overflow with water, providing a visual feature and movement in the pool. Also in the pool and opposite the bowls stand two umbrellas, matching the three umbrellas outside, providing shade and complementing the colour palette of the house.

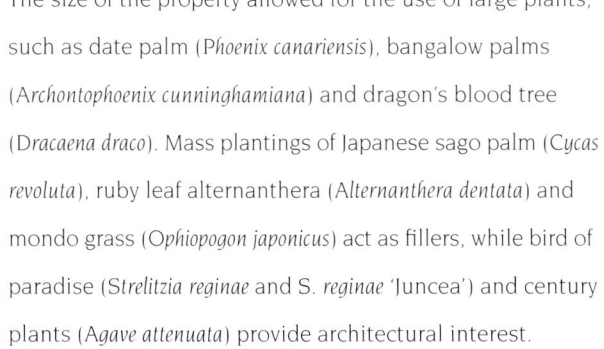

Large 600mm-by-1200mm porcelain tiles surround the pool, continuing into the alfresco area where the outdoor kitchen, dining and lounge areas are situated.

The size of the property allowed for the use of large plants, such as date palm (*Phoenix canariensis*), bangalow palms (*Archontophoenix cunninghamiana*) and dragon's blood tree (*Dracaena draco*). Mass plantings of Japanese sago palm (*Cycas revoluta*), ruby leaf alternanthera (*Alternanthera dentata*) and mondo grass (*Ophiopogon japonicus*) act as fillers, while bird of paradise (*Strelitzia reginae* and *S. reginae* 'Juncea') and century plants (*Agave attenuata*) provide architectural interest.

At the front of the property a large dam with a hardwood jetty was created and lined with basalt boulders and plantings, all assisting in the creation of an eco-environment. With a capacity of approximately 1.5 million litres, the dam is the lifeline of the garden, enabling the collection and reuse of water through the irrigation system.

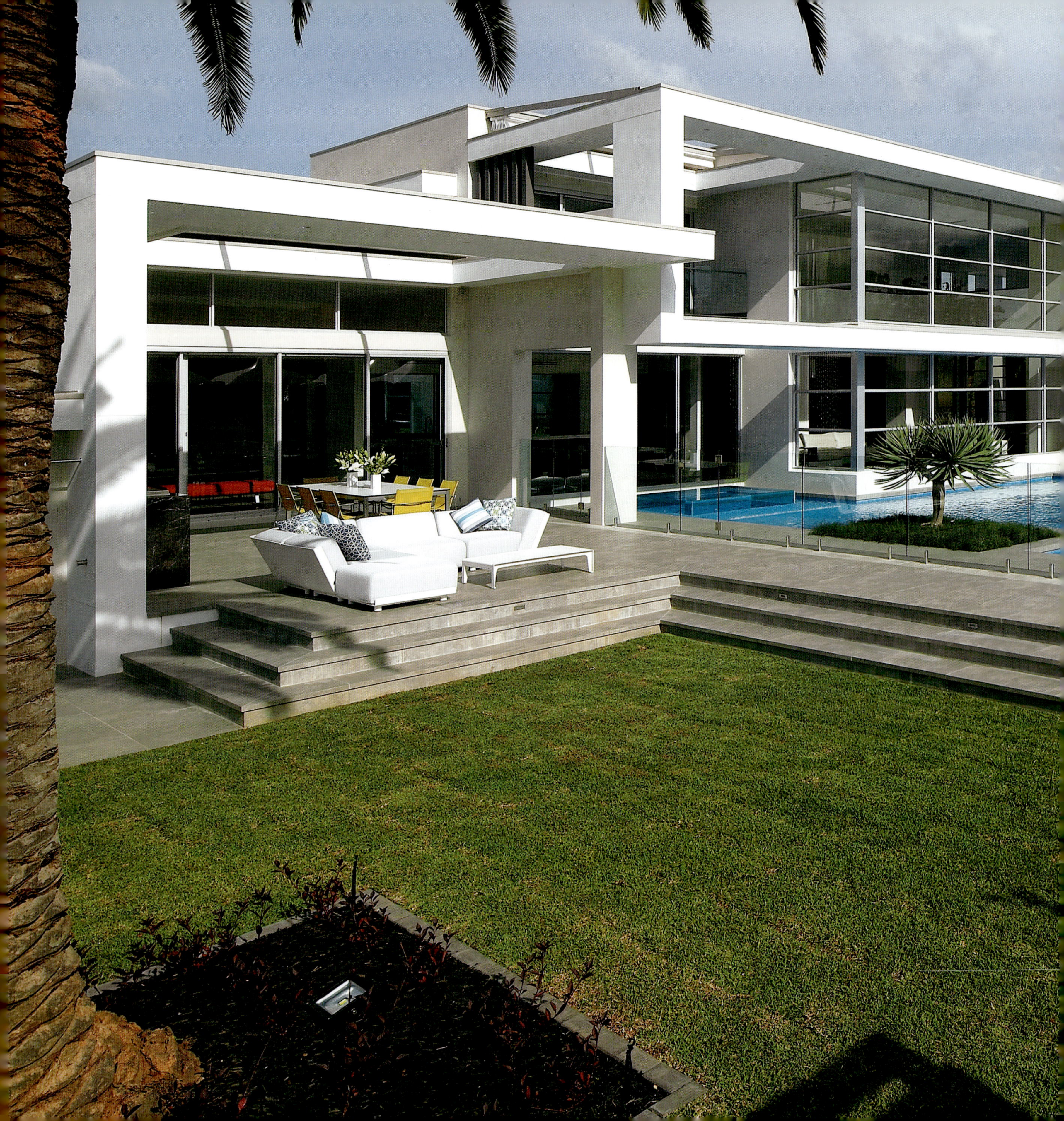

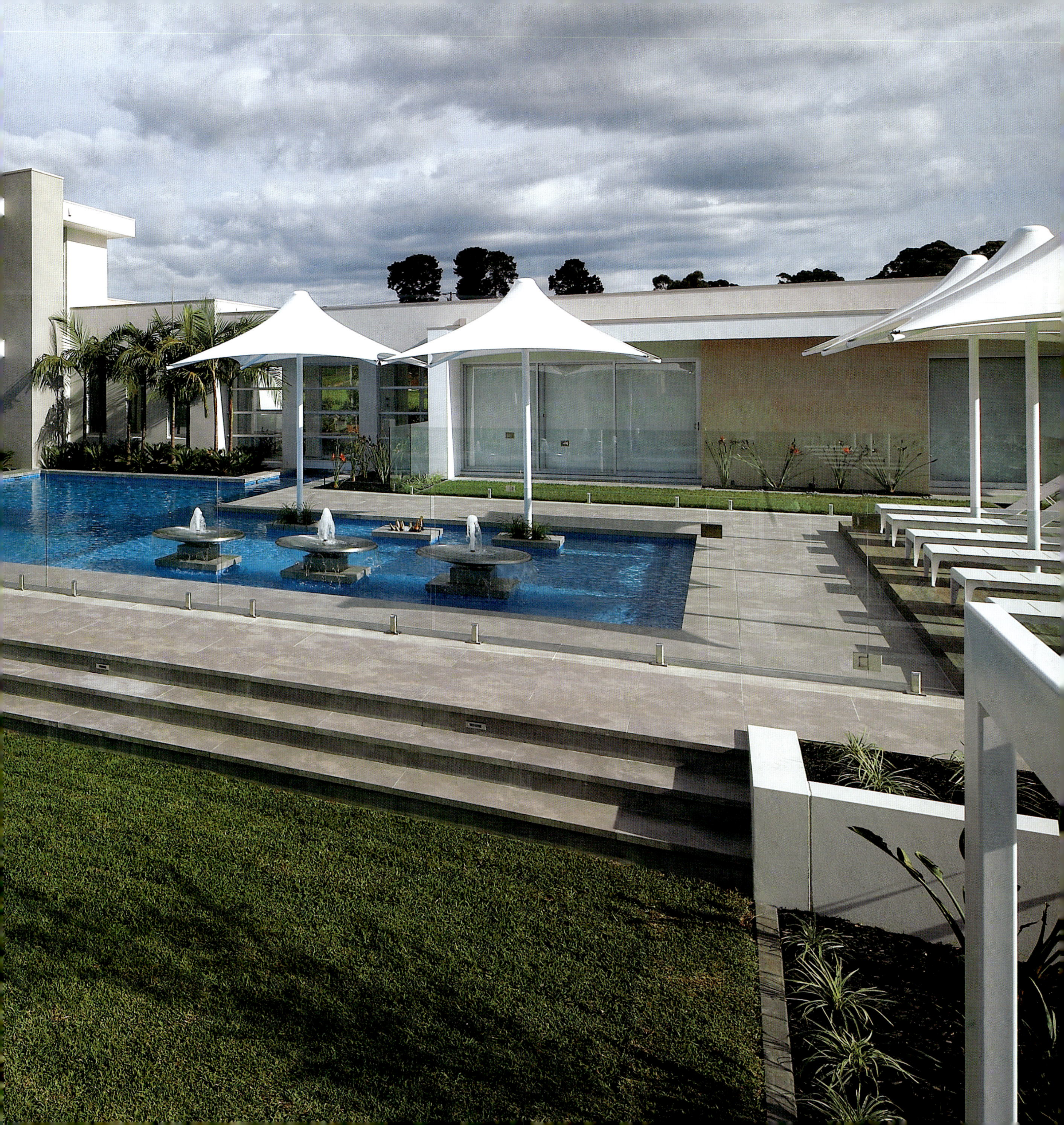

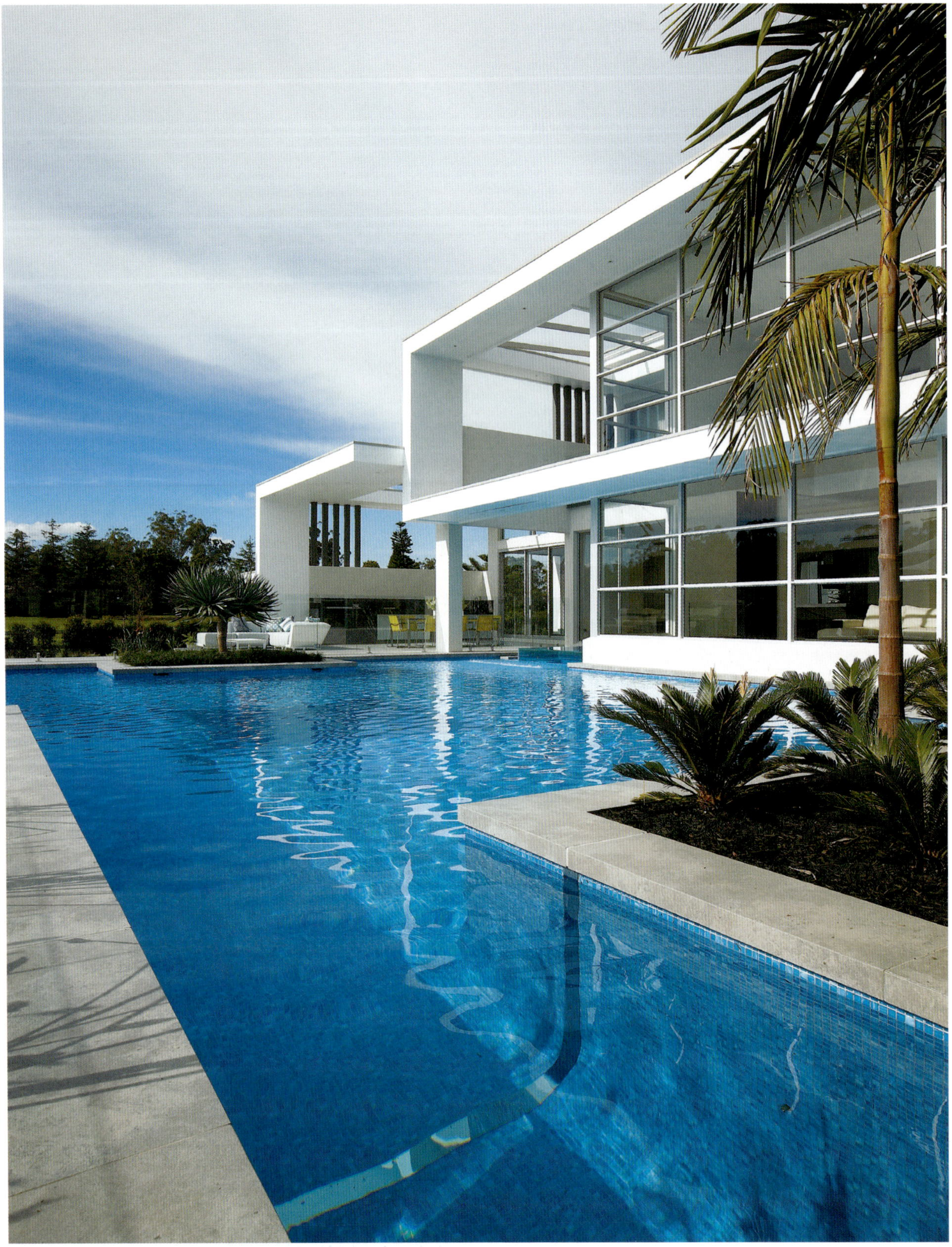

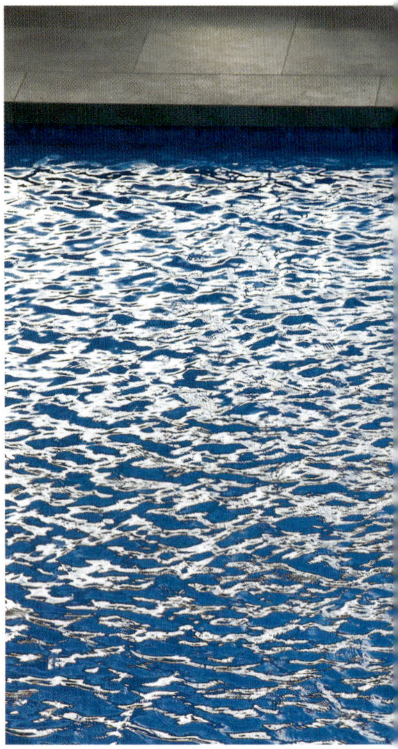

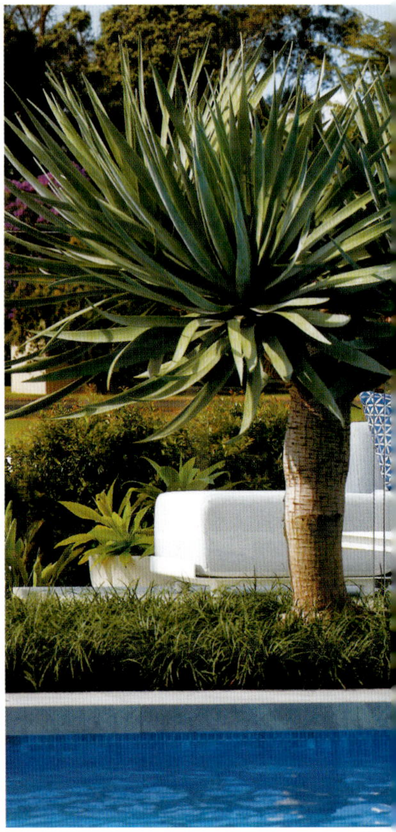

MODERN LIFE 115

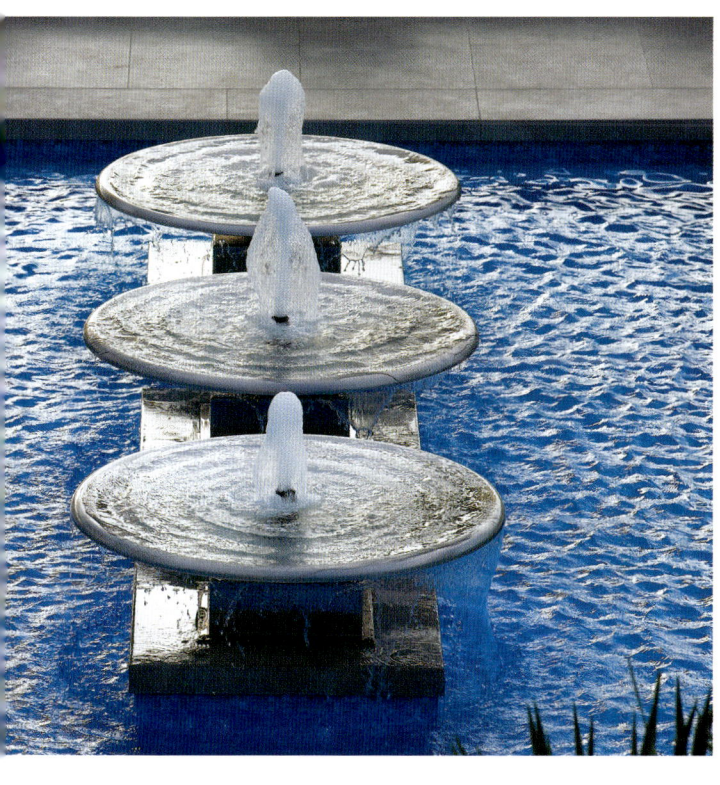

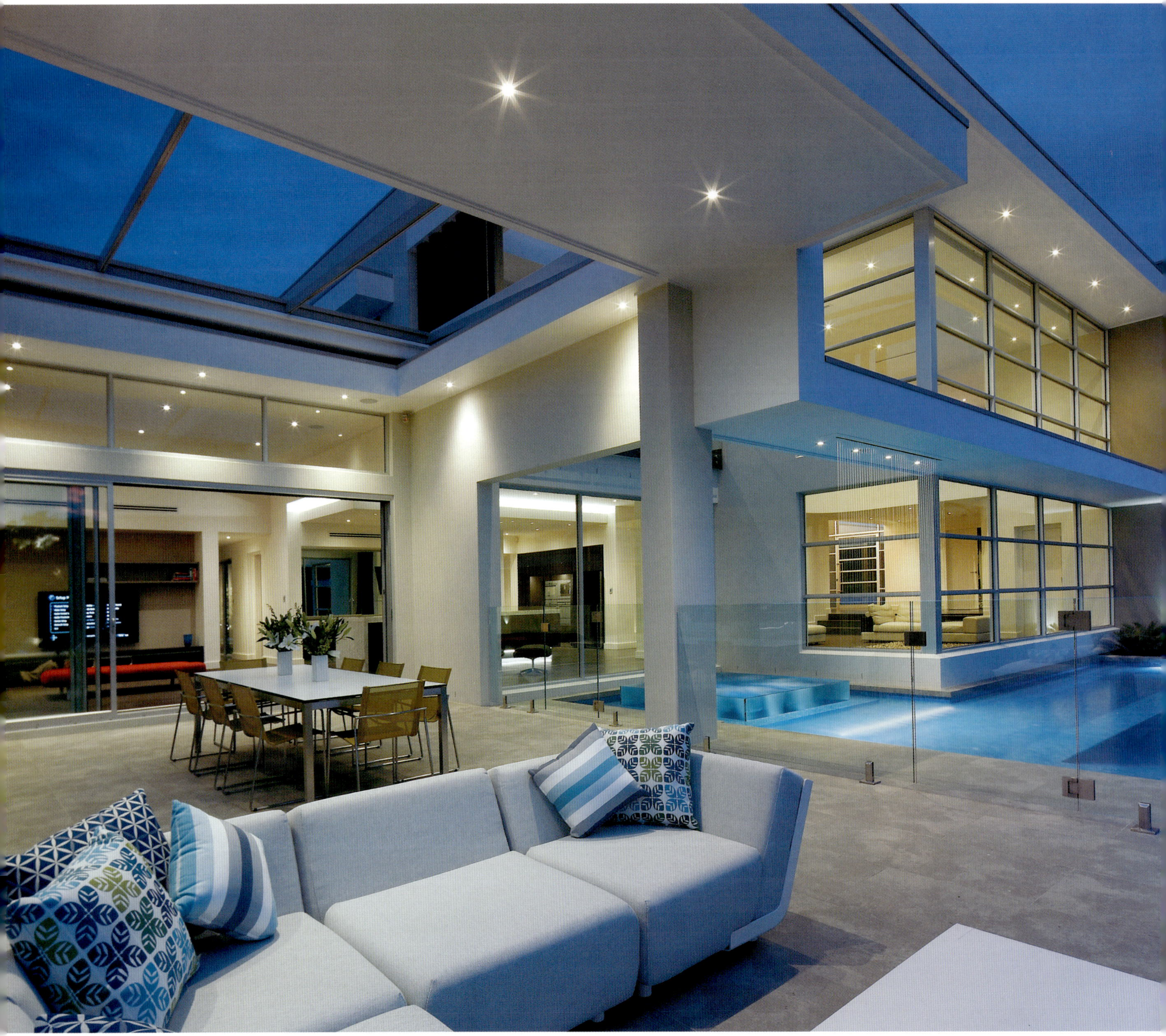

MODERN LIFE 117

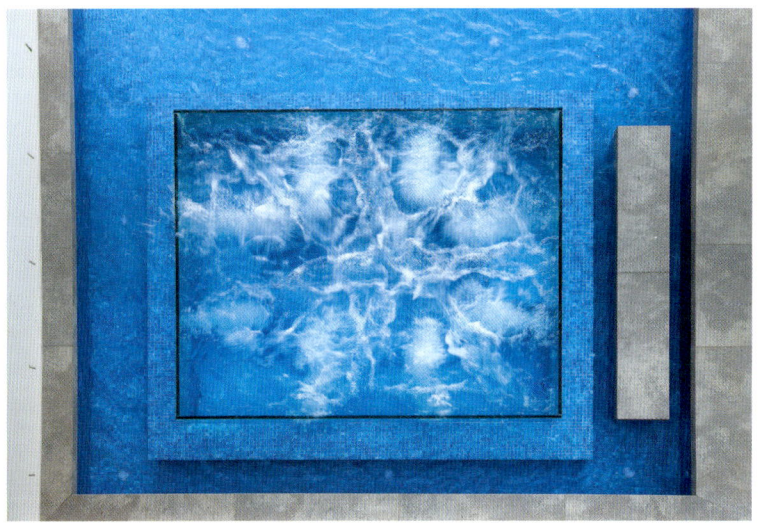

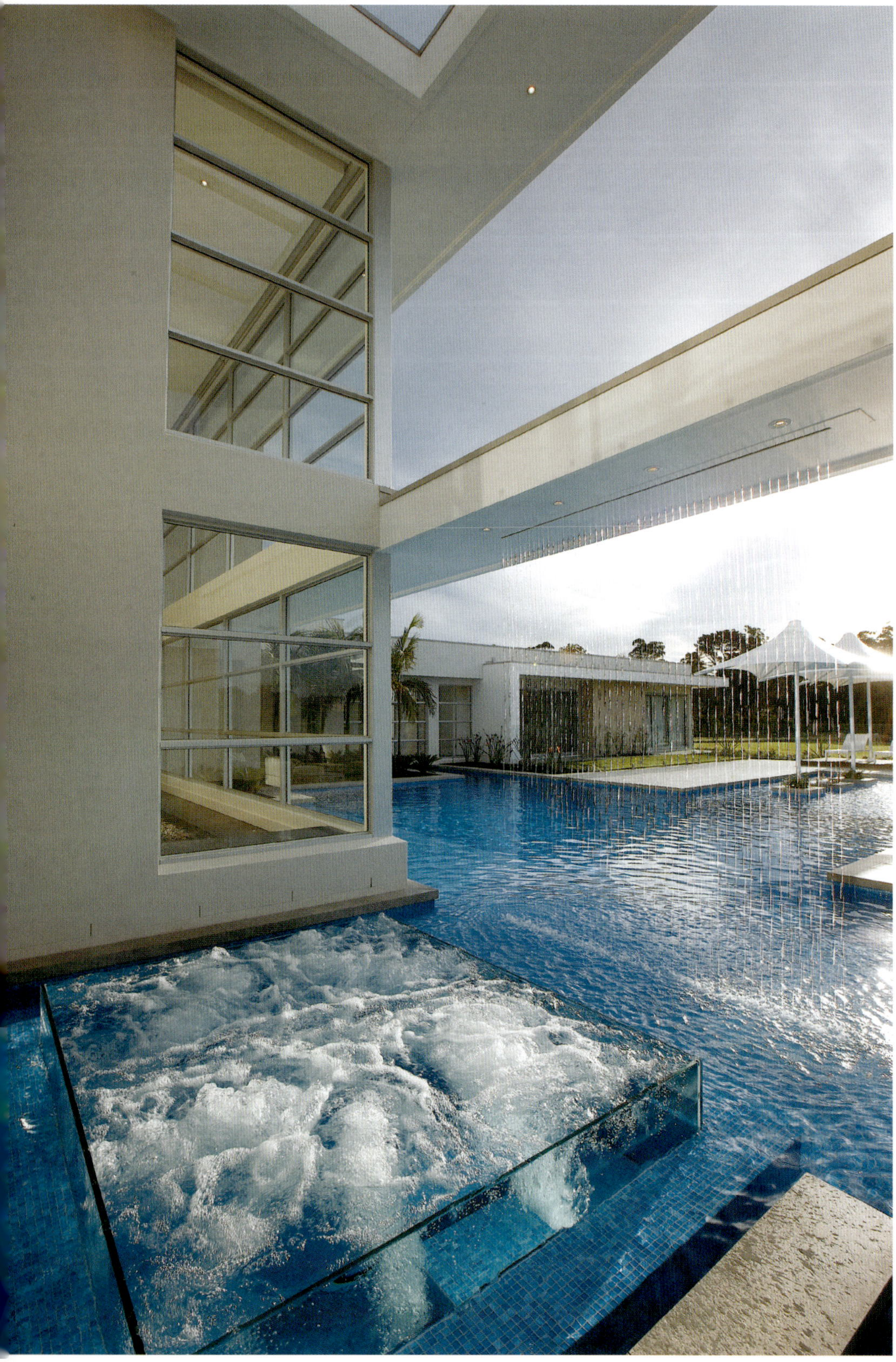

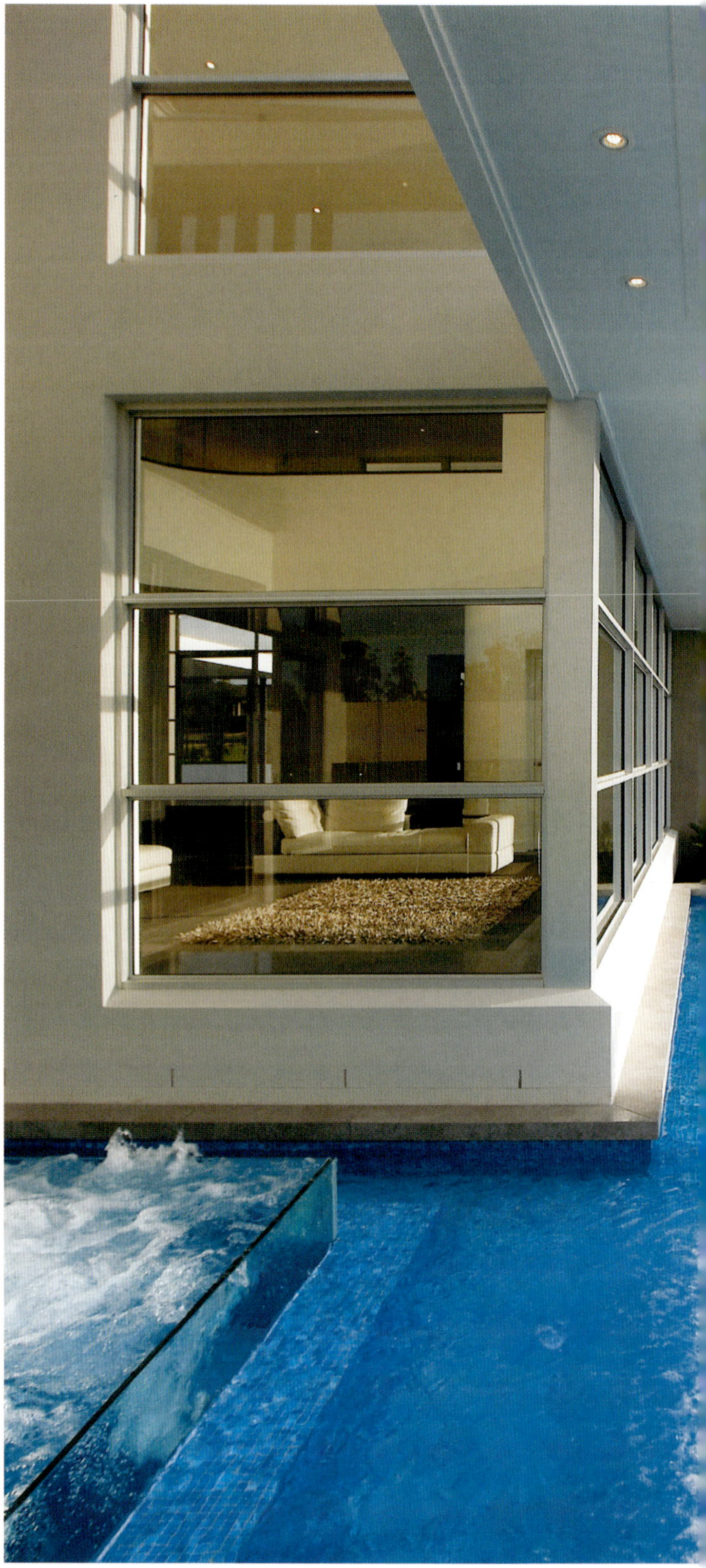

MODERN LIFE 119

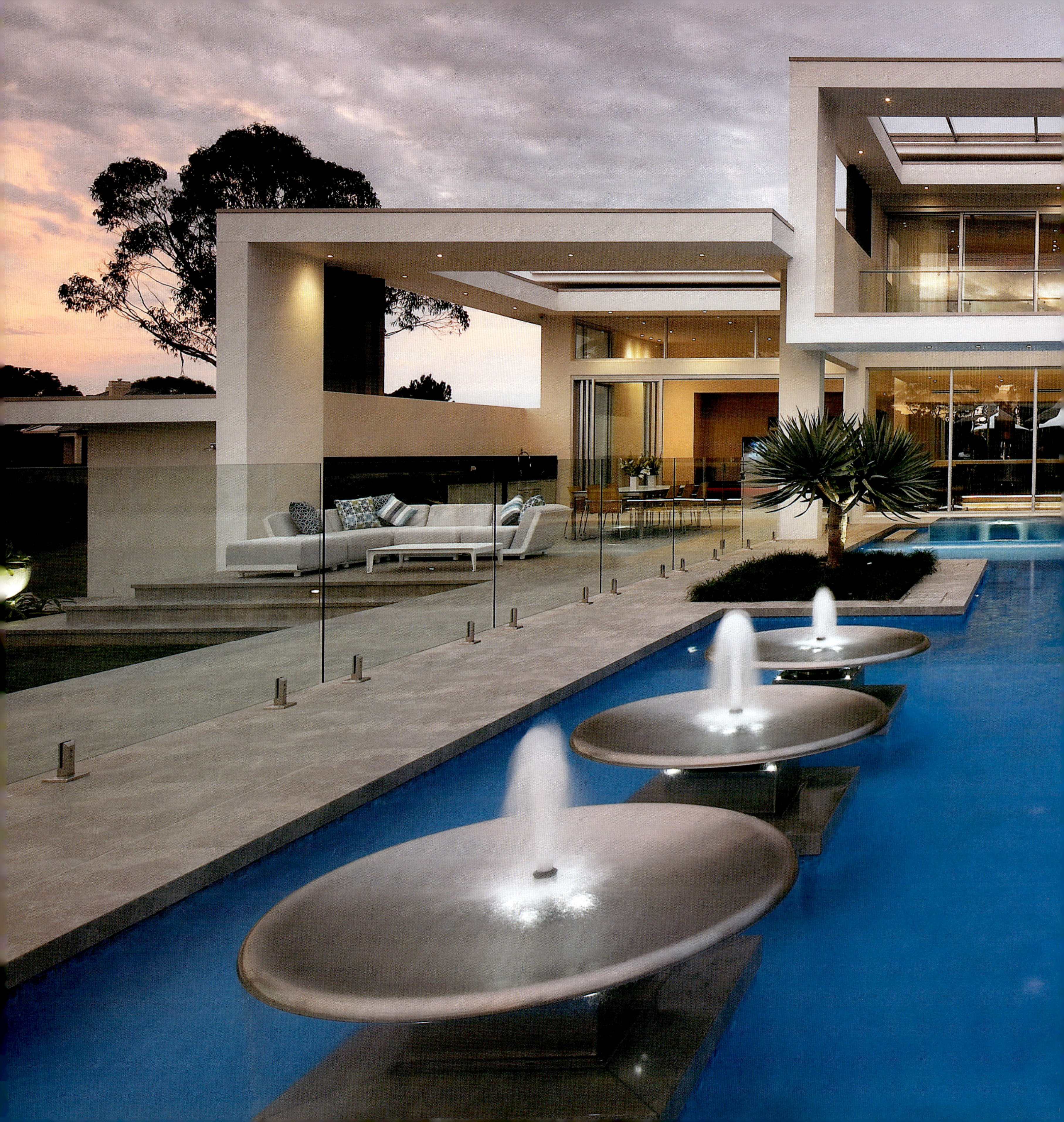

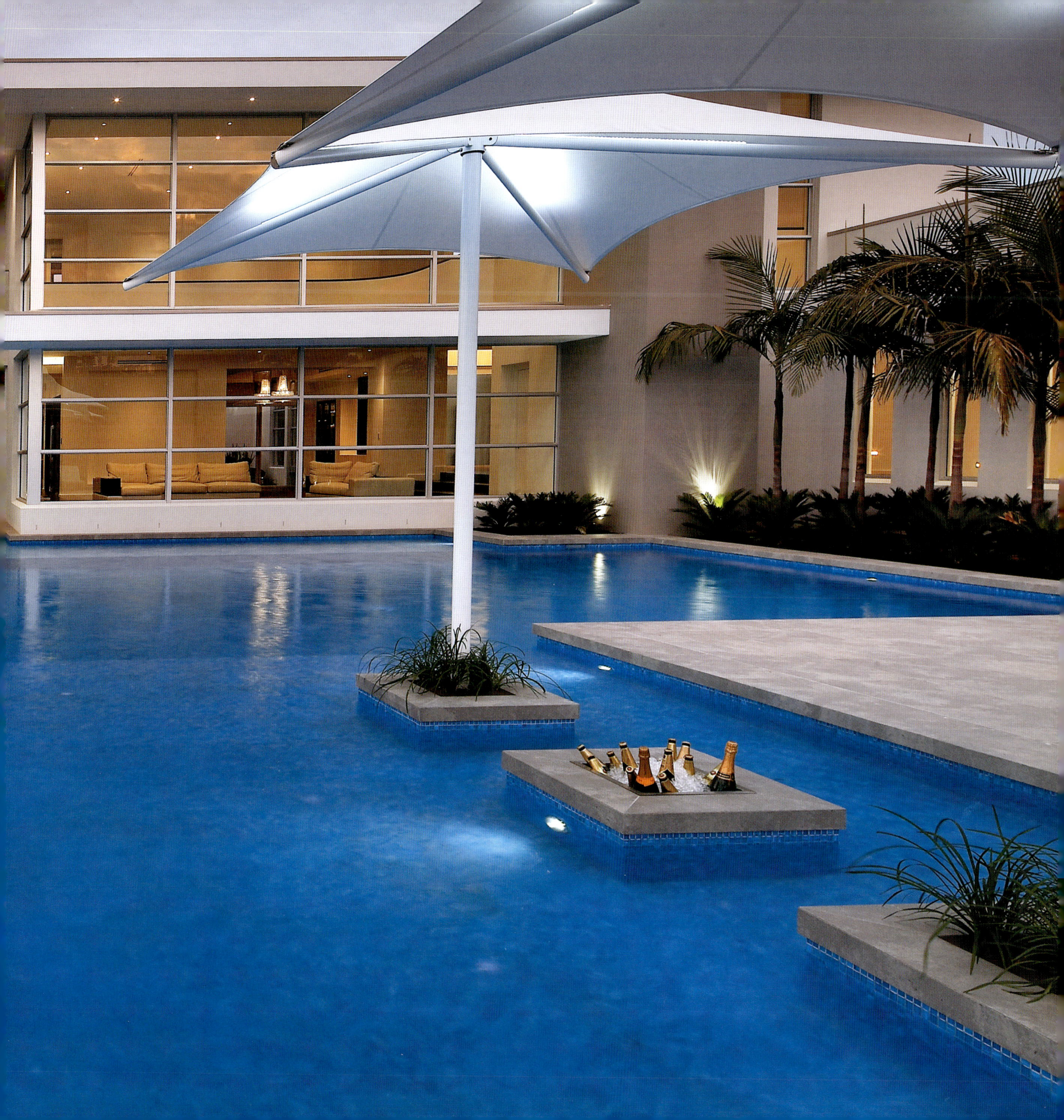

One of the most enjoyable aspects of landscape design is drawing on a theme or influence from one country and introducing it into a design to transform the look and atmosphere of a garden in another country.

For this client – a professional photographer with a downstairs studio – the vista of the garden from his studio and the entertaining deck above were of paramount importance. The client's desire to create a modern Asian ambiance in his garden was achieved by incorporating Zen-inspired architecture, materials and plants. When designing themed gardens I do tend to be inspired rather than replicate as rarely is there corresponding existing architecture or exact climate conditions for traditional plantings to work with.

Eastern Influence

CHATSWOOD

The area available for this project was at the rear of the property and called for a simplistic approach so that the theme could be felt without losing usability of the space. With this in mind, a black stone blade wall was installed with a circular steel vista window revealing a Japanese maple (*Acer palmatum*) and other soothing plant material behind it. The base of the wall is surrounded by a small pond with a basalt boulder placed within it – water falls onto the boulder from an outlet above. A hardwood deck was installed at the side of this water feature to provide a place to sit and experience the tranquil ambiance.

A lush green lawn works its way around the various structures, while maintaining straight lines to keep the space as generous as possible. Where small retaining walls were required, they were finished in a rendered texture and painted to complement the colour of the house. This colour also contrasts well with the installed stone paving. The paving consists of rectangular basalt tiles, which lend a dark tone to the layout. Hardwood timber inserts are also used – the same material used in the deck.

The planting of a themed garden is important in communicating a message. The slender weavers bamboo (Bambusa textilis 'Gracilis') used at the side boundary is perfect for the role of screen planting and best suits the theme. Also used were Japanese maple (Acer palmatum), little gem magnolia (Magnolia grandiflora 'Little Gem'), camellia (Camellia sasanqua), Japanese sago palm (Cycas revoluta), Japanese box (Buxus microphylla 'Japonica'), creeping juniper (Juniperus horizontalis), blue fescue grass (Festuca glauca) and mondo grass (Ophiopogon japonicus).

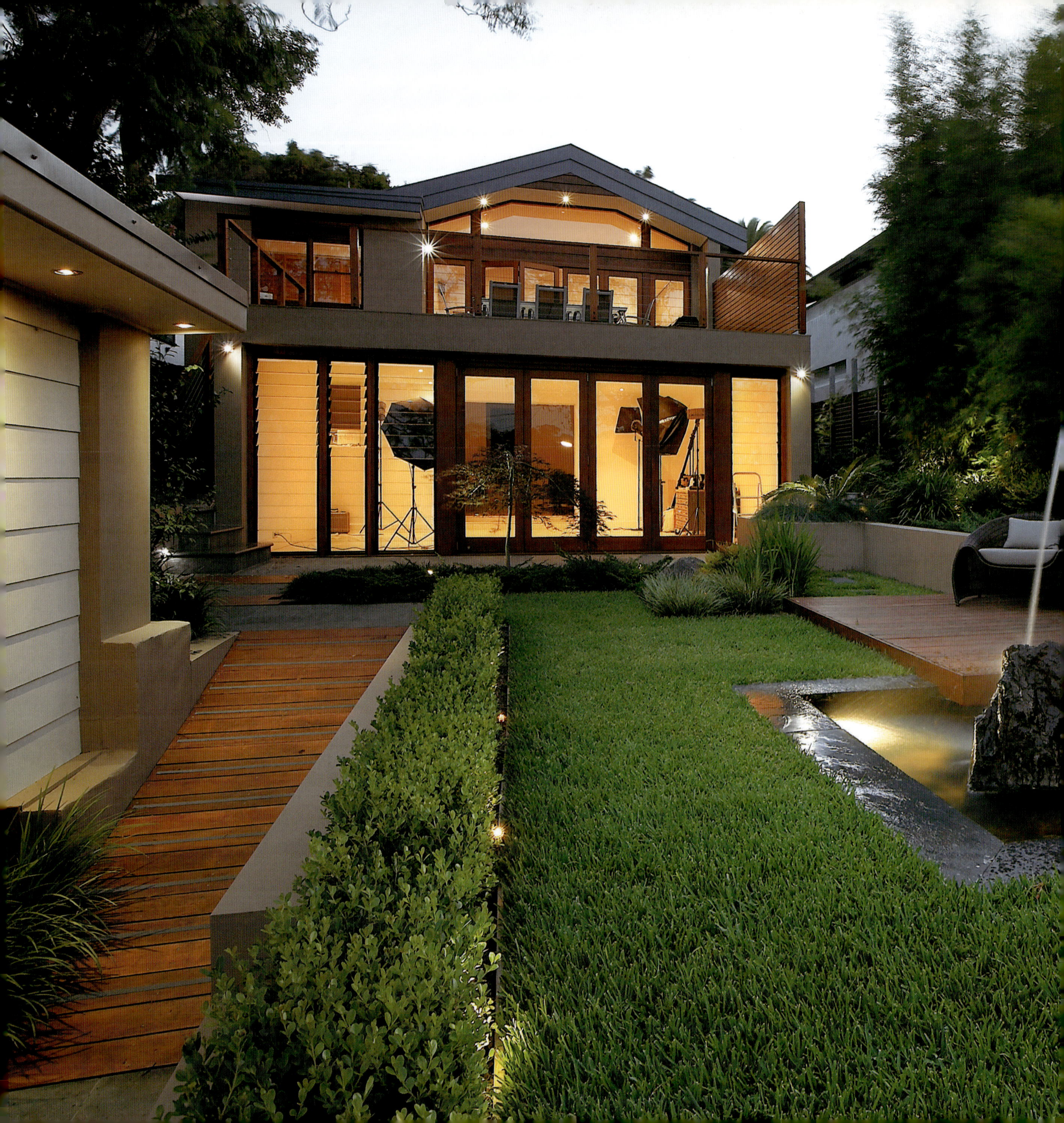

EASTERN INFLUENCE 125

126

EASTERN INFLUENCE 127

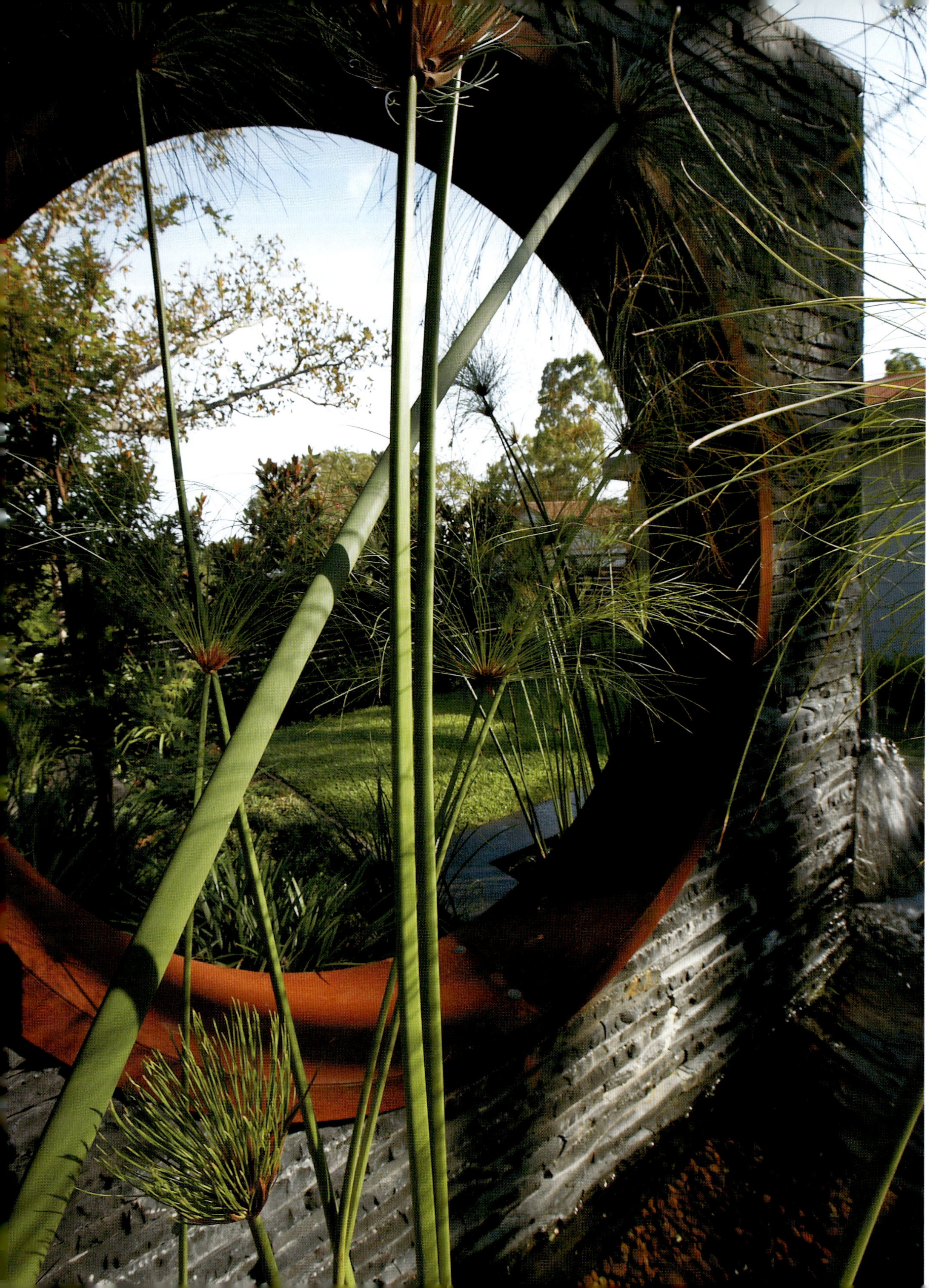

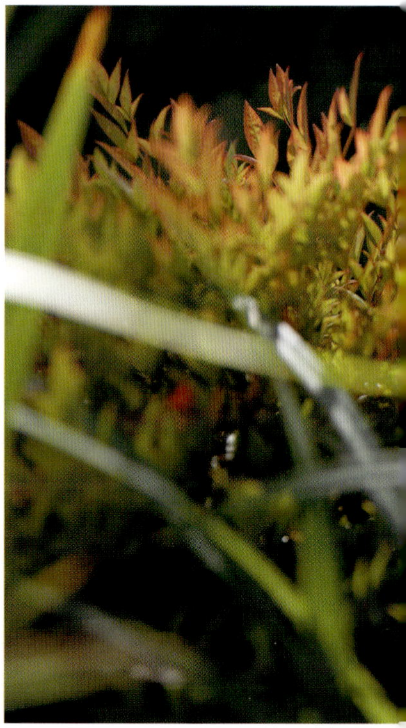

EASTERN INFLUENCE 129

I met the clients for this project shortly after they purchased a 5-acre property consisting mainly of natural bushland. They expressed a dream of having their own piece of paradise on this land. As the design team worked closely together on the home and its exterior, we also had to work with the local authorities due to some sensitive environmental factors on the site. As always, what at first seemed like an obstacle was transformed into an advantage and the house was given its location, satisfying the needs of the client along with those of the authorities.

The pool was designed to interact with the lines of the house, being positioned right against the living space. It stretches out as the land falls to the rear; a curved infinity edge

Infinity Blue

KENTHURST

enabling views out to the natural landscape. The water at the edge of the house is shallow enough to obviate the need for safety fencing, providing a great location for a sitting area. This central area is accessible from the master bedroom and study, and takes the form of a deck with a relaxing atmosphere enhanced by a stone-clad water-feature wall on the side of the house. Adding to the tranquil feel of the space, planted bangalow palms (*Archontophoenix cunninghamiana*), leafless bird of paradise (*Strelitzia reginae* 'Juncea') and variegated mondo (*Ophiopogon intermedians* 'Stripey White') fill the area. Furnished with two chairs, it sits ready for use at any time.

For entertaining purposes, the roofline of the home extends to cover the alfresco dining and outdoor kitchen areas that flow through to the pool. The same floor surface was used for all these areas to enhance the relationship between them. Elevated above the natural ground level, they offer the

SELECTED FEATURE PALM

OUTDOOR KITCHEN WITH SINK, DISHWASHER, FRIDGE & BBQ

OUTDOOR DINING AREA

OUTDOOR LOUNGE AREA

STEPPING STONES THROUGH POND

SELECTED FEATURE PALM

PROPOSED RESIDENCE

STONE-CLAD FEATURE WALL WITH WATER SPOUTS

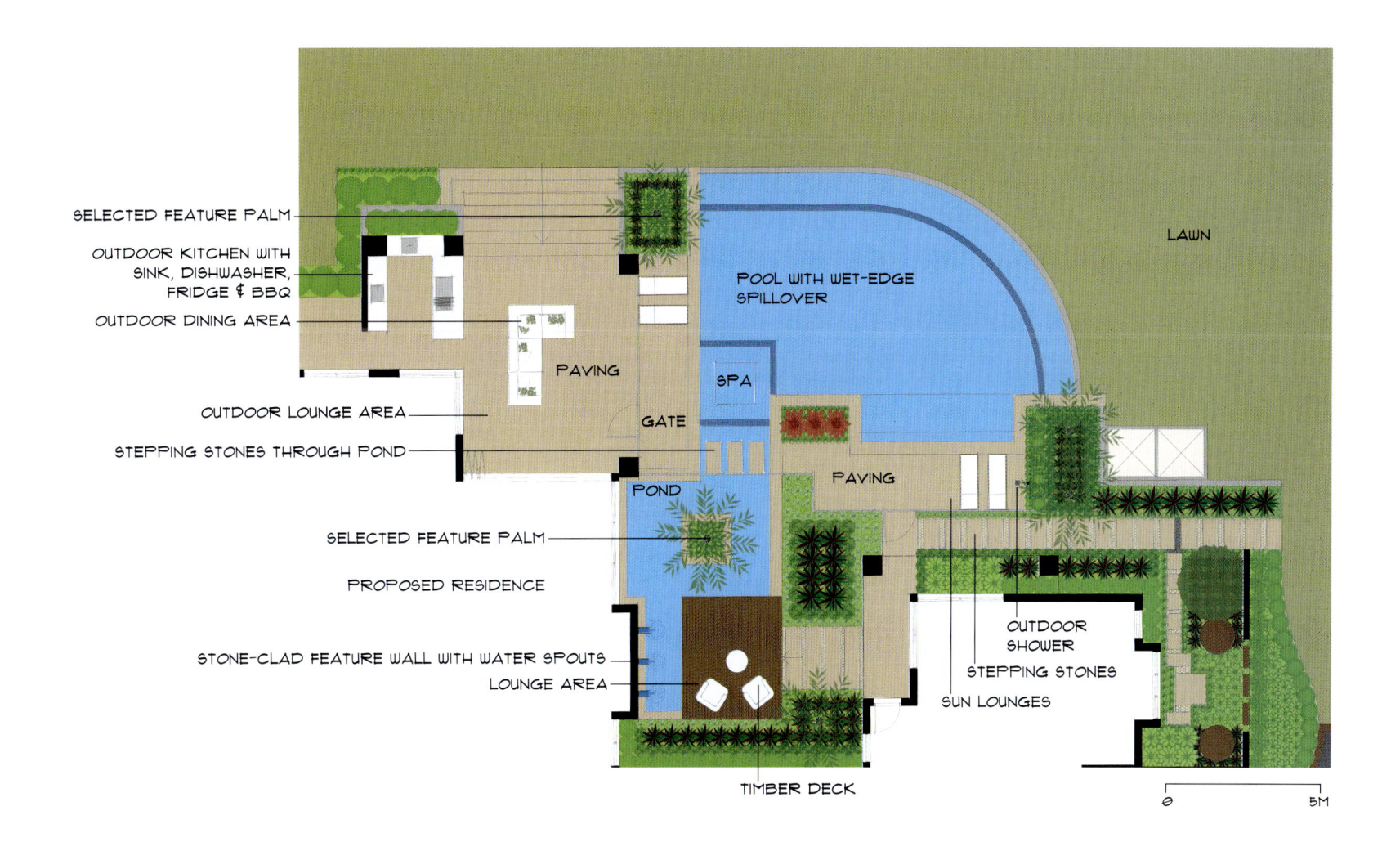

LOUNGE AREA

TIMBER DECK

LAWN

POOL WITH WET-EDGE SPILLOVER

PAVING

SPA

GATE

POND

PAVING

OUTDOOR SHOWER

STEPPING STONES

SUN LOUNGES

0 5M

best position from which to take in views of the mountains to the west that connect with the tree line of the existing eucalypts.

In addition to the aforementioned planting, century plant (*Agave attenuata*), Florida gardenia (*Gardenia augusta* 'Florida'), turf lily (*Liriope muscari*) and dwarf lilly pilly (*Acmena smithii* 'Allyn Magic') were included in the design to provide low-maintenance gardening that suits the clients' busy lifestyle.

131

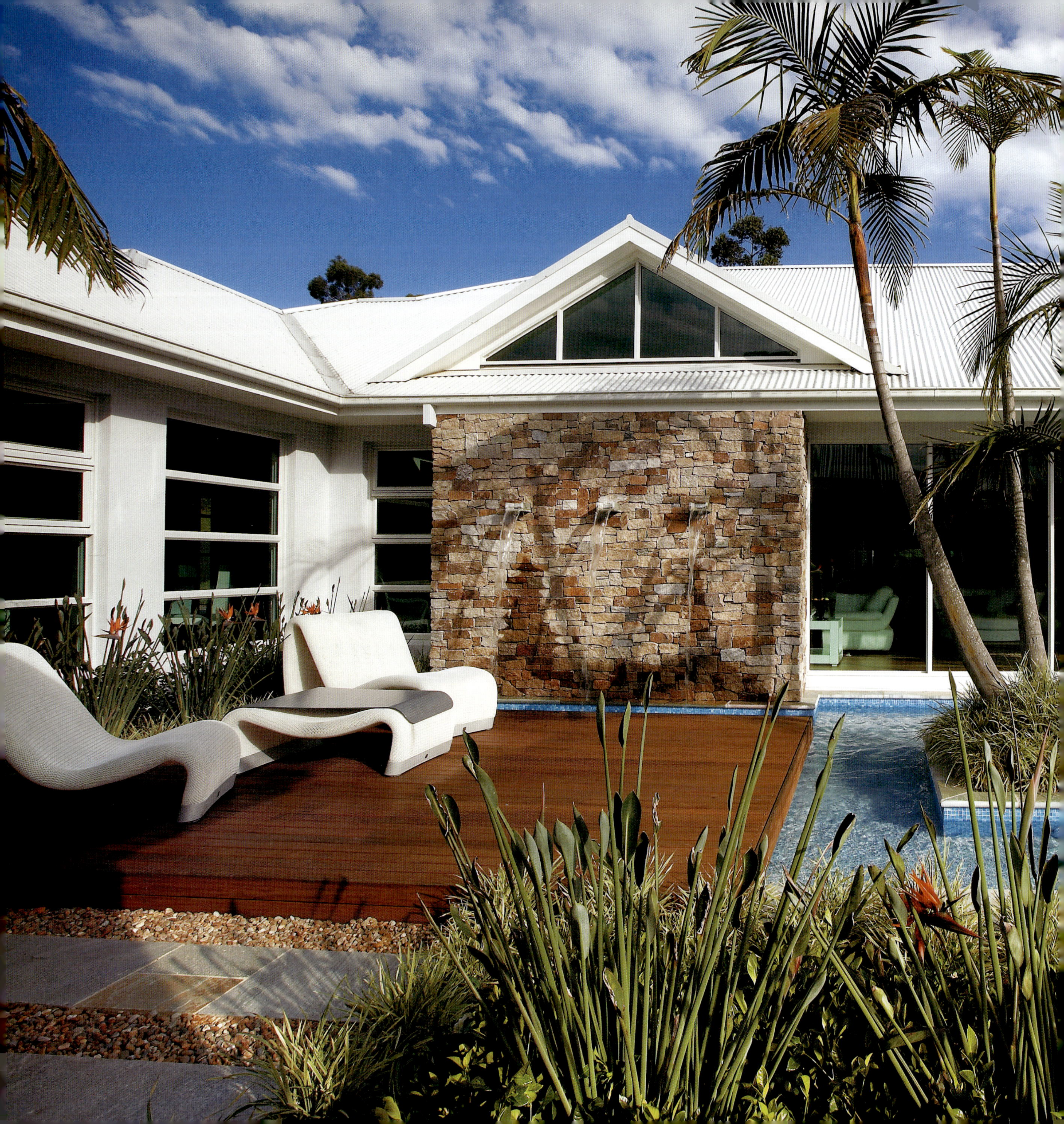

INFINITY BLUE 133

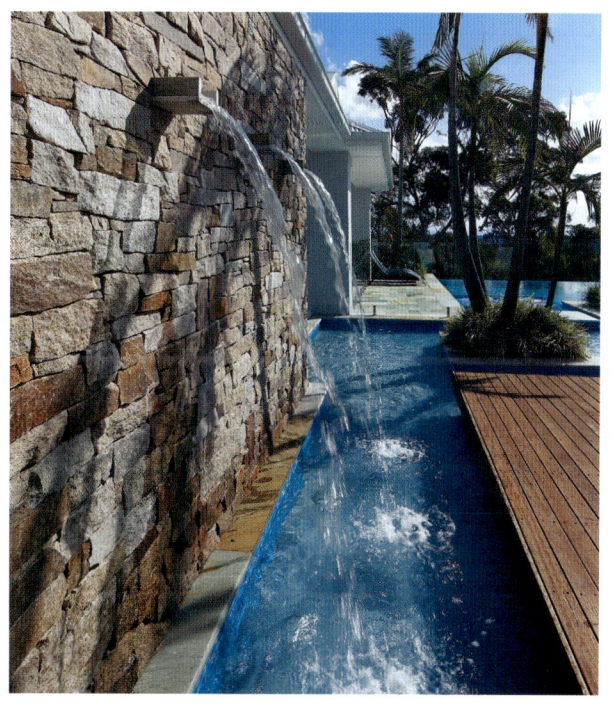

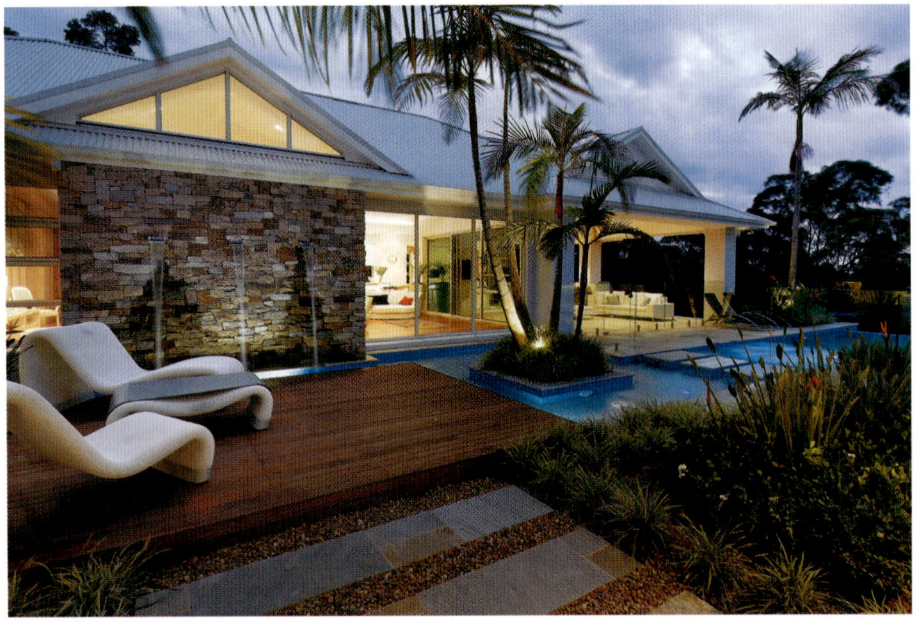

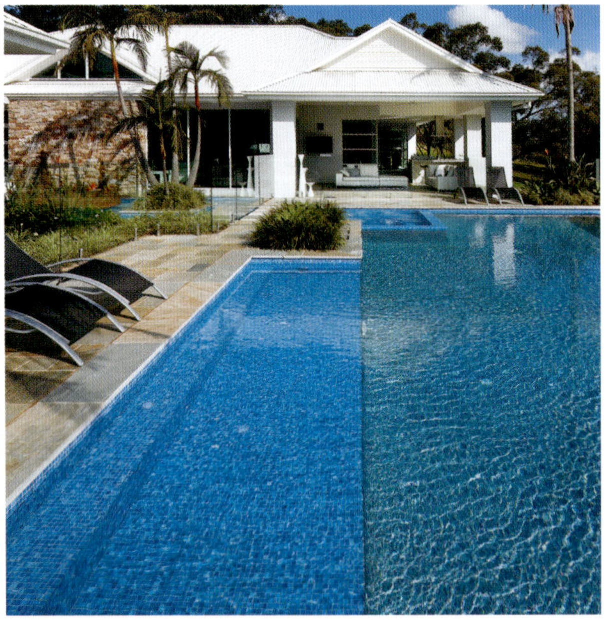

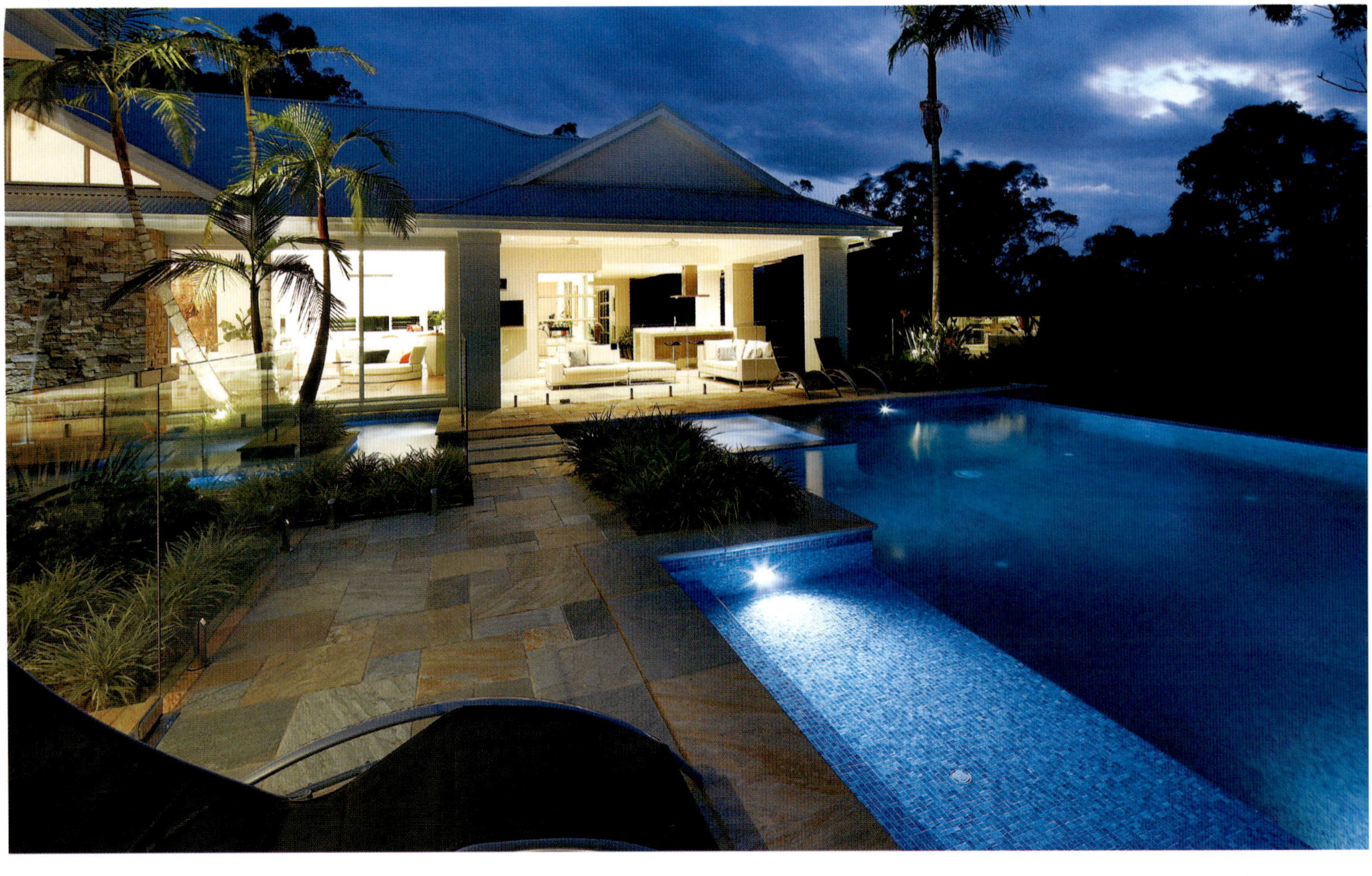

INFINITY BLUE 135

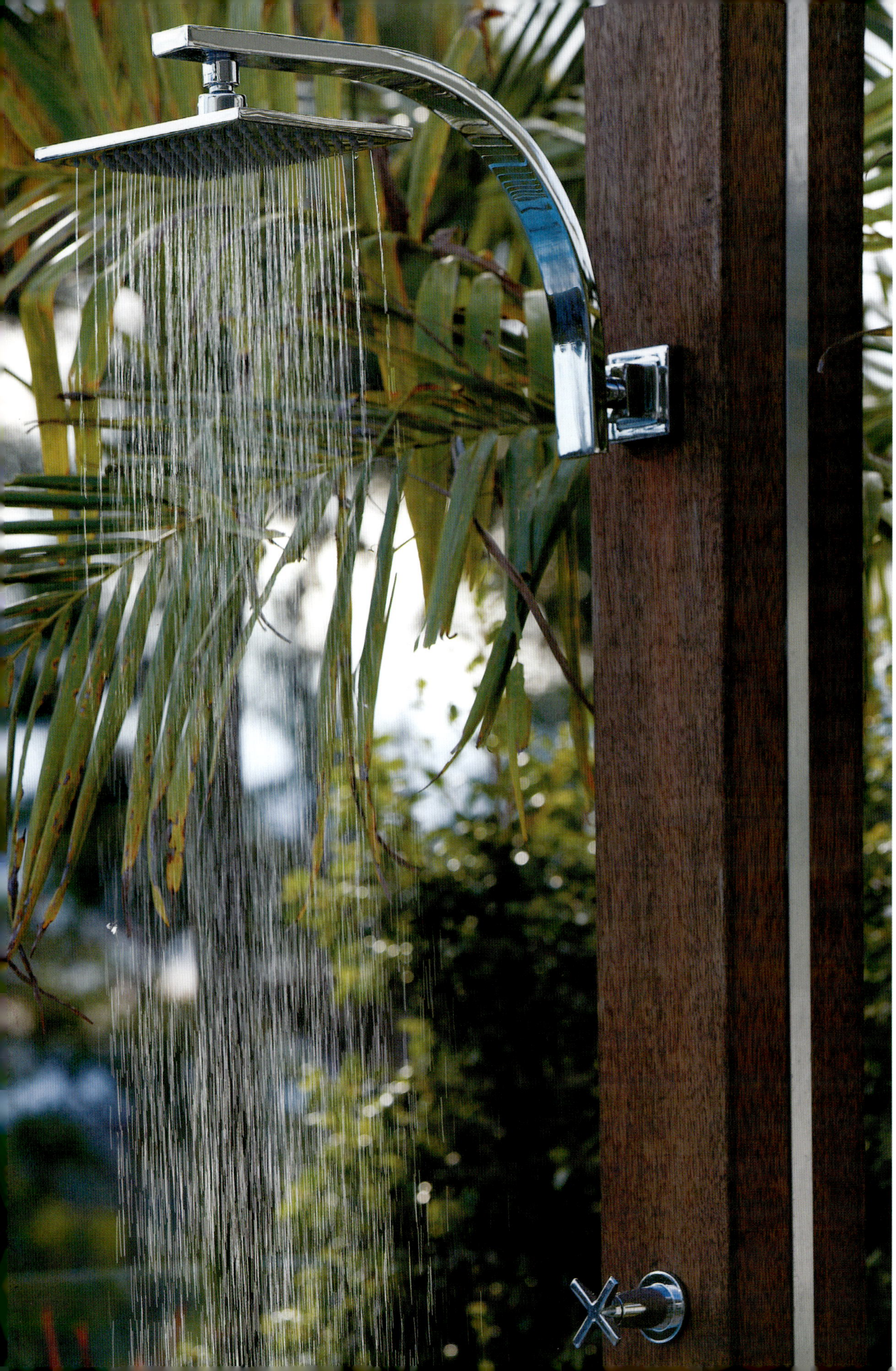

INFINITY BLUE 137

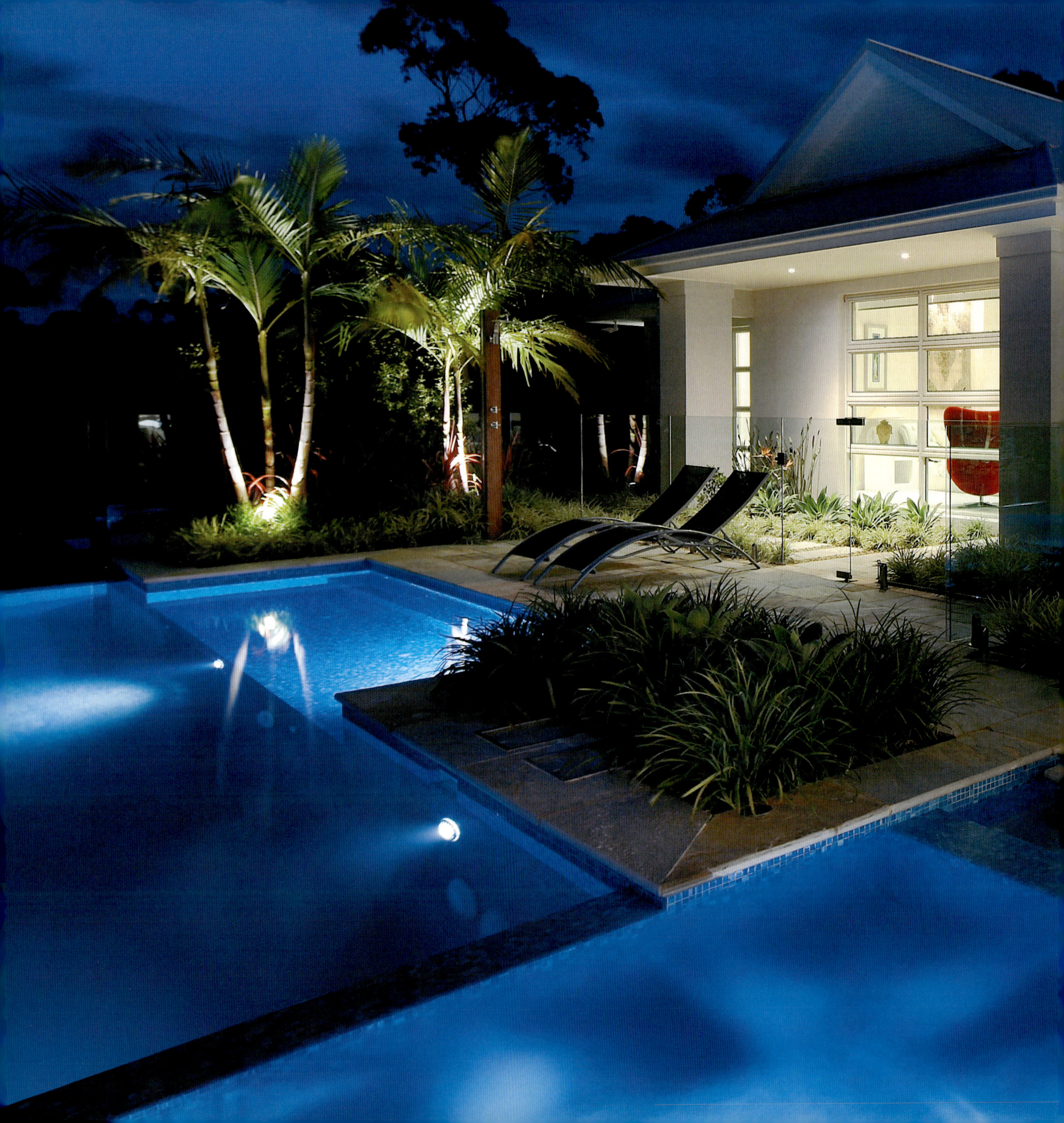

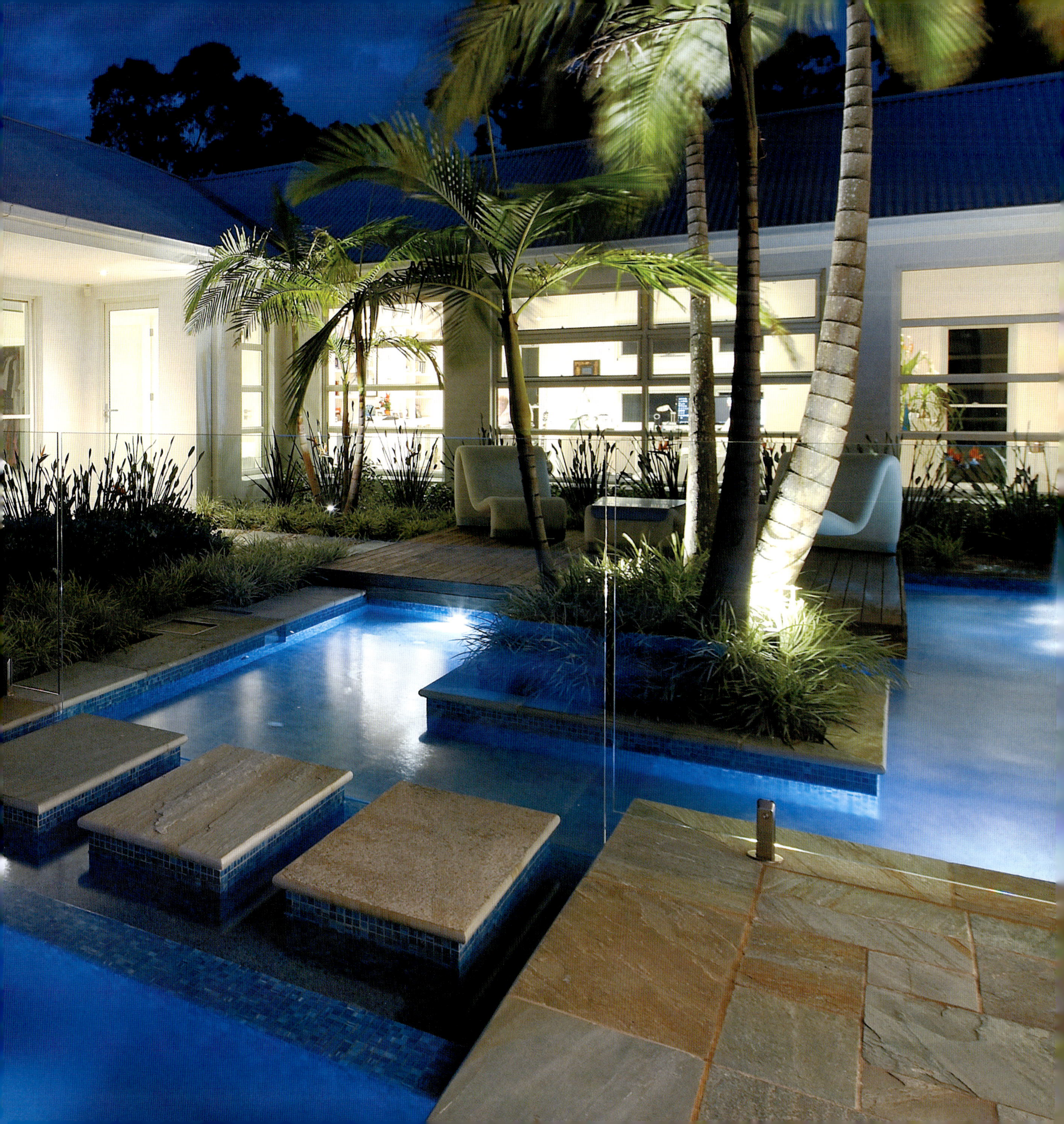

When the architecture of the house and landscape design are developed at the same time, the result is a seamless connection between the built form of the home and its relationship with the outdoor space. This was certainly the case for this project, which brought a unique opportunity to connect the architecture of the home to the internal courtyard.

To embrace the clients' love of cars, a glass showroom was designed to enable a display of prestige cars to become a focal point, visible from other areas within the home. The exotic appearance of these cars provides a unique sculptural element, framed like a piece of art on display.

On Show

DURAL

At the centre of the courtyard is a large pond, influenced by the lines of the home. The water feature continues under the home towards the front entry area, while a glass bridge allows access above it. This glass crossing enables a true connection with the water and the external structures when moving within the home.

To the side of the water feature, three fin walls were constructed to give elevation to the design while providing a position to mount the custom-designed stainless steel waterfall outlets, bringing life and movement to the pond. A large basalt boulder weighing more than 2 tonnes was moved into position over the house by crane, providing a great contrast between the smooth lines of the design and the natural form of the rock. A line of bubblers was installed beside the pond as an additional feature at the entry of the house, assisting in the movement of water.

To surround the pond and enable areas of usability, a large hardwood timber deck overlaps the water and cuts in around the basalt boulder. Large porcelain tiles were installed outside the doorways while matching tiles form stepping-stone paths in the garden and above the water. A darker matching tile was used to fully line the pond, enabling easier maintenance when required.

I thought it important that the planting would allow the clients to experience the changing seasons as the garden was to be used on a daily basis. To achieve this, three semi-advanced Japanese maples (*Acer palmatum*) were installed, providing stunning autumn foliage colour along with necessary height. Lady palm (*Rhapis excelsa*), bird of paradise (*Strelitzia reginae*), renga renga lily (*Arthropodium cirratum*), mother-in-law's tongue (*Sansevieria trifasciata*), turf lily (*Liriope muscari*) and dwarf mondo grass (*Ophiopogon japonicus* 'Nana') were also included.

141

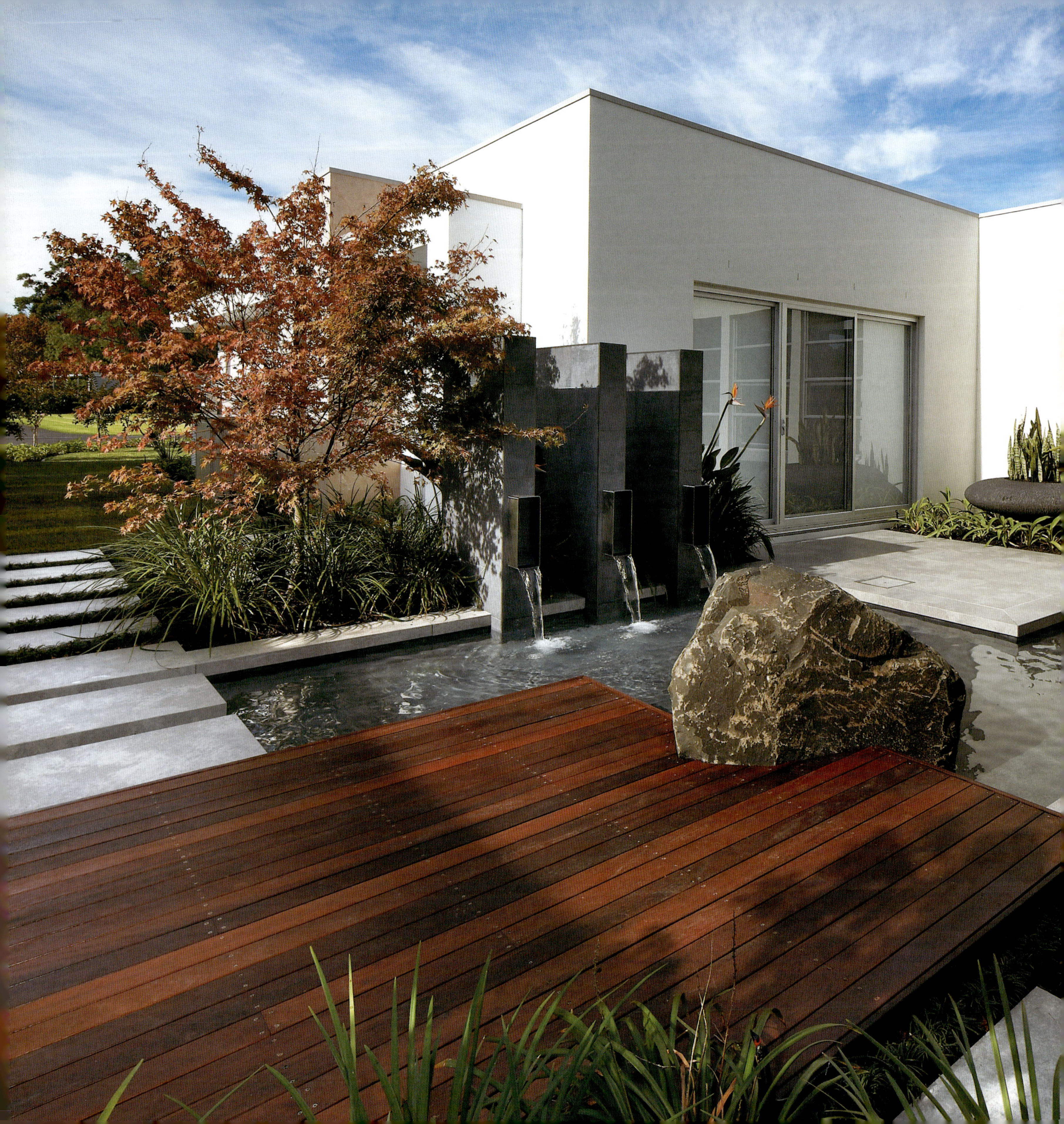

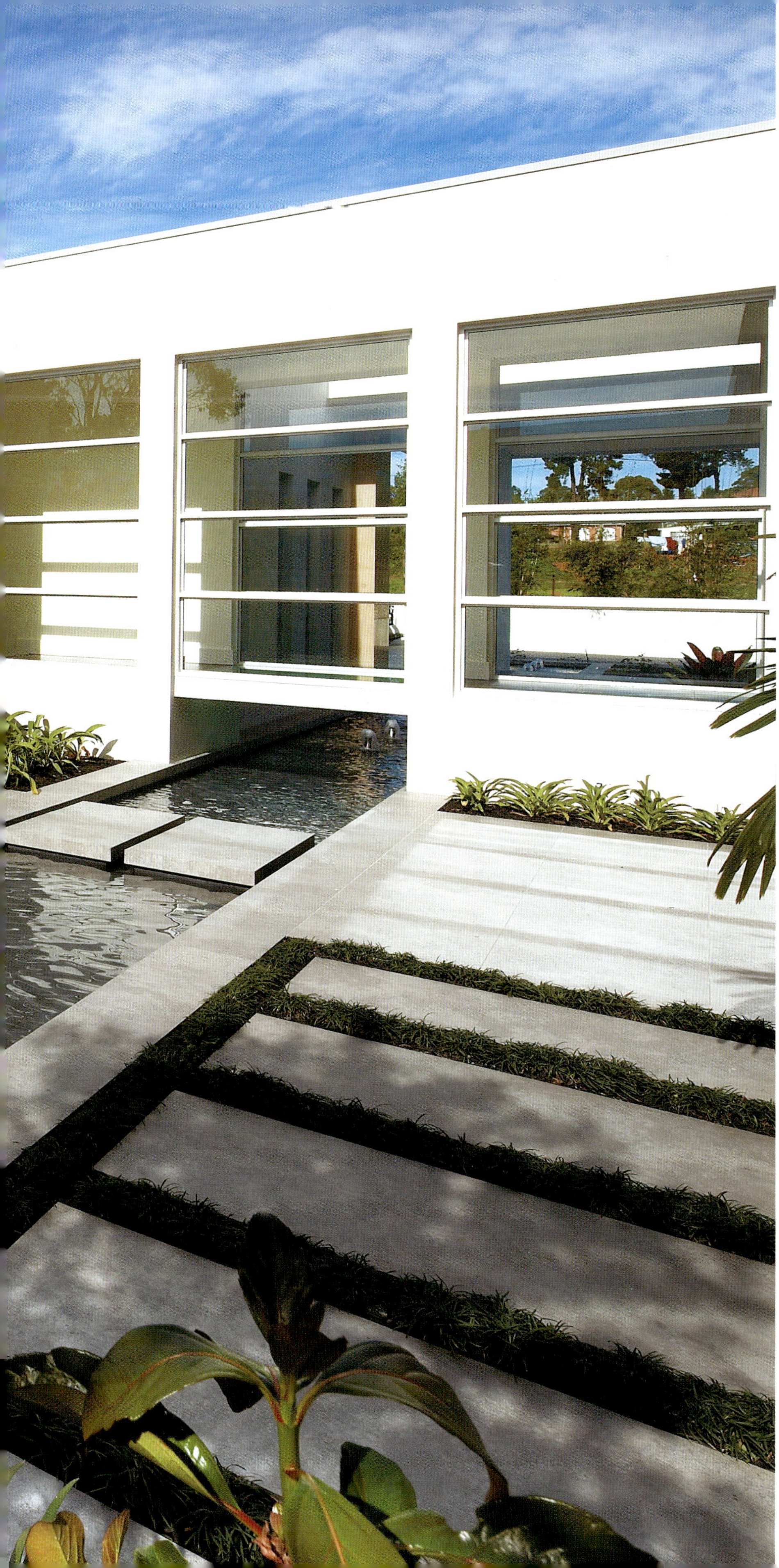
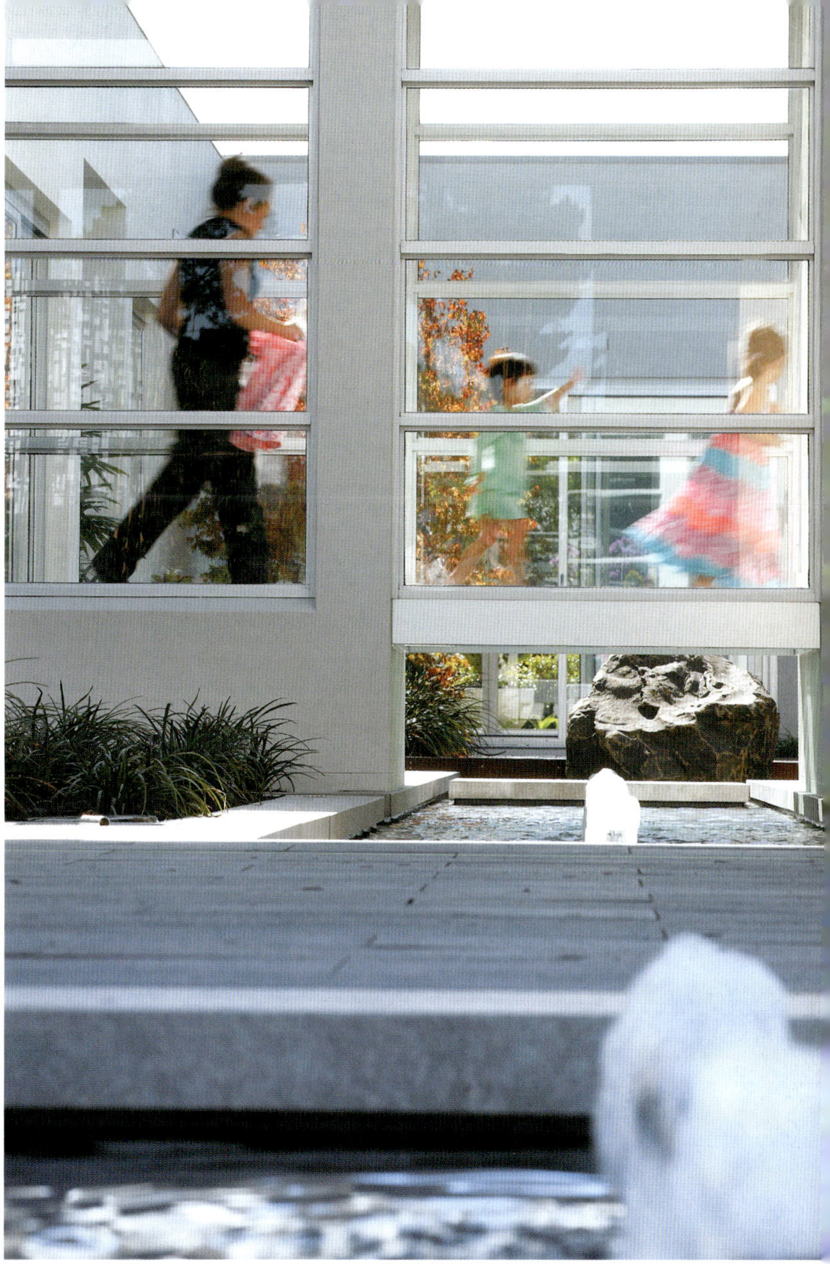
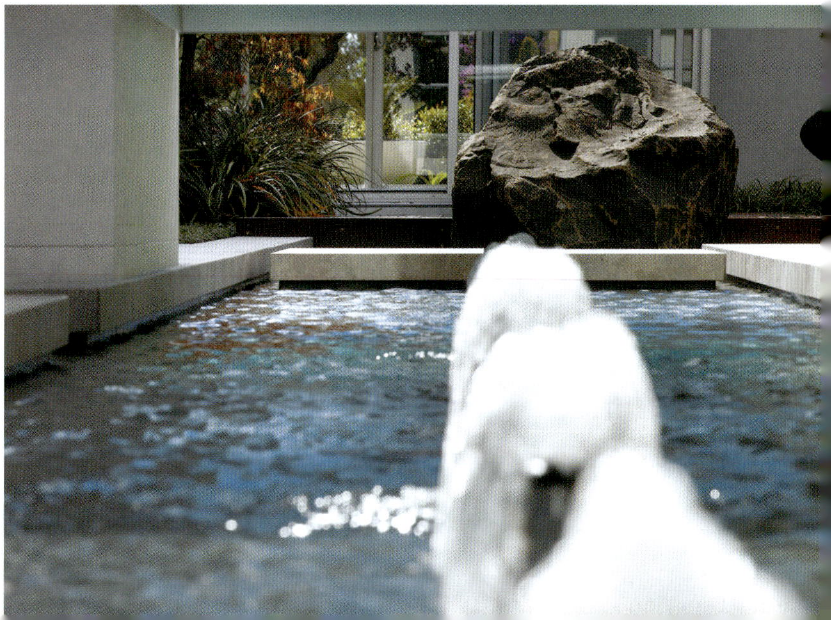

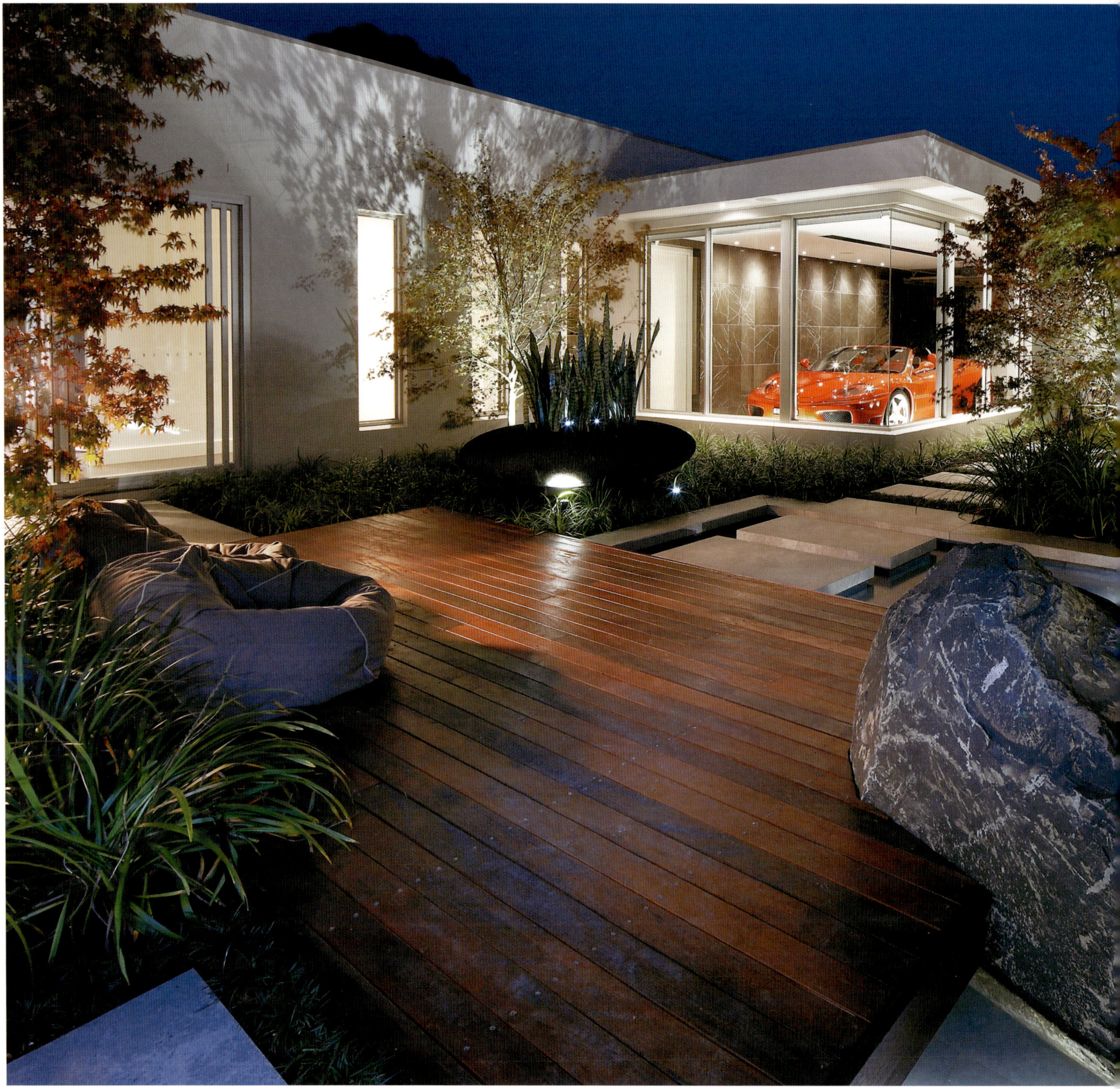

ON SHOW 145

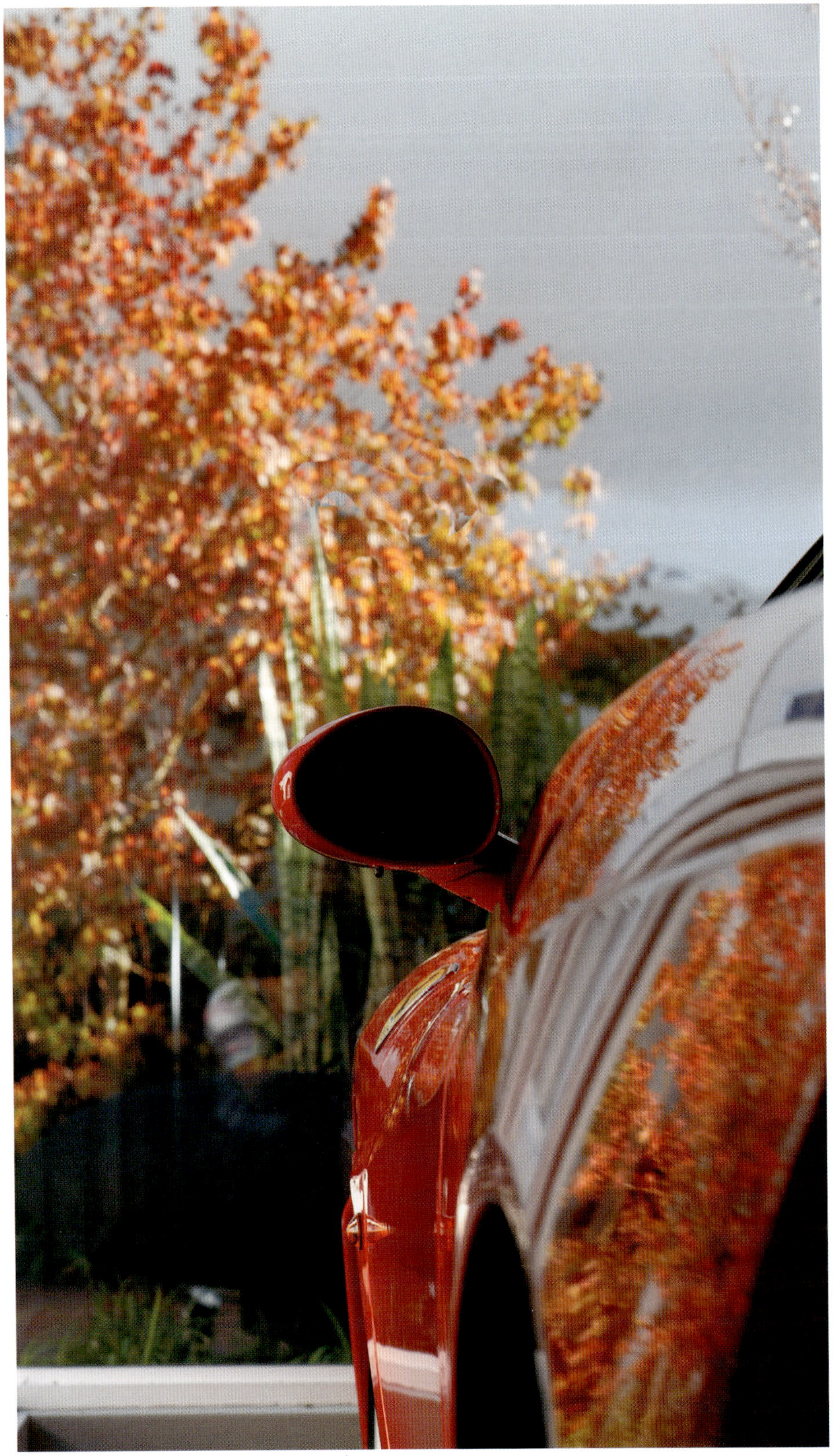

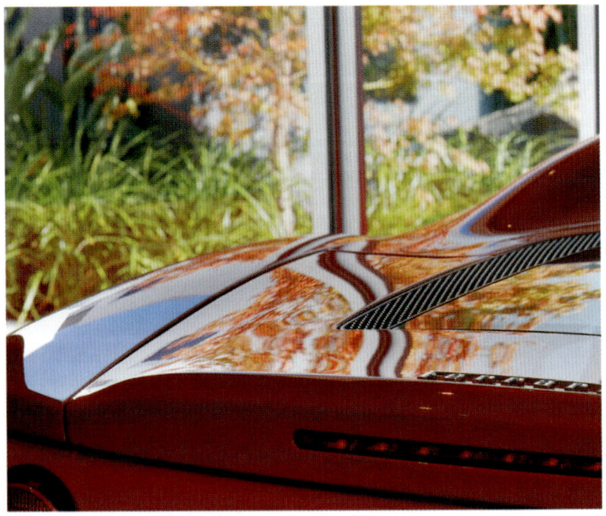

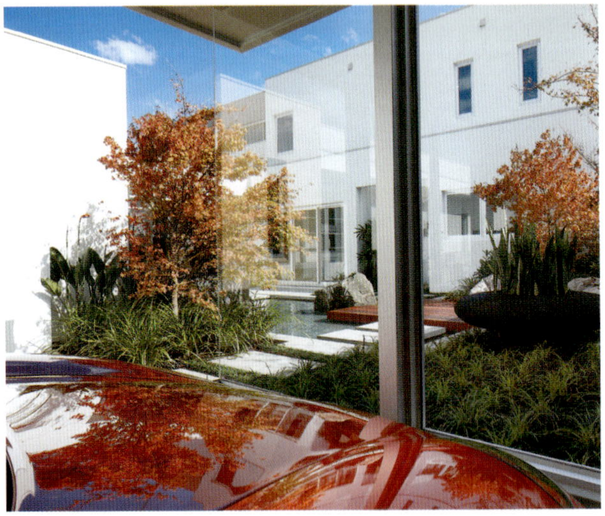

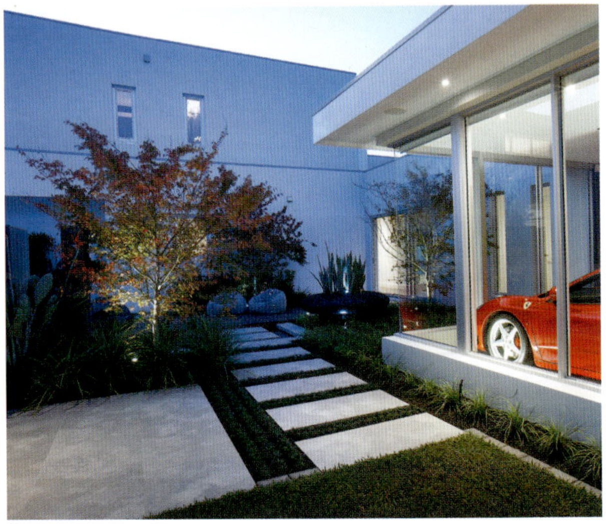

ON SHOW 147

With a natural bush backdrop, this property provided the opportunity to design a literal 'residential resort'. The brief was to deliver a resort-style getaway from everyday life – a place to spend quality time with friends and family.

Inspiration for the garden and entertaining areas was drawn from the clients' love of poolside relaxation at the various hotels and resorts they have visited around the world. It was important to bring a touch of that resort-style living into their backyard. The overall size and scale of the pool and pavilion had to be in keeping with the rest of the property and explore the use of the space and function of certain areas.

Resort Style Living

DURAL

Tiled with a blue glass mosaic, the pool features an infinity edge spillover and generous curves extending out towards the natural bushland. Together with a glass-sided spa that connects to the entertainment pavilion, the pool area creates a sense of luxury and relaxation.

The entertainment pavilion is the best place for the hosts and their guests to interact. A minimalistic cantilevered roof provides protection from the elements for the cooking, dining and relaxation areas while offering views over the pool and back towards the home. A self-contained outdoor kitchen including a teppanyaki-style barbecue, sink, integrated refrigerator and storage space ensures that there is no need for the hosts to travel back and forth continually from the main building. The dining area is positioned close to the kitchen, so there is no separation between the hosts and the guests. The lounge is positioned to take advantage of the outdoor fireplace – allowing use of the space in all seasons.

On the lower level of the pavilion is a swim-up bar containing a curved stainless steel ice trough for storing drinks. The stainless steel stools within the pool provide an opportunity to relax and enjoy a drink while taking in the atmosphere of resort-style living.

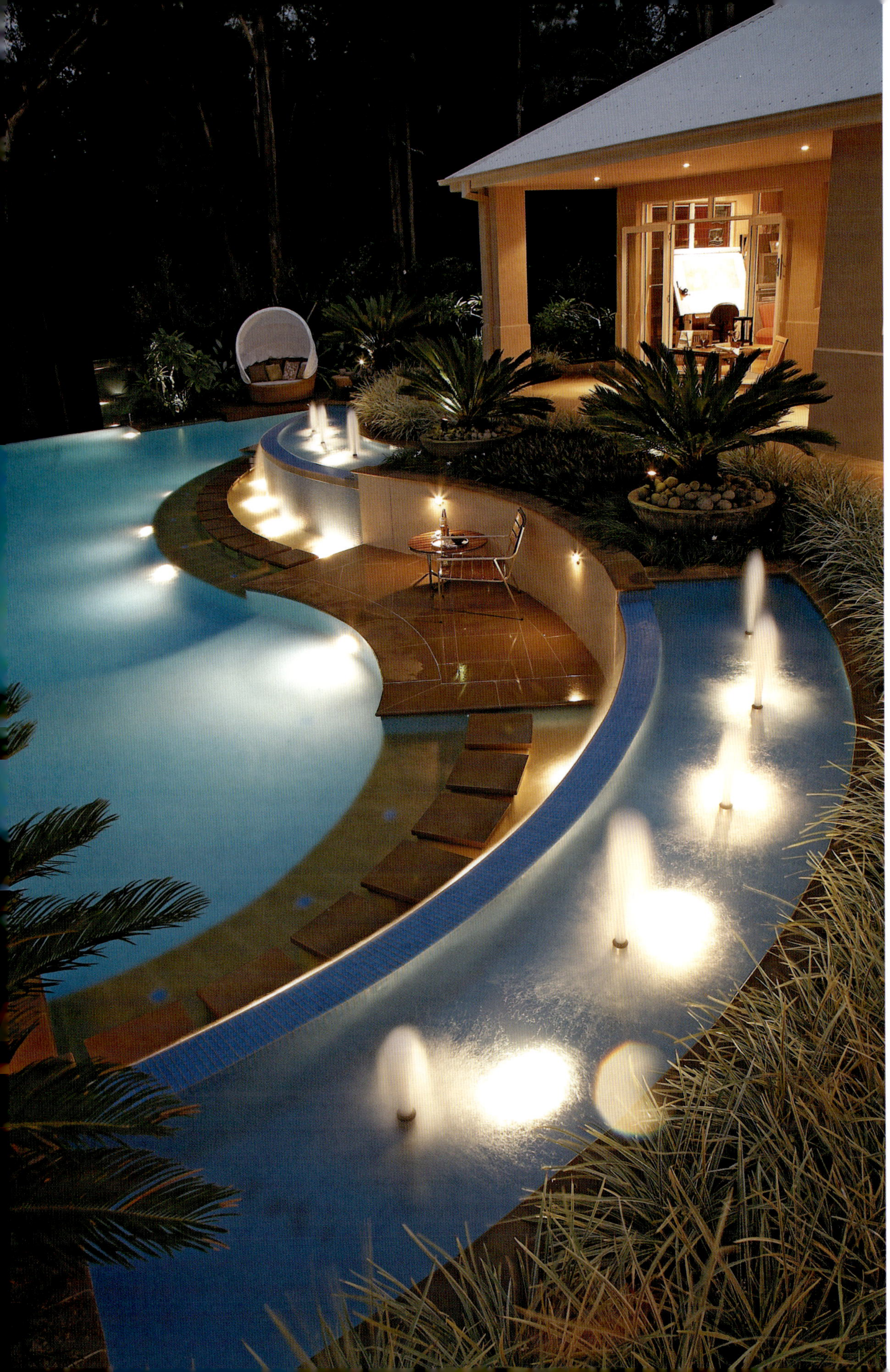
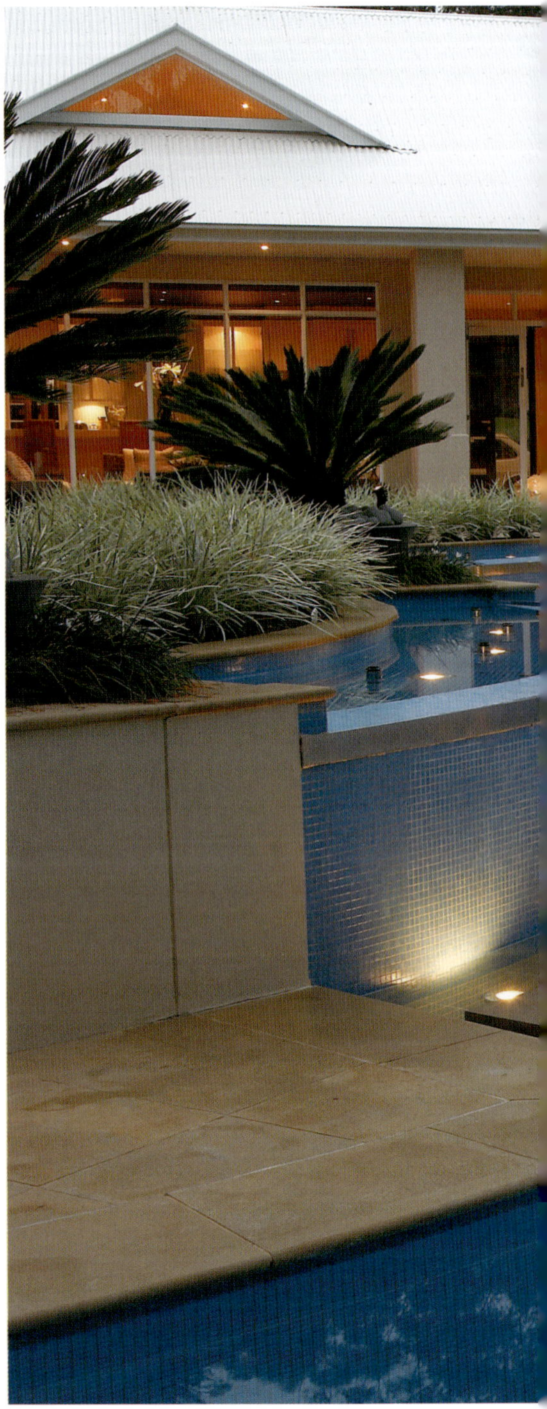

RESORT STYLE LIVING 151

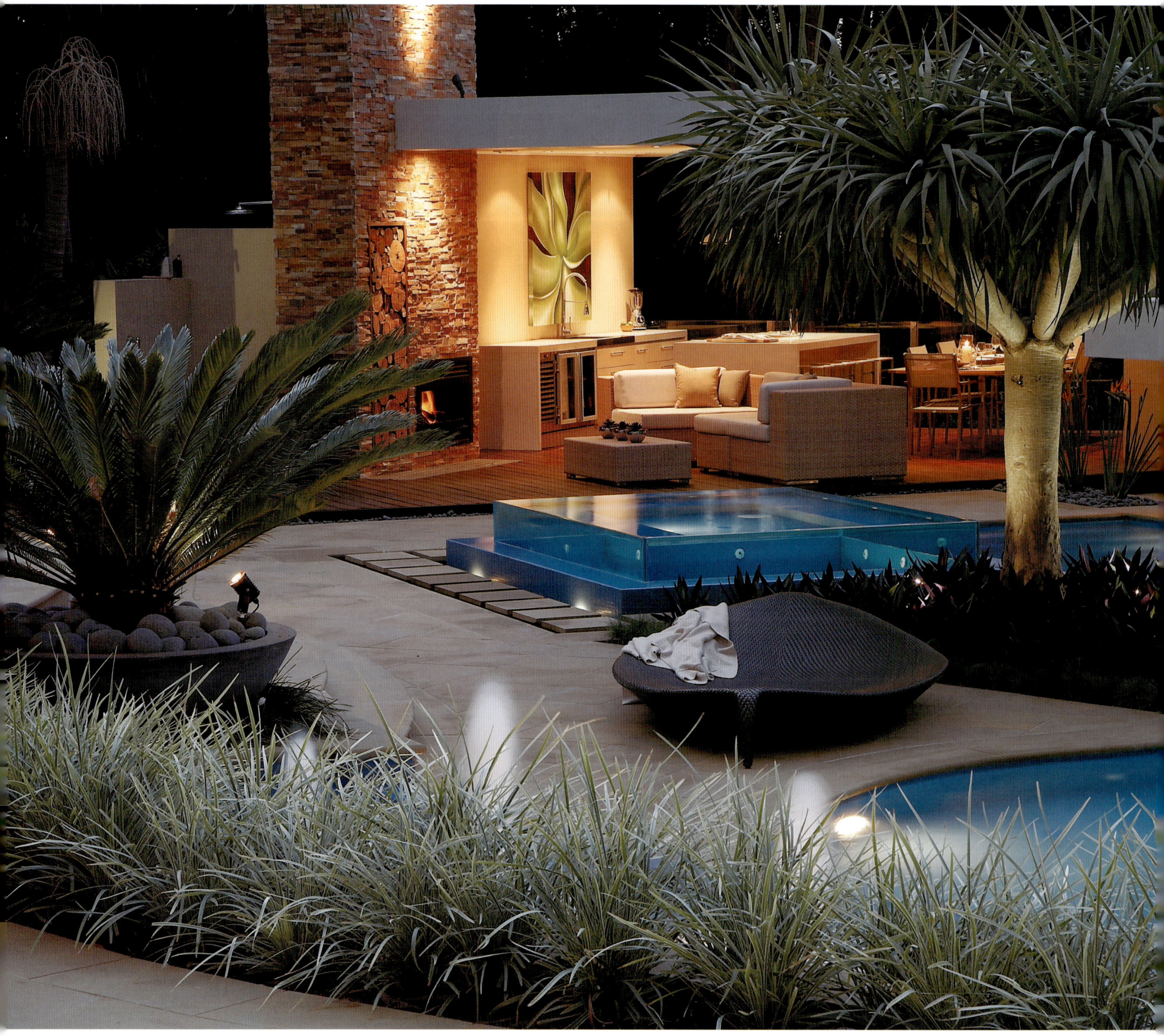

RESORT STYLE LIVING 153

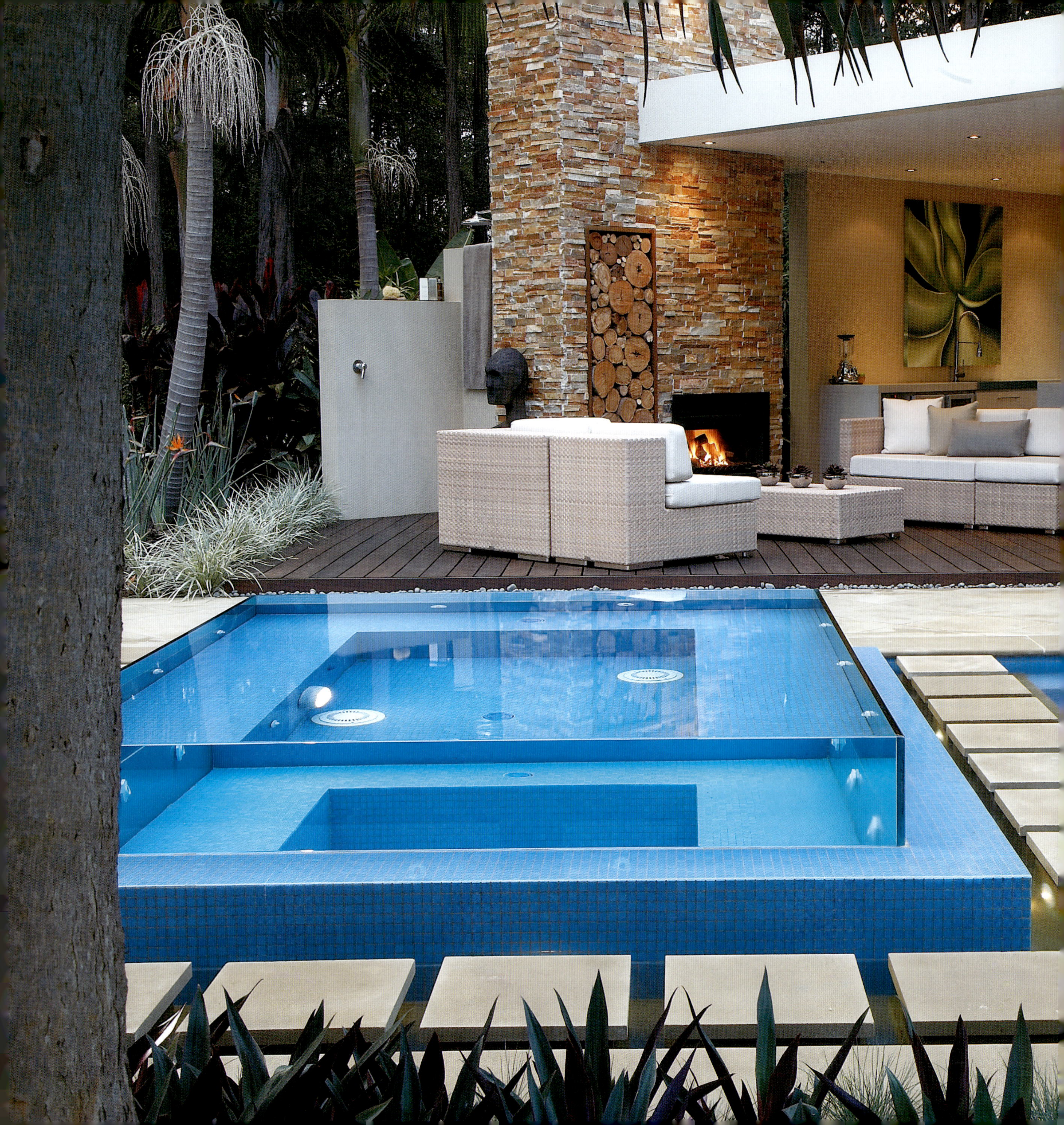

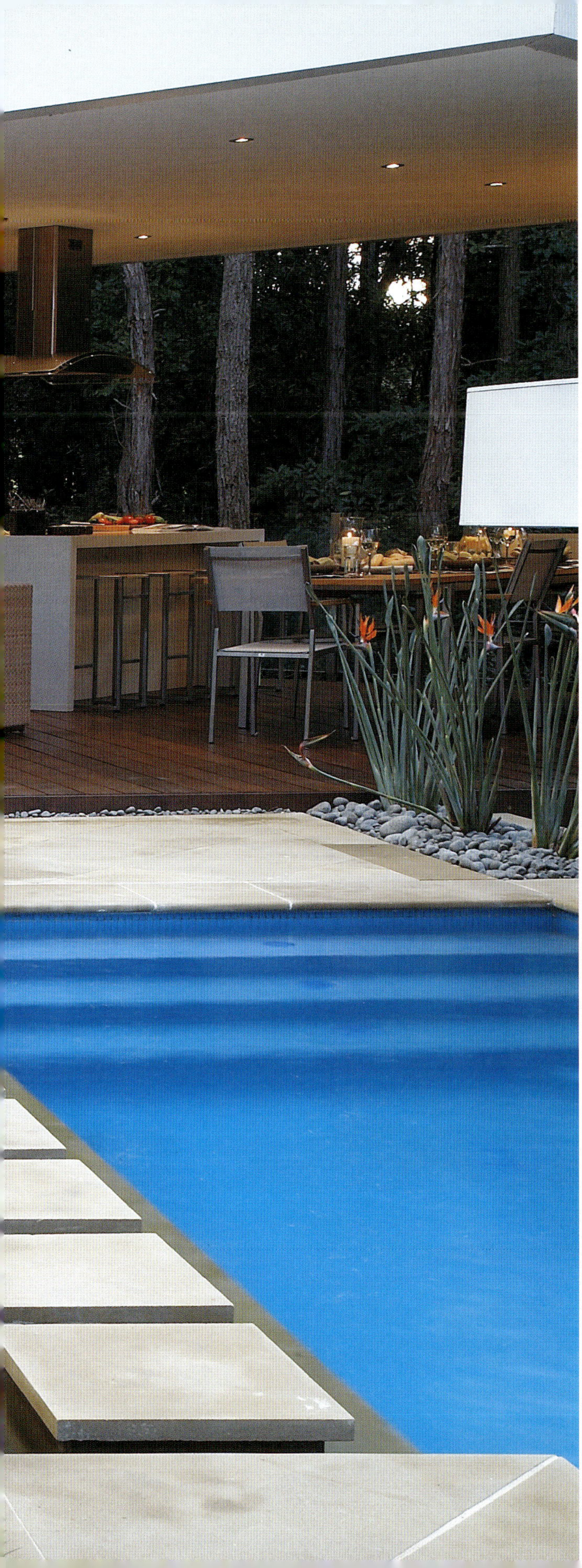
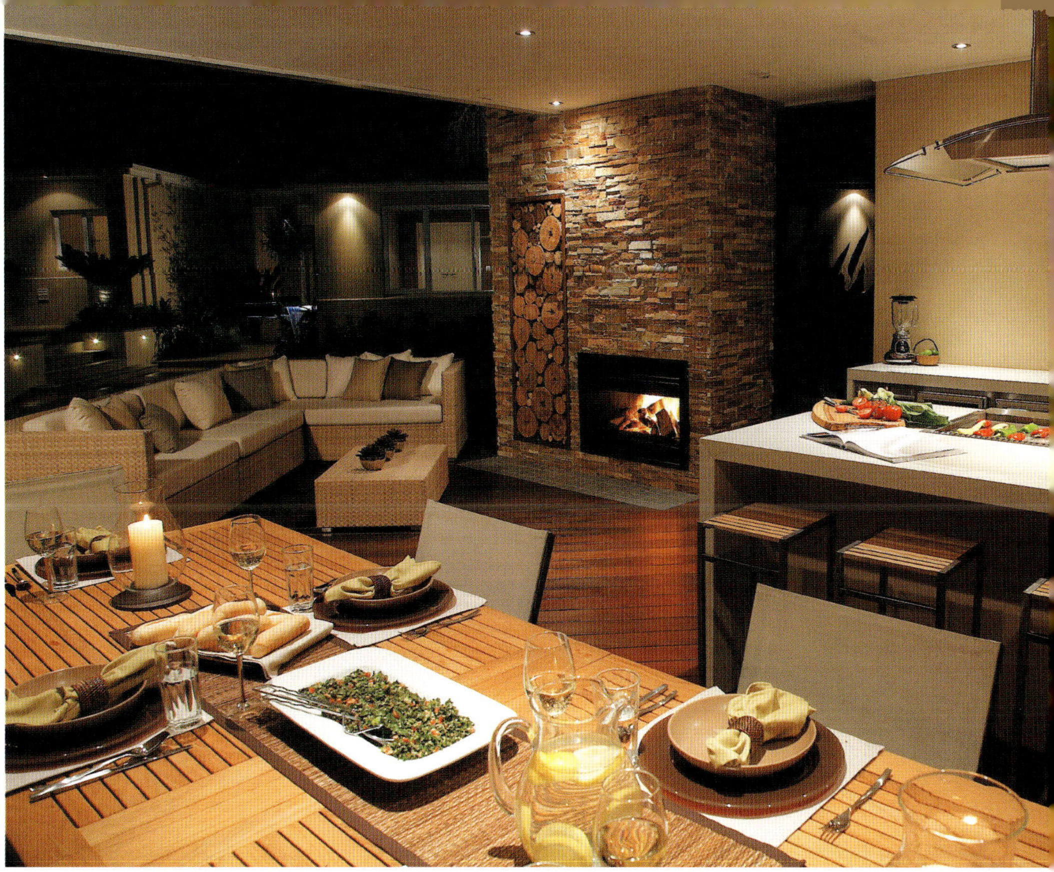
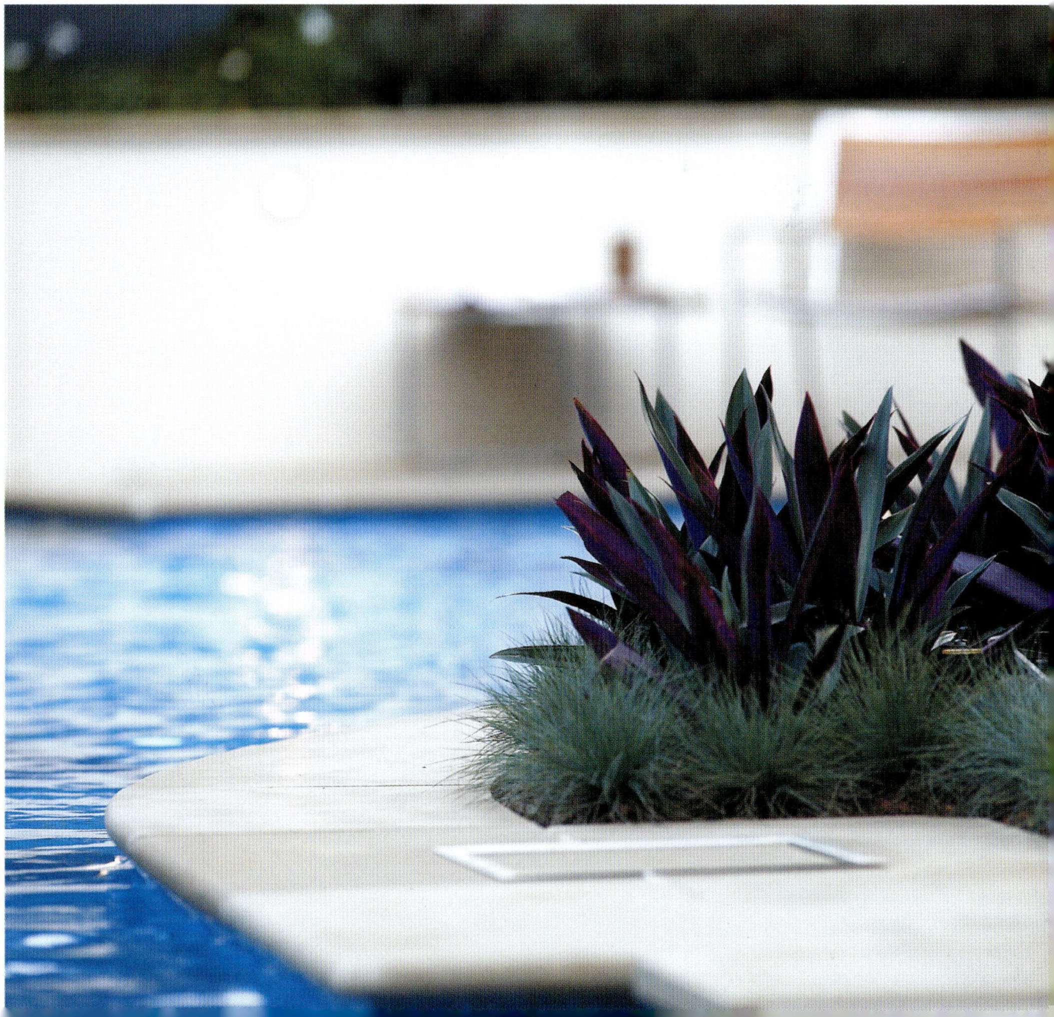

When well thought-out architecture is combined with an interesting location and an enthusiastic client, the combination is usually an enjoyable one and often ends in a spectacular result.

This home provided a unique space off the ensuite of the master bedroom to include an outdoor shower and sitting area, with a similarly distinctive space off the lower living room around the outdoor dining area. A blend of hardwood timbers and square concrete pavers was installed at a 45-degree angle to make the space appear larger through the use of long timber lines. This could not be achieved using a more conventional, square design.

Manly Hideaway

MANLY

This space also includes built-in bench seating with a slumped-glass water feature installed over a stone-clad wall. The water feature creates a tranquil effect that is visible from the dining area, and an interesting focal point when viewed from above, inside the house. With the two-storey glass architecture providing a backdrop to this space, the ambiance in the evening is stunning, with an illuminated view of the internal staircase through to the external space beyond.

Introducing planted areas adjacent to the home and at the boundary provided privacy screening. Lush, large-leaf plantings were used to achieve the desired sub-tropical

Plan labels:

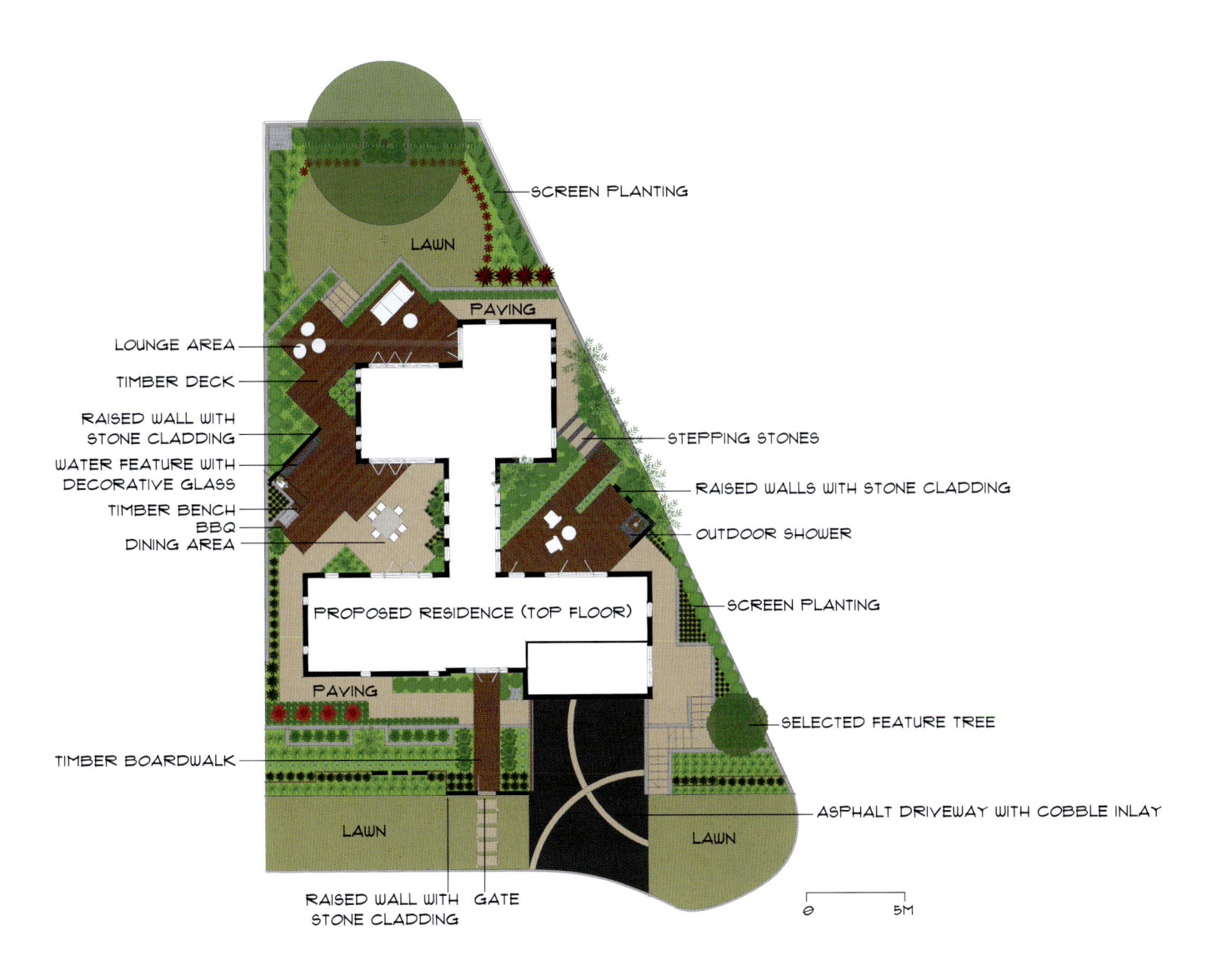

- SCREEN PLANTING
- LAWN
- PAVING
- LOUNGE AREA
- TIMBER DECK
- RAISED WALL WITH STONE CLADDING
- WATER FEATURE WITH DECORATIVE GLASS
- TIMBER BENCH
- BBQ
- DINING AREA
- STEPPING STONES
- RAISED WALLS WITH STONE CLADDING
- OUTDOOR SHOWER
- SCREEN PLANTING
- PROPOSED RESIDENCE (TOP FLOOR)
- PAVING
- SELECTED FEATURE TREE
- TIMBER BOARDWALK
- ASPHALT DRIVEWAY WITH COBBLE INLAY
- LAWN
- LAWN
- RAISED WALL WITH STONE CLADDING
- GATE

0   5M

Asian theme at the clients' request. The large glass windows of the house enable the plantings to be seen from inside, as they rest against the glass. Plants such as bird of paradise (*Strelitzia reginae*), grey star ctenanthe (*Ctenanthe setosa* 'Grey Star'), century plant (*Agave attenuata*), slender weavers bamboo (*Bambusa textilis* 'Gracilis'), orange jessamine (*Murraya panniculata*), variegated mondo (*Ophiopogon intermedians* 'Stripey White') and rhoeo (*Tradescantia spathacea*) were used to achieve abundant planting with the environment in mind.

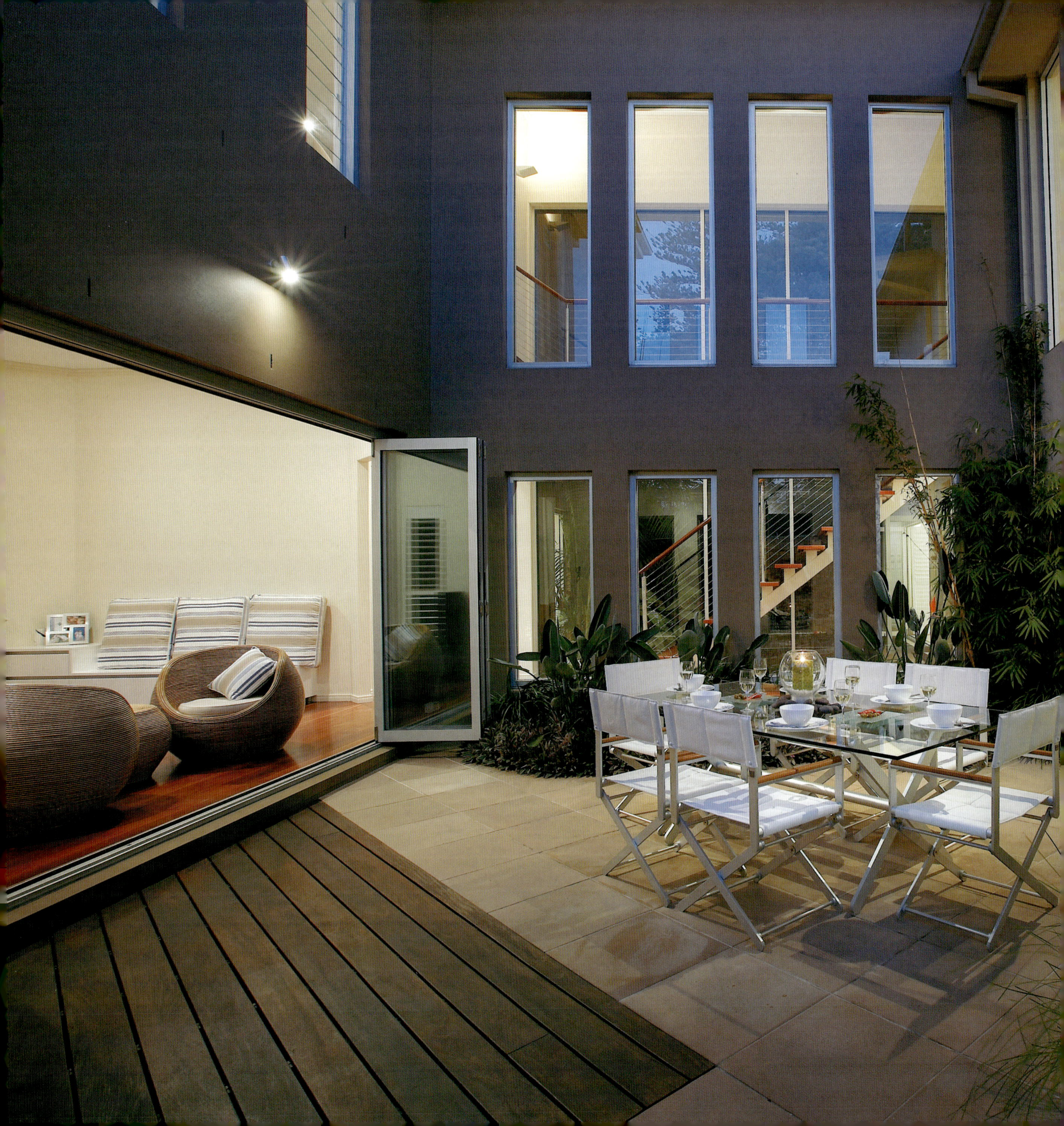

MANLY HIDEAWAY 159

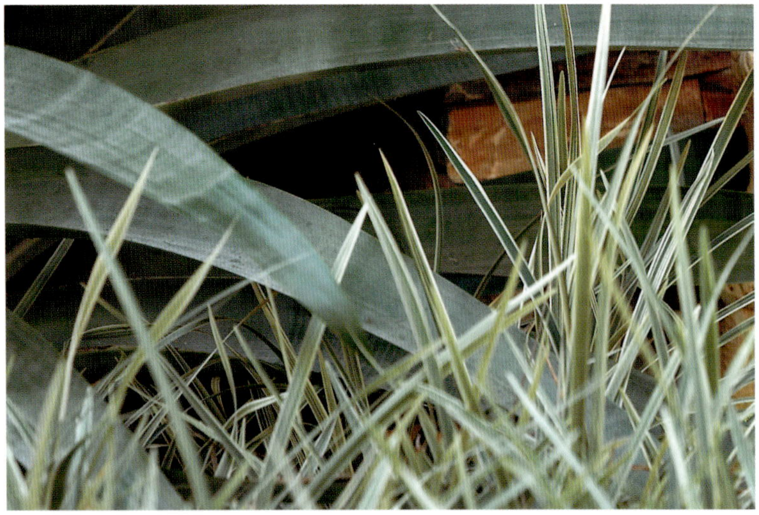
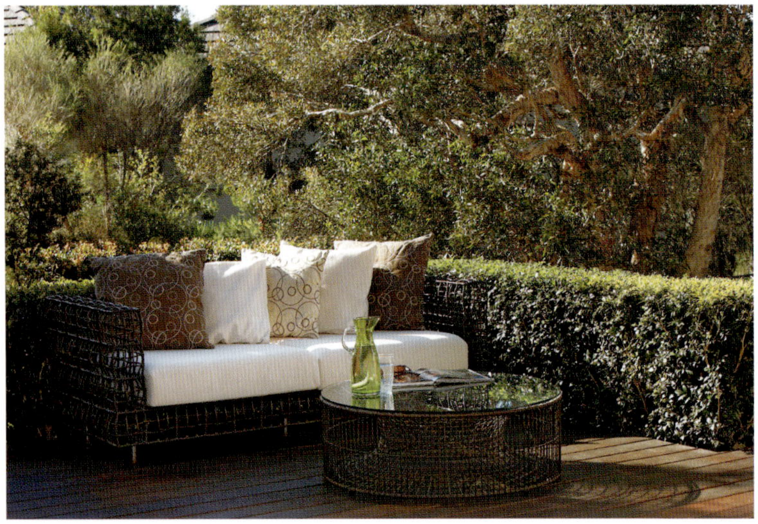
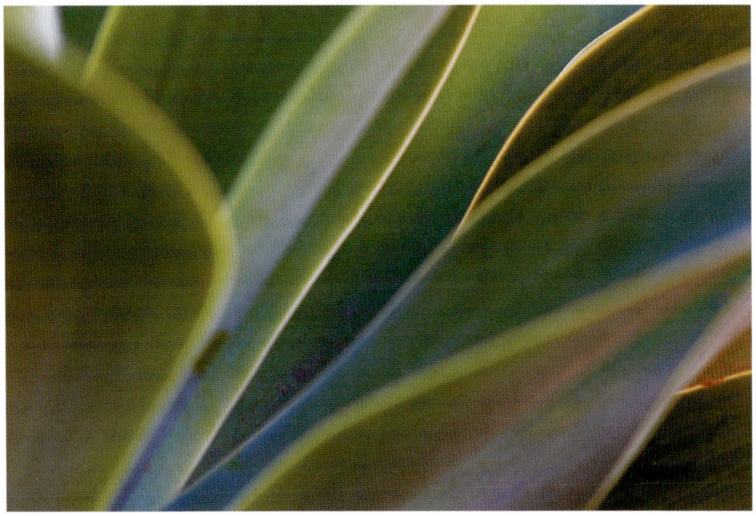
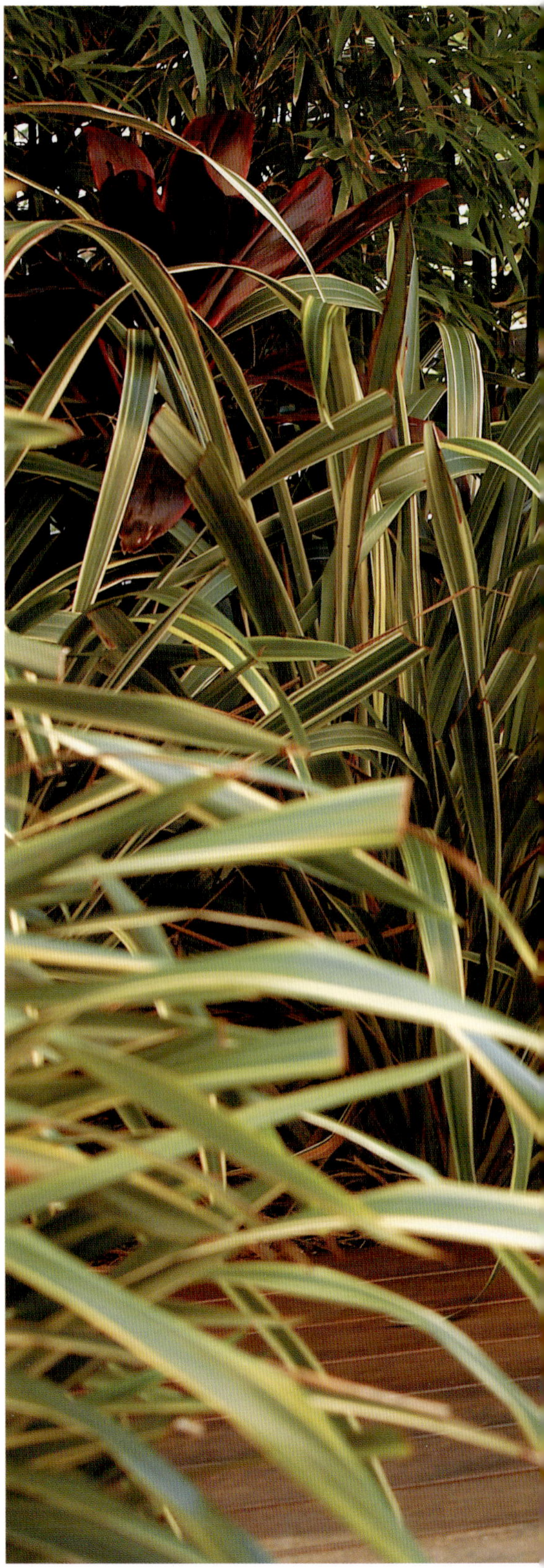

MANLY HIDEAWAY 161

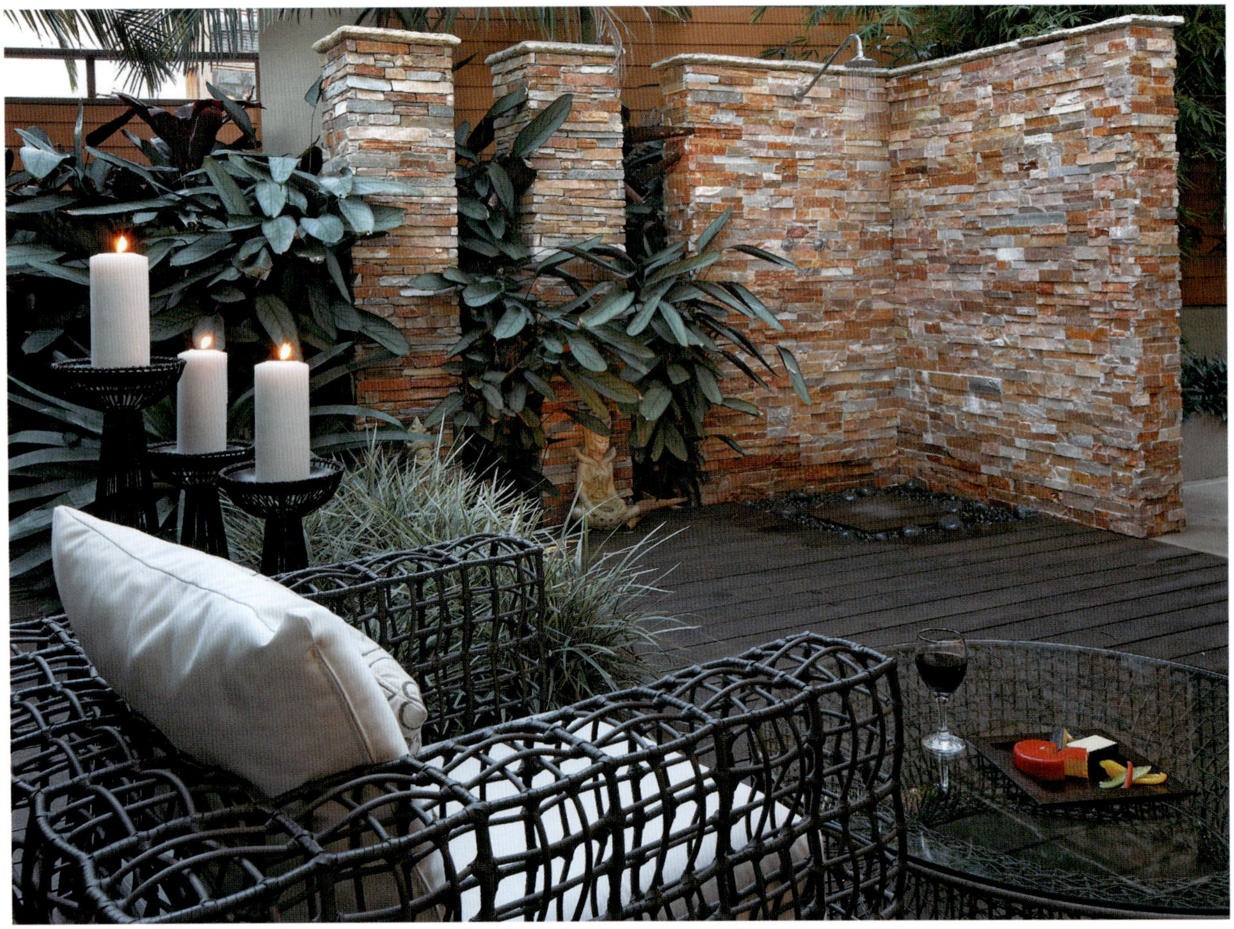

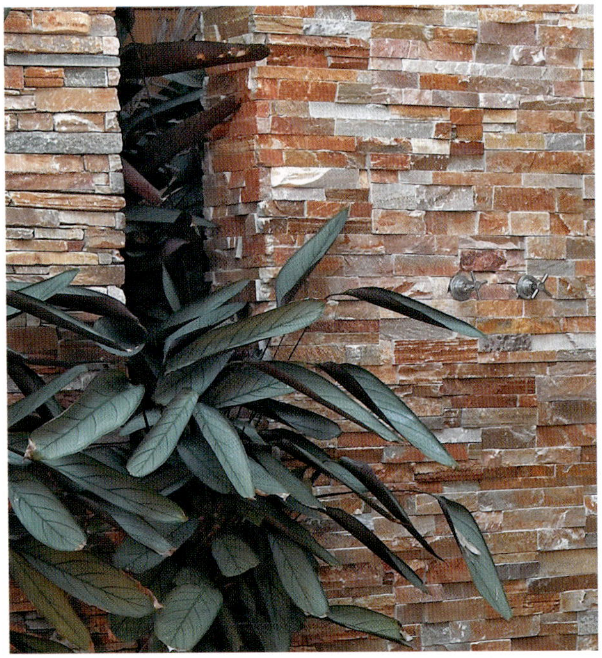

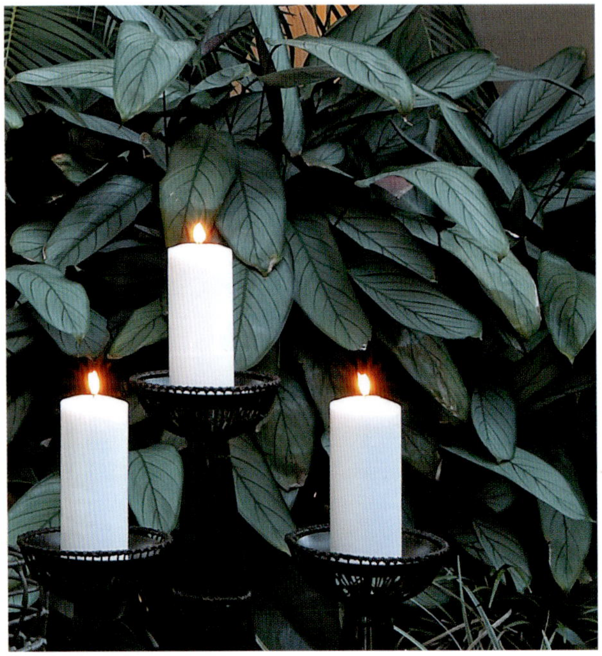

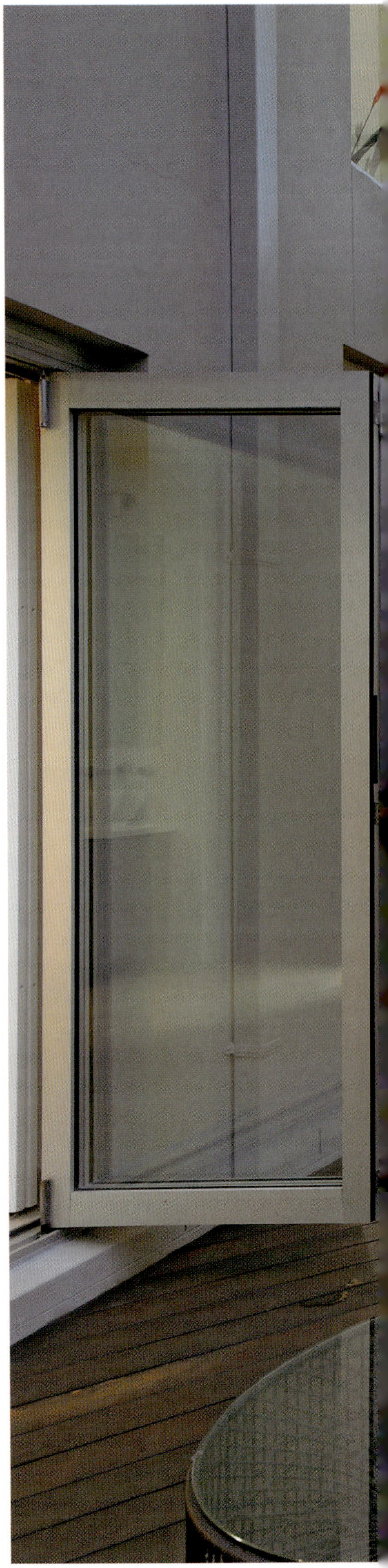

MANLY HIDEAWAY 163

Set In Stone

DURAL

When a family plans a new home, they have the freedom to design the space inside and out, to the specifications they want. This is different from a renovation, where existing structures do not always allow for such freedom of design.

The brief from these clients was to include a large family pool, visible from the kitchen and main living areas of the home, with an entertaining area between the pool and the house. It also aimed to capture the acreage lifestyle that comes with a new property like this, which includes large-scale lawns and gardens.

The first step, after reviewing the proposed house plans, was to position the pool, taking into consideration the sight lines from the home. The lie of the land provided an opportunity to design a vanishing edge along the outer line of the pool to give a smooth visual connection between the water and the lower lawn area. A large shallow area was incorporated into the pool design; fully covered in a green Balinese tile, the area also features a small cave with water falling from a ledge above. The position of the spa is paramount – set in a central location, it is only a few steps from the outdoor kitchen where drinks are chilled in the triple-door refrigerator. The outdoor kitchen is designed with full amenities for entertaining, including a barbecue and sink, along with plenty of storage space and a large stone bench top. At the end of the kitchen is a traditional wood-fired pizza oven, finished in glass mosaic tiles and positioned adjacent to the dining space.

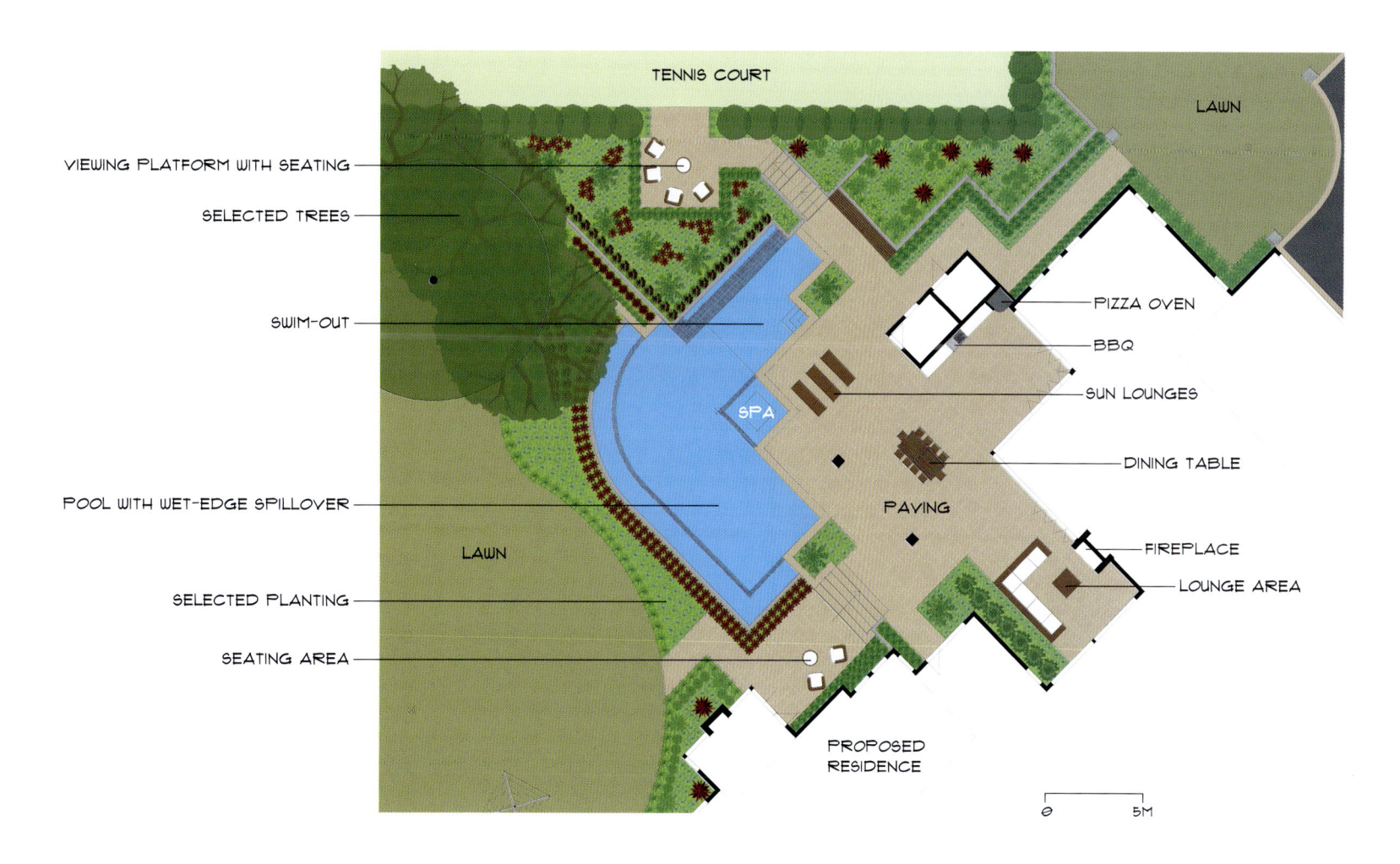

Plan labels:
- TENNIS COURT
- LAWN
- VIEWING PLATFORM WITH SEATING
- SELECTED TREES
- SWIM-OUT
- POOL WITH WET-EDGE SPILLOVER
- SELECTED PLANTING
- SEATING AREA
- LAWN
- SPA
- PAVING
- PIZZA OVEN
- BBQ
- SUN LOUNGES
- DINING TABLE
- FIREPLACE
- LOUNGE AREA
- PROPOSED RESIDENCE
- 0   5M

The outdoor lounge area faces a fireplace that is connected to the home. Clad in a natural stone it gives contrast to the rendered and painted texture of the house. It also worked well with the selected flooring – split stone laid out in a modular pattern.

Due to the business commitments of my clients it was important to ensure the plant materials used were low maintenance. The palette of plants includes Japanese sago palm (*Cycas revoluta*), century plant (*Agave attenuata*), purple fountain grass (*Pennisetum advena* 'Rubrum'), variegated mondo (*Ophiopogon intermedians* 'Stripey White'), New Zealand flax (*Phormium tenax*), dwarf lilly pilly (*Acmena smithii* 'Allyn Magic') and lady palm (*Rhapis excelsa*).

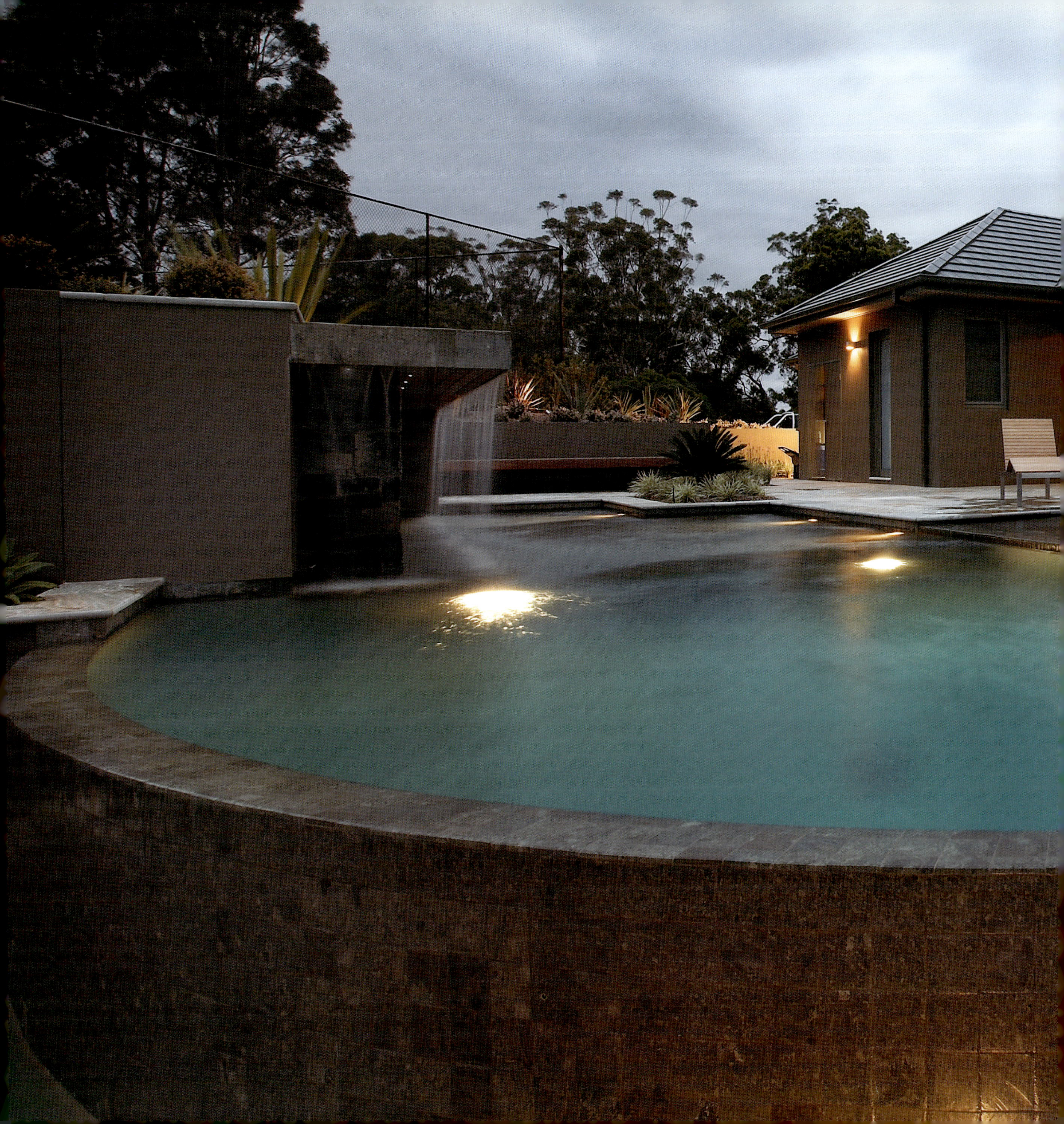

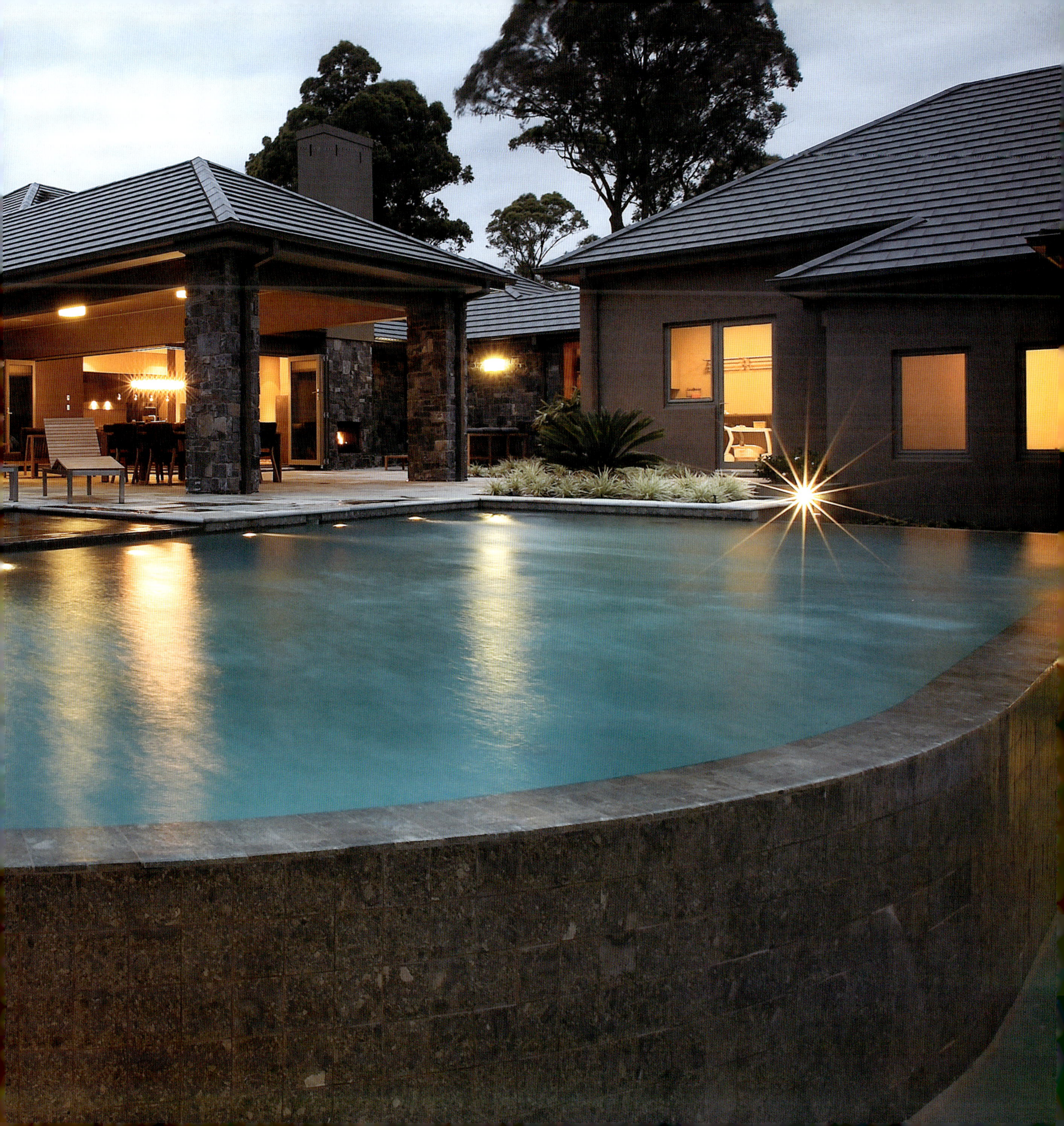

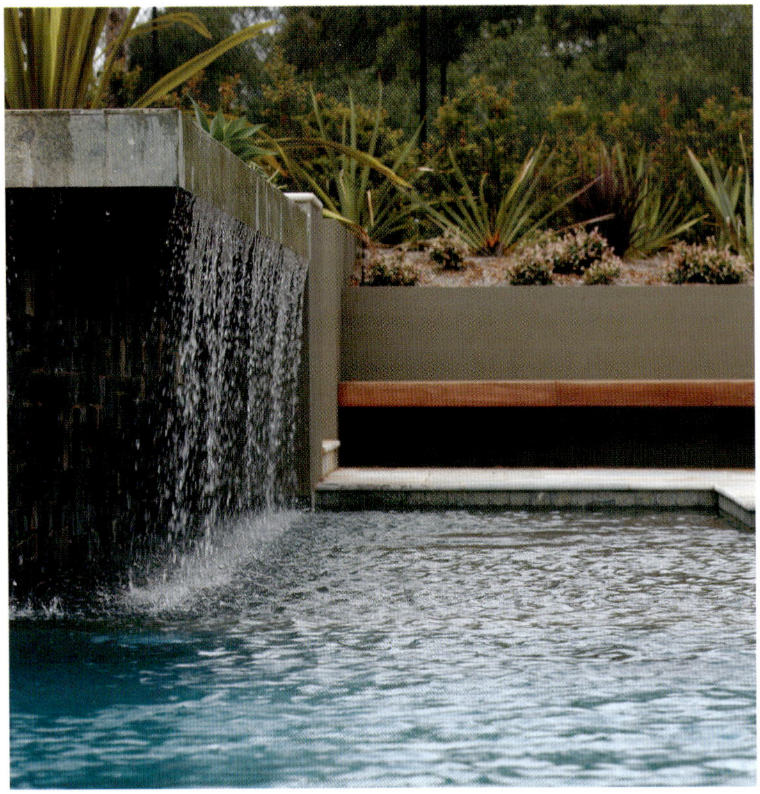

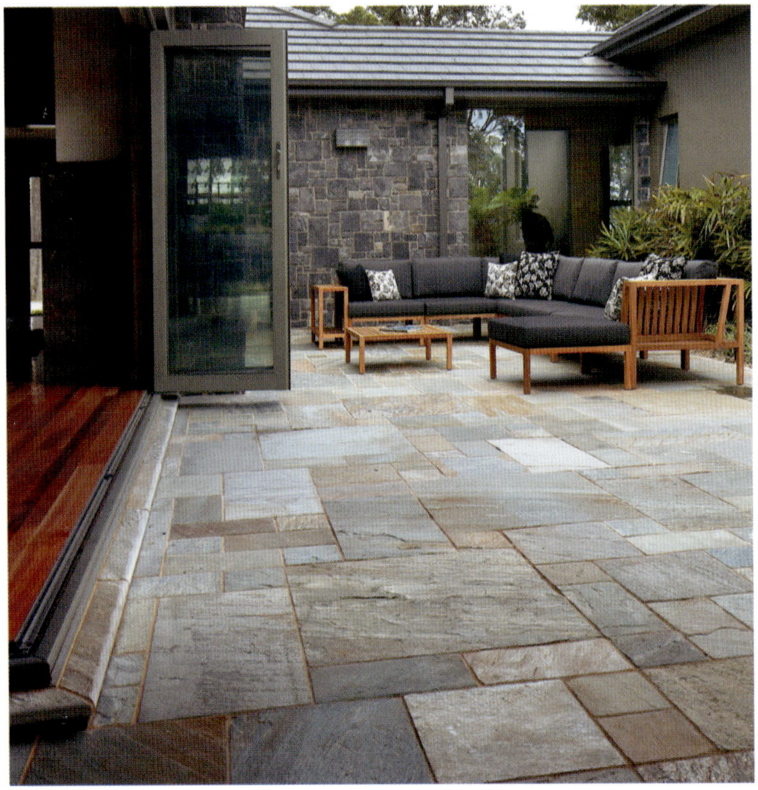

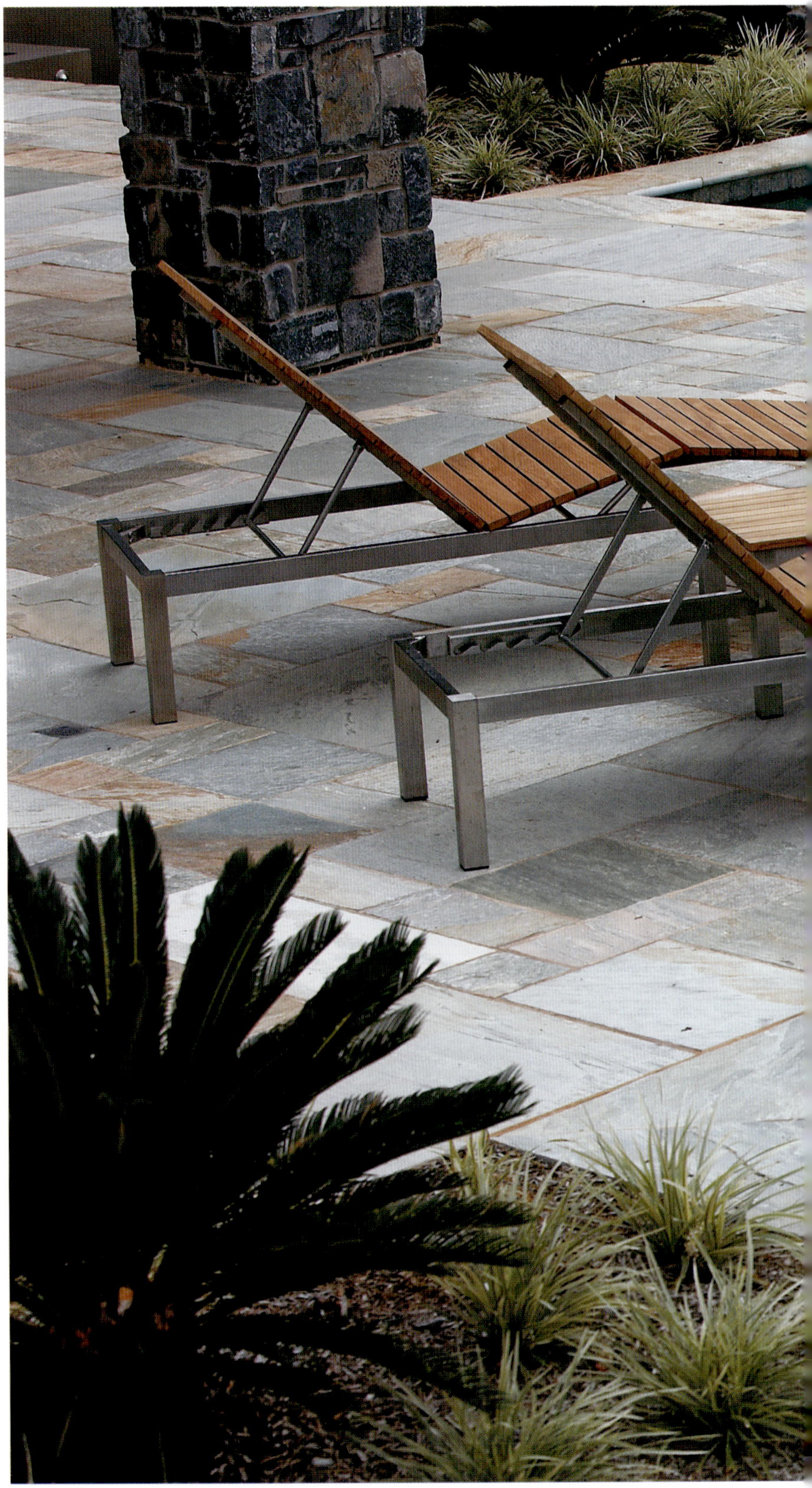

SET IN STONE 169

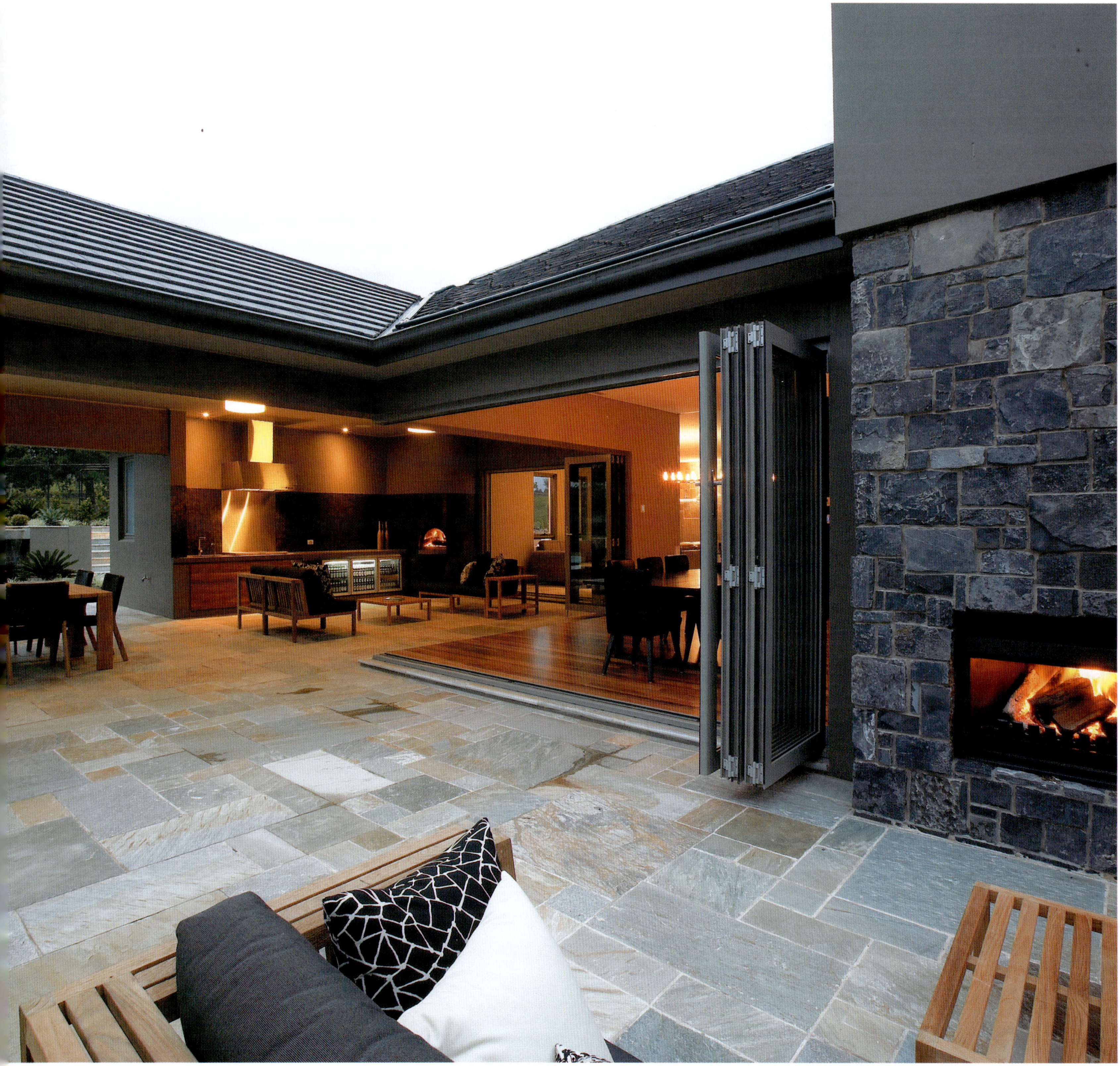

SET IN STONE 171

After purchasing this recently completed new home, my client invited me to view what was a blank canvas in the backyard of the property. The space had endless possibilities, with an existing covered entertaining area at the rear of the house, along with a small lap pool to the side. The garden itself lacked style and purpose and needed an aspect to draw people in.

One advantage of modern architecture is open-plan living, which results in wide spaces with large viewports, not only inside the house, but also in the external spaces. This was the case with this property, which provided the opportunity to complete a design that not only signifies use, but also

Urban Movement

RANDWICK

invites the occupant to interact with it. The sight lines from within the home offered a number of opportunities that played a strong part in influencing the complete project.

To express and stretch the view through the space, the floor was laid out in a linear fashion with long hardwood decking accompanying large porcelain tiles measuring 1200mm by 600mm. This combination of products gives interest to the space, drawing the eye through to the planting to the rear. On one side of the property two water-feature troughs were laid in the same linear manner, housing small bubblers for sight and sound, which are illuminated in the evening. At the end of one of the troughs a mirror was installed on the wall, giving an extended illusion of the water feature as viewed from the internal staircase. At the centre of the landscaping is a stunning lounge area set among the vegetation and communicating a clear message about the use of space. With a sculpture at the rear and an outdoor kitchen, the space conveys a mood of relaxation – a place to share with those closest.

The planting scheme continues this tone, consisting of a blend of modern and lush, leafy plantings of ornamental ginger (*Alpinia* spp.), Mexican lily (*Beschorneria yuccoides*), bangalow palms (*Archontophoenix cunninghamiana*), century plants (*Agave attenuata*) and variegated mondo (*Ophiopogon intermedians* 'Stripey White'). Two frangipani trees were moved into position by crane; once mature they will provide additional shelter during the summer months. The inclusion of rhoeo (*Tradescantia spathacea*) completes the theme, while small cape rush (*Chondropetalum tectorum*) at the side of the water feature emulates reeds among the pebbles.

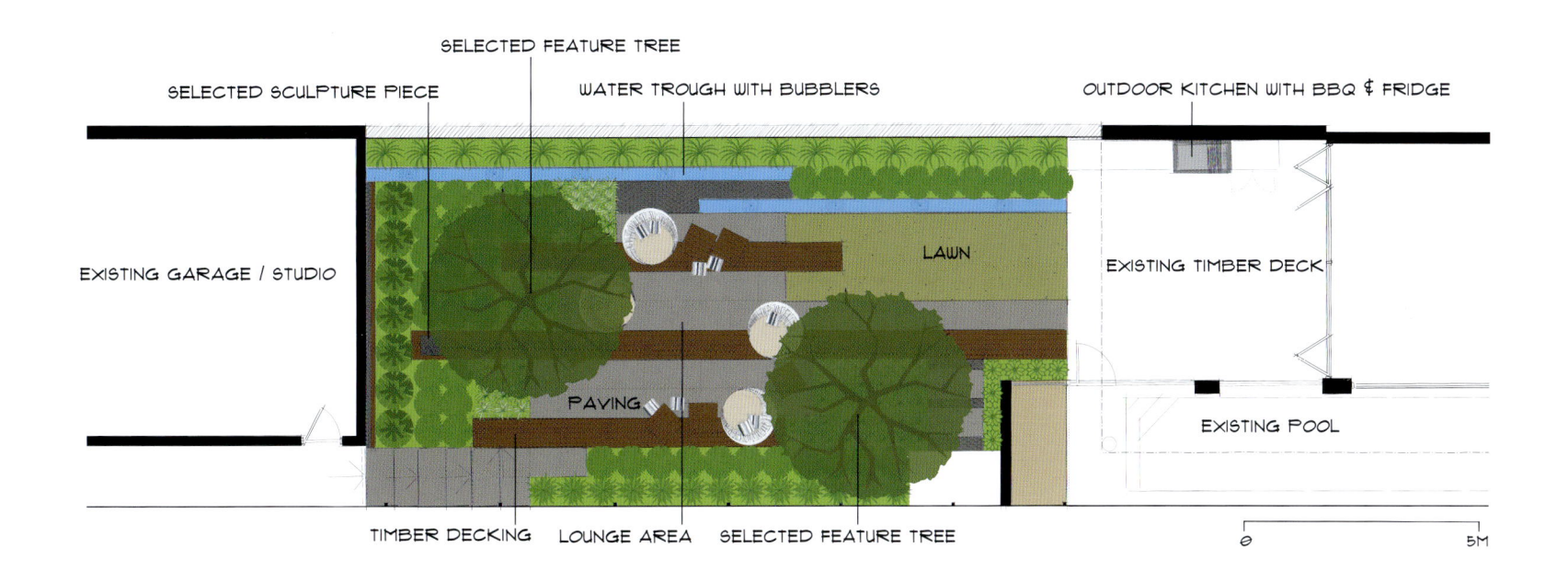

174

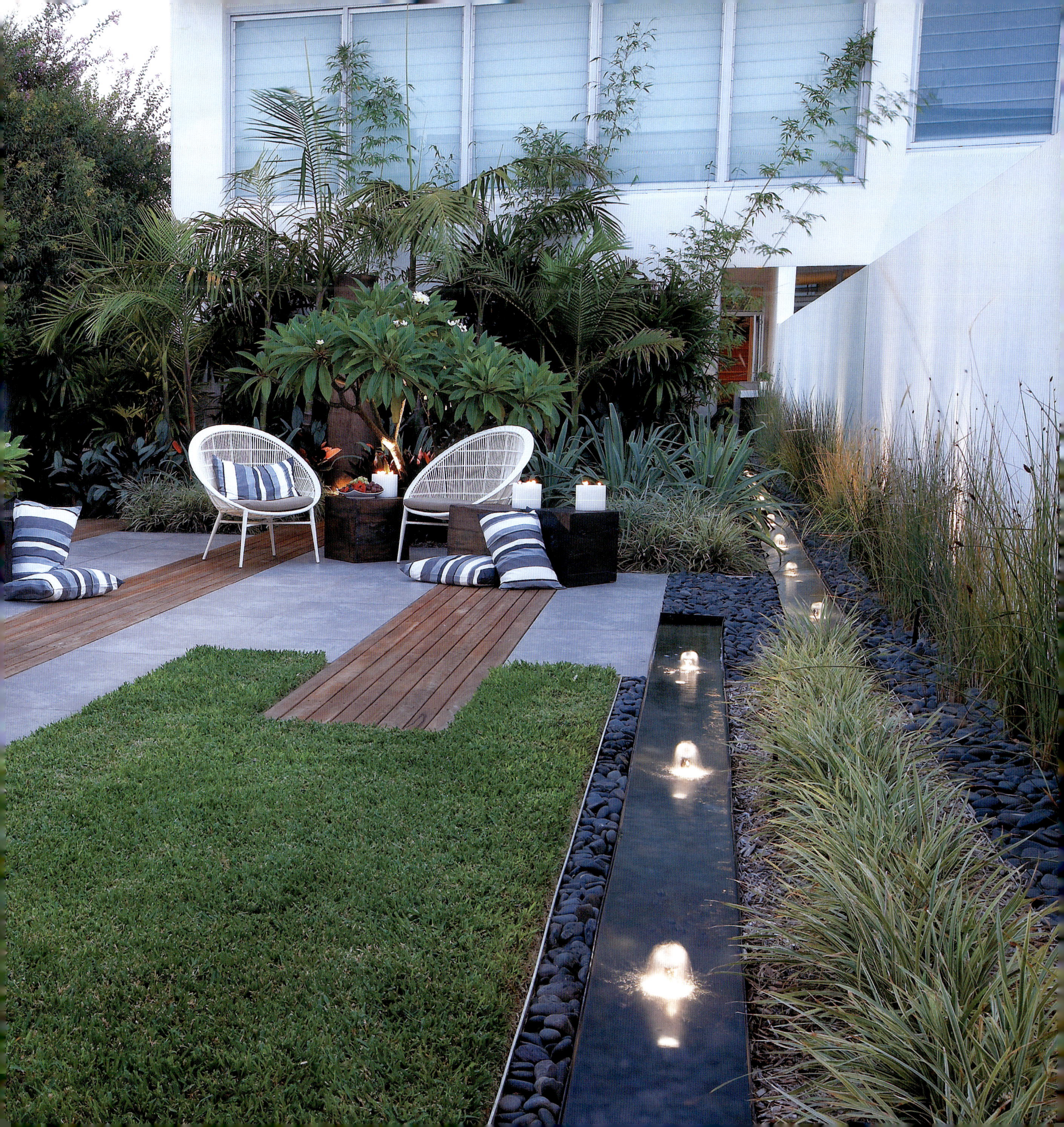

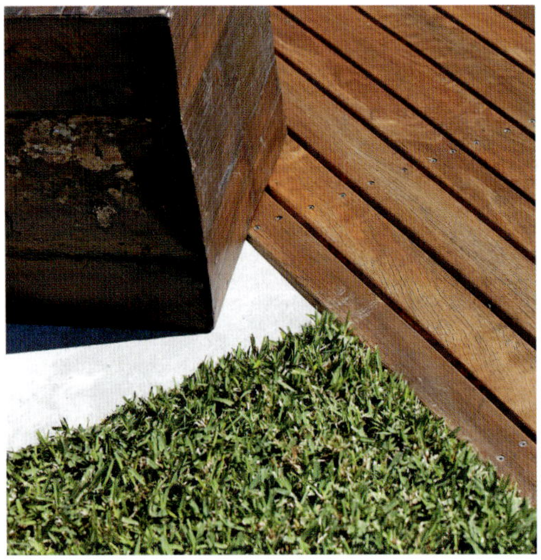
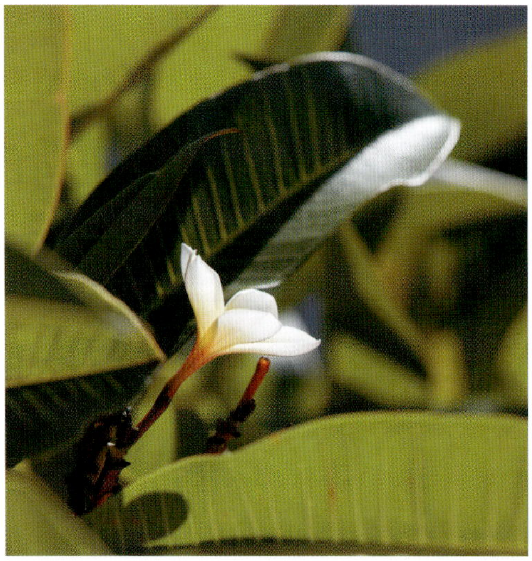
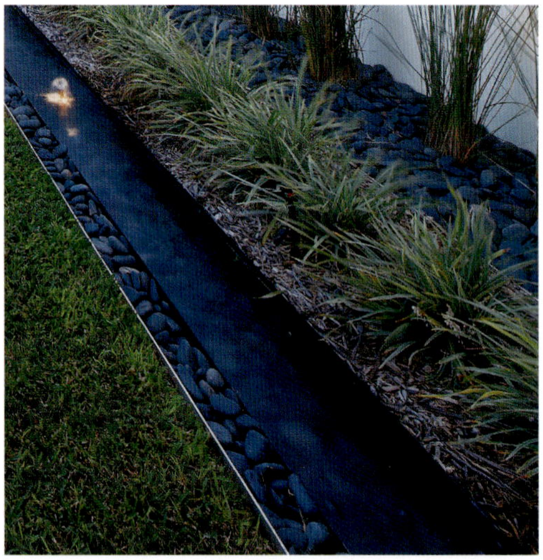
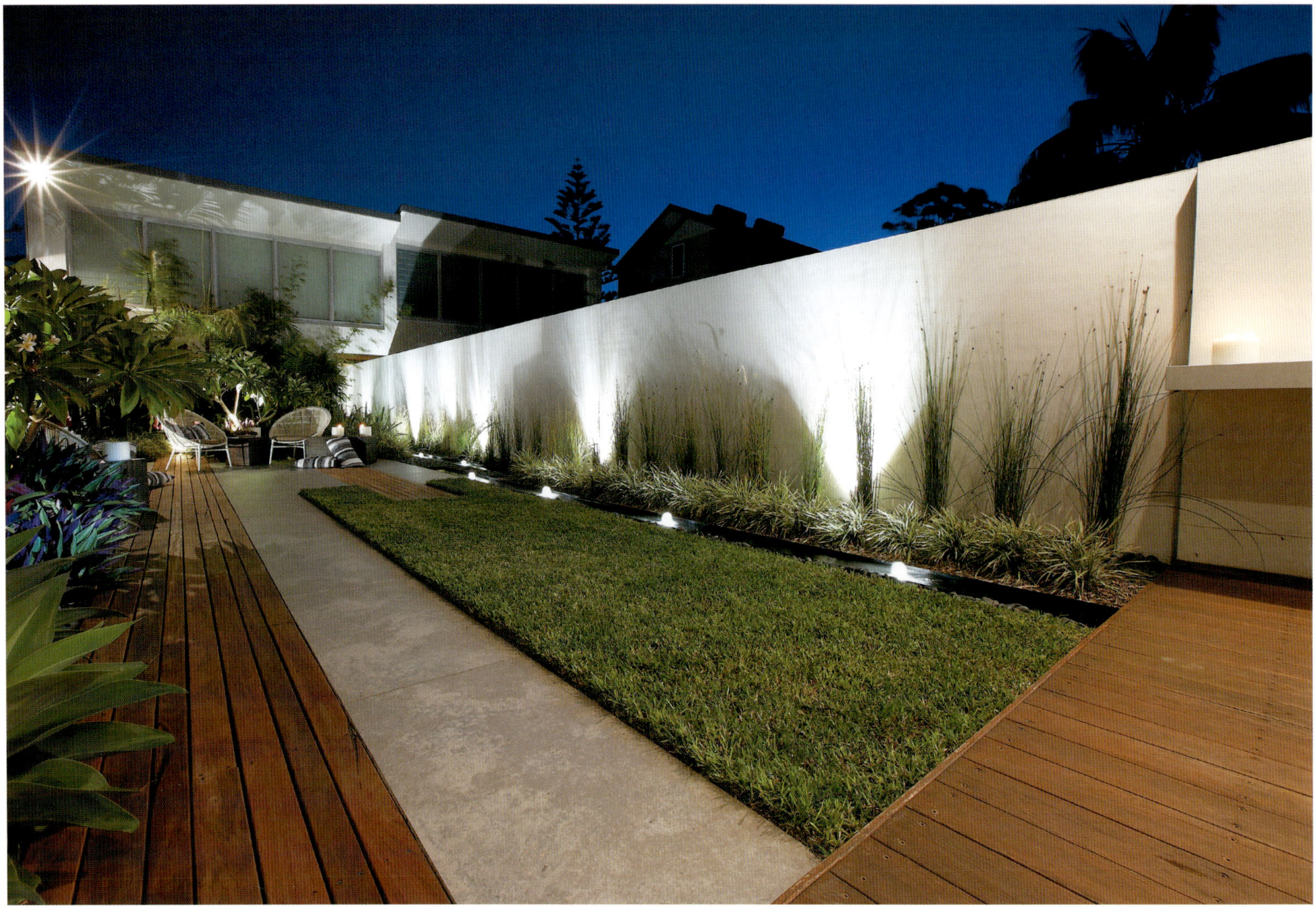

URBAN MOVEMENT 177

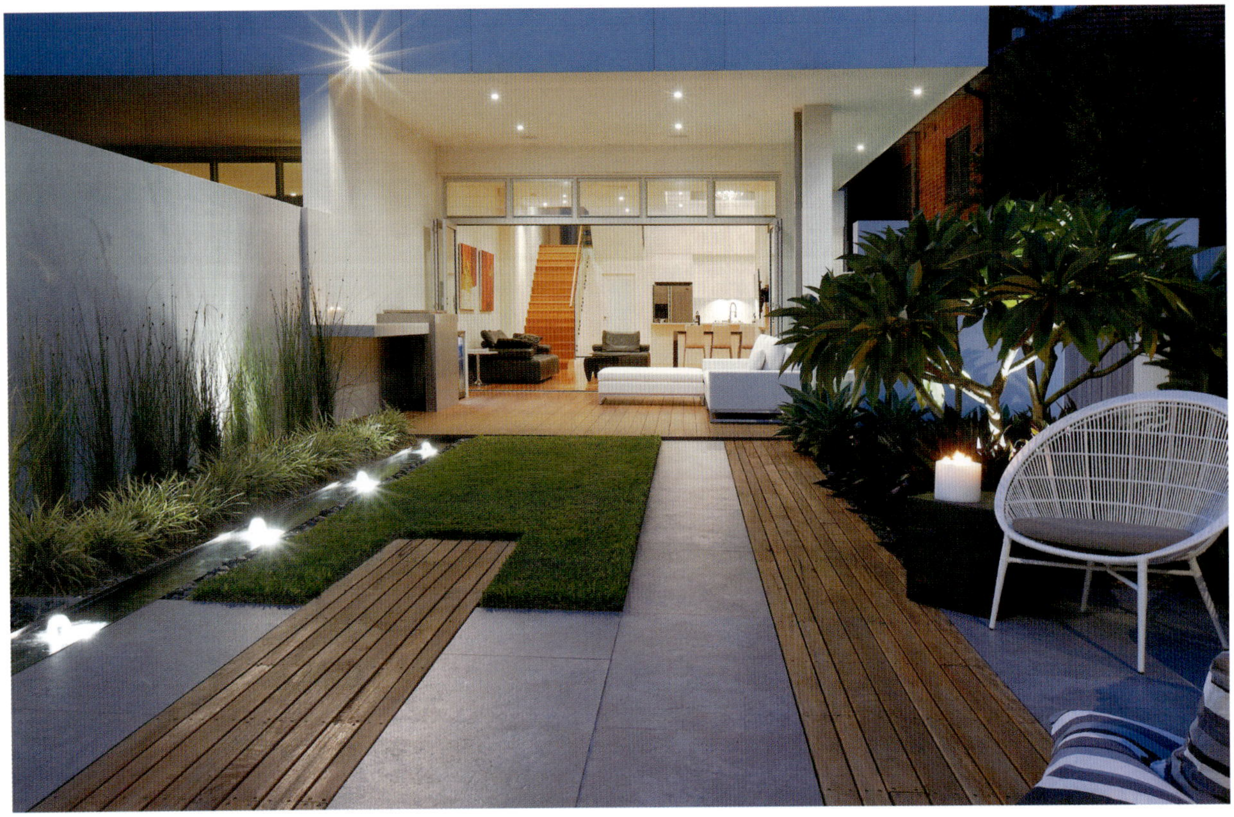

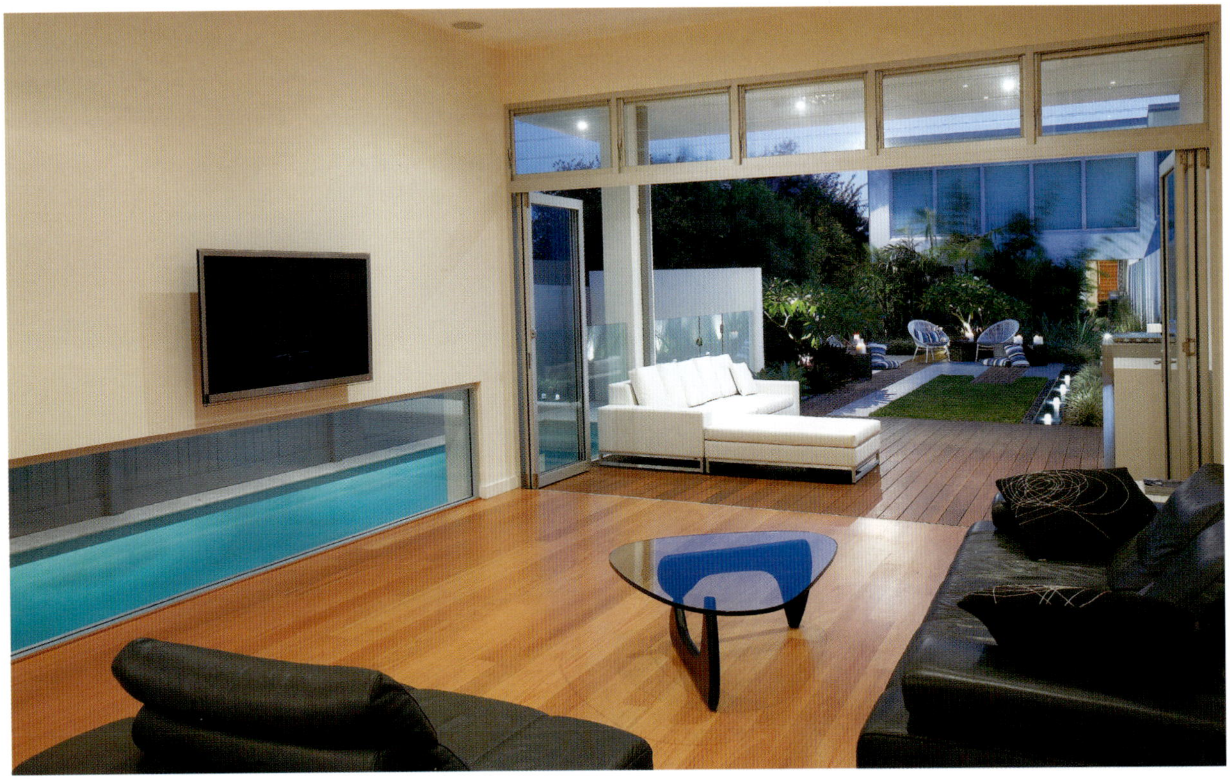

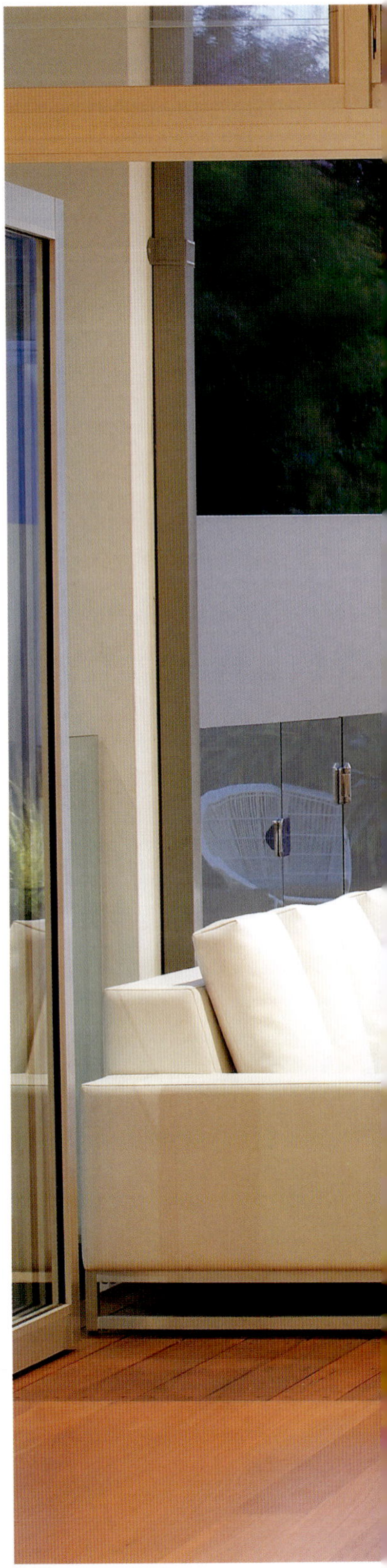

URBAN MOVEMENT 179

Set within a new estate, this contemporary home was designed to have a smooth connection to the outdoors with strong sight lines from the entry and living areas. With large bi-fold doors and two-storey windows, viewports were in place awaiting a design that would evoke relaxation and entice the observer to enter the space. With the boundary fences set and the neighbouring homes in view, a pavilion was designed to provide shading by the pool, and most importantly, to turn the view back towards the home and its architectural lines.

The pavilion was also designed to impose a hanging-ceiling effect and draw on the contemporary lines of the home. Cut-outs in the walls allow the garden to grow through,

Chill Out

BELLA VISTA

blending with the space. Hardwood timber decking was installed to provide a relaxing change to the tiled surround of the pool. The simplicity of the lounge setting provides the perfect 'chill out' space.

Between the pavilion and the home is a swimming pool designed to catch the reflection of the two-storey glass windows at the rear of the home. The pool has a 45-degree bend to allow for a greater body of water and room for the pavilion in the corner of the property. A large blade wall was installed at the end of the pool to provide complete privacy from neighbouring properties while the owners are swimming or entertaining, along with providing a room outside.

The planting selection enhances the relaxed nature of the project and the lush theme the clients desired. Taking into consideration the environment of this location, the design

SCREEN PLANTING

LAWN

SELECTED FEATURE TREE

STEPPING STONES

STEPPING STONES THROUGH WATER

OUTDOOR PAVILION

LOUNGE AREA

TIMBER DECK

DECO GRANITE PATH

BBQ

DINING AREA

POOL

PROPOSED RESIDENCE

0   5M

incorporates plants such as giant bird of paradise (*Strelitzia nicolai*), grey star ctenanthe (*Ctenanthe setosa* 'Grey Star'), slender weavers bamboo (*Bambusa textilis* 'Gracilis'), turf lily (*Liriope muscari*) and Japanese sago palm (*Cycas revoluta*).

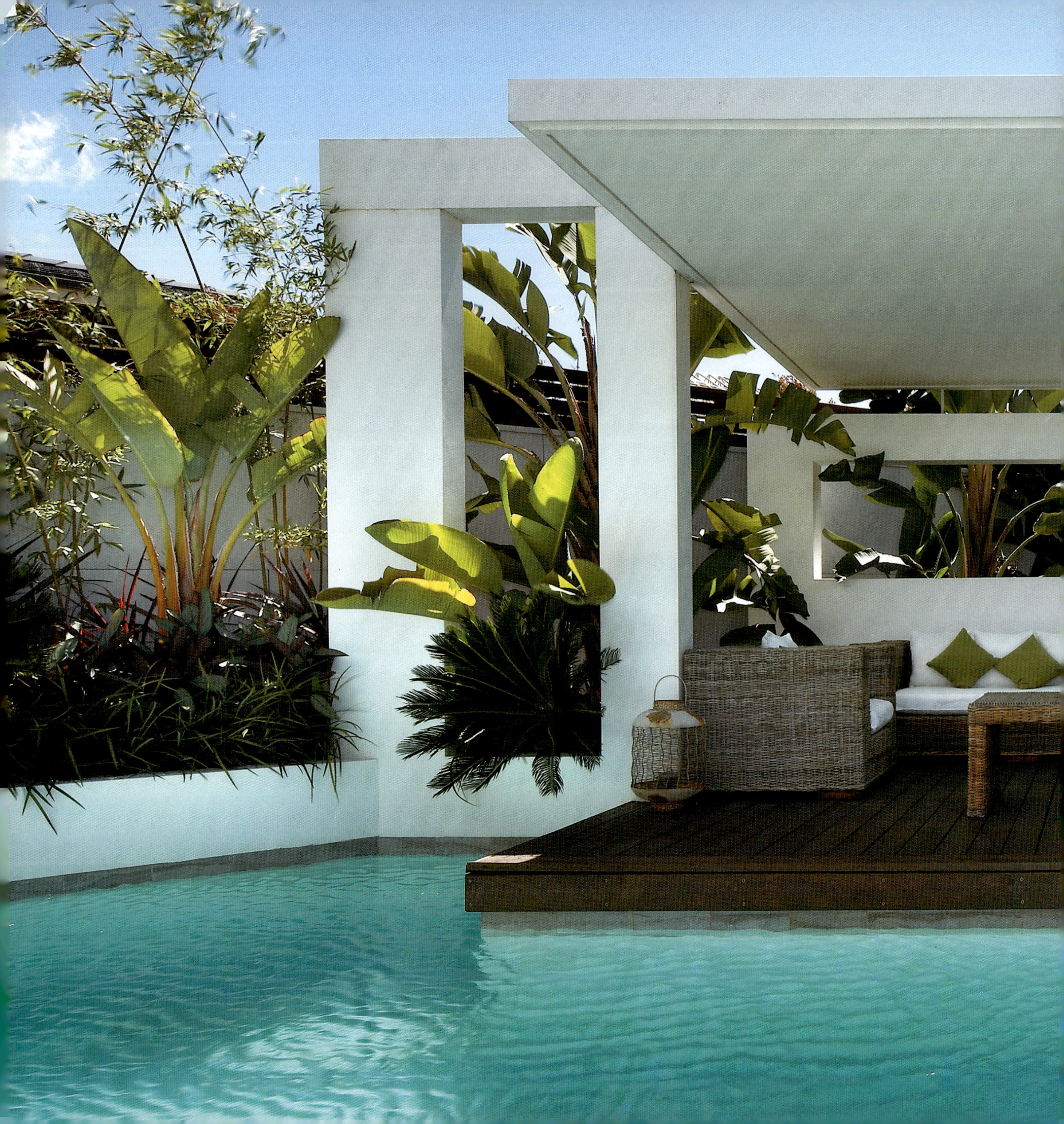

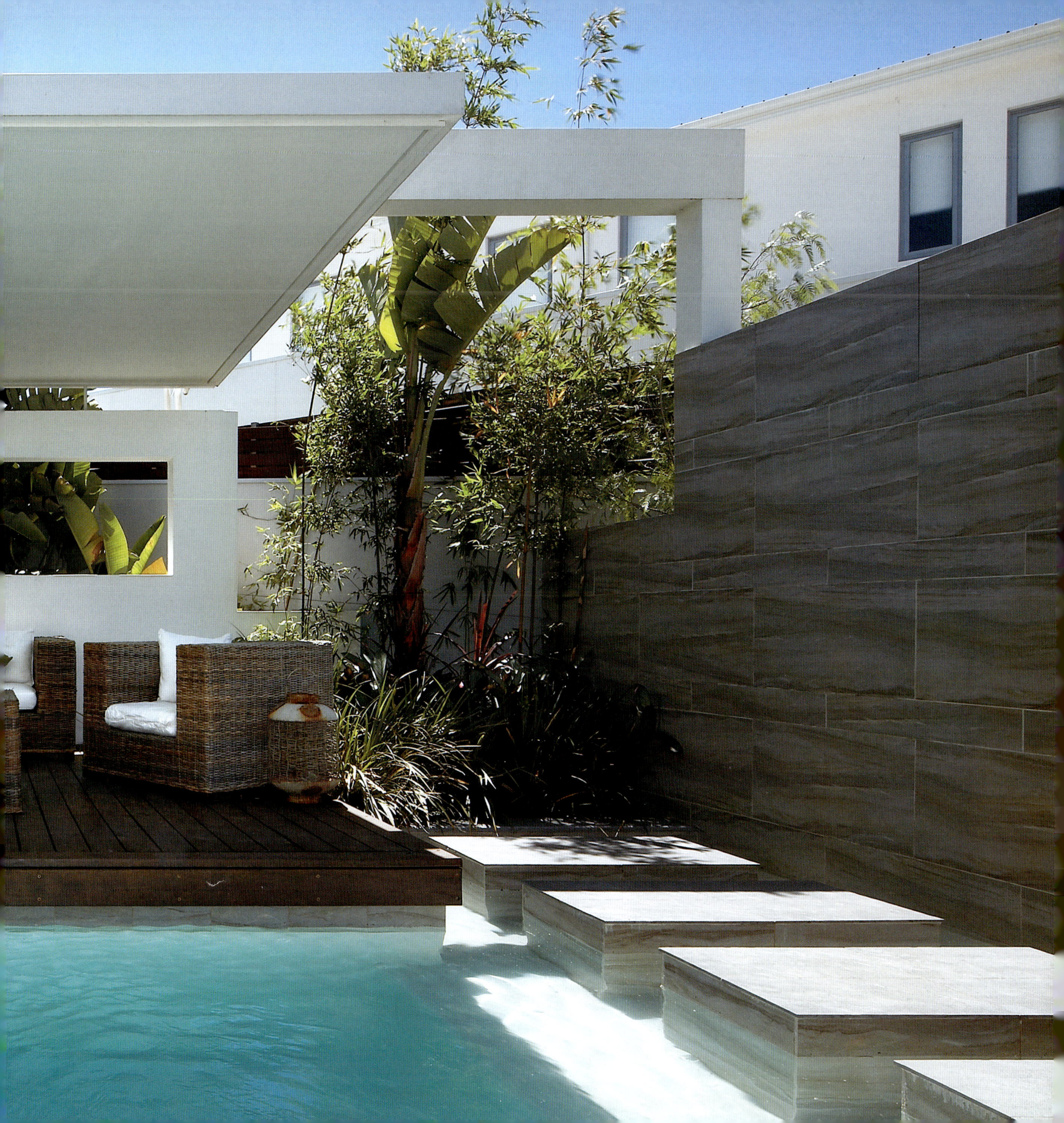

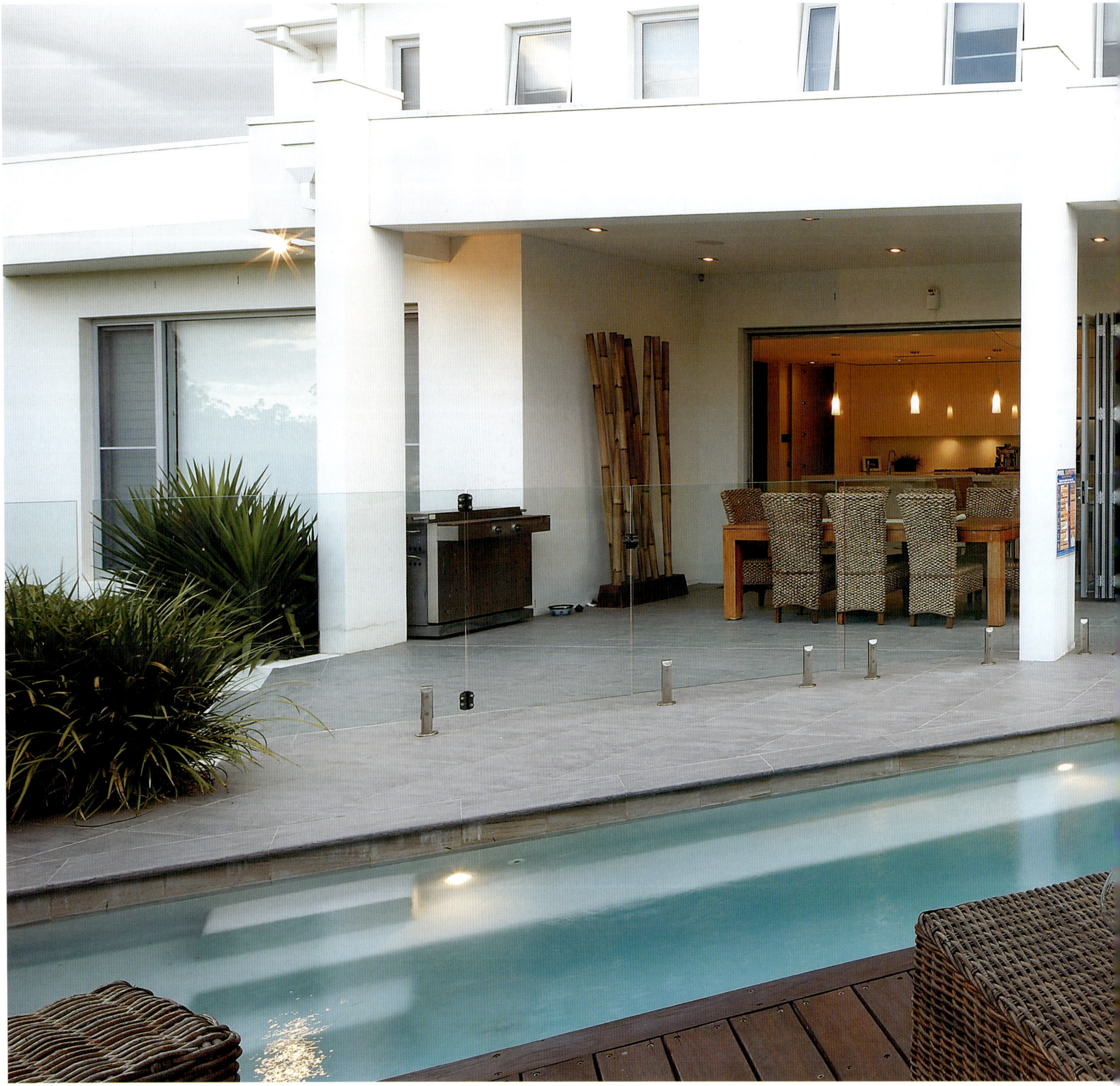

CHILL OUT 185

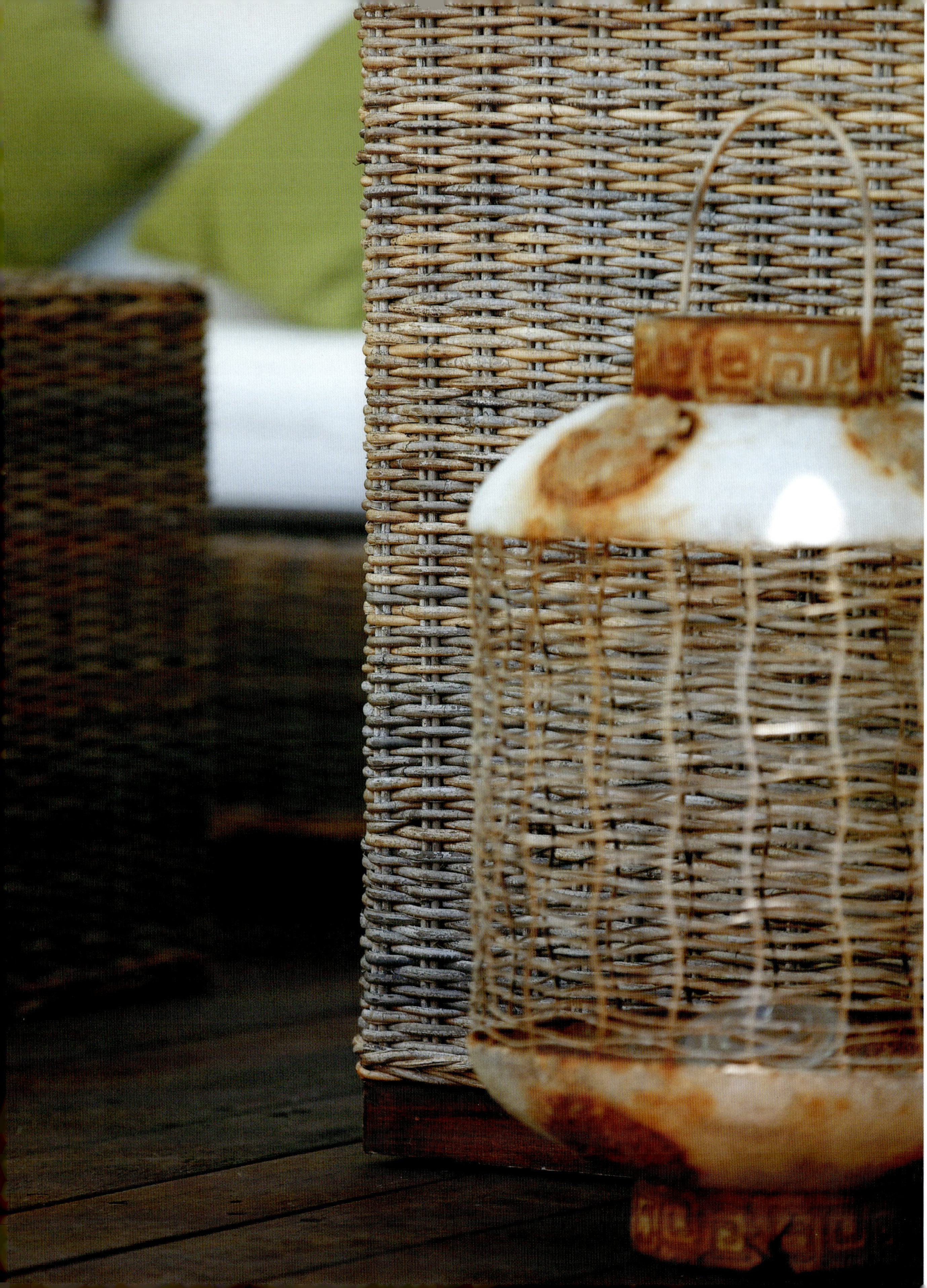
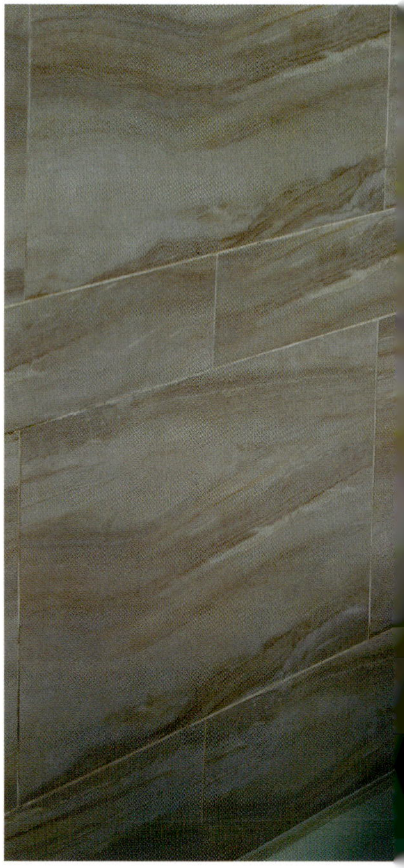

CHILL OUT 187

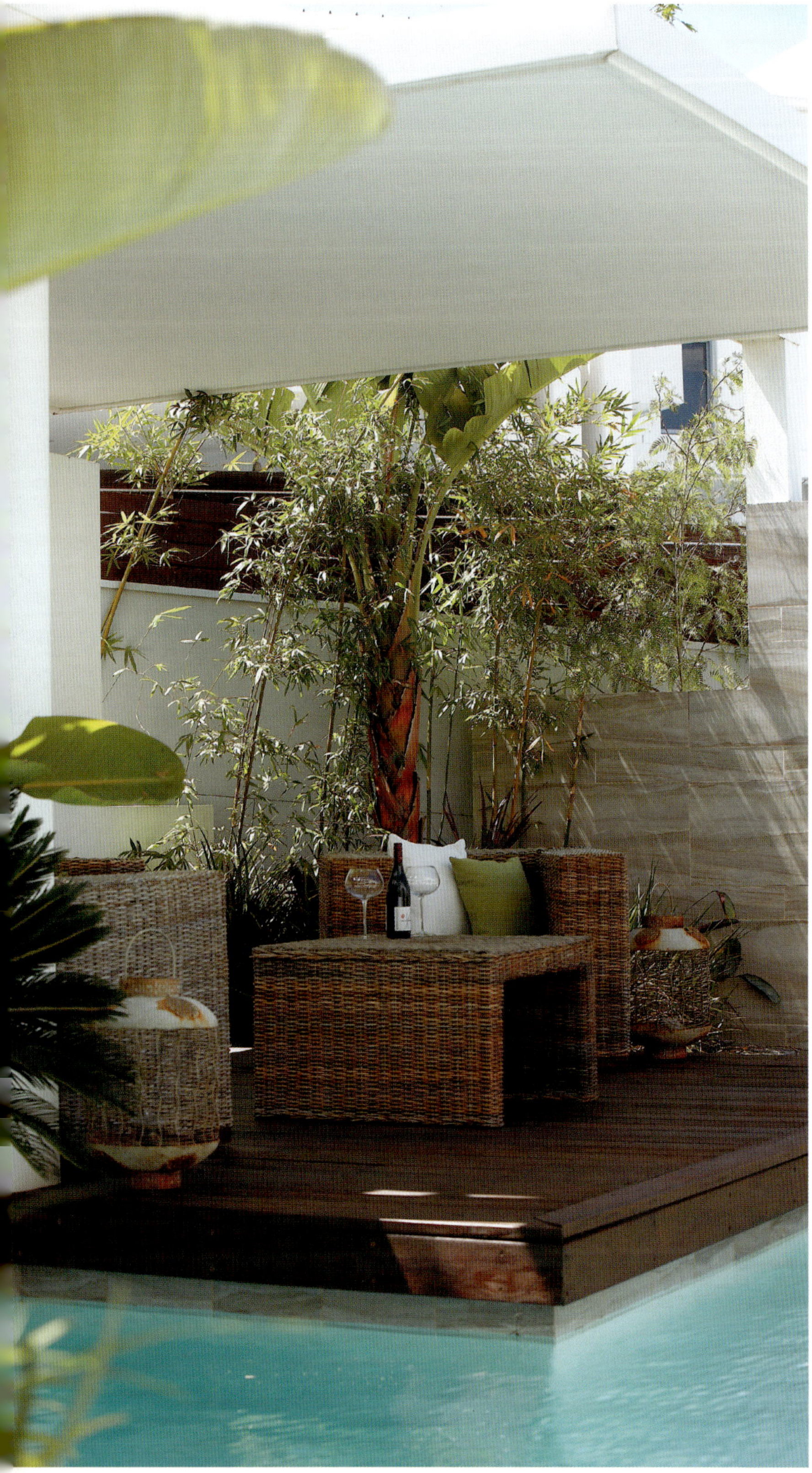

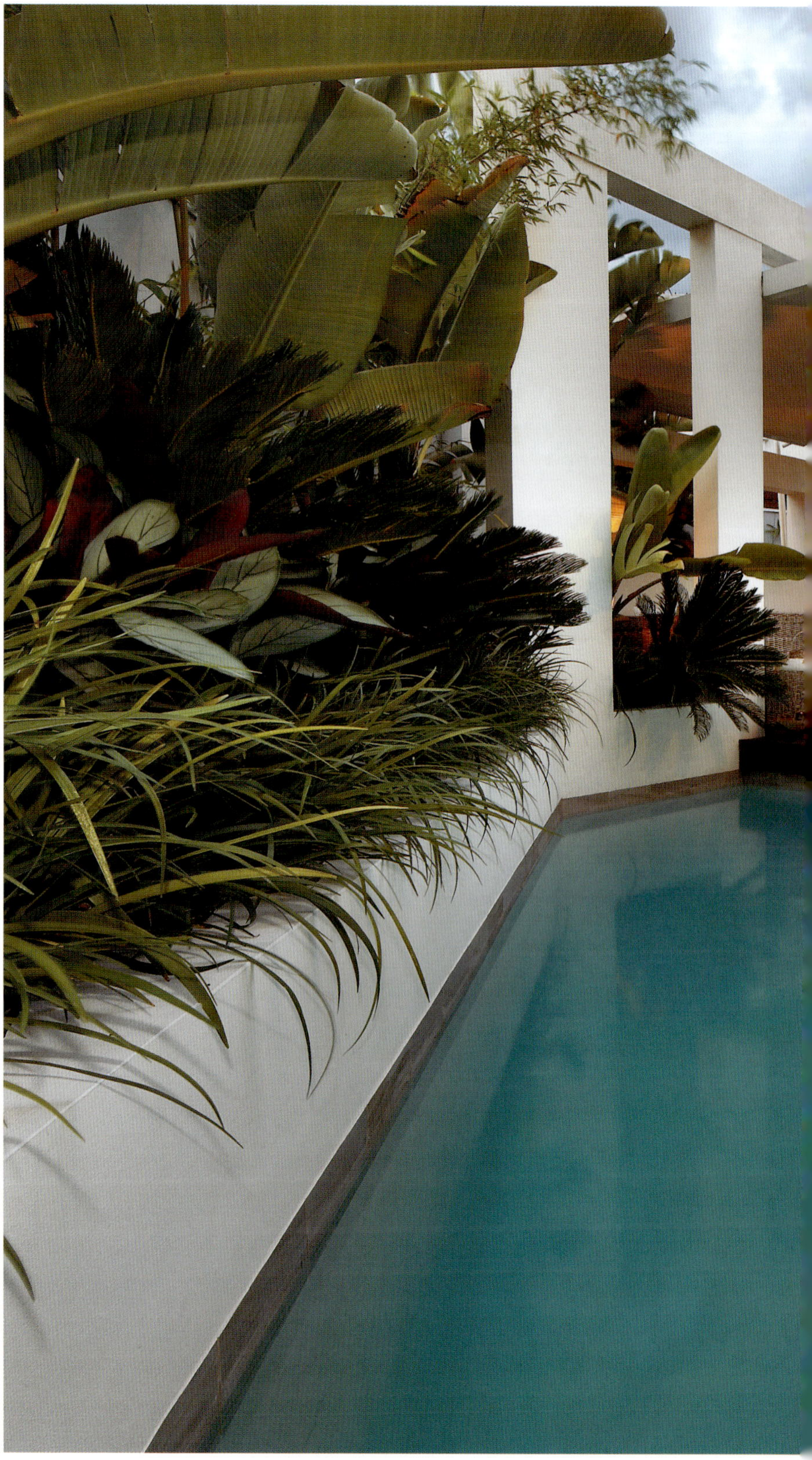

CHILL OUT 189

It is a distinct advantage to come into a project while the house is still in the early design phase. In this instance, entering the project at its preliminary stage gave me the opportunity to influence the design of a proposed ensuite and enhance it with the addition of an outdoor bathroom.

The main focus was to create an environment for pure relaxation. From a dark tile finish in the internal bathroom, a distinct change in material created a definitive day spa style in the outdoor area. Taking inspiration from the internal shape of the room, the view stretches from the indoors to the outdoors to draw you into the space.

A hardwood timber boardwalk, with all other items branching off it, enhances the strong lines of the room.

Boardwalk Bathing

DURAL

At the end of the boardwalk sits the outdoor bath, with clumping bamboo on either side. Two hardwood timber beams overhead conceal the outdoor shower plumbing and enable the showerhead to be placed centrally. Drainage is set under the decking to allow water to pass through when the shower is in use. For privacy, the space is surrounded by rendered and painted masonry walls that work in with the architecture of the house.

An atmosphere of rest and relaxation is the focus when planting for an outdoor bathroom. This unique opportunity allowed for the use of soft and lush plantings such as slender weavers bamboo (*Bambusa textilis* 'Gracilis'), grey star ctenanthe (*Ctenanthe setosa* 'Grey Star'), bromeliads (*Bromeliad* spp.), bird of paradise (*Strelitzia reginae*) and variegated mondo (*Ophiopogon intermedians* 'Stripey White').

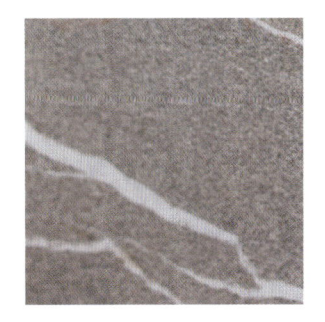

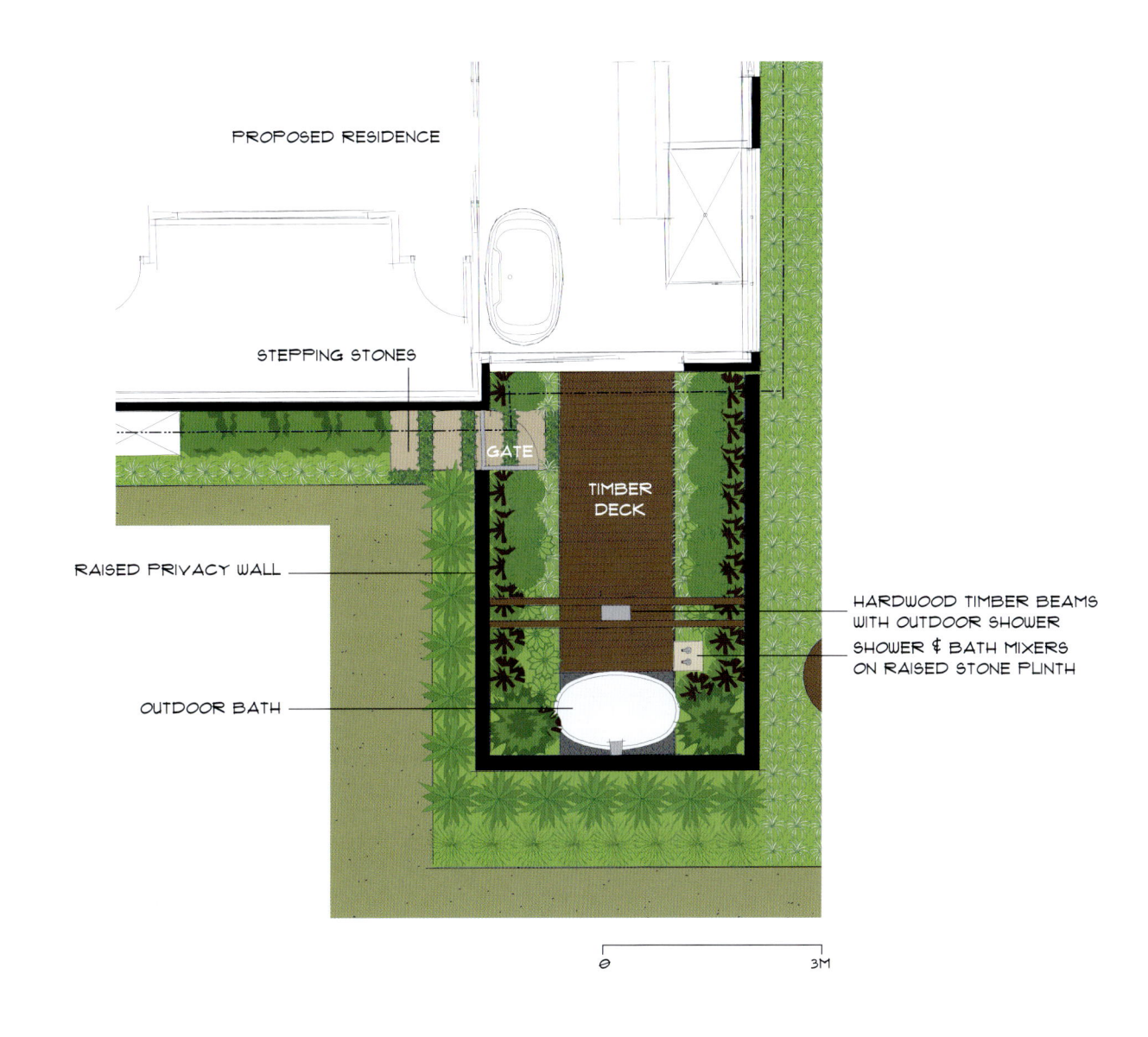

PROPOSED RESIDENCE

STEPPING STONES

GATE

TIMBER DECK

RAISED PRIVACY WALL

HARDWOOD TIMBER BEAMS WITH OUTDOOR SHOWER

SHOWER & BATH MIXERS ON RAISED STONE PLINTH

OUTDOOR BATH

0   3M

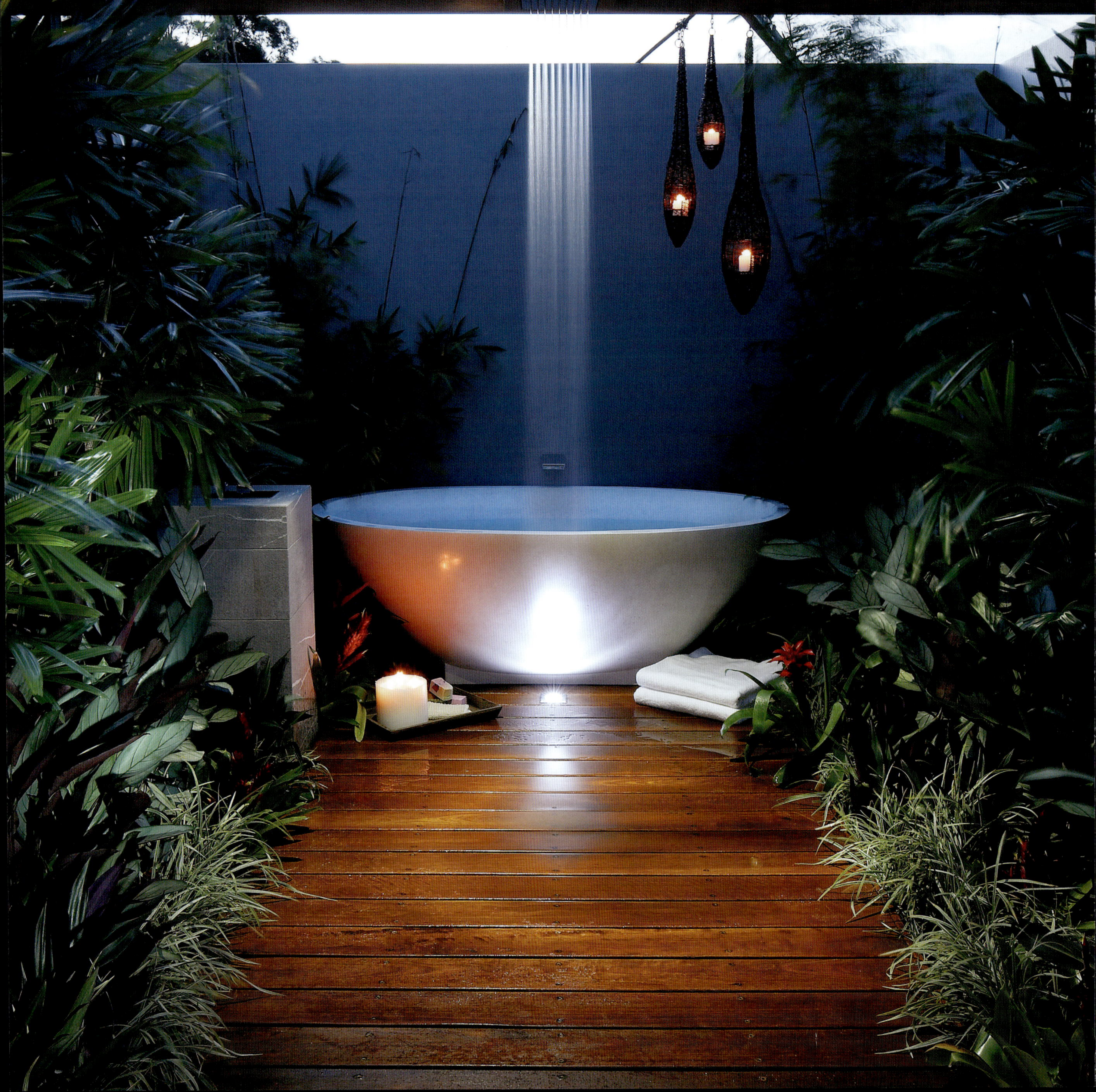

BOARDWALK BATHING 193

To be presented with an undeveloped 5-acre parcel of land and a client who is open to ideas and embraces the value a garden brings to a property can be an exciting opportunity. The success of this garden will be determined by its ability to handle the climatic changes each season brings, while blending harmoniously with the surrounding bushland.

With the fall of the land, the opportunity to collect, manage and reuse water on the property was a key component of the design and influenced how various elements were placed around it. This included the design and installation of two large dams with a combined holding capacity of more than 1 million litres of water. Both dams were constructed with an adjoining creek bed that acts as a large water feature,

On The Green

KENTHURST

allowing water to run down the streams before surging over the stone-clad walls. In addition to the beautiful visual effect of this structure, it is also the life-source of the entire property. Water is collected for storage from hard surfaces, including the roof of the house, along with swale catchment areas on the broad lawns. The irrigation system draws water from the dam feeds it to the surrounding plants and large lawn areas, making the property completely self-supportive for future growth.

With the goal of creating a natural landscape, material selection was key to the design process. Where possible, reclaimed rock from the site was used to line the dam, while the remaining material was brought in to line the edges of the stream. The landscape includes a four-hole golf course complete with manicured greens and bunkers.

The placement of the greens ensures a close interaction with the feature dams and creeks as players walk from hole to hole.

The plant selection matches the natural surroundings and existing mature trees on site, such as eucalypts, with other selected trees, such as honey locust (*Gleditsia tricanthos*) and a peppercorn tree (*Schinus molle* 'Areira'). Grasses including knobby club rush (*Ficinia nodosa*), fountain grass (*Pennisetum alopecuroides* and *P. advena* 'Rubrum') and border silver flax lily (*Dianella* 'Border Silver'), along with shrubs, coastal rosemary (*Westringia fruticosa*) and Florida gardenia (*Gardenia augusta* 'Florida') add another level to the landscape. Each plant provides a different form of colour and texture.

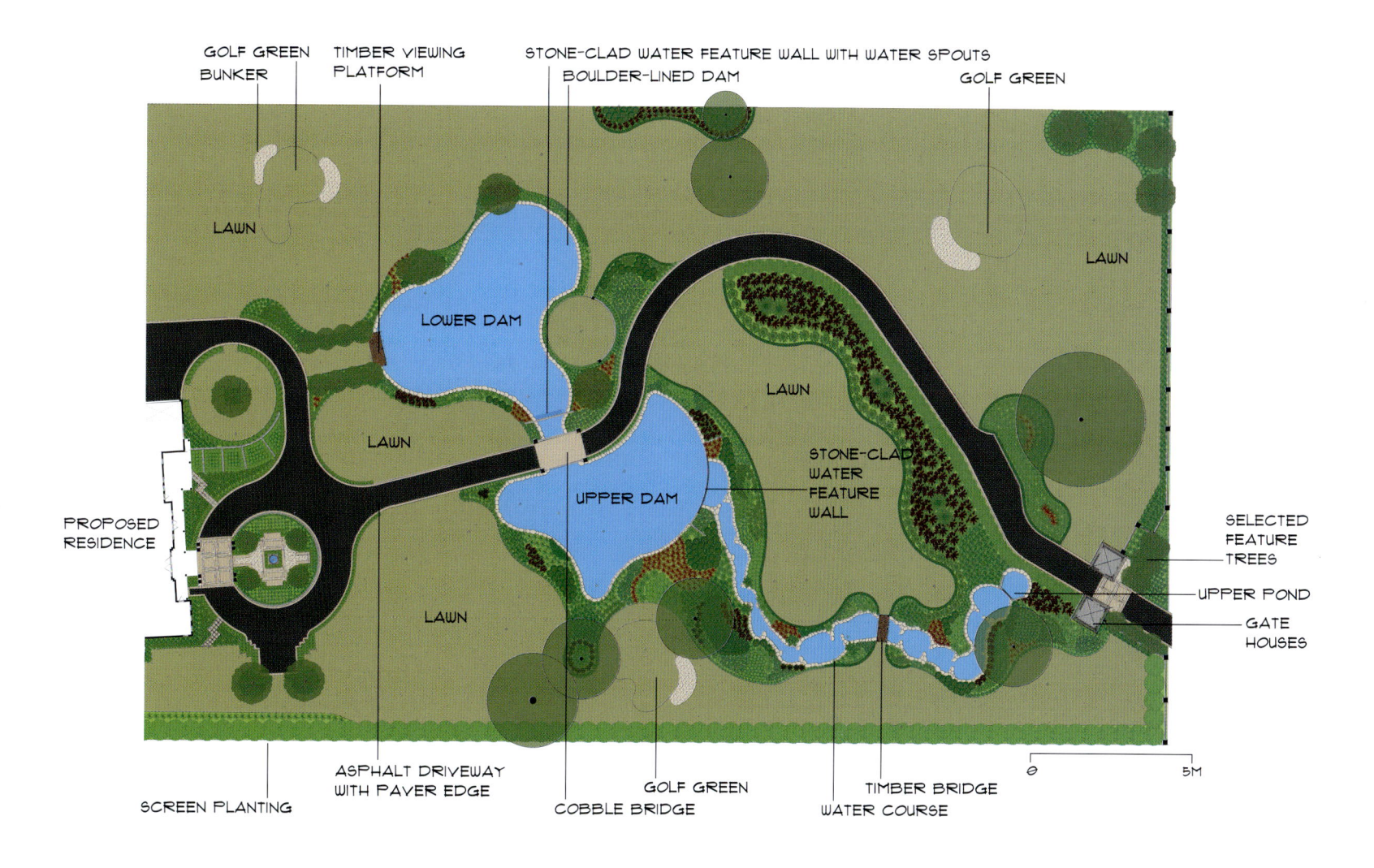

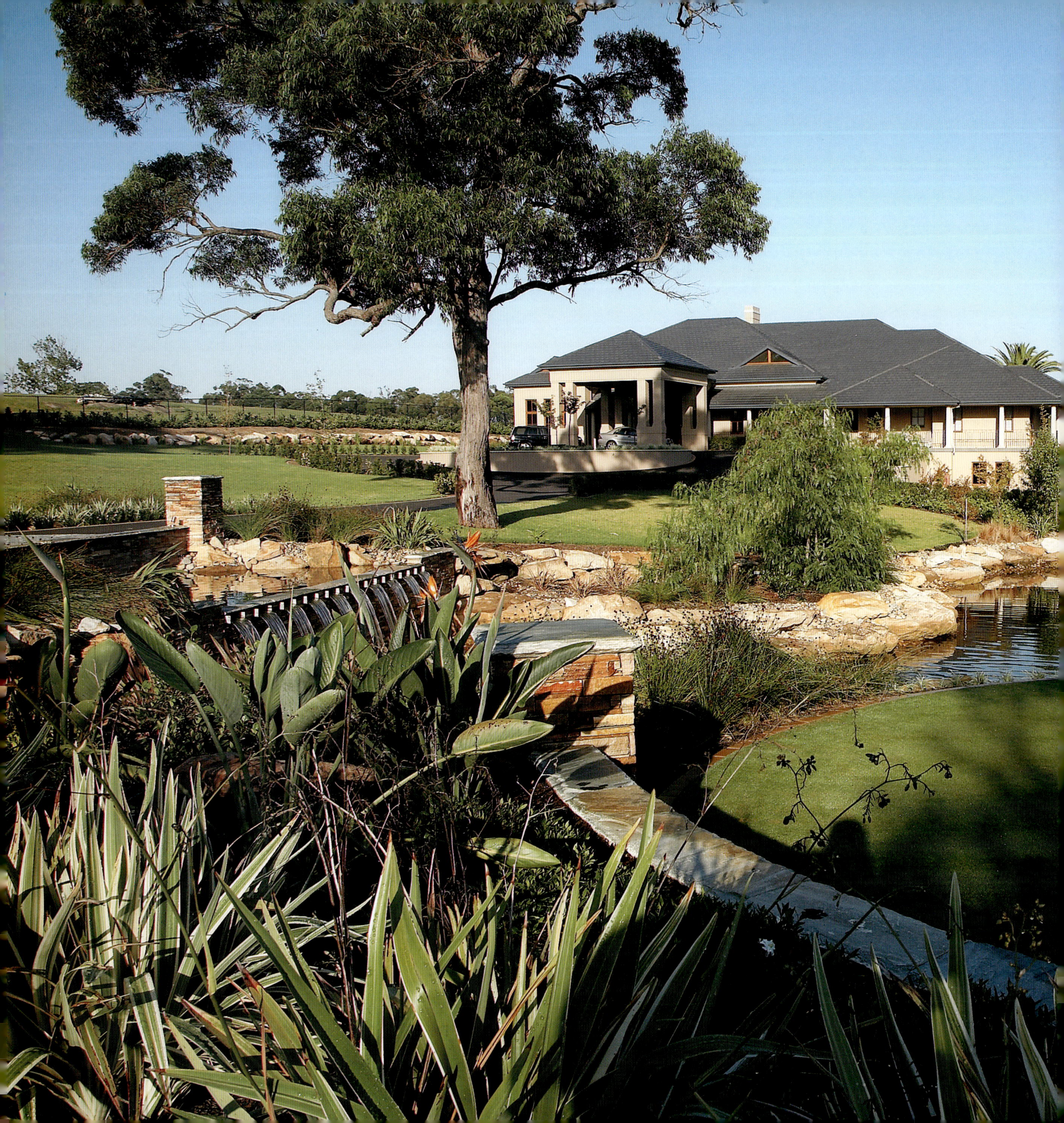

ON THE GREEN 197

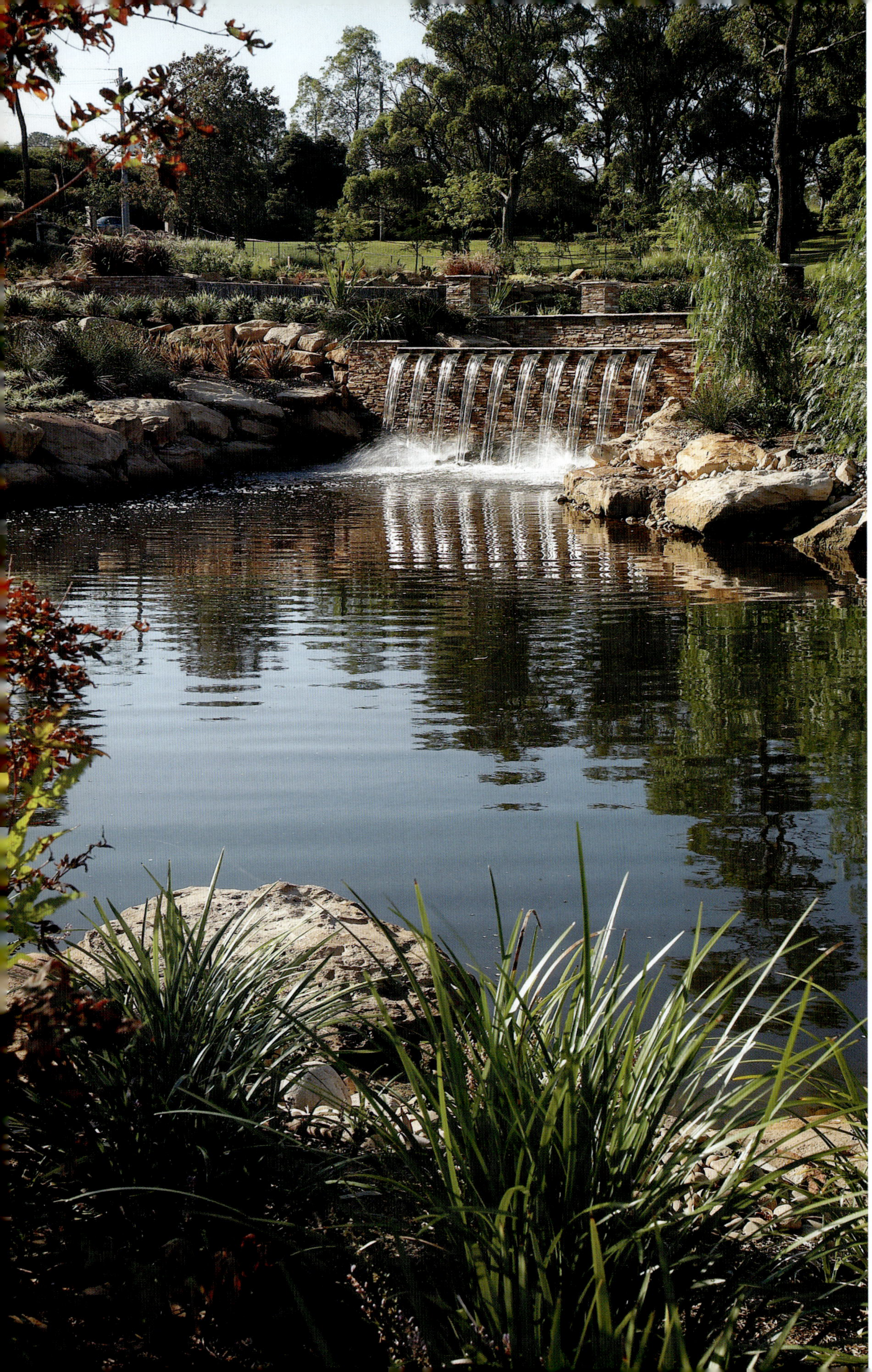

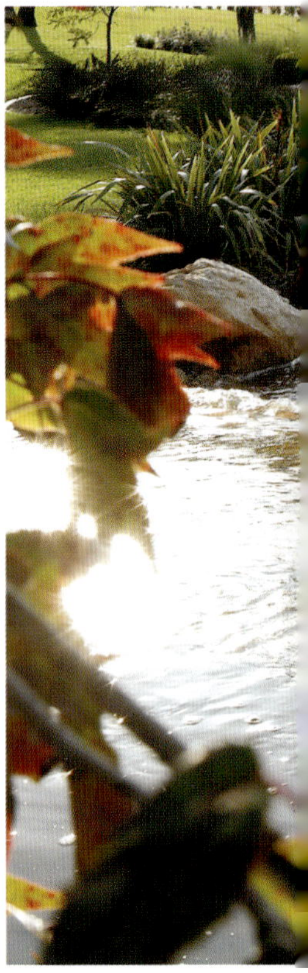

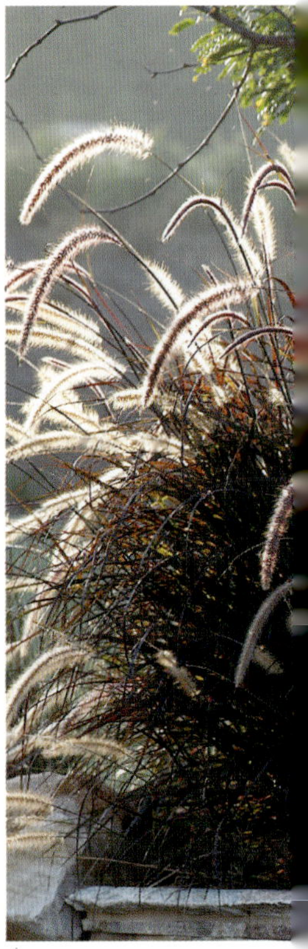

ON THE GREEN 199

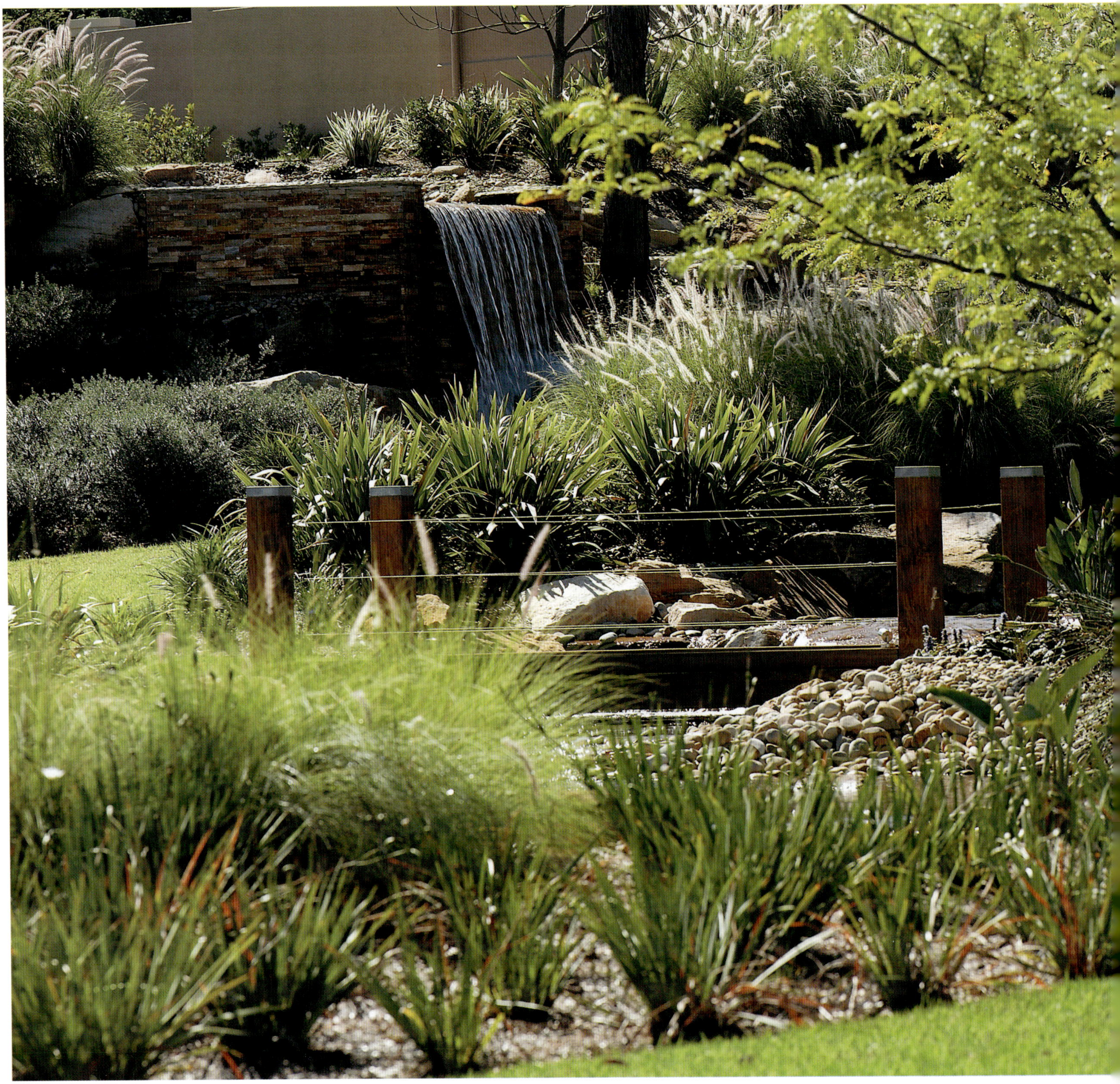

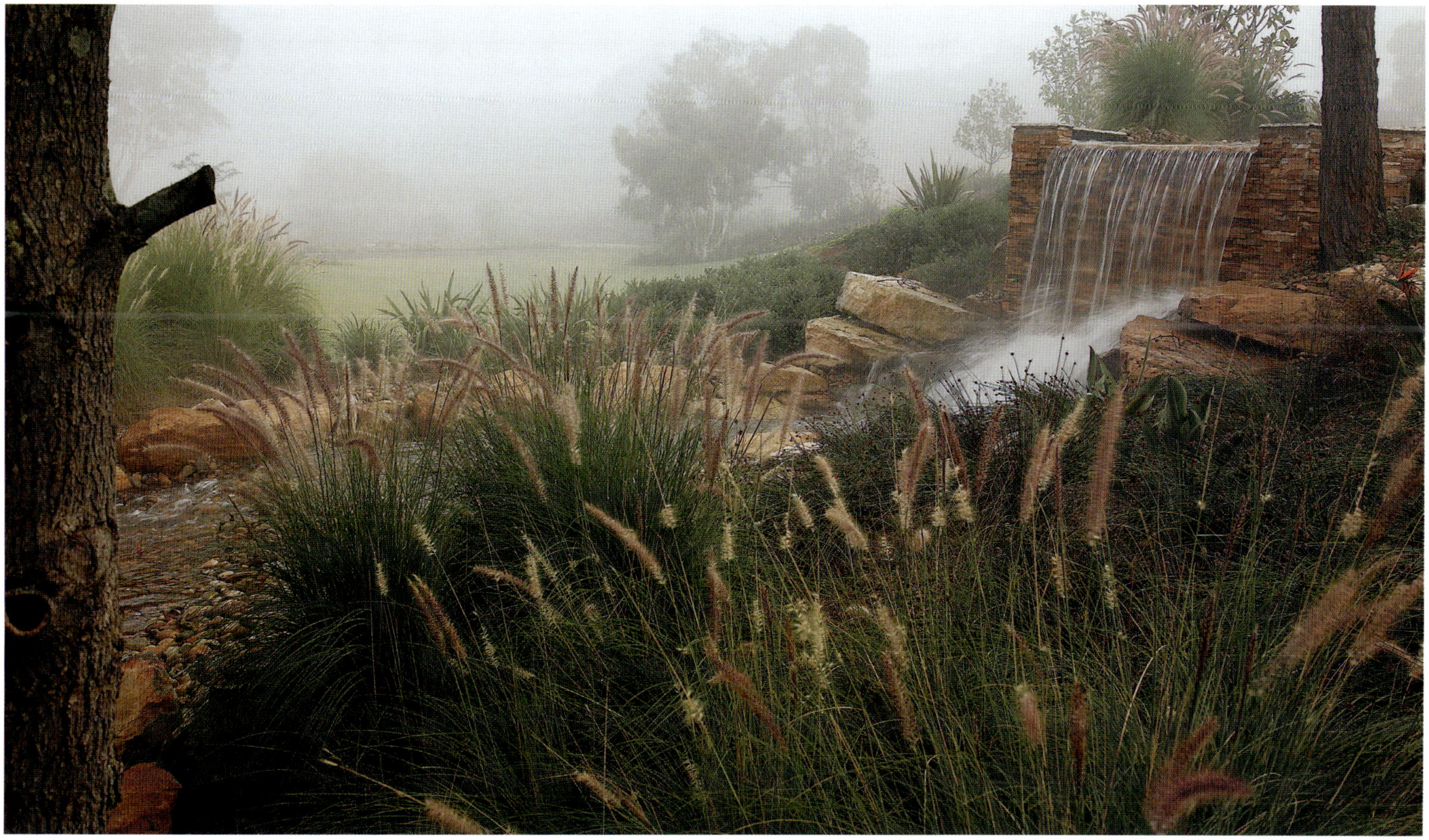

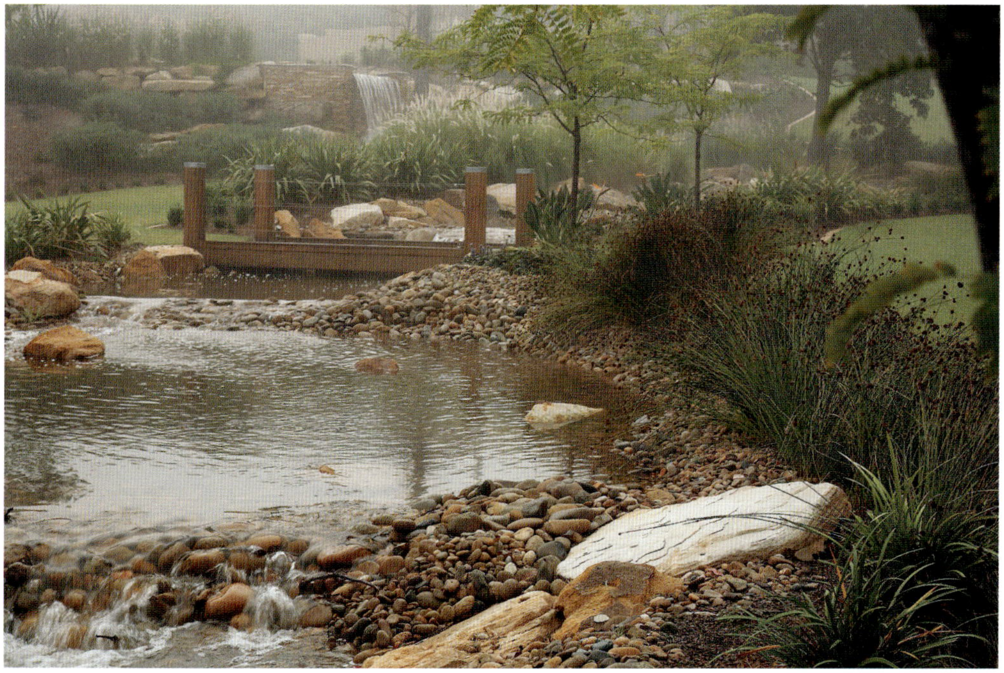

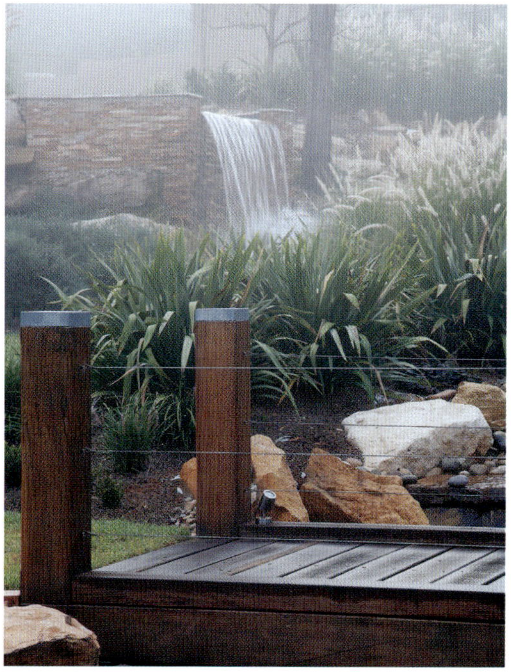

Hanging Out

SYDNEY

From time to time I get the opportunity to produce a display garden, similar to the larger show gardens that we have produced in Sydney, Melbourne and London. Display gardens are unique as there is no client brief to take into consideration and I have complete freedom to design a space of my choosing with a selection of materials that I feel will best communicate the message of the space.

My desire for this particular space was to evoke a discerning mood, not only when viewing it, but most importantly, when moving within it. This was achieved through the design, but mostly revealed by the products and colours selected. The three main colours of this space are: silver, which took in the stainless steel elements of the dining table and stools along with the grey tones of the floor tiles; lime-green plant material; and the stunning rust colour of the Cor-ten steel. Working together, these colours confer a smooth tone on the space and create a platform to be dressed with table settings and soft furnishings.

The function of the space is in common with most outdoor living areas and the requirements of cooking, dining and relaxing. A small outdoor kitchen was installed on one side, with a barbecue, sink and refrigerator, and lush planting overhead. For the dining area, one of my glass water feature tables (designed some time ago) takes pride of place. It not only provides practical use as a table, but also forms the central feature of the garden, with water pouring out of it. The table was engineered to cantilever from a wall, creating a floating effect and enabling it to sit within the landscape. Water is drawn from a lower pond and pumped between two layers of glass, flowing under the plates of diners before pouring out of the end. After the meal, there is the opportunity to retreat to the transparent hanging pod chairs that appear to float in the garden, around the fire pit.

For the planting, specific colours and heights embrace the characteristics of the design. Lush greens are achieved with the use of prickly rasp fern (*Doodia aspera*), lady palm (*Rhapis excelsa*), bird's nest fern (*Asplenium nidus*) and slender weavers bamboo (*Bambusa textilis* 'Gracilis'), while a splash of colour comes with the use of grey star ctenanthe (*Ctenanthe setosa* 'Grey Star') and rhoeo (*Tradescantia spathacea*).

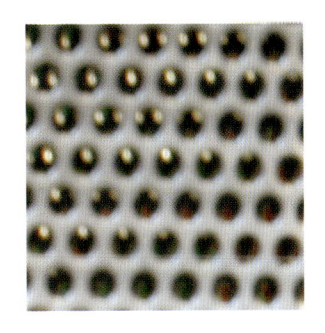

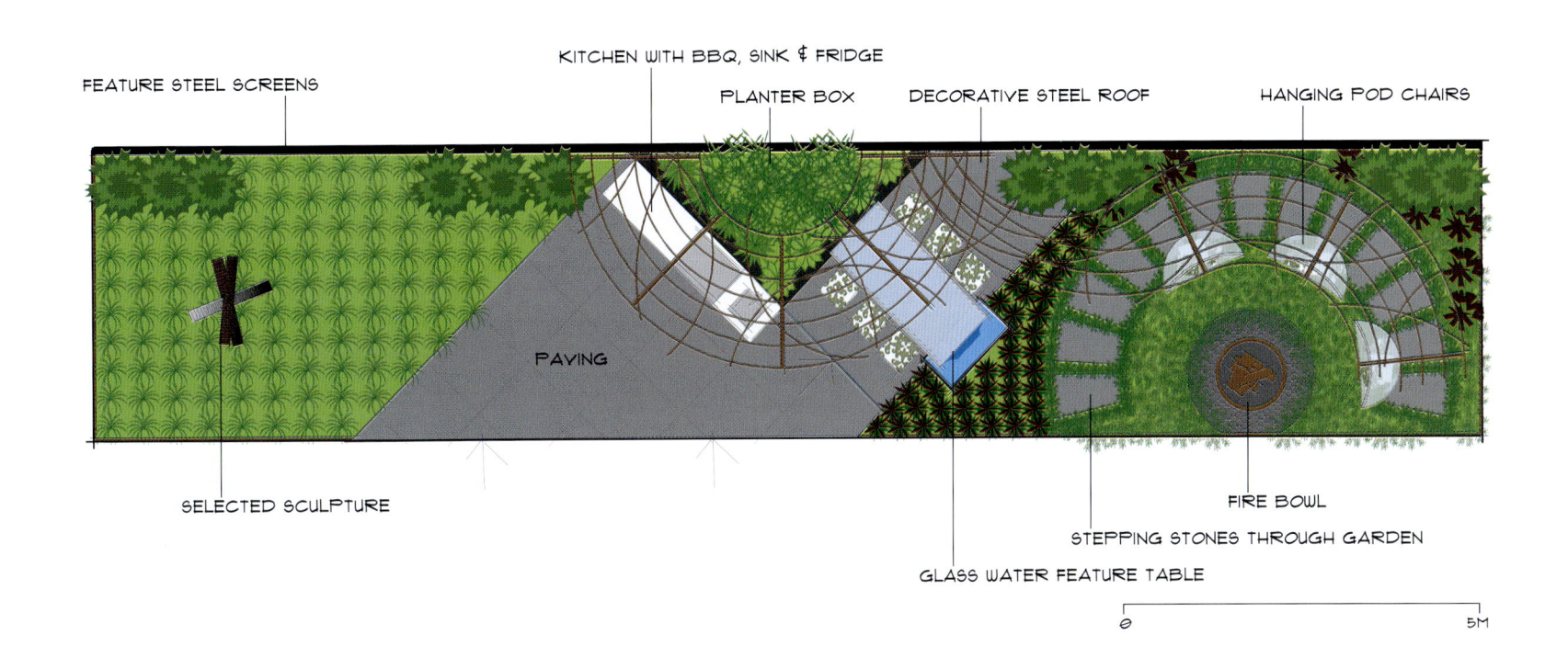

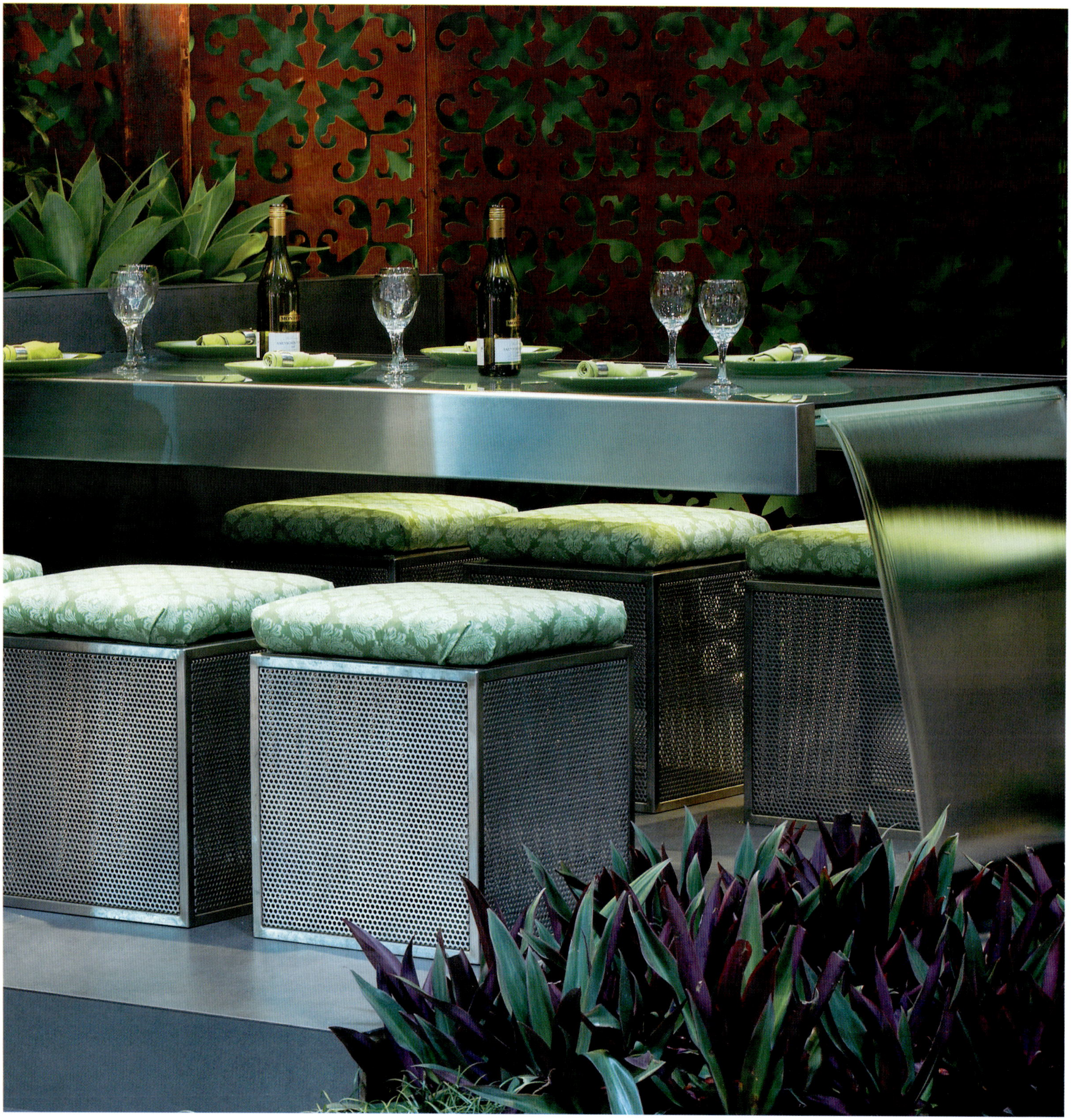

HANGING OUT 205

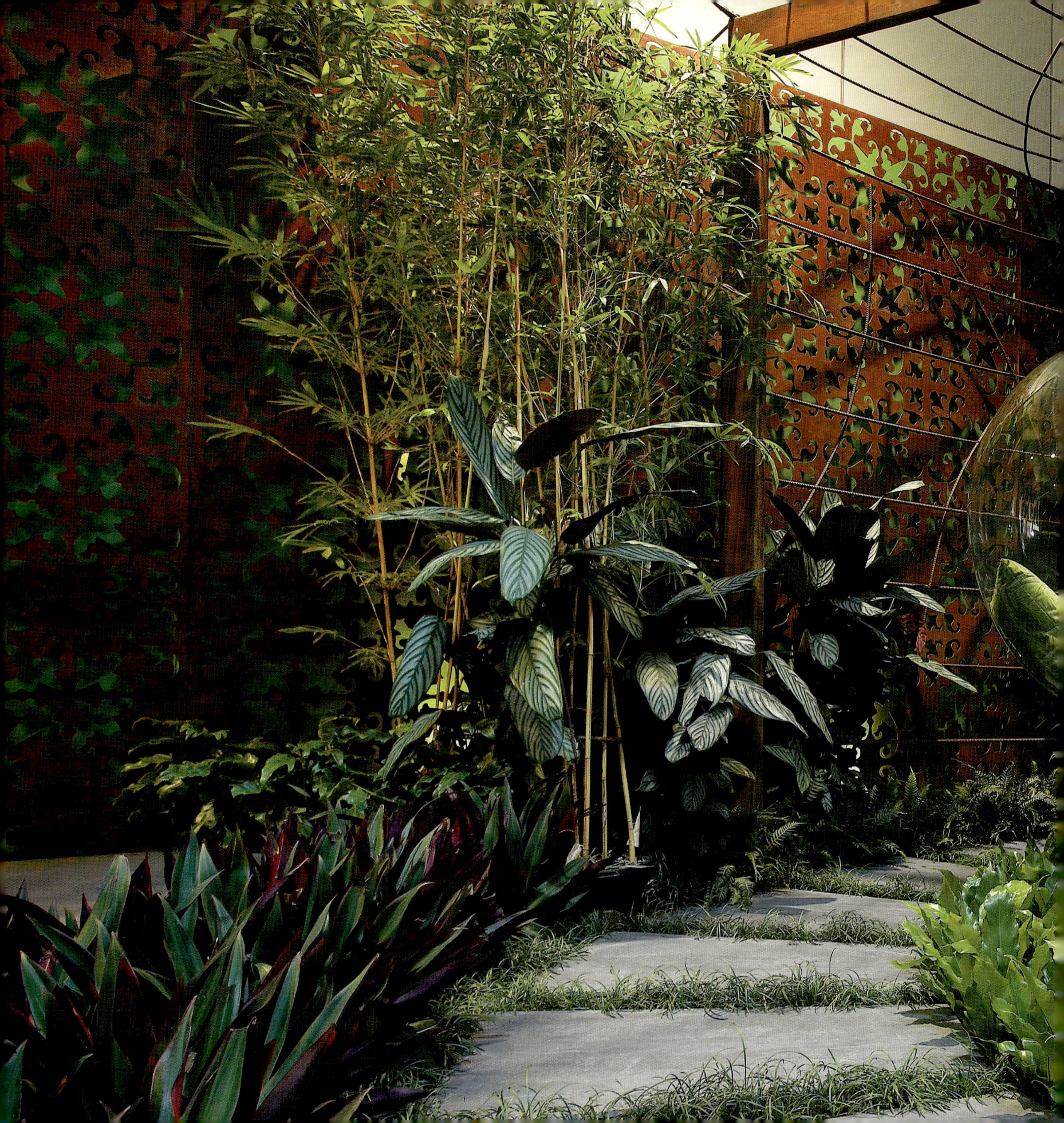

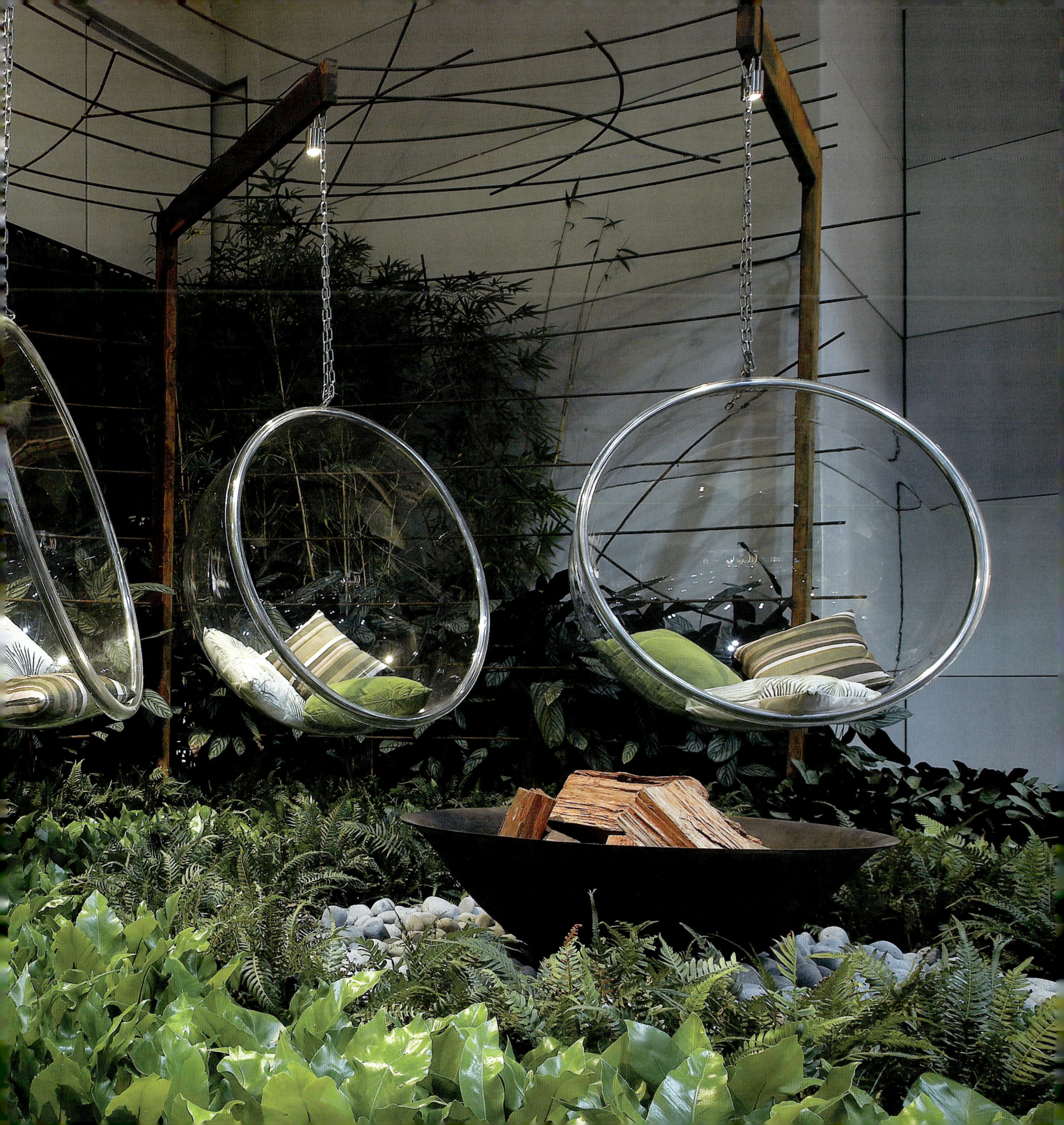

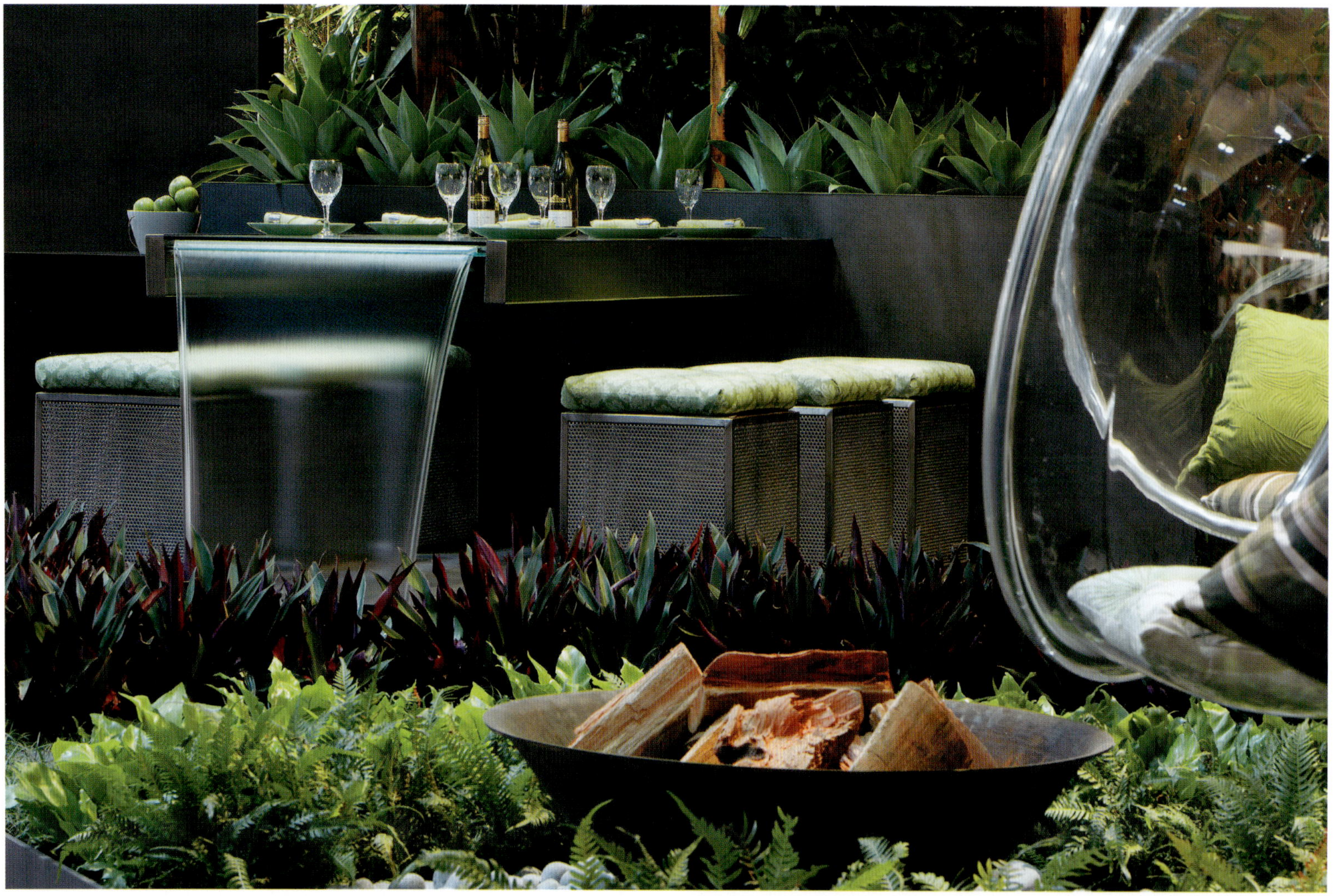

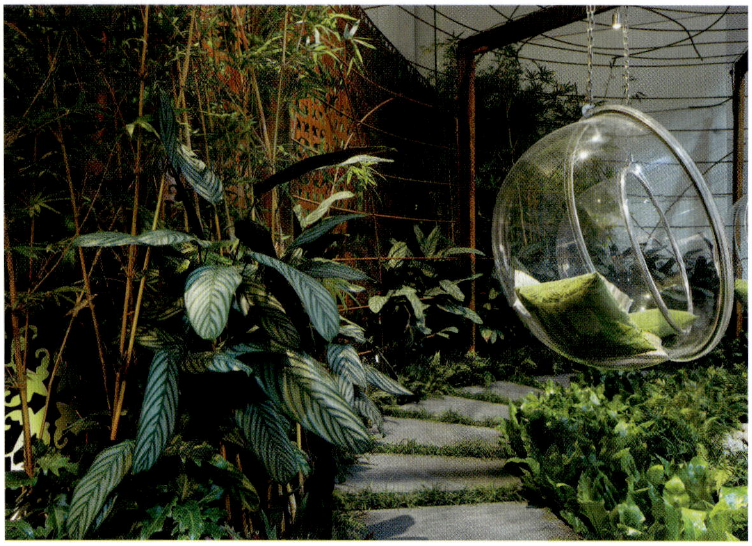

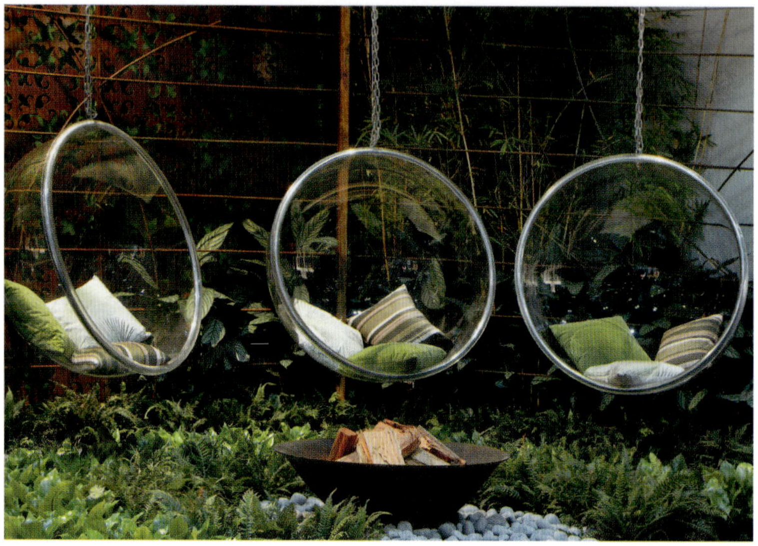

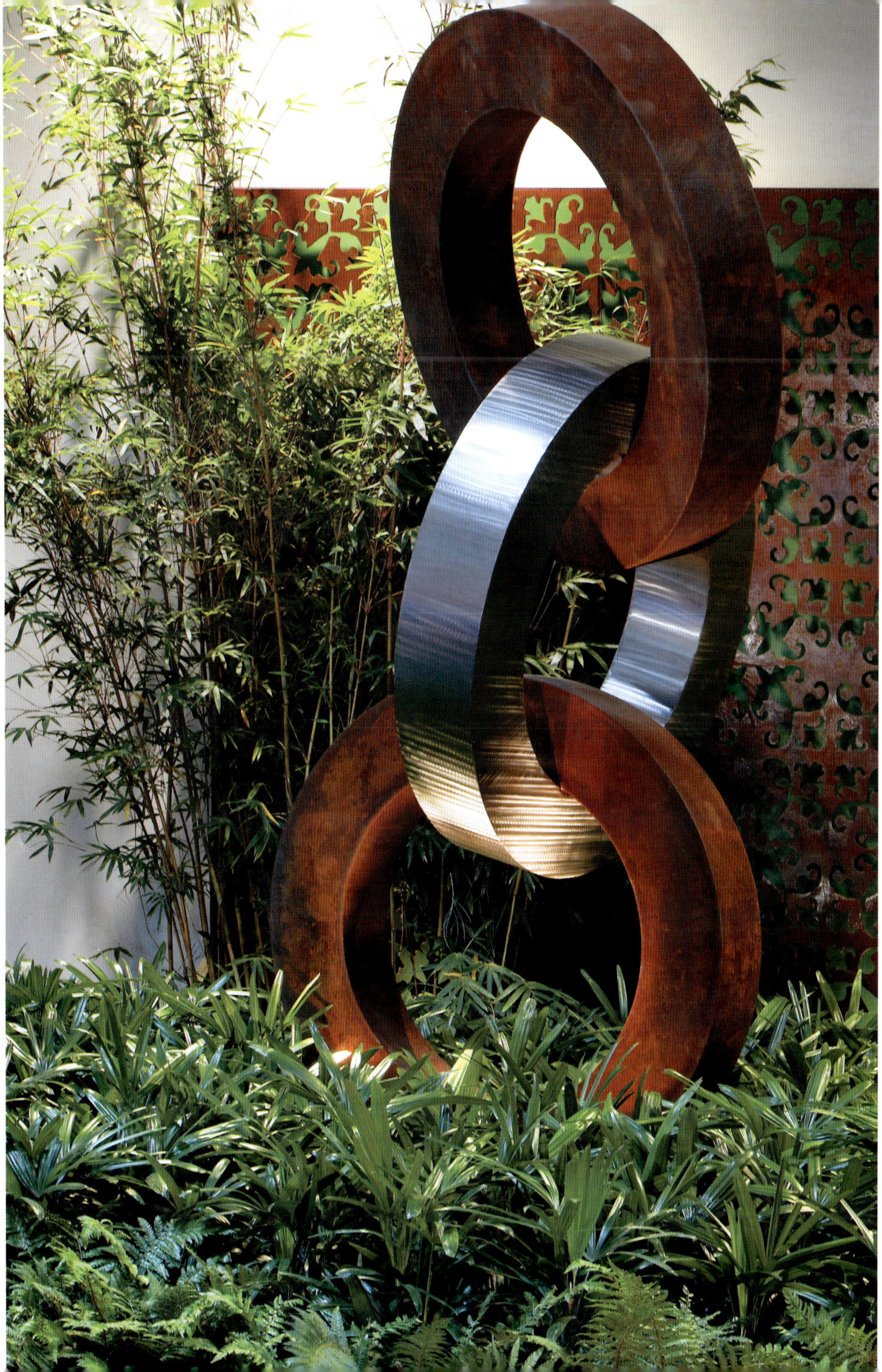

Every so often we are involved in a project that seems challenging due to the extreme site conditions. The challenges of this site actually turned out to be its best assets, which enabled the design team – for both the house and the landscape – to explore and express interesting and unusual solutions.

This site has a large rock shelf weaving its way from the front of the property to the rear. A natural stream that flows rapidly during rainfall crosses just in front of the entry to the house. With the garage set at the front of the house, I suspended a hardwood timber boardwalk over the natural watercourse at the front entry. This boardwalk ranges in height up to 5 metres above the undulating rock shelves

On Edge

ROSEVILLE CHASE

below. The zigzag pattern of the boardwalk provides articulating views on approach the house. A viewing platform was installed midway to protrude over the lower level of foliage and act as a transition point leading to the rear of the garage. With the structure in place, the planting layout will eventually mature to embrace the boardwalk and give a tree-top walk experience. Bangalow palms (*Archontophoenix cunninghamiana*) were planted to provide height and create a canopy. Mass plantings of ornamental ginger (*Alpinia* spp.) and grey star ctenanthe (*Ctenanthe setosa* 'Grey Star'), along with rough tree ferns (*Cyathea australis*) and New Zealand flax (*Phormium tenax*) perform their role as the ground-level foliage.

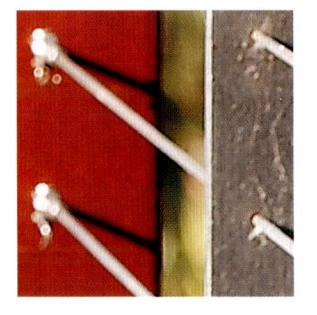

By the front door, a bluestone-clad blade wall was installed to provide a location for the entry statement of a slumped-glass water feature. On the other side of this wall sits the swimming pool, which was built in conjunction with the house so that the water laps against it. Due to the lie of the land, the pool is designed to project over the rock shelf with an infinity edge – a truly dramatic inclusion. A large mirror was inserted on the poolside of the blade wall; this serves to reflect the large jacaranda tree (*Jacaranda mimosifolia*) back to the sight line from the kitchen, inside the home. Positioned below the mirror are three stainless steel water spouts that provide a sight-and-sound experience to be enjoyed whether inside or out.

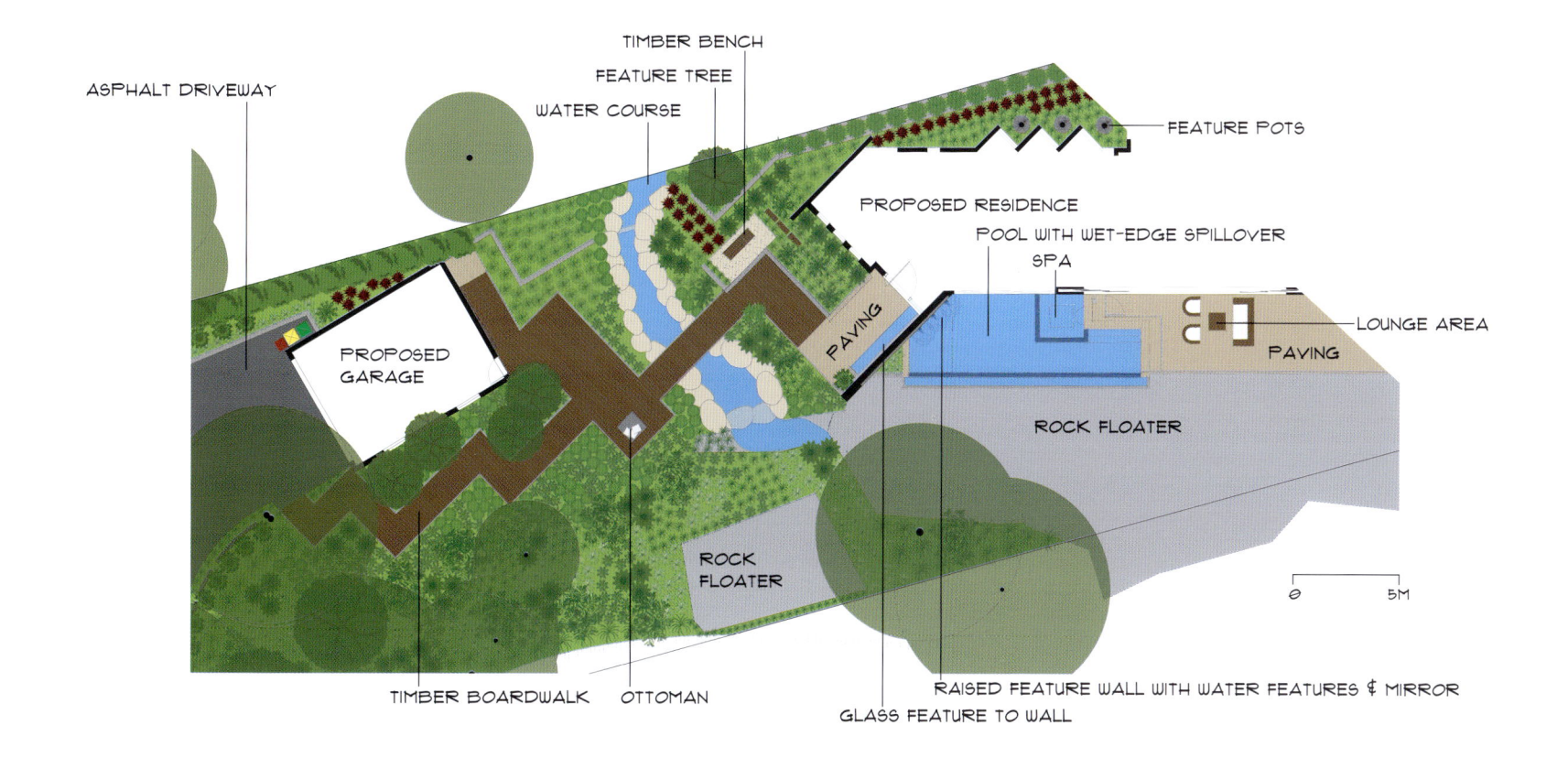

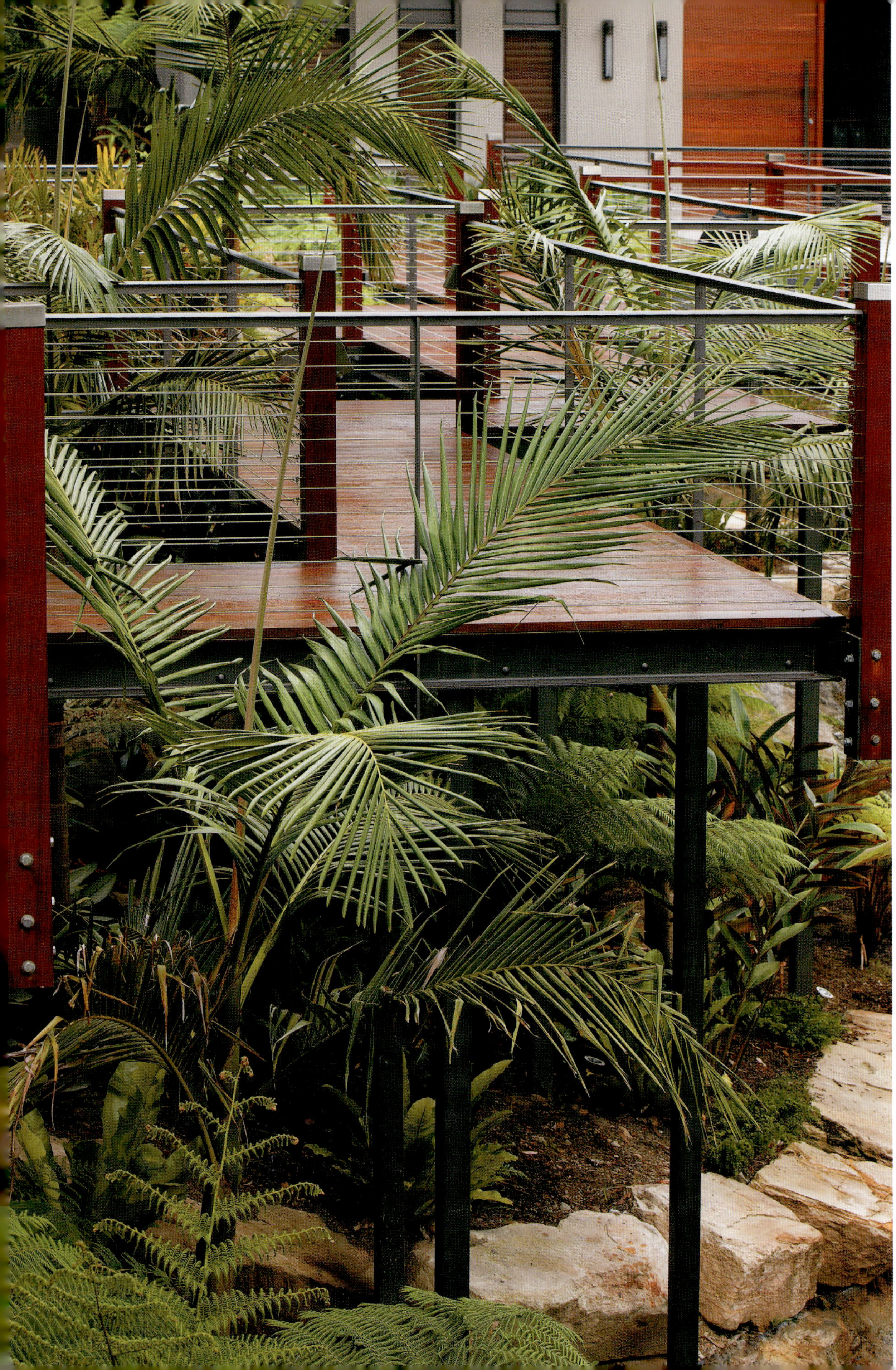

ON EDGE

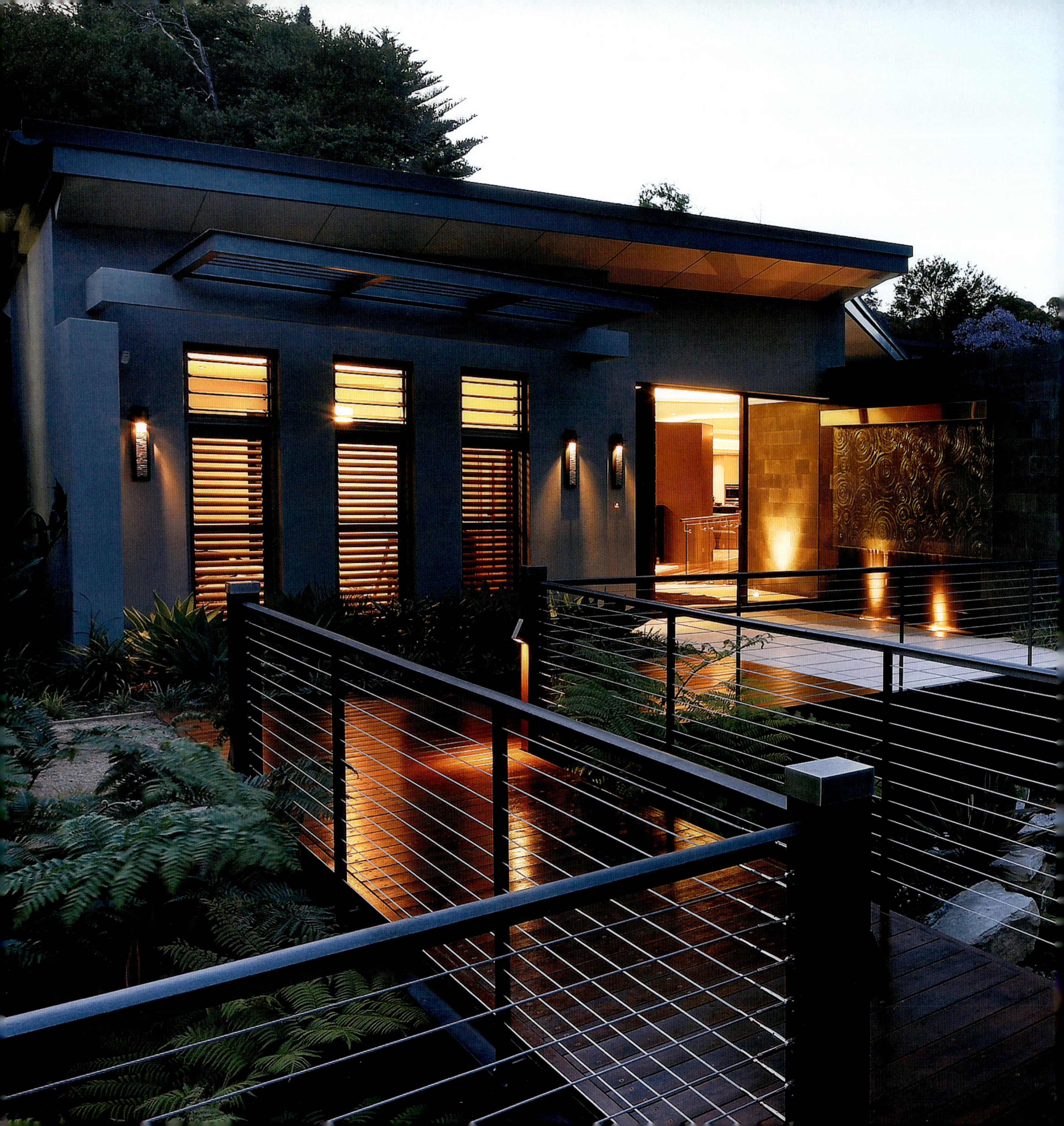

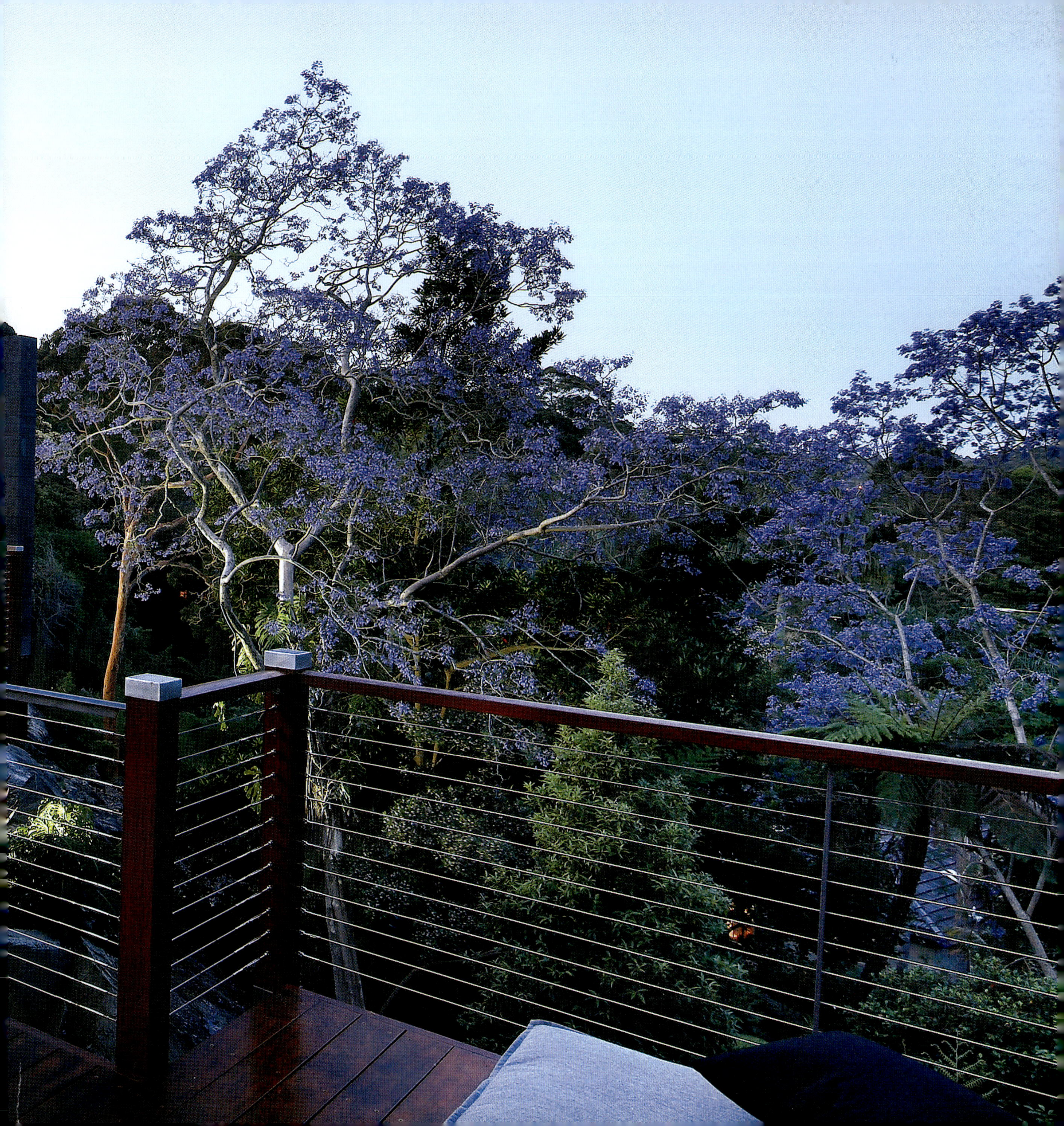

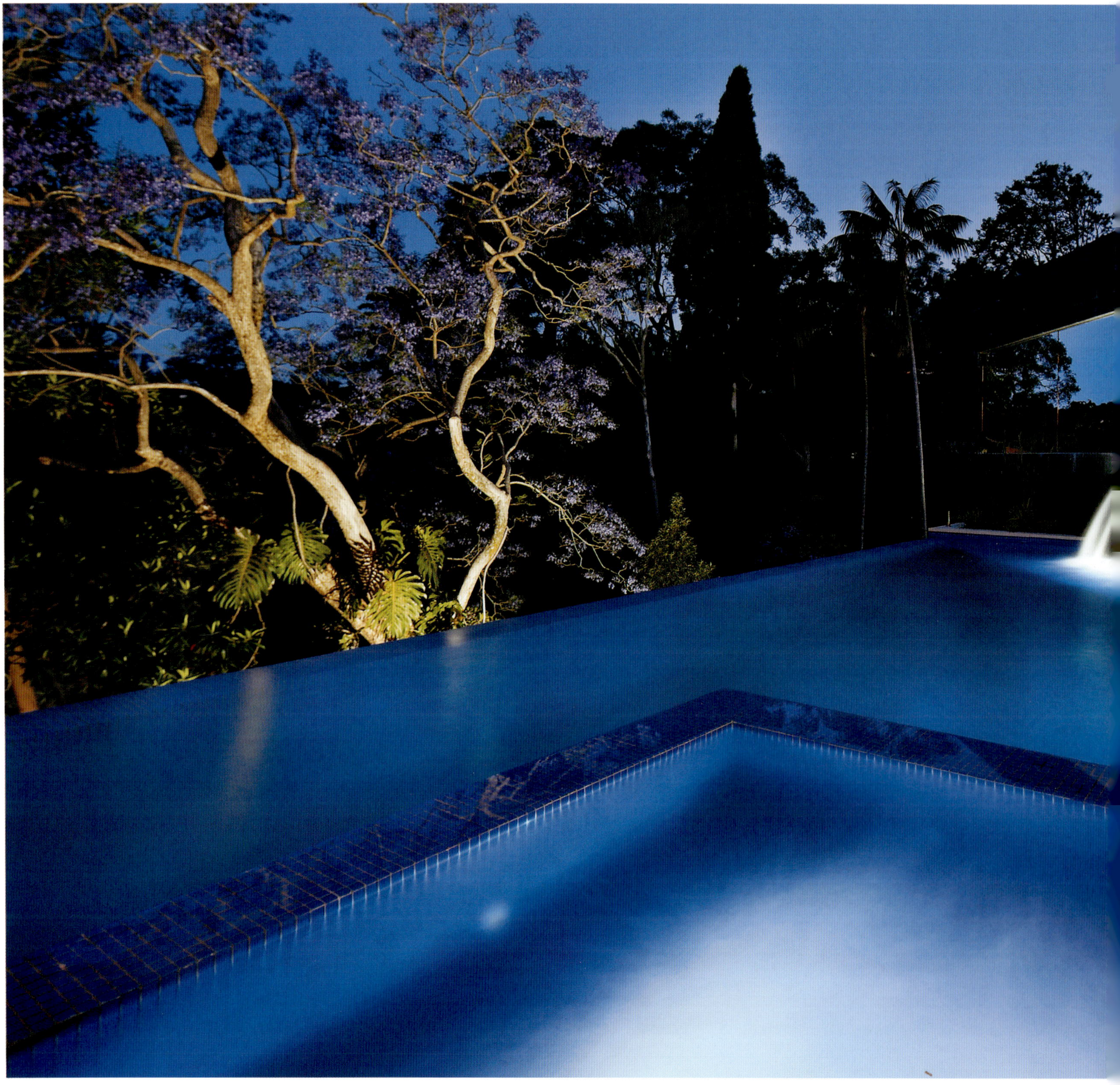

ON EDGE 217

Bushland Oasis

NIAGARA PARK

Located close to the coast, this acreage property is owned by clients who desired an area visible from the family home where they could entertain family and friends. The brief was for the space to embrace all the elements of modern outdoor living with a resort feel, while maintaining a connection with the existing home and surrounding natural environment.

Considering this, the pool was designed to be large in scale, offering many areas of use. The generous shallow end of the pool provides ample room for relaxation, along with a safe location for children to swim. The spa is designed to be functional, for use as a hot spa, as well as a spectacular sculptural piece when not in use. This was achieved with the spa sitting above the pool, suspended in glass that, when illuminated, becomes the central feature of the pool throughout the evening. Due to a rise in the land retaining was required to correctly address the cut and fill. This element provided the opportunity to incorporate a raised wall and waterfall at the higher elevation of the pool.

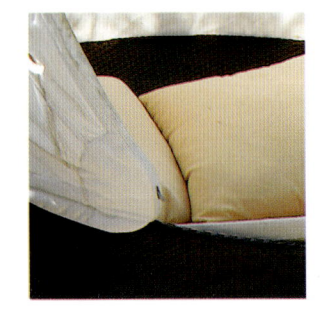

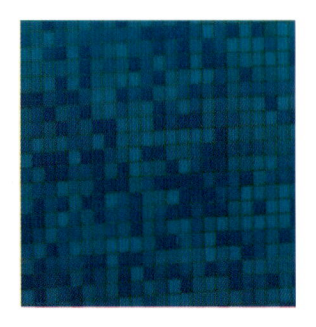

The pavilion, which is of a relevant scale to the pool, houses a fully equipped outdoor kitchen with an island bench and teppanyaki barbecue, along with a sink, refrigerators and storage facilities. The dining space is set off the kitchen, close to the edge of the pool – its hardwood decking hangs over the edge providing direct interaction with the water. A stone-clad fireplace forms part of the lounge area, ready for use after dining or swimming.

To the side of the main pavilion is a swim-up bar, with stainless steel stools submerged in the pool. This allows interaction between people in the water and those in the bar, as well as being a great location to sit in the pool and talk. A small roof structure was designed over the wet bar, enabling all-weather use and allowing the space to be fitted with glass backing and shelves. With a sink and refrigerator, this area is ready for entertaining.

A sub-tropical theme influenced the planting, which consists of bird of paradise (*Strelitzia reginae*), Japanese sago palm (*Cycas revoluta*), frangipani (*Plumeria rubra* 'Acutifolia'), bangalow palms (*Archontophoenix cunninghamiana*), gymea lily (*Doryanthes excelsa*), lilly pilly (*Acmena smithii*), purple fountain grass (*Pennisetum advena* 'Rubrum'), variegated mondo (*Ophiopogon intermedians* 'Stripey White') and variegated star jasmine (*Trachelospermum jasminoides* 'Tricolour').

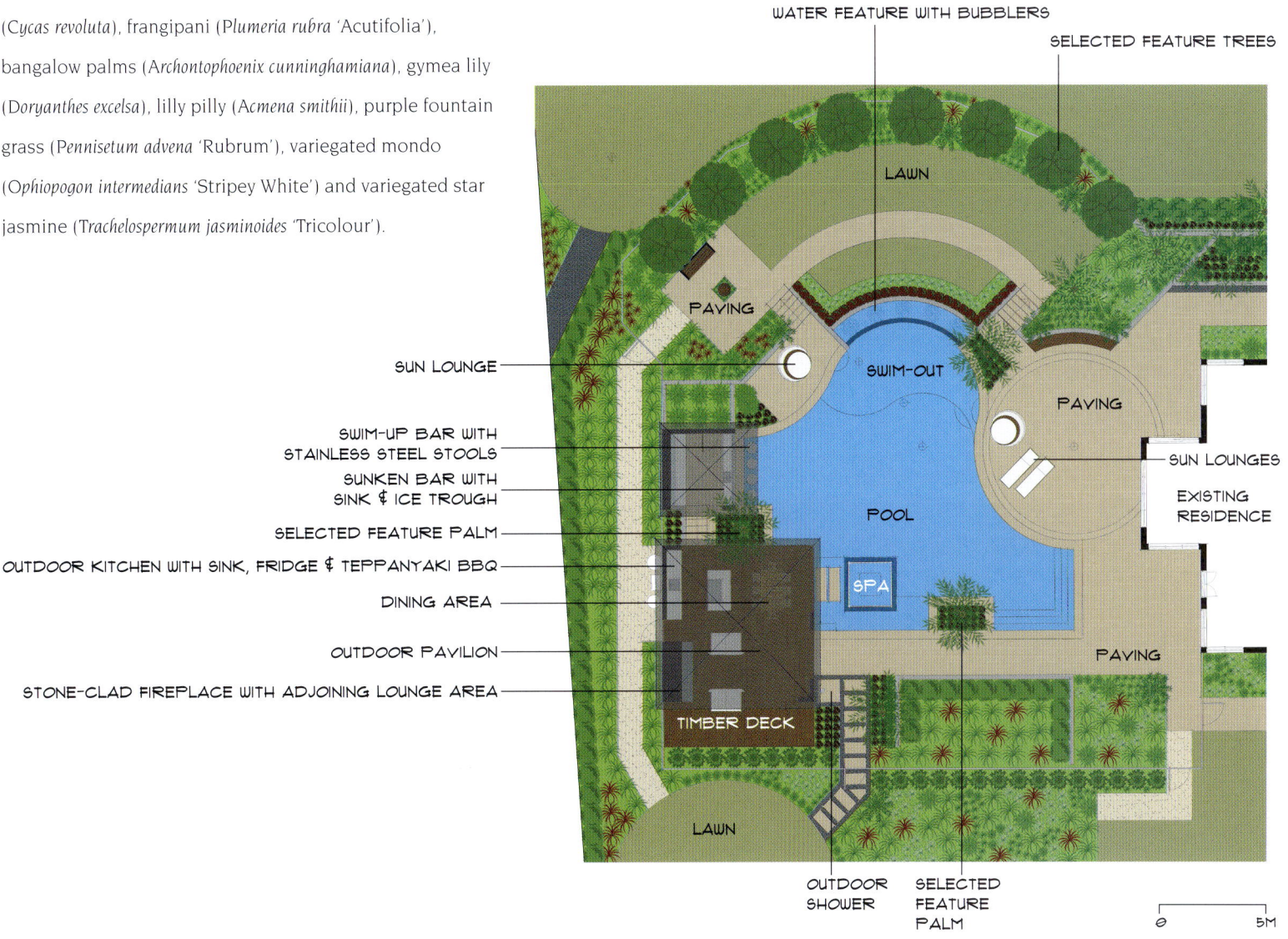

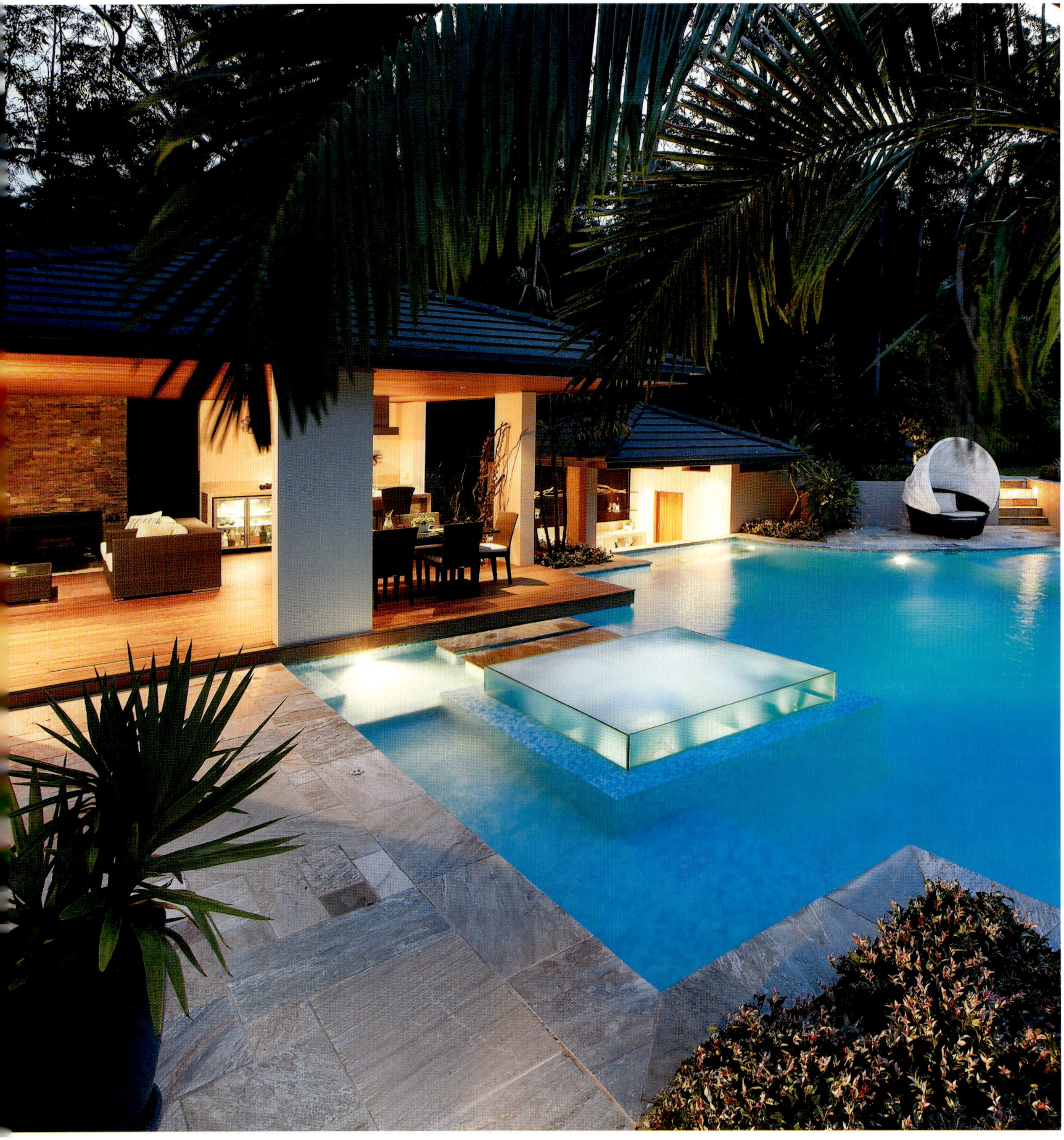

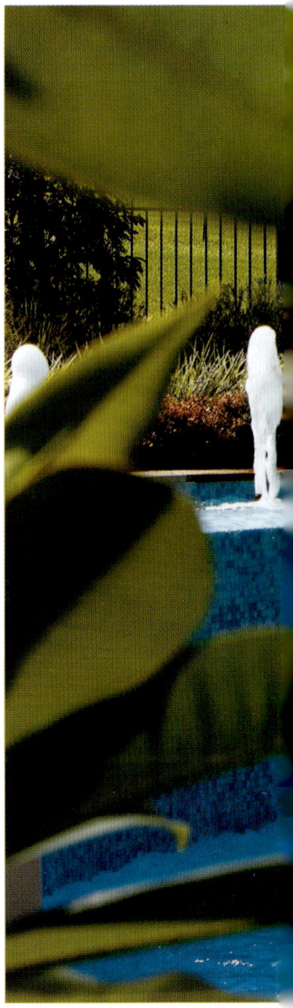

BUSHLAND OASIS 221

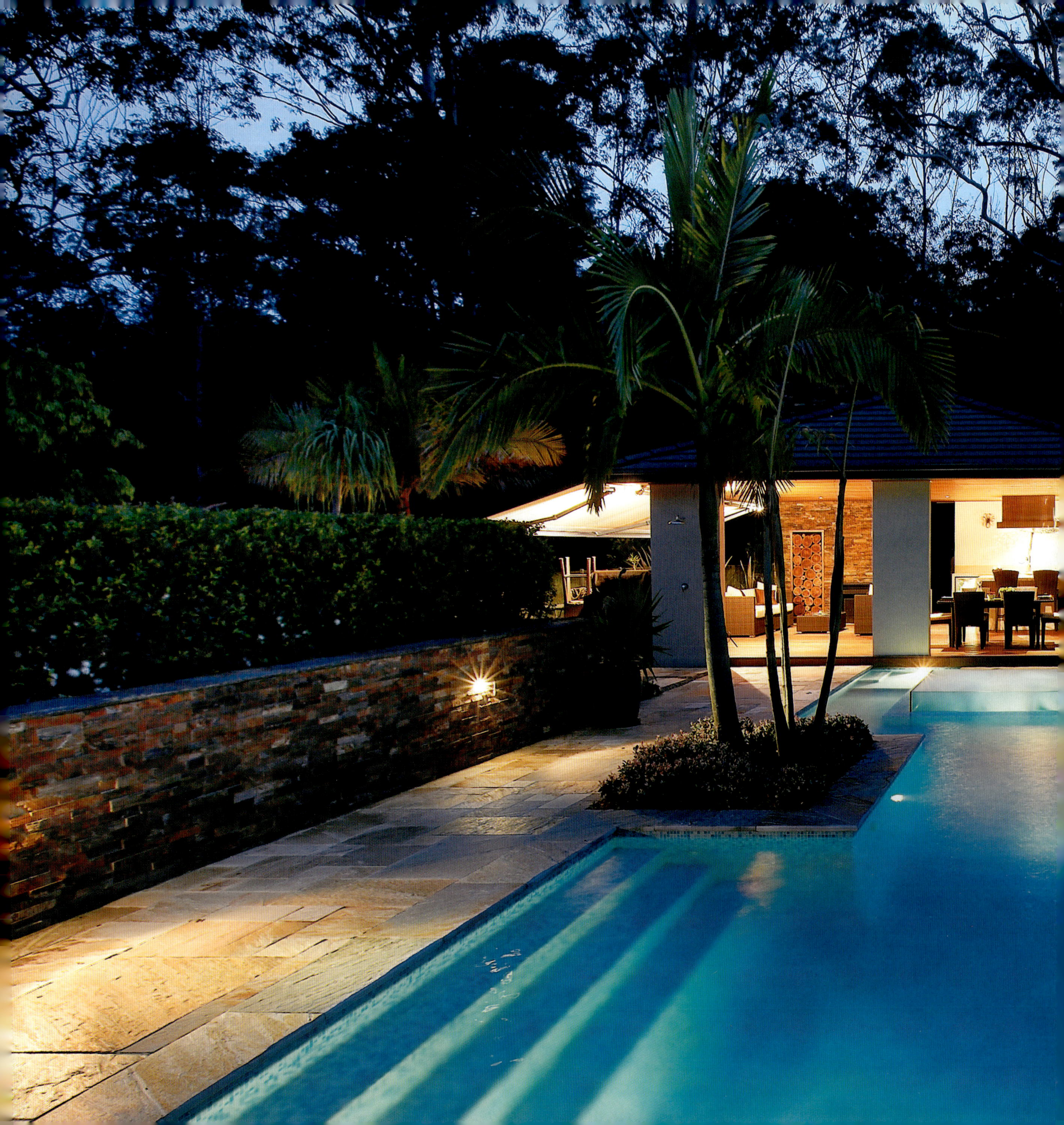

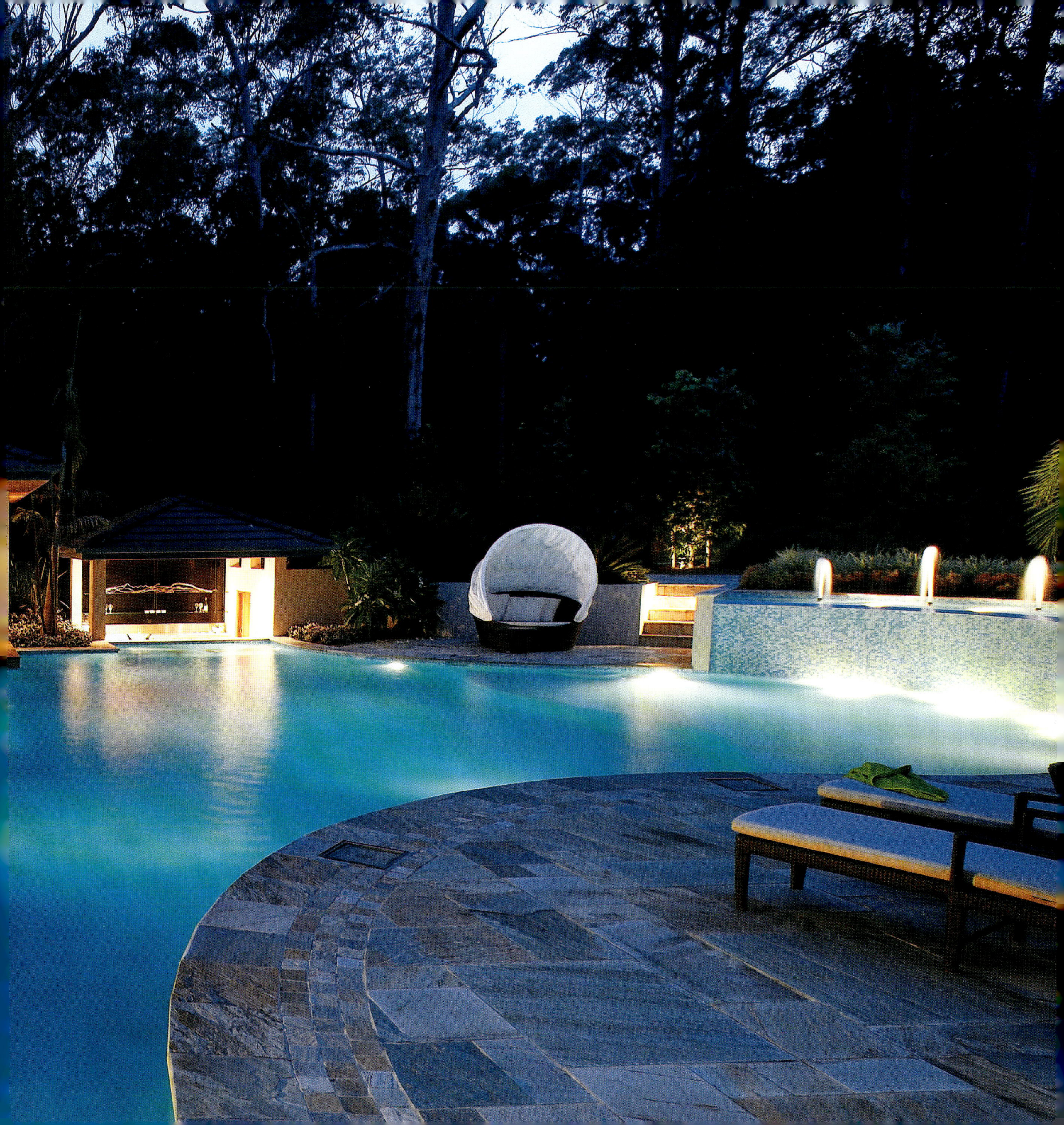

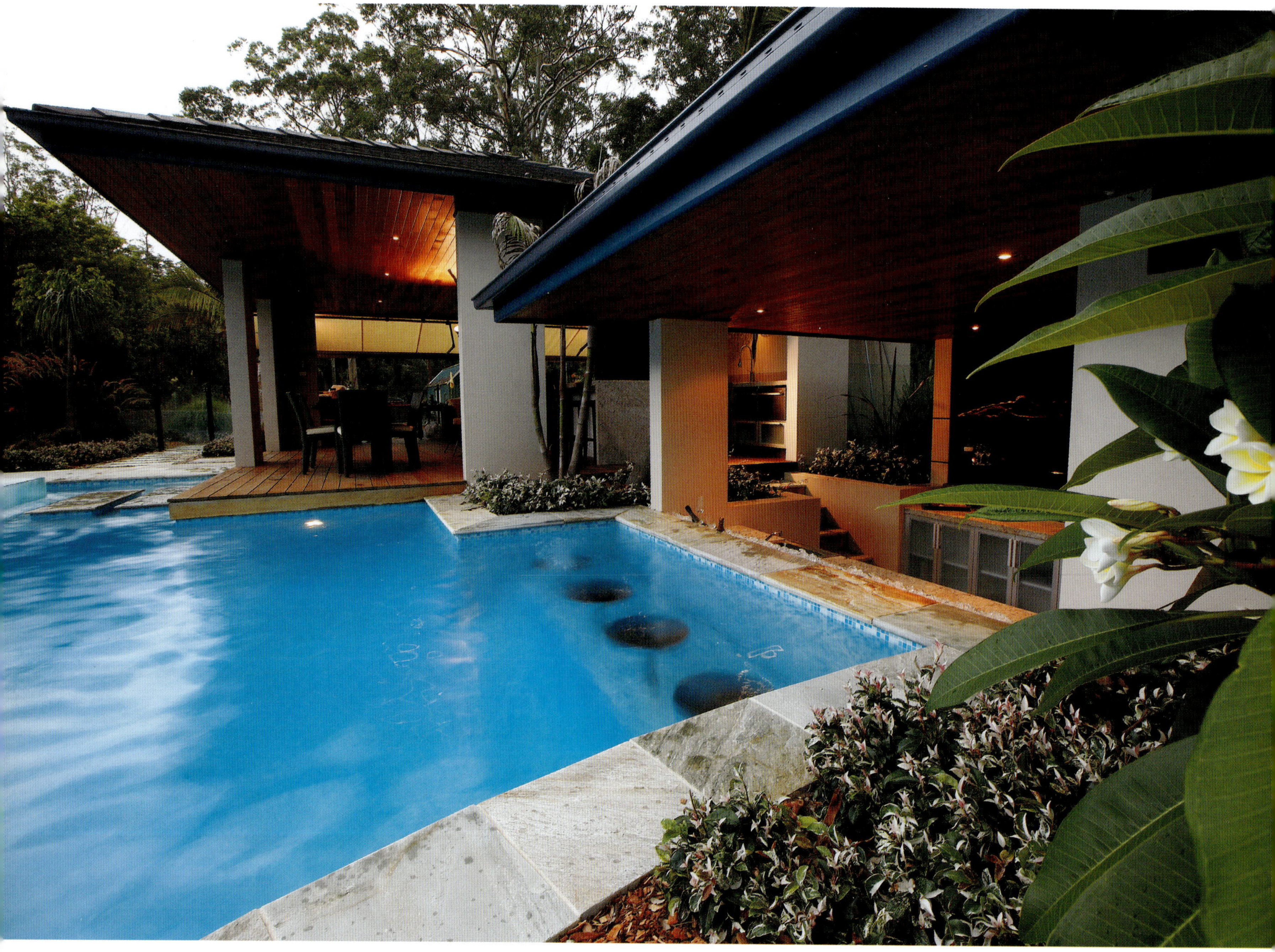

BUSHLAND OASIS 225

Acknowledgements

Thank you to all my clients for giving me the opportunity to develop their outdoor living environments and the trust and freedom to perfect the design process. Also a special thank you to all who allowed their properties to be showcased in this book.

I commend my design and construction teams, whose dedication and commitment to each project is represented in the outstanding quality of our finished projects. A special thank you to my management team Matt Denton, Mark Heath, Luke Passaro and Michael Lillyman for their continuous commitment to excellence in construction and the management of our projects. My designs are just ideas until your talents bring these projects to their full potential.

Thank you to James Caruso for your dedication within the design studio and your own design input into the projects we work together on, I would also like to acknowledge the time and effort you put into the photo shoots for this book along with Larissa Taylor and Rourke Hartwig.

Thank you to all the builders, pool builders and other landscape companies we work alongside throughout these projects, and a special thank you to David Denton of Denton Homes for his vision of creating stunning prestige homes and for embracing my vision to enhance them. Also to Aaron Davidson of Denton Homes for his close working relationship and his invaluable commitment to excellence on the projects we work together on.

Thank you to Matt Bramley of Splish Splash Pools for bringing my pool designs to life and finishing them to the highest quality for my clients.

I am grateful to the residential architects and designers I work with, and in particular Jeremy McCulla of Urban Harmony for our close working relationship on Modern Life, Infinity Blue, Rural Resort and On Show.

Great appreciation to my core group of suppliers in particular Eco Concepts, Kastell Kitchens, Alpine Nurseries, Lump Sculpture Studio, Marcus Engineering and Cosh Living. I would also like to acknowledge the commitment of my contractors and the expertise they bring to every project.

A special thank you to Paul Latham and Alessina Brooks of Images Publishing for your interest and belief in my work and to Rod Gilbert for his enthusiasm and creative direction, which has produced the finest book. Our dealings together have been a complete pleasure and you have produced a book that has truly captured my vision.

Many thanks to Danny Kildare – your photography has brought my work to life and captured it in a stunning way. Thank you for your dedication to excellence with every photograph you have taken.

And now to my amazing wife Bernice: thank you for your continuous support and belief in me. You have been by my side through this continuing journey and your loyalty is a priceless gift. To my two boys Nixon and Bryson: dream big, dream often and know that I love you both.

Every effort has been made to trace the original source of copyright material contained in this book. The publishers would be pleased to hear from copyright holders to rectify any errors or omissions.

The information and illustrations in this publication have been prepared and supplied by the author. While all reasonable efforts have been made to source the required information and ensure accuracy, the publishers do not, under any circumstances, accept responsibility for errors, omissions and representations express or implied.